JavaScript™
Professional Projects

Paul Hatcher
with
John W. Gosney

Premier

Press

The Premier Press logo and related trade dress are trademarks of Premier Press and may not be used without written permission.

JavaScript is a trademark of Netscape Communications Corporation.

Important: Premier Press cannot provide software support. Please contact the appropriate software manufacturer's technical support line or Web site for assistance.

Premier Press and the authors have attempted throughout this book to distinguish proprietary trademarks from descriptive terms by following the capitalization style used by the manufacturer.

ISBN: 1-59200-013-4

Library of Congress Catalog Card Number: 2002111222

Printed in the United States of America

03 04 05 06 07 BH 10 9 8 7 6 5 4 3 2 1

SVP, Retail and Strategic Market Group:
Andy Shafran

Publisher:
Stacy L. Hiquet

Senior Marketing Manager:
Sarah O'Donnell

Marketing Manager:
Heather Hurley

Manager of Editorial Services:
Heather Talbot

Associate Marketing Manager:
Kristin Eisenzopf

Project Editor/Copy Editor:
Estelle Manticas

Technical Reviewer:
Michelle Jones

Retail Market Coordinator:
Sarah Dubois

Interior Layout:
Shawn Morningstar

Cover Designer:
Mike Tanamachi

Indexer:
Kelly Talbot

Proofreader:
Linda Quigley

Premier Press, a division of Course Technology
25 Thomson Place
Boston, MA 02210

JavaScript™
Professional Projects

To Elaine

—P.H

To Melissa, Genna, George and Jackson

—J.G.

Acknowledgments

Paul Hatcher would like to thank John Gosney for making this all possible, Stacy Hiquet for keeping us on track, Michelle Jones ensuring that our technical material was correct, and Estelle Manticas for bringing it all together.

John Gosney would like to thank his co-author, Paul Hatcher, for his professionalism and desire to get the job done right. It's been great to work with you, Paul! Let's do it again very soon! John would also like to give special thanks to Estelle Manticas for doing such a great job in keeping the project on track, and for not losing her sense of humor, or her understanding that "the real world" sometimes gets in the way (at least for a few days) of meeting deadlines. Thanks as well to Stacy Hiquet for continuing to present terrific writing opportunities.

About the Authors

Paul Hatcher is currently attending Indiana University Purdue University Indianapolis where he is working towards a Computer Science degree. He started working in the IT field at an early age and has a great deal of experience with application development for the Web and other platforms.

John W. Gosney is currently Director of Technology Services for the Indiana University School of Dentistry. He has worked in both the publishing and pharmaceutical industries as an application developer, technical writer and training consultant. John writes extensively on all facets of the IT arena, from market analysis and forecasts to guidebooks for application developers. Additionally, he is an associate faculty member for the Indiana University School of Liberal Arts, Indianapolis.

John received his B.A. in technical writing and psychobiology in 1992 from Purdue University. In 1996 he was awarded an M.A. in English from Butler University. John enjoys spending time with his family, cheering for his favorite teams (Pacers, Colts and Boilermakers) and furthering his reputation as an expert in all things popular culture.

Contents at a Glance

Contents

Introduction

If you've purchased this book (or are standing in the bookstore thinking about purchasing it), you've probably already made up your mind to start integrating JavaScript into your Web projects—or at least you're interested in the multifaceted applications you can build with it. That said, this book is not beginner-level "basic tutorial," but a more advanced exploration of a real-world project that will show you how to implement JavaScript in actual applications. This book begins where most other tutorials leave off— by showing you how to pull together the basic operations of a software application in order to actually build practical and viable Web site for your organization.

What Are the Goals of This Book?

Although this book is divided into two parts, it has several specific goals in mind. Those goals include:

- **Presenting the fundamentals of JavaScript.** From programming basics to working with forms, from learning about JavaScript security to presenting you with code debugging tips and tricks, Part I (Chapters 1-13) will lay the necessary groundwork for both the project case study and your own specific JavaScript projects.

- **Teaching good coding practices and fundamental programming skills.** It could be said that programming all comes down to understanding some basic concepts. That is, if you know the foundational rules, you can quickly learn and implement new skills. With this in mind, we've written the chapters of Part I to give you this "ground-level understanding" of JavaScript. We've included lots of sample code in these early chapters, so that as you learn about the general concepts, you can immediately see them practically implemented.

- **Developing a "real world" JavaScript-enabled Web site.** Part II of the book puts you in the role of Web designer for the fictitious Center Park School. Rather than just throwing a bunch of sample code at you and asking you to make sense of it on your own, the project is divided into chapters that deal with a specific aspect of the final Web site. The first project chapter (Chapter 14) and the last (Chapter 21) present you with a before-and-after project view that will increase your larger understanding of the issues involved while working with JavaScript in an actual application.

♦ **Examining the entire Web development picture.** There's more to Web design than just simple code. Indeed, the actual coding of a project is often the "easy" part, and developing a design plan and project template the real challenge. Working with clients can be a daunting task, especially if those customers are not technically minded. To give you a sense of what it's like to plan and develop an entire Web project, we ask you to imagine that you are the actual designer of the Center Park site, and to address the requests put forward by the school administrators.

This book has been written from a holistic, total application-solution perspective. While you'll be presented with the functional foundations of JavaScript in the chapters that compose Part I, you also get a chance in Part II to examine a JavaScript-rich Web site and to study the code that makes the site function.

What Is the Project Case Study?

In Part II, you'll be presented with the Center Park School project, where you'll be asked to build a functional, feature-rich Web site for this made-up private secondary school.

By working through the project, you will:

♦ **Address the larger design issues of a Web site.** While this book is not about project management, it would be foolish to present you with a "real-world" project, and not address the process and procedural planning issues that must be dealt with in this arena. Again, you'll play the role of Web designer, working with the school administrators to ensure the final project is reflective of their requirements for each specific "customer"—parents, teachers and students.

♦ **Build on fundamental JavaScript skills from Part I.** In Part I we tried to avoid presenting you rudimentary information that you have little chance of using practically in your own work. We wanted to give you the real-world tools that you could turn around and use in a real world project like the Center Park project. The goal here is to show you JavaScript "in action" and in a format—the Center Park project—that is functional and practical for your study.

♦ **Develop an understanding of how different functional aspects of JavaScript work together.** If you work through the chapters of Part I in sequential order, you'll see how one functional component of JavaScript integrates with another to build larger, more complex (and interesting) Web applications. The Center Park school information has been presented in the same way. By gradually building the functionality of the site from the "ground up," you'll get to see all of the JavaScript features come together to create something functional, professional, and maybe even exciting!

PART I

JavaScript Essentials

Chapter 1

JavaScript, designed by Netscape Communications and Sun Microsystems, is a light-weight programming language that you can use to add dynamic effects to your Web pages. HTML (*Hypertext Markup Language*) can only describe the way a Web page's elements (text, forms, hyperlinks, and tables) look—it has no way of dictating how they behave. The ability to embed JavaScript scripts in a Web page gives you, the programmer, much more control over how your Web page behaves.

Scripting languages like JavaScript give Web pages far more processing power. JavaScript allows a Web page to interact with both a site visitor and the Web server from which the page originated. One common use for JavaScript is *form validation*, the process by which a form is checked prior to submission in order to verify that it contains all the required information and that it is in the correct format. By itself, HTML allows a visitor to retrieve a form from a server, fill in the required information, and send the form back to the server for processing. Unfortunately, if the user enters invalid data, the whole process must be repeated until entirely valid data is entered. As JavaScript is executed in the client browser, form validation can occur after the user has filled out the form and before it is sent back to the server. This saves both the client and server considerable time.

As you read through this book studying the projects and customizing the code I'll present, bear in mind that JavaScript is a scripting language that was created to run in browsers. Because of this, JavaScript cannot be used to create stand-alone programs, in the same way that HTML cannot be used to create stand-alone programs. Both JavaScript and HTML require a Web browser in order to be executed. More precisely, a JavaScript interpreter is required to understand and run JavaScript programs. JavaScript interpreters come prepackaged in almost all of today's mainstream Web browsers (including Netscape and Internet Explorer). This means that a client will not need to install any other programs on their computers before using Web sites with embedded JavaScript.

Unlike with many of today's common programming languages—such as C, C++, Visual Basic, and Java—you don't need any special development environment in order to write JavaScript applications. You can use the same text editor you're using to create your Web pages. To insert a script into a preexisting Web page, you need only enclose the JavaScript code between script tags (`<script>…</script>`). This will tell the Web browser to execute the code instead of trying to display it. As an example, here is a simple Web page that displays the classic Hello World!! message:

```
<html>

  <head>
    <title>
      JavaScript Professional Projects - "Hello World!!" Example
    </title>
  </head>

  <body>
    <center>
      <font size=6>JavaScript Professional Projects</font><br>
      <font size=4>Chapter 1: "Hello World!!" Example</font>
    </center>

    <br><br>
    <p>
      Not only can you display text as usual on your Web page,
      but you can also use JavaScript's built in 'document.write();'
      function to display dynamic information such as the current
      date and time.
    </p>
```

```
<script language="JavaScript">
<!--

   document.write( "Your current date and time is:   " +
                       new Date().toString() + "<br>" );

// -->
</script>

<br><br>
<p>
   You can also use JavaScript to display normal HTML
   elements repeatedly.  Here is an example of that:
</p>

<script language="JavaScript">
<!--

   for( i = 0 ; i < 5 ; i++ )
   {
     document.write( "Hello World!!<br>" );
   }

// --<
</script>

<br><br>
<p>
   As you can see, JavaScript has great power.
</p>
</body>

</html>
```

The statements enclosed in the script tags are considered executable code by the browser. It is important to specify the language attribute's value for the script tag because JavaScript is not the only scripting language that can be embedded within Web pages. In addition, it is always a good idea to include HTML comment tags within the script tags, to allow for older browsers that do not support JavaScript.

All of the commands used in the code example just presented will be explained in full in the following chapters. To run the example, type the HTML code into a text editor (such as Notepad for Windows, VI for Unix, or Applescript for Mac) and save it as HelloWorld.html. Opening the file in your browser will display the page that you see in Figure 1.1.

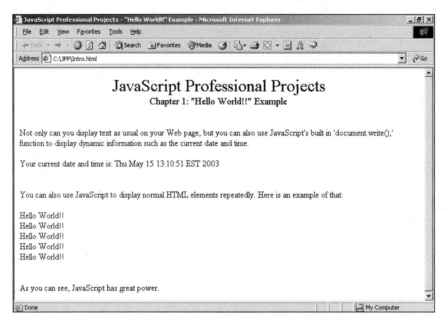

FIGURE 1.1 *A page displaying simple JavaScript capabilities.*

When JavaScript code is embedded into an HTML Web page, the browser will read and display the HTML as usual. When the browser encounters a script tag, it will interpret the JavaScript code. The JavaScript code can then be executed as the page loads, the entire time the page is being displayed, as the page is being unloaded, or along with programmer-designated events. It is important to remember that the interpretation occurs at the client side and after the Web page has been completely downloaded from the server. This has its advantages and disadvantages. Because JavaScript is run on the client's computer, it is unable to access resources located on the server from which it originated—most notable are databases. JavaScript does, however, run much faster than other server-side languages that do communicated directly with the server. When used in combination with the browser's Document Object Model (DOM), JavaScript can produce intricate, dynamic HTML effects as well as animation and sound.

Lexical Definition

The *lexical definition* of a language is simply the words that are used to write statements in that language. In the case of JavaScript, the lexical definition is borrowed in large part from languages such as C, C++, and Java. These languages, and JavaScript, have three basic types of statements or "words," that make up the language: assignment statements, selection statements, and iterative statements.

Assignment statements make up a majority of the program source. This type of statement includes variable declaration, class definition, and user-defined functions. *Selection statements* provide a way to choose between two or more execution paths in a program. *Iterative statements* provide a way for a block of code to be executed zero or more times consecutively. Assignment statements are covered later in this chapter, and selection and repetition statements are covered in Chapter 2, "Selection and Repetition Statements."

In addition to specifying the words that make up the language, the lexical definition of a language also specifies how a programmer can name variables and to what format literal definitions must conform. In JavaScript, the identifiers used to name variables must follow several rules; I'll explain these rules in the following section. Literals in JavaScript consist of strings and numbers. Strings are always enclosed in quotation marks (either single ' or double ") and numbers are not.

JavaScript Identifiers

Most of the JavaScript statements you write will request data from the client Web browser or from the server from which the Web page originated. In order for that data to be useful, you need a place to store it. To facilitate the storage of data, JavaScript gives you the ability to declare variables to store and to symbolically use the data. Each variable that is declared will have a name, or *identifier*, that allows the data to be referred to easily. Examples of identifiers that might be used in JavaScript are: `counter`, `userName`, and `listItem97`.

When creating an identifier, you should remember the following very important guidelines:

◆ The first character of an identifier must be an ASCII letter, an underscore (_), or a dollar sign ($).

◆ An identifier must never begin with a number.

◆ An identifier must never consist entirely of JavaScript reserved words. A complete list of JavaScript's reserved words can be found later in this chapter.

◆ JavaScript is a case-sensitive language, and so, for example, `casetest`, `CaseTest`, and `caseTest` can all be used simultaneously because they are considered different identifiers by the interpreter.

Identifiers are used not only to name variables, but also to identify user-defined functions and classes. Careful selection of identifier names will help promote readability and help with future code maintenance. See Table 1.1 for a short list of identifiers and their descriptions.

Table 1.1 Bad and Good Identifiers

Bad Identifier	Reason	Good Identifier
7th_element	Begins with number.	element_7
@address	Does not begin with _, $, or letter.	address
in	Is a JavaScript reserved word.	Input

Following is a simple example that demonstrates declaring variables and JavaScript case-sensitivity:

```
<html>

  <head>
    <title>
      JavaScript Professional Projects - Identifiers and literals
    </title>

    <script language="JavaScript">
    <!--
      var casetest = "Once apon a time";
      var CaseTest = 42;
      var caseTest = new Date();
    // -->
    </script>
  </head>

  <body>

    <center>
      <font size=6>JavaScript Professional Projects</font><br>
      <font size=4>Chapter 1: Identifiers and literals</font>
    </center>

    <br><br>

    <p>
    The value of <font face="Courier New">casetest</font> is: <b>"
    <script language="JavaScript">
```

```
<!--
   document.write( casetest );
// -->
</script>
"</b>. It was initialized to that string literal when
it was declared.

<br><br>

The value of <font face="Courier New">CaseTest</font> is: <b>
<script language="JavaScript">
<!--
   document.write( CaseTest );
// -->
</script>
</b>. It was initialized to that number literal when
it was declared.

<br><br>

The value of <font face="Courier New">caseTest</font> is: <b>
<script language="JavaScript">
<!--
   document.write( caseTest );
// -->
</script>
</b>. It was not initialized with a literal at all.
Instead it was declared as a date object.
</p>

   </body>

</html>
```

In this example, three variables—casetest, CaseTest, and caseTest (notice the different capitalization)—are declared, and each is assigned a different value. casetest was assigned a string value, CaseTest was assigned an integer value, and caseTest was declared as a Date object. In the body of the page, each variable is used in order to show the lack of ambiguity of JavaScript's case-sensitive design.

JavaScript Literals

A *literal* is data that has been entered directly into the source code of a program. Some examples of literals are 42, 3.14, and "Once upon a time". Literals are commonly used to initialize the value of a variable. For example, if a loop uses a counter, it might be declared as follows: var counter = 0; The name counter is an identifier and the name of the variable, while 0 is a literal and the initial value of counter. Literals can be used to initialize variables to a number, boolean, or string value.

Reserved Key Words

JavaScript, like almost all programming languages, has a list of reserved words that are used directly by the language itself and, consequently, cannot be used as variable names. Key words, or *lexemes*, make up the lexical definition of a language. A complete list of JavaScript's reserved words is as follows:

abstract	boolean	break	byte	case	catch
char	class	const	continue	debugger	default
delete	do	double	else	enum	export
extends	false	final	finally	float	for
function	goto	if	implements	import	in
instanceof	int	interface	long	native	new
null	package	private	protected	public	return
short	static	switch	synchronized	this	throw
throws	transient	true	try	typeof	var
void	while	with			

The list of reserved words makes up the vocabulary of the JavaScript language. By combining these words in various ways, the full power of the language is realized.

Although it is possible to use the reserved words as identifiers if you give them different capitalization, it is strongly discouraged because it hampers readability, as you can see in the following example:

```
var Var = 9 >= 7;
var True = false;
var If = Var && True;
if( If )
{
   document.write( "This is very confusing." );
}
```

Clearly, using key words in any form can lead to unreadable code.

Comments

Comments are a very helpful feature of every programming language. Adding comments allows a future reader of your source code to understand what you were thinking when you wrote the code.

There are two types of comments in JavaScript, *block comments* and *line comments*. Block comments are started by a /* symbol and terminated by a */. All text in between these two symbols will be ignored by the browser's interpreter. Block comments are useful when you need to leave a longer comment, such as a program header or description of user-defined functions. Line comments are preceded by the // symbol and have no terminator symbol. Line comments end at the next line break and are useful for describing the use of variables, leaving quick notes on program flow within functions, and for debugging purposes.

Following is an example showing both types of comments:

```html
<html>

  <head>
    <title>
      JavaScript Professional Projects - Comments
    </title>

    <script language="JavaScript">
    <!--
      /*
          This is a block comment. You should place these
          before each function you write to give the reader
          an idea of what it does.

          All text in this type of comment is ignored by the
          interpreter - including JavaScript commands!
      */
      function prototype()
      {
        // This is a one line comment
        // These comments are used to explain key steps
        // within a function.
      }
    // -->
```

```
    </script>
  </head>

  <body>

    <center>
      <font size=6>JavaScript Professional Projects</font><br>
      <font size=4>Chapter 1: Comments</font>
    </center>

  </body>

</html>
```

It is a good idea to get in the habit of using comments throughout a program during the coding process. The result of using comments will be a professional-looking and easy-to-maintain source program.

White Space and Line Breaks

The browser ignores all white space—including normal spaces, tabs, and line breaks,—during interpretation. The only exception to that rule is white space that is part of a literal. White space is used purely for aesthetic reasons, but even though white space has no direct effect on the execution of a program, it is still very important. A well-formatted source file will drastically increase the readability of a program and make maintaining it much less of a chore.

```
Following is an example of code without enough white space:
<html>

  <head>
    <title>
      JavaScript Professional Projects - White Space and Line Breaks
    </title>

  </head>

  <body>

    <center>
      <font size=6>JavaScript Professional Projects</font><br>
      <font size=4>Chapter 1: White Space and Line Breaks</font>
```

```
</center>

<br><br>

<p>
A poorly formatted function can be difficult to read and
difficult to debug.  Here is an example of a poorly
formatted function:<br><br>
<font face="Courier New">
function f1(var1,var2,var3){var answer;<br>
answer = 0; for( i = 0;<br>
    i < 10 ; i = i +1 ){<br>
         answer = answer + var1;<br>
    answer *= var2;<br>
answer--;<br>
}<br>
    return(answer-var3);<br>
    }<br>
</font>
<br>
This function does work, but it's not pretty.<br><br>
A much better way to write the same function would
be like this:<br><br>
<font face="Courier New">
function f2( var1, var2, var3 )<br>
{<br>
     var answer = 0;<br>
     for( i = 0 ; i < 10 ; i = i + 1 )<br>
     {<br>
          answer = answer + var1;<br>
          answer = answer * var2;<br>
          answer--;<br>
     }<br>
     return( answer - var3 );<br>
}<br>
</font>
<br>
```

```
    Although the extra spaces and line breaks will add slightly
    to the download time, it will add greatly to the readability
    and ease of updating.
    </p>

  </body>

</html>
```

During the life cycle of a program it will constantly be changed and updated. In most cases either you or someone else will have to go back and debug, rewrite, or make additions to the code you have written. It will be much easier and more efficient to do so if the original code has made good use of white space for clean, easy-to read formatting.

Optional Semicolon

Unlike in languages such as C, C++, and Java, the semicolon at the end of some JavaScript code lines is not necessary. The semicolon in JavaScript is used more for separation rather than termination. Because this is the case, you need not place a semicolon at the end of a single line of code. A semicolon is required, however, when there are two or more consecutive JavaScript statements in the same code block - such as a function.

At that time, it is common practice to place the semicolon at the end of the preceding line of code.

This example demonstrates some of the places a semicolon would and would not be needed:

```
<html>

  <head>

    <title>
      JavaScript Professional Projects - Comments
    </title>
    <script language="JavaScript">
      /*
          This function demonstrates an example where a
          semicolon is not needed.
      */
      function sayHello()
      {
        alert( "Hello visitor!" )
```

```
      }

      /*
          This function demonstrates an example where a
          semicolon is required.
      */
      function getDate()
      {
        var today = new Date();
        return( today )
      }
    </script>
  </head>

  <body onLoad="JavaScript: sayHello()">

    <center>
      <font size=6>JavaScript Professional Projects</font><br>
      <font size=4>Chapter 1: Optional Semicolon</font>
    </center>

    <br><br>
    <p>
    Today's date is
    <script language="JavaScript">
    <!--
      document.write( getDate() );
    // -->
    </script>
    . Have a nice day!

  </body>


</html>
```

Even though the semicolon is not always required, it is a good idea to get in the habit of using it. Doing so will avoid complications later on. If you were to make additions to a Web page and forgot to place a semicolon at the end of the old lines of code before adding new lines, the result would be some very confusing error messages.

Data Types

Data types are the way that data can be represented. For example, if you saw the characters 123, you would most likely assume that they were a number, and correctly so. What you may not think of is that the same three characters can also be a string "123". Both ways of thinking about the three characters are correct, but sometimes one way has advantages over the other. For instance, you would want to worry about using the string representation in an arithmetic operation. On the other hand, the string representation of the characters 123 is easier to print to the screen than the number representation. This is an example of choosing the correct primitive data type for a specific job.

Primitive data types are not the only group in a language's data type collection. Many languages, including JavaScript, also have a collection of *abstract* data types. In the case of JavaScript, the abstract data types are usually objects. Objects are most easily thought of as a collection of primitive data types all kept in one place. You will see in Chapter 5 that an object has many properties that are a part of its definition. These properties are usually instances of primitive data types. In addition to a collection of primitive data, objects can also have functions that are part of their definition.

Primitive Types

Because JavaScript is an interpreted language, it has the added advantage of being loosely typed. What that means exactly is that a variable does not need to be implicitly declared as one of the built-in JavaScript types. Instead, a variable can be declared using one type of literal (number, string, or boolean) and used as one or the other. There are three primitive types in the JavaScript programming language: number, string, and boolean.

The *number* primitive type is used to perform arithmetic operations such as addition, subtraction, multiplication, and division. Any whole number or floating-point literal that does not appear between quotation marks is considered a number.

The *string* primitive type is used to handle text. A string represents any sequence of zero or more characters that are to be considered strictly text—that is, no mathematical operations can be performed on them.

The boolean primitive type is used with logical operations and can have one of two values: true or false.

Table 1.2 lists each primitive data type that is part of the JavaScript language, as well as several examples of each.

These three data types comprise the majority of data you will encounter while using JavaScript.

Table 1.2 Primitive Data Types

Data Type	Examples
Number	`57, 3.14, 1001`
String	`"Hello", 'a string', "2001"`
Boolean	`true, false`

Abstract Data Types

JavaScript's abstract data types are extremely useful. Abstract data types include objects, arrays, and functions.

An object represents a collection of data and functions that work together to perform a related task. One of JavaScript's most powerful features is its object-based approach. All abstract data types, including strings, arrays, and functions, are objects. This approach makes objects very efficient and easy to use. Although strings and arrays are considered objects in JavaScript, their behavior is slightly more specialized than the other general objects, which is why they are covered in their own chapter, Chapter 3. Objects are covered in depth in Chapter 5, "Object-Oriented JavaScript."

An *array* facilitates the storing of like data in a logical way. For more information on arrays, see Chapter 3, "JavaScript Arrays and Strings."

A *function* is a piece of executable code that is written once but is called repeatedly from different parts of your program. Functions are covered in Chapter 4, "JavaScript Functions."

Special Data Types

There are three built-in special data types in the JavaScript programming language. They are `null`, `undefined`, and `NaN` and are explained in Table 1.3.

Table 1.3 Special Data Types

Data_type	Description
`null`	This value is given to a variable to indicate that no value exists.
`undefined`	This value is given to a variable to indicate that it has not been previously defined.
`NaN`	Not-a-Number is used to signify that a number variable is in fact not a legal number.

Following is an example demonstrating how each of the special data types are produced:

```html
<html>

  <head>
    <title>
      JavaScript Profesional Projects - Special Data Types
    </title>

    <script language="JavaScript">
    <!--
      var myNumber;
      var myDate = new Date();
      delete( myDate );
      myDate = null;
    // -->
    </script>
  </head>

  <body onLoad="javascript: sayHello()">

    <center>
      <font size=6>JavaScript Professional Projects</font><br>
      <font size=4>Chapter 1: Special Data Types</font>
    </center>

    <br><br>

    <p>
    The variable 'myNumber' currently has the value: <b>
    <script language="JavaScript">
    <!--
      document.write( myNumber );
    // -->
    </script>
    </b>because it has not been defined yet.
    <br><br>
    The variable 'myNumber' is now being assigned the value 'text'.<br>
```

```
The variable 'myNumber' currently <b>
<script language="JavaScript">
<!--
  document.write( isNaN( myNumber ) ? "is not" : "is" );
// -->
</script>
</b>a number!
<br><br>
The object 'myDate' currently has the value: <b>
<script language="JavaScript">
<!--
  document.write( myDate );
// -->
</script>
</b>because it was deleted before being used!
</p>

</body>

</html>
```

Variables

Variables are a very important part of any programming language. Without being able to declare variables, the programmer's ability to create useful programs would be severely hindered. A *variable* is a place to store program-generated data that may or may not change as the program runs. A variable can hold anything from the number of visits to a Web page to a list of items in a customer's shopping cart. A variable consists of two parts, an identifier and a value.

Every variable has an *identifier*, or name, so that it may be referred to later in the program. The name of the variable can be any legal identifier and is usually chosen so that it will accurately describe the variable's purpose. For example, if a variable is intended to hold the user name of a Web page visitor, an appropriate name for that variable would be userName. Variable names that are not easily understood will seriously impede the readability of a source program.

The second, and most important, part of a variable is its *value*, or the data that it holds. This can be any of the primitive or abstract data types mentioned above. All variables have the value undefined after they are declared and before they are initialized.

Variable Typing

As I mentioned previously, JavaScript is a loosely typed scripting language. This means that all variables will have the same generic type 'var' assigned to them when they are declared. The type of the variable will change behind the scenes as you use it, which could be confusing later on, as you may lose track of what the current variable type is. Luckily, JavaScript has a built-in operator to handle this situation: typeof. The typeof operator returns the type of an uneval- uated variable. The typeof operator can return the values 'number', 'string', 'variable', 'object', or 'keyword'. Some examples of typeof use are listed in Table 1.4.

Table 1.4 typeof() return values

Call to typeof	Return Value of typeof Operator
typeof(123);	'number'
typeof('a string');	'string'
typeof(new Date());	'object'
typeof(true);	'boolean'
typeof(null);	'object'
typeof(parseInt);	'function'

The typeof operator is very useful in preventing errors before performing arithmetic opera- tions on variables about whose type you are unsure.

Great, so you know the type of your variable. It just so happens that it is the wrong variable type for the job. What can you do? Once again, the designers of JavaScript have provided for that eventuality. There are two built-in functions for converting strings to numbers: parseInt() and parseFloat().

The top-level function parseInt (string, radix) takes a mandatory string as a parameter, from which the first integer will be extracted and returned. If the function fails to find a num- ber at the beginning of the string, the value NaN will be returned. The optional parameter radix allows you to specify the number base. The default is 10 for decimal numbers. You might also use a radix of 16 for hexadecimal numbers or a radix of 2 for binary numbers. Any number from 2 to 36 can be used here.

The top-level function parseFloat (string) takes a string as a parameter, from which the first floating-point number will be extracted. If the function fails to find a number at the beginning of the string, the value NaN will be returned.

The isNaN(var) function was designed to determine if the value returned from either parseInt() or parseFloat() is in fact a number. Calling isNaN() with the return value of either of these functions will determine whether they are numbers. Remember, isNaN returns true if the value passed to it was *not* a number.

Variable Declaration

Most JavaScript statements you write will have the browser do something with data. The data may come from the site visitor as he enters information into a form element, it may be saved and loaded by the browser from a special file called a *cookie*, or it may be generated from within the program itself. Regardless of how the data is received, it will most likely be stored within a named memory location, which, as you know, is called a *variable*. This process can only happen if you reserved the space to store the data.

There are four parts to declaring a variable.

1. First is the key word `'var'`.
2. `'var'` is followed immediately by the name you would like to use for the variable. The name must be a legal identifier.
3. The variable name is followed by an equals sign (=).
4. The equals sign is followed by a literal you would like your variable to contain the value of.

Here is the variable declaration syntax:

```
var <identifier> = <literal>
```

This will make `<identifier>` the name of the variable and `<literal>` the initial value of the variable. The equals sign and literal are optional, but I highly recommend initializing your variables so that they don't contain the value `undefined` when your program starts.

Variable Scope

The scope of a variable determines where in the program it can be used. JavaScript uses *static scoping*, which means that if you declare your variables outside of a function, they can be used throughout the program. Variables declared within a function, however, can only be used within the function body.

Following is an example that demonstrates JavaScript's static variable scoping:

```
<html>
  <head>
    <title>
      JavaScript Professional Projects - Variable Scope
    </title>

    <script language="JavaScript">
    <!--
      var number = 10;
```

```
    function func1()
    {
      return( number );
    }

    function func2()
    {
      var number = 35;
      return( number );
    }

    function func3()
    {
      var number = 35;
      return( func1() );
    }
  // -->
  </script>

</head>

<body>

  <center>
    <font size=6>JavaScript Professional Projects</font><br>
    <font size=4>Chapter 1: Variable Scope</font>
  </center>

  <br><br>

  <p>
  The value returned from func1 is <b>
  <script language="JavaScript">
  <!--
    document.write( func1() );
  -->
  </script>
  </b>-  func1 used the global variable 'number'.<br><br>
```

```
The value returned from func2 is <b>
<script language="JavaScript">
<!--
  document.write( func2() );
-->
</script>
</b>- func2 used the local variable 'number'.<br><br>
The value returned from func3 is <b>
<script language="JavaScript">
<!--
  document.write( func3() );
-->
</script>
</b>- func3 declared a local variable 'number', but
then used the returned value from func1 - the global 'number'.
</p>

  </body>

</html>
```

This example demonstrates one peculiarity that may arise from having local and global variables of the same name. In the example, a global variable 'number' is declared and the value 10 is assigned to it. That variable is returned by the function func1 and displayed on the page. In func2, however, a local variable, also named 'number', is declared and has the value 35 assigned to it. When the return statement in the function func2 returns 'number', it is no longer the global value. The local variable temporarily overrides the global variable. As soon as the end of the second function is reached, all other references to 'number' will have the global value of 10 just like before. That means that the variable 'number' in the second function only has a local scope and temporarily replaces the global variable of the same name.

When the function func3 is called, it creates a local variable named 'number', but then calls the function func1. Because func1 uses the global variable, it returns that value to func3, which is then returned and displayed on the page. This demonstrates that local variables can only be used within the local context in which they were created.

Garbage Collection

In any programming language that allows you to dynamically create new objects (such as with the new operator in JavaScript), there must be some way for you to free up memory that is no longer needed by objects. If you didn't have this ability, your program would continue to use more and more memory until there was none left and the program crashed. This is called a *memory leak*. In C and C++, *garbage collection*, the process of freeing up memory, is manual. The programmer has to manually use the delete operator on each object created. In Java, reclaiming memory is automated. The Java Virtual Machine can detect when an object is no longer needed and automatically reclaim the memory used by that object.

Thankfully, JavaScript takes after Java and has automatic garbage collection. In Internet Explorer 3.0 and later, and in Navigator 4.0 and later, garbage collection is implemented without flaw and you need not understand the details. Unfortunately, in earlier versions of Navigator, garbage collection has some problems and you must take certain steps to avoid any errors or crashes. Garbage collection will be covered in depth in Chapter 5, "Object-Oriented JavaScript."

Operators

Variables are only useful to a programmer if they can be manipulated. JavaScript has many built-in operators that can be used to manipulate variables. JavaScript operators are symbols and keywords you can use to assign values to variables or perform operations with those values. Using operators, you can combine variable and literal values into expressions that perform calculations and produce results. Your script can display onscreen the result from an expression, store the result within another (or the same) variable, and use the result within another expression. In the preceding section you learned how to use the basic assignment operator, the equals sign (=), to store values in variables within a script. This section will show you many more operators in the JavaScript language.

Arithmetic Operators

There are several operators that you can use to perform arithmetic operations on numbers. JavaScript has two kinds of arithmetic operators, unary and binary. *Unary* operators change the value of a single value or expression, while *binary* operators change the value of two values or expressions—one on each side of the operator. An assignment operator is used to store the results of the arithmetic to a variable. Table 1.5 lists both kinds of operators, as well as the assignment operators.

Some assignment operators perform arithmetic operations with the right-hand expression before assigning a new value to the variable on the left. For example, the expression counter += 2; would add counter and 2 and then save the new value back to counter.

The increment and decrement unary operators increase or decrease by one, respectively, the variable they are used with, and then they assign the new value to the original variable. Unary operators are most commonly used with loop counters, which are discussed in Chapter 2, "Selection and Repetition Statements." The negation unary operator changes the sign of a variable or expression.

Each binary operator does exactly what you would expect it to do—performs basic mathematical operations. The modulus operator only works on integer numbers and returns a whole number remainder resulting from integer division.

Table 1.5 Arithmetic Operators

Symbol	Description	Example
	Assignment Operators	
=	Assign to	variable = expression
+=	Add to	variable += expression
-=	Subtract from	variable -= expression
*=	Multiply by	variable *= expression
/=	Divide by	variable /= expression
	Unary Operators	
++	Increment	++variable or variable++
--	Decrement	--variable or variable--
-	Negation	-expression
	Binary Operators	
+	Addition (overloaded)	expression + expression
-	Subtraction	expression - expression
*	Multiplication	expression * expression
/	Division	expression / expression
%	Modulus	expression % expression

The following example demonstrates the use of each unary operator:

```
<html>
  <head>
    <title>
      JavaScript Professional Projects - Arithmetic Operators
    </title>

    <script language="JavaScript">
    <!--
      var number = 10;
    // -->
    </script>

  </head>
```

```
<body>

  <center>
    <font size=6>JavaScript Professional Projects</font><br>
    <font size=4>Chapter 1: Arithmetic Operators</font>
  </center>

  <br><br>

  <p>
  <font size=4><b>Unary Operators (++, -- and -)</b></font><br><br>
  The original value of 'number' is <b>
  <script language="JavaScript">
  <!--
    document.write( number );
  // -->
  </script>
  </b>.<br><br>
  The value of 'number++' is <b>
  <script language="JavaScript">
  <!--
    document.write( number++ );
  // -->
  </script>
  </b>, but after the operation completes, 'number' it is <b>
  <script language="JavaScript">
  <!--
    document.write( number );
  // -->
  </script>
  </b>.<br><br>
  The value of '++number' is <b>
  <script language="JavaScript">
  <!--
    document.write( ++number );
  // -->
  </script>
  </b>, and after the operation completes, 'number' it is <b>
```

```
<script language="JavaScript">
<!--
  document.write( number );
// -->
</script>
</b>.<br><br>
The value of '-number' is <b>
<script language="JavaScript">
<!--
  document.write( -number );
// -->
</script>
</b>.<br><br><br><br>
<font size=4><b>Binary Operators
                (+, -, *, / and %)</b></font><br><br>
The value of 'number + 12' is <b>
<script language="JavaScript">
<!--
  document.write( number + 12 );
// -->
</script>
</b>.<br><br>
The value of 'number - 9' is <b>
<script language="JavaScript">
<!--
  document.write( number - 9 );
// -->
</script>
</b>.<br><br>
The value of 'number * 33' is <b>
<script language="JavaScript">
<!--
  document.write( number * 33 );
// -->
</script>
</b>.<br><br>
The value of 'number / 2' is <b>
<script language="JavaScript">
```

```
<!--
  document.write( number / 2 );
// -->
</script>
</b>.<br><br>
The value of 'number % 7' is <b>
<script language="JavaScript">
<!--
  document.write( number % 7 );
// -->
</script>
</b>.<br><br>
</p>

</body>

</html>
```

You'll notice that the addition operator is marked as overloaded. This means that the same symbol can be used in more than one way. In the case of the plus sign, it can be used to add two numbers together or concatenate one string with another—two altogether very different operations.

Relational Operators

Relational operators are used primarily with selection statements because they produce a boolean result—either true or false. Here is an example of using the relational operators with an if/else if statement:

```
var var1 = 99;
var var2 = -12;

if( var1 == var2 )
{
  // This relation is false
}
else if( var1 > var2 )
{
  // This relation is true
}
else if( var1 < var2 )
```

```
{
  // This relation is false
}
```

The relational operators and their names are listed in Table 1.6.

Table 1.6 Relational Operators

Symbol	Description
==	Equal to
!=	Not equal to
>	Greater than
>=	Greater than or equal to
<	Less than
<=	Less than or equal to

When performing complex operations that involve relational operators, it is possible to split the statements into their corresponding parts. For example, if you were writing code that used the fact that var1 and var2 are equal or not, you could do the following:

```
...
var areEqual = var1 == var2;
if( areEqual )
{
  // Statement to run if var1 is equal to var2
}
else
{
  // Statement to run if var1 is not equal to var2
}
```

This allows you to use the fact that var1 is or is not equal to var2 without repeatedly performing the evaluation. This method will decrease the amount of time it takes for your program to run, but it may make the program harder to read.

JavaScript Bitwise and Logical Operators

There are many bitwise operators that will allow you to easily change the bit values of numeric variables. Bitwise operators can be either unary or binary, and they always result in a numeric value. Logical operators are used in correlation with the relational operators mentioned in the previous section. Bitwise operators may be a bit difficult to understand, but will be very useful once you get the hang of them. Table 1.7 lists the symbol and name of each bitwise and logical operator.

Table 1.7 Bitwise and Logical Operators

Symbol	Description
&	Bitwise AND
|	Bitwise OR
^	Bitwise XOR
~	Bitwise NOT
<<	Left shift
>>	Right shift
>>>	Zero fill right shift
&&	Logical AND
||	Logical OR
!	Logical NOT

The logical operators are most commonly used with selection statements, which are explained in the next chapter. Bitwise operators can be very useful for mathematical operations. Using bitwise operators is generally faster than multiplying or dividing by powers of two.

Bitwise Operator Example

Because bitwise operators are best explained using examples, I've included a lengthy one:

```
<html>

  <head>
    <title>
      JavaScript Professional Projects - Shift Operators
    </title>

    <script language="JavaScript">
    <!--
```

```
  function toBinary( n )
  {
    var answer = "";
    while( n != 0 )
    {
      answer = Math.abs(n % 2) + answer;
      n = parseInt( n / 2 );
    }
    if( answer.length == 0 ) answer = "0";
    return( answer );
  }
// -->
</script>

</head>

<body>

<center>
  <font size=6>JavaScript Professional Projects</font><br>
  <font size=4>Chapter 1: Shift Operators</font>
</center>

<br><br>

<p>
  <table width="85%">
    <tr>
      <td width="10%"></td>
      <td width="33%"><b>Decimal</b></td>
      <td width="34%"><b>Binary</b></td>
    </tr>
    <tr>
      <td width="10%"> </td>
      <td width="33%"> </td>
      <td width="34%"> </td>
    </tr>
    <tr>
```

```html
  <td width="10%">Bitwise AND</td>
  <td width="33%">117 &amp; 7 =
    <script language="JavaScript">
    <!--
      document.write( 117 & 7 );
    // -->
    </script>
  </td>
  <td width="34%">
    <script language="JavaScript">
    <!--
      document.write( toBinary( 117 ) + " & " + toBinary( 7 ) +
                  " = " + toBinary( 117 & 7 ) );
    // -->
    </script>
  </td>
</tr>
<tr>
  <td width="10%"></td>
  <td width="33%">42 &amp; 21 =
    <script language="JavaScript">
    <!--
      document.write( 42 & 21 );
    // -->
    </script>
  </td>
  <td width="34%">
    <script language="JavaScript">
    <!--
      document.write( toBinary( 42 ) + " & " + toBinary( 21 ) +
                  " = " + toBinary( 42 & 21 ) );
    // -->
    </script>
  </td>
</tr>
<tr>
  <td width="10%"> </td>
  <td width="33%"> </td>
```

```html
    <td width="34%"> </td>
</tr>
<tr>
  <td width="10%">Bitwise OR</td>
  <td width="33%">117 | 7 =
    <script language="JavaScript">
    <!--
      document.write( 117 | 7 );
    // -->
    </script>
  </td>
  <td width="34%">
    <script language="JavaScript">
    <!--
      document.write( toBinary( 117 ) + " | " + toBinary( 7 ) +
                      " = " + toBinary( 117 | 7 ) );
    // -->
    </script>
  </td>
</tr>
<tr>
  <td width="10%"> </td>
  <td width="33%">42 | 21 =
    <script language="JavaScript">
    <!--
      document.write( 42 | 21 );
    // -->
    </script>
  </td>
  <td width="34%">
    <script language="JavaScript">
    <!--
      document.write( toBinary( 42 ) + " | " + toBinary( 21 ) +
                      " = " + toBinary( 42 | 21 ) );
    // -->
    </script>
  </td>
</tr>
```

```html
<tr>
  <td width="10%"> </td>
  <td width="33%"> </td>
  <td width="34%"> </td>
</tr>
<tr>
  <td width="10%">Bitwise XOR</td>
  <td width="33%">117 ^ 7 =
    <script language="JavaScript">
    <!--
      document.write( 117 ^ 7 );
    // -->
    </script>
  </td>
  <td width="34%">
    <script language="JavaScript">
    <!--
      document.write( toBinary( 117 ) + " ¦ " + toBinary( 7 ) +
                " = " + toBinary( 117 ¦ 7 ) );
    // -->
    </script>
  </td>
</tr>
<tr>
  <td width="10%"> </td>
  <td width="33%">42 ^ 21 =
    <script language="JavaScript">
    <!--
      document.write( 42 ^ 21 );
    // -->
    </script>
  </td>
  <td width="34%">
    <script language="JavaScript">
    <!--
      document.write( toBinary( 42 ) + " ¦ " + toBinary( 21 ) +
                " = " + toBinary( 42 ¦ 21 ) );
    // -->
```

```
    </script>
  </td>
</tr>
<tr>
  <td width="10%"> </td>
  <td width="33%"> </td>
  <td width="34%">
     </td>
</tr>
<tr>
  <td width="10%">Bitwise NOT</td>
  <td width="33%">~117 =
    <script language="JavaScript">
    <!--
      document.write( ~117 );
    // -->
    </script>
  </td>
  <td width="34%">
    <script language="JavaScript">
    <!--
      document.write( "~" + toBinary( 117 ) +
                      " = " + toBinary( ~117 ) );
    // -->
    </script>
  </td>
<tr>
  <td></td>
  <td width="33%">~42 =
    <script language="JavaScript">
    <!--
      document.write( ~42 );
    // -->
    </script>
  </td>
  <td width="34%">
    <script language="JavaScript">
    <!--
```

```
                document.write( "~" + toBinary( 42 ) +
                                " = " + toBinary( ~42 ) );
        // -->
        </script>
      </td>
  </tr>
  <tr>
    <td> </td>
    <td width="33%"> </td>
    <td width="34%"> </td>
  </tr>
  <tr>
    <td>Left Shift</td>
    <td width="33%">117 &lt;&lt; 1 =
      <script language="JavaScript">
      <!--
        document.write( 117 << 1 );
      // -->
      </script>
    </td>
    <td width="34%">
      <script language="JavaScript">
      <!--
        document.write( toBinary( 117 ) + " << 1 = " +
                        toBinary( 117 << 1 ) );
      // -->
      </script>
    </td>
  </tr>
  <tr>
    <td> </td>
    <td width="33%">42 &lt;&lt; 3 =
      <script language="JavaScript">
      <!--
        document.write( 42 << 3 );
      // -->
      </script>
    </td>
```

```
  <td width="34%">
    <script language="JavaScript">
    <!--
      document.write( toBinary( 42 ) + " << 3 = " +
                        toBinary( 42 << 3 ) );
    // -->
    </script>
  </td>
</tr>
<tr>
  <td> </td>
  <td width="33%"> </td>
  <td width="34%"> </td>
</tr>
<tr>
  <td>Right Shift</td>
  <td width="33%">117 &gt;&gt; 1 =
    <script language="JavaScript">
    <!--
      document.write( 117 >> 1 );
    // -->
    </script>
  </td>
  <td width="34%">
    <script language="JavaScript">
    <!--
      document.write( toBinary( 117 ) + " >> 1 = " +
                        toBinary( 117 >> 1 ) );
    // -->
    </script>
  </td>
</tr>
<tr>
  <td> </td>
  <td width="33%">42 &gt;&gt; 3 =
    <script language="JavaScript">
    <!--
      document.write( 42 >> 3 );
```

```
        // -->
        </script>
      </td>
      <td width="34%">
        <script language="JavaScript">
        <!--
          document.write( toBinary( 42 ) + " >> 3 = " +
                          toBinary( 42 >> 3 ) );
        // -->
        </script>
      </td>
    </tr>
  </table>


  </body>


</html>
```

This example demonstrates the use of each bitwise operator (except the zero fill right shift [>>>], which behaves identical to the regular right shift [>>]). I encourage you to modify the example above and discover the true power of the bitwise operators.

Logical Operators

The logical operators are comparatively simple, compared to the bitwise operators. Tables 1.8-1.10 display every combination that you will encounter with the logical operators.

Table 1.8 Logical AND

True	&&	True	=	True
True	&&	False	=	False
False	&&	False	=	False

Table 1.9 Logical OR

True	||	True	=	True
False	||	True	=	True
True	||	False	=	True
False	||	False	=	False

Table 1.10 Logical NOT

!True	=	False
!False	=	True

The AND operator only returns true when both operands evaluate to `true`, the OR operator returns `true` if either of the operands evaluate to `true`, and the NOT operator returns the opposite of its single operand.

The most common use for logical operators is with selection statements. Here is a very simple example of a few situations you may encounter:

```
if( true && false )
{
  // These statements will never run
}


if( true ¦¦ false )
{
  // These statements will always run
}


if( !false )
{
  // These statements will always run
}
```

In the first `if` statement, `true && false` will always result in a `false` value, as you can see in Table 1.8. This means that the statements inside the `if` block will never get a chance to run. On the other hand, in the last two `if` statements, `true ¦¦ false` and `!false` will always evaluate to `true`. This means that the statements inside these `if` blocks will always run.

Miscellaneous Operators

There are many other very useful operators that do not fit into the above sections, but are included with JavaScript. All of them are listed in Table 1.11

Table 1.11 Miscellaneous Operators

Symbol	Description
?:	Ternary condition operator.
delete	Used to delete an object and free up its memory.
new	Used to create an instance of a user defined object.
this	Used to refer to the current object.
typeof	Returns the type of an unevaluated operand.
void	Evaluates an expression without returning a value.
+	String concatenation operator.

The ternary operator is closely related to the if/else structure covered in the next chapter. This operator takes three operands. The first operand is a condition, the second operand is the value for the entire expression if the condition evaluates to true, and the third operand is the value for the entire expression if the condition evaluates to false. For example, the output statement

```
document.write( new Date().getHour() < 12 ? "Good morning" :
                                            "Good afternoon" );
```

contains a conditional expression that evaluates to true during the first 12 hours of the day (if new Date().getHour() == true) and false to the last 12 hours of the day (if new Date().getHour() == false). This entire statement can be used to replace the following if/else structure:

```
if( new Date().getHour() < 12 )
{
  document.write( "Good morning" );
}
else
{
  document.write( "Good afternoon" );
}
```

The precedence of this operator is low, so it is a good idea to surround the entire statement in parentheses to avoid undesired results, such as the interpreter evaluating the relational operator and not knowing what to do with the rest of the statement.

Void Operator

The void operator is used to evaluate an expression without returning any results. The most popular way to use the void operator is in a link that goes nowhere. For example:

```
<a href="JavaScript: void" onClick="<some JavaScript command>">
```

This link will not change the currently displayed page when the visitor clicks on it, but will perform some other JavaScript-related action.

+ Operator

The plus (+) operator is an overloaded operator. This means that it can perform more than one operation depending on its operands. When both operands of the plus sign are numbers, they are added together and the result is returned. If one or both of the operands are strings, the operands are concatenated together and a new string is formed. The plus operator in both cases is left-associative. This means that the values to the left of the operator are calculated first, and then the appropriate operation is performed with the left and right operands.

Summary

JavaScript is a client-side programming language that is embedded into Web pages to add dynamic effects to an otherwise static Web page. JavaScript closely resembles the language Java from which it inherits much of its syntax and functionality. To embed JavaScript in your Web page, enclose it in HTML <script> tags.

Chapter 2

Selection and Repetition Statements

This chapter covers two of the most important features of the JavaScript language, selection and repetition statements. Normally, statements in a program are executed sequentially, in the order that they were written. Often it is useful to transfer control in the middle of execution to another section of code—sort of like changing trains at the terminal. The transfer might be just a couple lines of code away, as is the case with loops, or might be a different block of code all together, which is what selection statements do. So that you can accomplish this, several statements that alter the sequential flow of a program are included in the JavaScript programming language. Together, selection and repetition statements are known as *control structures*.

Selection Statements

Selection statements are the decision-making control structure in JavaScript; they are used to choose among alternative courses of action. A program would not be useful at all if it did the same thing no matter what the conditions were while it was running. Selection statements are very easy to translate from English into JavaScript and back again.

Using if and if-else if Statements

Selection statements are your basic decision-making statements in JavaScript. The `if` structure is the single most used selection statement in the JavaScript language. The syntax of the `if` statement is as follows:

```
if( <condition> ){ <statements> }
```

The condition part of the statement can be any statement or relational operator that returns a boolean value. The statements inside the brackets will be executed only if the condition evaluates to `true`. As I stated earlier, selection statements are easily translated to and from English statements. The following statement:

```
If theVar is greater than 2
  Set theVar equal to 1.
```

determines whether the variable `theVar` is greater than 2. If it is, then assign the value 1 to it. This English sentence can be literally translated into the following JavaScript statement:

```
if( theVar > 2 )
{
   theVar = 1;
}
```

This example would have a practical purpose if you were trying to create a table with rows that have alternating colors. The full function might be the following:

```
<html>

  <head>
    <title>
      JavaScript Professional Projects - Selection Statements - if/else
    </title>

    <script language="JavaScript">
    <!--
      var rowNumber = 1;
      function getColor()
```

```
    {
      var color;
      if( rowNumber > 2 )
      {
        rowNumber = 1;
      }

      if( rowNumber == 1 )
      {
        color = "gray";
      }
      else
      {
        color = "white";
      }

      rowNumber++;
      return( color );
    }
  // -->
  </script>

</head>

<body>

  <center>
    <font size=6>JavaScript Professional Projects</font><br>
    <font size=4>Chapter 2: Selection Statements - if/else</font>
  </center>

  <br><br>

  <p>
    <table width="85%" border="1">
      <script language="JavaScript">
      <!--
        document.write( "<tr bgcolor='" + getColor() + "'>" );
```

```
        // -->
        </script>
          <td> </td>
          <td> </td>
        </tr>
        <script language="JavaScript">
        <!--
          document.write( "<tr bgcolor='" + getColor() + "'>" );
        // -->
        </script>
          <td> </td>
          <td> </td>
        </tr>
        <script language="JavaScript">
        <!--
          document.write( "<tr bgcolor='" + getColor() + "'>" );
        // -->
        </script>
          <td> </td>
          <td> </td>
        </tr>
        <script language="JavaScript">
        <!--
          document.write( "<tr bgcolor='" + getColor() + "'>" );
        // -->
        </script>
          <td> </td>
          <td> </td>
        </tr>
        <script language="JavaScript">
        <!--
          document.write( "<tr bgcolor='" + getColor() + "'>" );
        // -->
        </script>
          <td> </td>
          <td> </td>
        </tr>
      </table>
```

```
    </p>


    </body>

</html>
```

This very simple code creates a table with two columns and five rows. The odd-numbered rows have a background color of `"gray"` and the even-numbered rows have a background color of `"white"`. The technique of alternating row colors could be very useful if you are displaying a lot of data in a table because it makes the individual rows easier to distinguish.

You'll notice that in the function there is a regular `if` statement, like in the original example, but then there is an `if` statement with an `else` attached to it. The statements contained within the `else` block will be executed only when the condition in the preceding `if` is determined to be `false`. In the preceding example, the `if` statement will run when `rowNumber` is equal to 1, and at all other times the `else` statement will be run. The syntax for the `if`/`else` structure is

```
if( <condition> ){ <statements> }
else{ <statements> }
```

That is not the end of the story with `if` statements, however. If you have a lot of conditions that you wanted to check and you want only one block of code run for each one, you may end up doing something like the following which prints a grade letter based on a given score:

```
if( n >= 90 )
{
   document.write( "A" );
}
else
{
   if( n >= 80 )
   {
      document.write( "B" );
   }
   else
   {
      if( n >= 70 )
      {
         document.write( "C" );
      }
      else
      {
```

```
          if( n >= 60 )
          {
            document.write( "D" );
          }
          else
          {
            document.write( "F" );
          }
        }
      }
    }
```

If n is greater or equal to 90, then the first four conditions will be evaluated to be `true`, but only the letter A will be displayed. After the first condition is evaluated to be `true`, the `else` attached to it will be skipped. This is a perfectly legal way to check for multiple conditions. It does, however, result in deep indentations that can be hard to read. Many programmers prefer to write the preceding `if` structure as:

```
if( n >= 90 )
{
  document.write( "A" );
}
else if( n >= 80 )
{
  document.write( "B" );
}
else if( n >= 70 )
{
  document.write( "C" );
}
else if( n >= 60 )
{
  document.write( "D" );
}
else
{
  document.write( "F" );
}
```

The two forms behave in exactly the same way. On average, the nested if/else statements in the first form can run faster than the series of if/else if statements in the second form. To increase the runtime of your programs, test the conditions that have a greater chance of evaluating to true early; doing so will cause the structure to exit earlier.

The complete syntax for if/else if/else structures is as follows:

```
if( <condition> ){ <statements> }
else if( <condition> ){ <statements> }

...

else{ <statements> }
```

To avoid extra characters in the source file—which increase download time—omit the curly braces surrounding a single statement in an if structure. The second form in the example above could be rewritten as

```
if( n >= 90 )
   document.write( "A" );
else if( n >= 80 )
   document.write( "B" );
else if( n >= 70 )
   document.write( "C" );
else if( n >= 60 )
   document.write( "D" );
else
   document.write( "F" );
```

This is an overall more compact, but slightly harder to read, version that accomplishes the same goal. When omitting braces, it is important to understand how the else statement matches up with preceding if statements. For example, the following piece of code might not do what you would expect:

```
if( n > 0 )

   if( n < 10 )
      document.write( "n is > 0 but < 10" );


else
   document.write( "n is <= 0" );
```

This is a perfectly legal if structure. If n is 8, then "n is > 0 but < 10" is output. But what happens when n is 11? You might expect that nothing will be output, but that is not the case. The message "n is <= 0" is output when n is 11—but that is obviously not accurate. What happens is that the else statement is really attached to the inner if statement. This is another case in which not formatting your code correctly may confuse the reader. The JavaScript inter-preter in your browser does not know that the `else` statement was supposed to go with the first `if` statement. All that the interpreter knows is that there is an `if` statement followed by another `if` statement and an `else`. Its natural response is to connect the `else` with the `if` statement that immediately preceded it. To avoid this problem, you will need to be more specific and use curly braces. A better version of the same code would be as follows:

```
if( n > 0 )
{

  if( n < 10 )
    document.write( "n is > 0 but < 10" );
}
else
  document.write( "n is <= 0" );
```

This code does exactly what you would expect it to do. When n is equal to 11, nothing is dis-played, and when n is less than or equal to 0, the message `"n is <= 0"` is displayed.

Using the Ternary Operator in Lieu of if Statements

As I mentioned in Chapter 1, the ternary operator can be used to replace simple `if`/`else` structures. In the alternating row color example given previously, the `if`/`else` structure,

```
if( rowNumber == 1 )
{
  color = "gray";
}
else
{
  color = "white";
}
```

can be replaced by the single line of code:

```
color = ( rowNumber == 1 ? "gray" : "white" );
```

This, of course, is a little harder to read, but it will decrease the overall download time of your Web page. The revised function,

```
var rowNumber = 1;
function getColor()
{
  var color;
```

```
  if( rowNumber > 2 ) rowNumber = 1;


  color = ( rowNumber == 1 ? "gray" : "white" );


  rowNumber++;
  return( color );
}
```

can be simplified even further with the use of the modulus operator. As you learned in Chapter 1, the modulus operator, %, returns the remainder that results from integer division. Keeping this in mind, the entire function could be rewritten as a single line function:

```
var rowNumber = 0;
function getColor()
{
  return( rowNumber++ % 2 == 0 ? "gray" : "white" );
}
```

This trades readability for overall speed.

You could even replace the nested if/else structure above what was used to print grade letters with the following nested ternary operators:

```
document.write
  ( n >= 90 ? "A" :
    ( n >= 80 ? "B" :
      ( n >= 70 ? "C" :
        ( n >= 60 ? "D" : "F" )
      )
    )
  );
```

This results in a singe statement that is very hard to read, but it reduces the number of character required to download from 168 to 66.

Using switch Statements

Switch statements are the other selection structure that is supported by JavaScript. While you can replace a switch statement with an if/else if/else statement in any instance, they are not interchangeable—you cannot replace all if/else if/else statements with switch statements. This means that the switch structure is slightly less powerful, but no less useful. Switch statements are used primarily for comparing a handful of values to a variable that contains a primitive value.

Occasionally, an algorithm will test a single variable against a list of different values and execute separate commands depending on the variable's value. An example of this might be

```javascript
if( n == 0 )
{
   document.write( "zero" );
}
else if( n == 12 )
{
   document.write( "One dozen" );
}
else if( n == 13 )
{
   document.write( "Baker's dozen" );
}
else
{
   document.write( "Some number" );
}
```

This checks three different values for n, but is a rather lengthy way of testing for three simple values. An alternative would be to use a `switch` statement:

```javascript
switch( n )
{
   case 0:
     document.write( "zero" );
     break;
   case 12:
     document.write( "One dozen" );
     break;
   case 13:
     document.write( "Baker's dozen" );
     break;
   default:
     document.write( "Some number" );
     break;
}
```

The `switch` structure is made up of a series of `case` labels and an optional `default` case.

Each `case` consists of one or more statements followed by an optional `break` statement. The complete syntax for the `switch` statement is as follows:

```
switch( <variable> )
{
  case <possible value>:
    <statements>
    break;
  case <possible value>:
    <statements>
    break;

  ...

  default:
    <statements>
    break;

}
```

There really is no advantage of using a `switch` statement instead of an `if/else if/else` structure if both are suitable for a situation. As a rule of thumb, use a `switch` statement when you are comparing a list of values against a single variable and an `if/else if/else` structure all other times.

Let's expand on our alternating row color example given previously. If you wanted to use more than two colors in your table, then that would be an excellent time to use a `switch` statement. Here is an example:

```
<html>

  <head>
    <title>
      JavaScript Professional Projects - Selection Statements - switch
    </title>

    <script language="JavaScript">
    <!--
      var rowNumber = 0;
      function getColor()
      {
        var color;

        switch( rowNumber )
```

```
        {
          case 0:
            color = "gray";
            break;
          case 1:
            color = "white";
            break;
          case 2:
            color = "blue";
            break;
          case 3:
            color = "green";
            break;
          case 4:
            color = "red";
            break;
        }

        rowNumber = ( rowNumber + 1 ) % 5;
        return( color );
      }
    // -->
    </script>

  </head>

  <body>

    <center>
      <font size=6>JavaScript Professional Projects</font><br>
      <font size=4>Chapter 2: Selection Statements - switch</font>
    </center>

    <br><br>

    <p>
      <table width="85%" border="1">
        <script language="JavaScript">
```

```
<!--
   document.write( "<tr bgcolor='" + getColor() + "'>" );
// -->
</script>
   <td> </td>
   <td> </td>
</tr>
<script language="JavaScript">
<!--
   document.write( "<tr bgcolor='" + getColor() + "'>" );
// -->
</script>
   <td> </td>
   <td> </td>
</tr>
<script language="JavaScript">
<!--
   document.write( "<tr bgcolor='" + getColor() + "'>" );
// -->
</script>
   <td> </td>
   <td> </td>
</tr>
<script language="JavaScript">
<!--
   document.write( "<tr bgcolor='" + getColor() + "'>" );
// -->
</script>
   <td> </td>
   <td> </td>
</tr>
<script language="JavaScript">
<!--
   document.write( "<tr bgcolor='" + getColor() + "'>" );
// -->
</script>
   <td> </td>
   <td> </td>
```

```
            </tr>
          </table>
        </p>


      </body>

  </html>
```

This example is identical in functionality to the previous example, except that it allows you to alternate between five different colors instead of two.

Another example of where `switch` statements are a logical choice is when determining the postscript for a number. For example: 1st, 2nd, 3rd, 4th, and so on. This could be useful if you are designing a calendar that displays the number for each day of the month. For now, here is a slightly simpler example:

```
<html>

  <head>
    <title>
      JavaScript Professional Projects - Selection Statements - switch
    </title>

    <script language="JavaScript">
    <!--
      function getEnding( number )
      {
        switch( number % 10 )
        {
          case 0:
          case 4:
          case 5:
          case 6:
          case 7:
          case 8:
          case 9:
            return( "th" );
          case 1:
            return( "st" );
          case 2:
```

```
          return( "nd" );
        case 3:
          return( "rd" );
      }
    }
  // -->
  </script>

</head>

<body>

  <center>
    <font size=6>JavaScript Professional Projects</font><br>
    <font size=4>Chapter 2: Selection Statements - switch</font>
  </center>

  <br><br>

  <p>
    <table width="85%" border="1">
      <tr>
        <td>1
          <script language="JavaScript">
          <!--
            document.write( getEnding( 1 ) );
          // -->
          </script>
        </td>
      </tr>
      <tr>
        <td>2
          <script language="JavaScript">
          <!--
            document.write( getEnding( 2 ) );
          // -->
          </script>
        </td>
```

```
    </tr>
    <tr>
      <td>3
        <script language="JavaScript">
        <!--
          document.write( getEnding( 3 ) );
        // -->
        </script>
      </td>
    </tr>
    <tr>
      <td>4
        <script language="JavaScript">
        <!--
          document.write( getEnding( 4 ) );
        // -->
        </script>
      </td>
    </tr>
    <tr>
      <td>5
        <script language="JavaScript">
        <!--
          document.write( getEnding( 5 ) );
        // -->
        </script>
      </td>
    </tr>
  </table>
</p>


</body>

</html>
```

This example is an oversimplification of the true power of the `getEnding()` function, which will be explored fully later on.

There are two peculiar things about the example just given. First of all, there are six case labels in a row that do not have any break or return associated with them. Because they don't have a break statement, the empty case labels all share the statements in the following case statement—in this case, return("th");. The second interesting part of the example is the total lack of break statements. Normally, without a break statement, every statement in each case label would be executed until the end of the switch block was reached. In the example just given, the return statements do the job of the break statement by "breaking" out of the switch block.

The importance of the break statement, or in the previous example return statements, cannot be over emphasized. The following example illustrates what would happen if the break statements were left out of the switch structure.

```
function func( n )
{
  switch( n )
  {
    case 1:
      document.write( "One<br>" );
    case 2:
      document.write( "Two<br>" );
    case 3:
      document.write( "Three<br>" );
    case 4:
      document.write( "Four<br>" );
    case 5:
      document.write( "Five<br>" );
    default:
      document.write( "Some number<br>" );
  }
}
```

The output from this example would not be what the programmer had in mind. If the function were to be called with the number 2 as an operand, the output would be

Two
Three
Four
Five
Some number

Although sometimes this result might be desirable, most of the time it is not. In the previous example, you might expect the output to only print Two, but because I left off the `break` statements, it prints Two, Three, Four and Five. In the example that printed the number postscripts, leaving the `break` statements out was a good thing; in this example it is not.

Repetition Statements

Selection statements may be the most used of all JavaScript statements, but repetition statements make up the biggest time slice of the total running time of your program. On average, repetition statements (or *loops*) will take up 95 to 99 percent of the total running time of any given program. Because of this fact, it is necessary not only to write working loops, but to write efficient loops. This is especially necessary with an interpreted language such as JavaScript because the interpretation tends to run slower than identical natively compiled programs.

Using while

The simplest type of repetition statement, or loop structure, is the `while` loop. A `while` loop is adequate for meeting all of your looping needs. The syntax for a `while` loop is very simple:

```
while( <condition> )
{
  <statements>
}
```

A `while` loop executes all of the statements between curly braces over and over again until the condition is evaluated to `false`. Just like with the `if` statement, the curly braces are optional *if and only if* there is a single statement within the loop body. Take a look at the following example, which creates a table with five rows:

```
<html>

  <head>
    <title>
      JavaScript Professional Projects - Repetition Statements - while
    </title>

  </head>

  <body>

    <center>
```

```
      <font size=6>JavaScript Professional Projects</font><br>
      <font size=4>Chapter 2: Repetition Statements - while</font>
   </center>


   <br><br>


   <p>
      <table width="85%" border="1">
        <script language="JavaScript">
        <!--
          var n = 1;
          while( n <= 5 )
          {
            document.write( "<tr><td>" +
                            "This is row #" + n +
                            "</td></tr>" );
            n++;
          }
        // -->
        </script>
      </table>
   </p>




   </body>


</html>
```

The while loop in the body runs as long as the variable n is less than or equal to five incrementing ns each time through the loop. The loop runs a total of five times and creates a new row in the table each time. The last line in the body of the loop, n++;, is very important. If that one line were not there, the condition would never evaluate to false and would cause the loop to run forever—an *infinite loop*. You can tell if you have written an infinite loop because your computer will appear to slow down, and the Web page will never be displayed in the browser. The only way to stop an infinite loop is to close your browser or, if you are unable to close your browser, hit Alt + F4 in Windows or Command + Option + Escape in Mac OS.

The alternating row color example presented earlier would be an excellent candidate for the while loop.

```
<html>

  <head>
    <title>
      JavaScript Professional Projects - Alternating row
    </title>

    <script language="JavaScript">
    <!--
      var rowNumber = 1;
      function getColor()
      {
        var color;

        switch( rowNumber )
        {
          case 0:
            color = "gray";
            break;
          case 1:
            color = "white";
            break;
          case 2:
            color = "blue";
            break;
          case 3:
            color = "green";
            break;
          case 4:
            color = "red";
            break;
        }

        rowNumber = ( rowNumber + 1 ) % 5;
        return( color );
      }
    // -->
    </script>
```

```
</head>

<body>

  <center>
    <font size=6>JavaScript Professional Projects</font><br>
    <font size=4>Chapter 2: Alternating row background colors</font>
  </center>

  <br><br>

  <p>
    <table width="85%" border="1">
      <script language="JavaScript">
      <!--
        var n = 1;
        while( n <= 15 )
        {
          document.write( "<tr bgcolor='" + getColor() + "'>" );
          document.write( "<td>Row number " + n + "</td></tr>" );
          n++;
        }
      // -->
      </script>
    </table>
  </p>


</body>

</html>
```

With the while loop, not only does the Web page become much smaller as far as the amount required to download, but it also becomes much more flexible. If you wanted a table with more or fewer rows, all you would have to do is change the condition in the while loop. This is especially useful if you don't know how many rows are required before the page is loaded. Take a look at the following code fragment for a simple example of dynamic row counts:

```
var n = 1;
var totalRows = Math.random() * 20 + 1;
```

```
while( n <= totalRows  )
{
   document.write( "<tr bgcolor='" + getColor() + "'>" );
   document.write( "<td>Row number " + n + "</td></tr>" );
   n++;
}
```

If you replace this code fragment for the script in the above example, you will get a randomly generated number of rows—anywhere from 1 to 21.

Using do-while

The do-while statement is very similar to the regular while statement. The condition in while loops is tested before the body of the loop is run. This means that it is possible for the loop not to run at all. The difference in the do-while loop is that the condition is tested *after* the loop body has run. This ensures that the loop will run at least one time before the condition statement is reached. Here is the syntax for the do-while statement:

```
do
{
   <statements>
}
while( <condition> );
```

One important difference in the syntax is the fact that the do-while statement ends in a semicolon and the while statement does not. The semicolon at the end of the do-while loop is needed to set the while portion off from the next line of code and to make your source easier to read.

Using for

A for loop is slightly more complicated than a while loop because it takes three operands and can create/update variables. A while loop can do everything a for loop can do. Likewise, everything a for loop can do is also possible with a while loop. Choosing between a for or while loop is really up to the programmer, as there is no inherit benefit from using one instead of the other. The syntax of a for loop is as follows:

```
for( <declaration> ; <condition> ; <increment> )
{
   <statements>
}
```

The declaration part of the for loop is where you can declare and initialize the control variable for the loop. The condition part of the for loop is identical to the condition portion of the while loop and will cause the loop to run until evaluated to `false`. The increment portion of the `for` loop is where the control variable is updated. All three parts of the `for` loop header are optional, but the semicolons must always be present. Just as with the `while` loop and `if` statement, the curly braces are optional *if and only if* there is a single statement in the body of the loop.

The order in which the portions of a `for` statement are executed is very important to how a program behaves. When the loop is reached, the declaration portion of the statements is executed and then the condition is checked. If the condition evaluates to `true`, the loop body is run and the increment portion is executed. Once again, the condition is checked and if it evaluates to `true`, the body and increment portions of the loop are each executed. The whole process continues until the condition evaluates to `false`.

To illustrate the ease of switching between `for` and `while` loops, here is the alternating row color example with `for` loops:

```html
<html>

  <head>
    <title>
      JavaScript Professional Projects - Alternating row
    </title>

    <script language="JavaScript">
<!--
    var rowNumber = 1;
    function getColor()
    {
      var color;

      switch( rowNumber )
      {
        case 0:
          color = "gray";
          break;
        case 1:
          color = "white";
          break;
        case 2:
          color = "blue";
          break;
```

```
      case 3:
        color = "green";
        break;
      case 4:
        color = "red";
        break;
    }

    rowNumber = ( rowNumber + 1 ) % 5;
    return( color );
  }
// -->
</script>


</head>

<body>

  <center>
    <font size=6>JavaScript Professional Projects</font><br>
    <font size=4>Chapter 2: Alternating row background colors</font>
  </center>

  <br><br>

  <p>
    <table width="85%" border="1">
      <script language="JavaScript">
      <!--
        var totalRows = Math.random() * 20 + 1;
        for( n = 1 ; n <= totalRows ; n++ )
        {
          document.write( "<tr bgcolor='" + getColor() + "'>" );
          document.write( "<td>Row number " + n + "</td></tr>" );
        }
      // -->
      </script>
```

```
    </table>
  </p>


  </body>


</html>
```

The examples produce identical results. It is up to you to choose which loop you want to use.

One thing that you can do with a for loop that's not so easy to do with a while loop is to declare variables that will only be used within the scope of the loop. In the preceding example, the variable n was part of the declaration portion of the for loop. This variable will only be available as long as the loop is running. As soon as the loop ends, the variable is "forgotten" as the memory it occupied is freed. You are not limited to only one variable declaration in the for loop. In the same example, it would be possible to declare the variable totalRows within the declaration portion of the for loop.

```
for( n = 1, totalRows = Math.random() * 20 + 1 ; n <= totalRows ; n++ )
{
  document.write( "<tr bgcolor='" + getColor() + "'>" );
  document.write( "<td>Row number " + n + "</td></tr>" );
}
```

This loop and the one used in the previous example are nearly identical. A comma-separated list of variables in the declaration portion of the for loop means that each will be initialized before the loop begins. The only drawback to the second approach is that the variable totalRows will no longer be available after the loop completes. You may also have a comma-separated list of increments in the increment portion of the for loop.

Using for-in Loops

for-in loops are used to easily iterate through a list of items such as an array or properties of an object. Here is the syntax for a for-in statement:

```
for( <variable> in <object> )
{
  <statements>

}
```

In the for-in loop, "variable" is the name of a new variable that will hold the next element of "object" during each pass through the loop. This concept is best illustrated with an example.

```html
<html>

<head>
  <title>
    JavaScript Professional Projects - Repetition Statements - for-in
  </title>

  <script language="JavaScript">
  <!--
    var daysArray = new Array( "Sunday",
                               "Monday",
                               "Tuesday",
                               "Wednesday",
                               "Thursday",
                               "Friday",
                               "Saturday" );
  // -->
  </script>

</head>

<body>

  <center>
    <font size=6>JavaScript Professional Projects</font><br>
    <font size=4>Chapter 2: Repetition Statements - for-in</font>
  </center>

  <br><br>

  <p>
    <script language="JavaScript">
    <!--
      for( day in daysArray )
      {
        document.write( daysArray[day] + "<br>" );
      }
    // -->
```

```
    </script>
  </p>


  </body>


</html>
```

In this example, `daysArray` is an array holding the days of the week. The `for-in` loop in the body of the Web page iterates through each element in the array and prints the value of the array element. One advantage of using a `for-in` loop to iterate through arrays is that you do not need to know the size of the array. This allows you to write faster and more efficient code.

`for-in` loops will be covered in depth in Chapter 3, "Arrays and Strings" and in Chapter 5, "Object-Oriented JavaScript."

break and continue Statements

Sometimes it is necessary to alter the flow of a loop from within the loop itself. For example, if erroneous data is encountered while looping through all the elements in a form, the `break` command will allow the loop to be prematurely exited. A situation in which you might use the `break` command would be when a loop is finding the sum of an array of integers and encounters an element that is not a number.

```
var total = 0;
for( number in theArray )
{
  if( !isNaN( theArray[number] ) )
  {
    total += theArray[number];
  }
  else
  {
    break;
  }
}
```

As soon as the loop encounters an array element that is not a number and, consequently, cannot be added to the total, the loop breaks. If all of the array elements are numbers, the loop will successfully iterate through the entire array, adding each element to the total.

Another way to handle the erroneous array elements would be to simply skip each one that is not a number. The `continue` command tells the loop structure to break out of the current loop, but continue as if everything was fine. The example above could be rewritten as

```
var total = 0;
for( number in theArray )
{
  if( !isNaN( theArray[number] ) )
  {
    total += theArray[number];
  }
  else
  {
    continue;
  }
}
```

This program segment would find the sum of all of the numbers in an array, ignoring anything that is not a number.

The break and continue commands are most often used for error checking and error recovery while processing data in loops.

Optimizing Loops

Because so much of the time that a program is running is taken up by executing repetition statements, a lot of study has gone into making them as efficient as possible. The total running time of a program can be greatly improved by decreasing the number of instructions inside a loop, even if those instructions are simply moved outside the loop structure.

There are two techniques for the optimization of loops: *code motion* and *reduction in strength*. These techniques are very advanced concepts that are usually discussed in books on compiler writing. Feel free to consider this section optional reading. If, on the other hand, you want to know even more than is presented here, I would recommend the book *Compilers: Principles, Techniques and Tools* by Alfred V. Aho.

One of the simplest things you can do to decrease the amount of time spent in loops and improve the runtime of your programs is to move constant instructions outside of a loop. The easiest way to do this is to identify statements in the body of the loop that do not change as the loop runs, such as declarations and comparisons. To understand this process, take a look this example of a bad loop:

```
var i = 0;
var limit = 57;
while( i <= limit - 2 )
{
  var pi = 3.14;
```

```
    if( new Date().getDay() > 0 )
      document.write( pi * i + "<br>" );
    i++;
}
```

There are three places where this loop can be improved. First of all, the quantity limit − 2 does not need to be evaluated each time through the loop. Secondly, the variable `pi` does not change throughout the program, so it can be moved outside of the loop. Lastly, the `if` statement creates a new `Date` object, then gets the day value and compares it to a literal—this does not need to be done every time through the loop. A better version of the same program would be

```
var i = 0;
var limit = 57;
var pi = 3.14;
var t = limit - 2;
var show = new Date().getDay() > 0;
while( i <= t )
{
  if( show )
    document.write( pi * i + "<br>" );
  i++;
}
```

These three changes will probably not noticeably change the runtime of your program, but if all these optimizations are applied to each of your loops, you will see a difference—especially on slower computers.

The other type of optimization, reduction of strength, might not be quite so obvious. Replacing complex operations with simpler ones inside your loops can have surprising effects on the amount of time it takes for your program to run. Here is an example program segment that would be a good candidate for reduction in strength:

```
for( i = 0 ; i < 100 ; i++ )
{
  document.write( "2^" + i + " = " +
                  Math.pow( 2, i ) + "<br>" );

}
```

This rather straightforward loop calculates and displays the first 50 powers of two. The `Math.pow()` statement in particular is very costly in time. An alternative to calling this costly method 50 times is to use the left shift operator (<<). Here is the same code segment rewritten with reduction in strength applied:

```
for( i = 0 ; i < 100 ; i++ )
{
  document.write( "2^" + i + " = " +
                     ( 1 << i ) + "<br>" );

}
```

The left shift operator is much less costly as far as its time requirements. Unfortunately, the left shift operator is only useful when multiplying by powers of two. Although the reduction in strength technique of loop optimization is not as common or easy to use as code motion, it generally yields more noticeable results.

Summary

Together, selection and repetition statements are known as *control structures*. JavaScript supports two selection statements and three repetition statements. The `if`/`else` selection statement is the basic decision-making statement in JavaScript. `switch`/`case` statements perform the same basic type of selection but only on lists of primitive values. The `for` and `while` loops are nearly identical in function and are used for repeating several statements many times. The `for-in` repetition statement is designed to loop through arrays or collections of data very efficiently. The total running time of a program can be greatly improved by decreasing the number of instructions inside a loop. There are two ways you can optimize your loops, *code motion* and *reduction in strength*.

Chapter 3

Arrays and Strings

Arrays and strings are two of the most commonly used objects in the JavaScript language. *Arrays* are used to hold large amounts of data of the same type logically in memory so that each element can be accessed directly from the array name and index. *Strings* are collections of characters that can be manipulated with special built-in functions. You have already seen strings in the code examples in previous chapters. Any term surrounded by either single or double quotes is considered a *string literal* and is used to create a string object.

JavaScript Arrays

What would you do if you had 100 names you wanted to keep track of throughout the length of your program? One solution would be to create a separate variable for each name. Having done so, if you wanted to display each name on your Web page, you would have to write a separate output statement for each variable. Not only would this process be lengthy and inefficient, it would also make the size of your Web page much larger than it needed to be. A better solution would be to keep track of all the names in an array. Then, when you wanted to output them, you could just loop through the array and use the same output statement to display each one.

Single and Multi-Dimensional Arrays

The most commonly used type of array is a single-dimension array that holds a list of numbers or strings that are related in some way. For example, you might use an array to store the ISBN numbers of books your Web page visitor would like to check out of a library. Similarly, you might want to keep track of the title of each book so that you could display the list later on. Both would be valid uses for an array. The syntax for declaring an array is as follows:

```
var <identifier> = new Array( <size> );
```

or

```
var <identifier> = new Array( <element>, <element>, ... );
```

The first way to declare an array is with only the size as an operand. This will create an array of the desired size, with empty elements. The second way of declaring an array is to provide a comma-separated list of elements that you would like to include in the array. The size of the array will depend on the number of elements you provide. Here is an example of declaring, filling, and outputting an array:

```
<html>

  <head>
    <title>
      JavaScript Professional Projects - Arrays
    </title>

    <script language="JavaScript">
    <!--
      var arraySize = 100;
      var theArray = new Array( arraySize );

      for( i = 0 ; i < arraySize ; i++ )
      {
        theArray[i] = parseInt( Math.random() * 100 );
```

```
        }
      // -->
      </script>

  </head>

  <body>

    <center>
      <font size=6>JavaScript Professional Projects</font><br>
      <font size=4>Chapter 3: Arrays</font>
    </center>

    <br><br>

    <p>
      <table>
        <script language="JavaScript">
        <!--
          for( i = 0 ; i < arraySize ; i++ )
          {
            if( i % 10 == 0 ) document.write( "<tr>" );
            document.write( "<td>" );

            document.write( theArray[i] );

            document.write( "</td>" );
            if( i % 10 == 9 ) document.write( "</tr>" );
          }
        // -->
        </script>
      <table>
    </p>


  </body>

</html>
```

This example creates a single-dimension array with size `arraySize`, which is declared as 100. The array is then filled with randomly generated integer numbers from 0 to 99. This way, in the body of the Web page, each element of the array is displayed in a 10 × 10 table. This example demonstrates one important point: It is always a good idea to keep a variable that holds the desired size of the array. This will make iterating through the array easier because you already know how large the array is. This technique will also make updating your code easier. If, in the example just given, the integer literal 100 had been used to declare the array, then you might be tempted to use the literal 100 while looping through the array. This would cause a problem later on if you decided to change the size of the array. Not only would you have to change the literal where you declared the array, but you would also have to find every other place where you used 100 as the array length and change that, too. By declaring a variable to keep track of the array length, you need only change the value of it in that one place in order for it to take effect throughout the page.

Unfortunately, single-dimension arrays do no always provide enough functionality for every problem you will have. If you decided to keep track of not only the ISBN number, but also the title, author, and publisher of books your Web page visitor wanted to check out of the library, you could do one of two things. You could create four parallel arrays—one to hold the ISBN, a second to hold the title, a third to hold the author's name, and a fourth to hold the name of the book's publisher. This approach works, but may lead to confusion later on. A better way to keep track of all that information would be to use a two-dimension array.

```
<html>

  <head>
    <title>
      JavaScript Professional Projects - Multi-Dimensional Arrays
    </title>

    <script language="JavaScript">
    <!--
      var numBooks = 5;
      var bookInfo = new Array( numBooks );

      bookInfo[0] = new Array( 4 );
      bookInfo[0][0] = "0-201-10088-6";
      bookInfo[0][1] = "Compilers - Principles, Techniques, and Tools";
      bookInfo[0][2] = "Alfred V. Aho etc.";
      bookInfo[0][3] = "Addison-Wesley Publishing Company";

      bookInfo[1] = new Array( 4 );
      bookInfo[1][0] = "0-201-89685-0";
```

```
    bookInfo[1][1] = "The Art of Computer Programming Vol.3";
    bookInfo[1][2] = "Donald E. Knuth";
    bookInfo[1][3] = "Addison-Wesley";

    bookInfo[2] = new Array( 4 );
    bookInfo[2][0] = "0-13-899394-7";
    bookInfo[2][1] = "Java - How to Program";
    bookInfo[2][2] = "Deitel & Deitel";
    bookInfo[2][3] = "Prentice Hall";

    bookInfo[3] = new Array( 4 );
    bookInfo[3][0] = "0-7645-4003-3";
    bookInfo[3][1] = "HTML & Web Publishing Secrets";
    bookInfo[3][2] = "Jim Heid";
    bookInfo[3][3] = "IDG Books Worldwide, Inc.";

    bookInfo[4] = new Array( 4 );
    bookInfo[4][0] = "0-13-091013-9";
    bookInfo[4][1] = "Assembly Language for Intel-Based Computers";
    bookInfo[4][2] = "Kip R. Irvine";
    bookInfo[4][3] = "Prentice Hall";
  // -->
  </script>

</head>

<body>

  <center>
    <font size=6>JavaScript Professional Projects</font><br>
    <font size=4>Chapter 3: Multi-Dimensional Arrays </font>
  </center>

  <br><br>

  <p>
    <table border="1" cellpadding="2" cellspacing="1">
      <tr>
```

```
    <td><b>ISBN</b></td>
    <td><b>Title</b></td>
    <td><b>Author</b></td>
    <td><b>Publisher</b></td>
  <script language="JavaScript">
  <!--
    for( i = 0 ; i < numBooks ; i++ )
    {
      document.write( "<tr>" );

      document.write( "<td>" + bookInfo[i][0] + "</td>" );
      document.write( "<td>" + bookInfo[i][1] + "</td>" );
      document.write( "<td>" + bookInfo[i][2] + "</td>" );
      document.write( "<td>" + bookInfo[i][3] + "</td>" );

      document.write( "</tr>" );
    }
  // -->
  </script>
  <table>
</p>


</body>

</html>
```

This example essentially uses an array of arrays to hold all of the information for each book. The first array declaration creates the first dimension of the multi-dimension array. Afterwards, each element in the first array—representing each book—is initialized as another array of size 4. Each element in the second-dimension array will hold the information for the book. The only limit to the number of dimensions an array can have is the amount of memory the program is running on.

Elements in an Array

Easy access to any element in an array is one of the biggest benefits of using arrays. You can get or set the value of any element in an array simply by specifying its index. For example, an array declared as

```
var theArray = new Array("January","February","March","April");
```

has a length of 4. The string "January" has an index of 0, "February" has an index of 1, "March" has an index of 2, and "April" has an index of 3. It is important to remember that arrays in JavaScript have a zero-based indexing system. In the previous array, referencing the element at index 4 will cause an error in your program. The largest index of any array will be its length − 1. To reference the elements of an array in your program, you simply put the index within square braces after the array name:

```
document.write( theArray[0] + " is the first month" +
                "of the year.<br>" );


document.write( theArray[1] + " is the shortest month" +
                "of the year.<br>" );


document.write( "Spring begins in " + theArray[2] + ".<br>" );


document.write( theArray[3] + " showers bring" +
                "May flowers.<br>" );
```

Using elements in a multi-dimensional array is just as easy. Instead of a single set of square braces, you will need to use the same number as there are dimensions in the array. If an array is declared as

```
var bookInfo = new Array( 1 );
bookInfo[0] = new Array( 4 );
```

then referencing the elements in the second dimension could be done like this:

```
bookInfo[0][0] = "0-201-10088-6";
bookInfo[0][1] = "Compilers - Principles, Techniques, and Tools";
bookInfo[0][2] = "Alfred V. Aho etc.";
bookInfo[0][3] = "Addison-Wesley Publishing Company";
```

The first set of square braces refers to the elements in the first dimension of this two-dimensional array, and the second set refers to elements in the second dimension.

Most of the time, you will be referencing the elements of an array within some type of loop. for loops are ideal for iterating through arrays. The basic structure of a for loop that iterates through a single-dimension array would be as follows:

```
var theArray = new Array( <some size> );
for( index = 0 ; index < theArray.length ; index++ )
{
   <statements referencing theArray[index]>
}
```

The `for` loop is not the only way to loop through all of an array's elements. The `for-in` loop structure was designed specifically to iterate through an array of elements. The previous example could just as easily be written as

```javascript
var theArray = new Array( <some size> );

for( index in theArray )
{
    <statements referencing theArray[index]>
}
```

It is up to you, as the programmer, to decide which loop structure suits your needs.

Iterating through multi-dimensional arrays usually requires nested loops like this:

```javascript
var theArray = new Array( <some size> );

// Create the second dimension
for( index in theArray )
{
    theArray[index] = new Array( <some size> );
}


// Iterate through both dimensions of the array
for( i = 0 ; i < theArray.length ; i++ )
{
    for( j = 0 ; j < theArray[i].length ; j++ )
    {
        <statements referencing theArray[i][j]>
    }
}
```

This example will loop through each element in a two-dimensional array. The last nested `for` loops could just as easily be written with nested `for-in` loops, like this:

```javascript
// Iterate through both dimensions of the array
for( i in theArray )
{
    for( j in theArray[i] )
    {
        <statements referencing theArray[i][j]>
    }
}
```

Again, both methods accomplish the same result.

Array-Specific Properties and Methods

As you'll recall, I stated back in Chapter 1 that arrays were nothing more than specialized objects. Like all objects, an array has many properties, and methods are built into the Array object to make working with it much easier.

Array Properties

The following subsections contain descriptions of the Array object's properties.

length

The `length` property is the total number of element spaces allocated in the array. If the array constructor specified a size, this property reflects that amount, even if data is not stored in each element.

prototype

The `prototype` property is a static property of the Array object. Use the `prototype` property to assign new properties and methods to the Array object in the current document.

To add an additional method to the Array object, all you'd need to do is write the corresponding function:

```
function print()
{
  for( index = 0 ; index < this.length ; index++ )
  {
    document.write( this[index] + "<br>" );
  }
}
```

Then simply add it to the `prototype` property of the static Array object:

```
Array.prototype.print = print;
```

Then, whenever a new instance of the Array object is created, a new method, `print`, will be available to it:

```
var theDays = new Array( "Sun", "Mon", "Tues", "Wed",
                         "Thurs", "Fri", "Sat" );


theDays.print();
```

When the print method is called, each element in the array will be printed on its own line in the Web page.

Array Methods

There are some very useful methods that are part of the Array object definition. The following subsections name and describe them.

concat (array2)

The concat (array2) method combines the current array with the array specified as the parameter.

Following is an example of using the concat() method:

```
var myArray3 = myArray1.concat( myArray2 );
```

The array instance myArray3 will now contain all the elements in myArray1 followed by myArray2. Neither of the original arrays is altered in any way.

join (delimiter)

The join(delimiter) method returns a string containing each element in the array separated by delimiter.

Following is an example of the join() method:

```
var myArray = new Array( "Yesterday", "Today", "Tomorrow" );
document.write( myArray.join( "," ) + "<br>" );
```

The output of this code segment would be:

> Yesterday, Today, Tomorrow.

pop()

The pop() method removes the last elements in the array and returns its value; the size of the array is decreased by one.

Following is an example of the pop() method:

```
var myArray = new Array( "Yesterday", "Today", "Tomorrow" );

for( i = 0 ; i < myArray.length ; i++ )
{
  document.write( myArray[i] + ", " );
}
```

```
myArray.pop();
```

```
for( i = 0 ; i < myArray.length ; i++ )
{
   document.write( myArray[i] + ", " );
}
```

The output from this code segment would be the original array,

> Yesterday, Today, Tomorrow

followed by the altered array,

> Yesterday, Today

The length of the original array is now equal to two.

push (value)

The push() method appends values to the end of the array; the size of the array is increased by one.

Following is an example of the push() method:

```
var myArray = new Array( "Yesterday", "Today" );
```

```
for( i = 0 ; i < myArray.length ; i++ )
{
   document.write( myArray[i] + ", " );
}
```

```
myArray.push( "Tomorrow" );
```

```
for( i = 0 ; i < myArray.length ; i++ )
{
   document.write( myArray[i] + ", " );

}
```

The output from this code segment would be the original array,

> Yesterday, Today

followed by the altered array,

> Yesterday, Today, Tomorrow

The length of the original array is now equal to three.

reverse()

The reverse() method reverses the order of the elements in the array and returns a new array with the reversed elements. The order of the original array is changed after this method is executed.

Following is an example of the reverse() method:

```
var myArray = new Array( "Yesterday", "Today", "Tomorrow" );


for( i = 0 ; i < myArray.length ; i++ )
{
   document.write( myArray[i] + ", " );
}


myArray.reverse();


for( i = 0 ; i < myArray.length ; i++ )
{
   document.write( myArray[i] + ", " );

}
```

The output from this code segment would be the original array,

> Yesterday, Today, Tomorrow

followed by the altered array,

> Tomorrow, Today, Yesterday

The length of the original array does not change.

shift()

The shift() method removes the first element in the array and returns its value; the size of the array is decreased by one.

Following is an example of the shift() method:

```
var myArray = new Array( "Yesterday", "Today", "Tomorrow" );


for( i = 0 ; i < myArray.length ; i++ )
{
   document.write( myArray[i] + ", " );
}
```

```
myArray.shift();

for( i = 0 ; i < myArray.length ; i++ )
{
  document.write( myArray[i] + ", " );
}
```

The output from this code segment would be the original array,

>Yesterday, Today, Tomorrow

followed by the altered array,

>Today, Tomorrow

The length of the original array is now equal to two.

slice(startIndex, endIndex)

The `slice(startIndex, endIndex)` method returns a subset of the array starting from `startIndex` and ending with `endIndex`. If `endIndex` is omitted, the last element of the array is taken to be `endIndex`. The total number of elements in the subset array is equal to `endIndex` - `startIndex`.

Following is an example of the `slice()` method:

```
var theDays = new Array( "Sun", "Mon", "Tues", "Wed",
                         "Thurs", "Fri", "Sat" );

var days1 = theDays.slice( 2, 6 );

var days2 = theDays.slice( 4 );
```

At the end of execution, the array `days1` will contain 4 elements of the original array:

>"Tues", "Wed", "Thurs" and "Fri"

The array `days2` will contain three elements of the original array:

>"Thurs", "Fri" and "Sat"

sort (compare Function)

The `sort (compare Function)` method sorts the values of the array by the ASCII value of string by default or by a `compareFunction` function of your own design. The comparison function should take two parameters and return an integer value. The comparison function is optional. The `sort` function not only rearranges the elements in the array, but also returns a copy of the array.

Following is an example of the `sort()` method:

```
var theDays = new Array( "Sun", "Mon", "Tues", "Wed",
                         "Thurs", "Fri", "Sat" );
```

```
theDays.sort();
```

After execution, the elements in the `theDays` array will be in sorted order:

"Fri", "Mon", "Sat", "Sun", "Thurs", "Tues", "Wed"

If you want to sort the elements of an array in a way other than the default, you can create your own compare function, like this:

```
function compare( a, b )
{
  return( a - b );
}
```

This compare function would be ideal for sorting numerical data. The return value is interpreted by the arrays `sort` method, as shown in Table 3.2.

Table 3.2 Compare Function Return Value

Return Value	Meaning
Less than zero	The second value should appear before the first.
Equal to zero	Both values are equal.
Greater than zero	The first value should appear before the second.

To sort an array with this compare function, you could do the following:

```
var numbers = new Array( 8888, 3561, 0, 4133, 5555, 62, 1 );
```

```
numbers.sort( compare );
```

```
document.write( numbers.join( "<br>" ) );
```

The output from this code segment would be

0
1
62
3561

      4133

      5555

      8888

unshift(value)

The unshift(value) method inserts value at the beginning of the array; the size of the array is increased by one.

Following is an example of using the unshift() method:

```
var myArray = new Array( "Today", "Tomorrow" );


for( i = 0 ; i < myArray.length ; i++ )
{
  document.write( myArray[i] + ", " );
}


myArray.unshift( "Yesterday" );


for( i = 0 ; i < myArray.length ; i++ )
{
  document.write( myArray[i] + ", " );
}
```

The output from this code segment would be the original array,

> Today, Tomorrow

followed by the altered array,

> Yesterday, Today, Tomorrow

The length of the original array is now equal to three.

Using Arrays

The built-in methods of the Array object lend themselves greatly to using arrays as dynamic data structures. Together, the Array object's push(), pop(), shift(), and unshift() methods can be used to simulate many common dynamic data structures, such as linked lists (the most commonly used data structure in computer science), stacks, and queues. To use an array as a stack, use the push() method to insert elements into the array and the pop() method to remove elements from the array. To use an array as a queue, use only the push() and shift() methods to insert and remove elements from the array. A linked list uses any of the insert/remove methods that are part of the array methods and still allows the use of array indexing.

Some functionality needed from the default array object to make array instances easily usable as a linked list is missing—mainly the insertAt() and removeAt() methods. Thanks to the prototype property, this problem is easily solved. Both functions are simple enough to design:

```
function insertAt( index, value )
{
  var part1 = this.slice( 0, index );
  var part2 = this.slice( index );
  part1.push( value );
  return( part1.concat( part2 ) );
}
Array.prototype.insertAt = insertAt;
```

This method will allow you to insert an element anywhere within an array bounds.

The removeAt() function is equally simple:

```
function removeAt( index )
{
  var part1 = this.slice( 0, index );
  var part2 = this.slice( index );
  part1.pop();
  return( part1.concat( part2 ) );
}
Array.prototype.removeAt = removeAt;
```

Both of these new methods will allow you to make an array a fully functional linked list. Here is a brief example of these two methods in use:

```
<html>

  <head>
    <title>
      JavaScript Professional Projects - Using Arrays
    </title>

    <script language="JavaScript">
    <!--
      function insertAt( index, value )
      {
        var part1 = this.slice( 0, index );
        var part2 = this.slice( index );
```

```
      part1.push( value );
      return( part1.concat( part2 ) );
    }
    Array.prototype.insertAt = insertAt;

    function removeAt( index )
    {
      var part1 = this.slice( 0, index );
      var part2 = this.slice( index );
      part1.pop();
      return( part1.concat( part2 ) );
    }
    Array.prototype.removeAt = removeAt;
  // -->
  </script>

</head>

<body>

  <center>
    <font size=6>JavaScript Professional Projects</font><br>
    <font size=4>Chapter 3: Using Arrays</font>
  </center>

  <br><br>

  <p>
    <b>Before:</b><br>
    <script language="JavaScript">
    <!--
      var numbers = new Array( 8888, 3561, 0, 4133, 5555, 62, 1 );
      document.write( numbers.join( "<br>" ) );
    // -->
    </script>
    <br><br>
    <b>After:</b><br>
    <script language="JavaScript">
    <!--
```

```
        numbers = numbers.removeAt( 5 );
        numbers = numbers.insertAt( 2, 666 );
        document.write( numbers.join( "<br>" ) );
      // -->
    </script>
  </p>


  </body>


</html>
```

The ability to use linked lists in your programs will open many doors for organizing, sorting, and manipulating data. Using dynamic data structures, such as linked lists, will decrease the amount of memory your program requires to run, but will also increase its complexity.

Strings

Strings are the most commonly used object in the JavaScript language. The examples given in previous chapters and in this one have almost all used strings. The most commonplace strings have been used in the document.write statements. In the statement

```
document.write( "Hello World!!" );
```

the character sequence "Hello World!!" is considered a string literal. This is not the only way to create a string, however. You can also implicitly create a String object with the new operator. A String object represents any sequence of zero or more characters that are to be considered strictly text—that is, no mathematical operations can be performed on them. The String object comes equipped with a large number of built-in methods, just like the Array object, for handling normal string operations. The two ways to declare a string are as follows:

```
var <identifier> = "someString";
```

and

```
var <identifier> = new String( "someString" );
```

Using Strings

The first method of declaring a string given in the section above would result in a String literal. The second method would create an instance of a String object. Both literals and objects are functionally the same. Passing arguments to Java applets often requires that strings be objects instead of literals.

As I mentioned in Chapter 1, the plus sign is an overloaded operator. It can either perform addition on two numbers or concatenate two strings together. This can occasionally be slightly tricky. Take a look at the following example to see why:

```html
<html>

  <head>
    <title>
      JavaScript Professional Projects - Strings
    </title>
  </head>

  <body>

    <center>
      <font size=6>JavaScript Professional Projects</font><br>
      <font size=4>Chapter 3: Strings</font>
    </center>

    <br><br>

    <p>
      The command:<br>
      <code>
           
        <b>document.write( "The sum of 123 and 89 is " +
                          123 + 89 + "." );</b>
      </code>
      <br><br>
      produces the following output:<br>
      <code>   <b>
      <script language="JavaScript">
      <!--
        document.write( "The sum of 123 and 89 is " +
                       123 + 89 + "." );
      // -->
      </script>
      </code></b>
      <br><br>
```

```
Not quite what you expect was it?
<hr>
The command:<br>
<code>
      
   <b>document.write( "The sum of 123 and 89 is " +
                     (123 + 89) + "." );</b>
</code>
<br><br>
however, produces this output:<br>
<code>   <b>
<script language="JavaScript">
<!--
   document.write( "The sum of 123 and 89 is " +
                     (123 + 89) + "." );
// -->
</script>
</code></b>
<br><br>
Now that's more like it!
</p>


</body>


</html>
```

The problem with the first statement,

```
document.write( "The sum of 123 and 89 is " + 123 + 89 + "." );
```

is that the interpreter does not know which overloaded operation the plus sign is to perform. Because the plus sign is left-assistive (it performs the operations on its left first), the first operation it performs is between the string `"The sum of 123 and 89 is "` and the literal 123. Because strings cannot have mathematical operations performed on them, only the concatenation operation can be performed. Afterwards, the interpreter encounters the second plus sign. At this point it has a string, `"The sum of 123 and 89 is 123"`, as one operand and the literal 89 as the second operand. Once again, the only thing that can be done is to concatenate the two operands, resulting in the string `"The sum of 123 and 89 is 12389."`!

This is probably not what you want. The problem is solved in the second statement,

```
document.write( "The sum of 123 and 89 is " + (123 + 89) + "." );
```

by placing the addition within parentheses and making the interpreter evaluate the operation (123 + 89) before any string concatenation is performed.

String Specific Properties and Methods

There are many properties and methods that are built into the String object to make working with them much easier.

String Properties

The following subsections list and describe the string properties.

length

length is the total number of characters that make up the string. This number will change automatically as characters are either added or removed from the string.

prototype

The prototype property is a static property of the String object. Use the prototype property to assign new properties and methods to the String object in the current document. Refer to the Array.prototype property for further description and examples.

String Methods

The following subsections list and describe the many available string methods.

anchor(name)

The anchor() method is used to create an HTML anchor (<A>). The value of the original string will be the text that goes along with the anchor, and name will be the name of the anchor.

Following is an example of the anchor() method:

```
var myString = "Anchor text";


document.write( myString.anchor( "anchorName" ) );
```

This code would be comparable to the HTML tag

```
<A NAME="anchorName">Anchor text</A>
```

big()

The big() method creates a string that would be displayed as if it were embedded in a <BIG> tag.

Following is an example of the big() method:

```
var myString = "Biger text";
```

```
document.write( myString.big() );
```

This code would be comparable to the HTML tag

```
<BIG>Biger text</BIG>
```

blink()

The blink() method creates a string that would be displayed as if it were embedded in a <BLINK> tag.

Following is an example of the blink() method:

```
var myString = "Blinking text";
```

```
document.write( myString.blink() );
```

This code would be comparable to the HTML tag

```
<BLINK>Blinking text</BLINK>
```

bold()

The bold() method creates a string that would be displayed as if it were embedded in a <B> tag.

Following is an example of the bold() method:

```
var myString = "Bolded text";
```

```
document.write( myString.bold() );
```

This code would be comparable to the HTML tag

```
<B>Bolded text</B>
```

charAt(index)

The charAt(index) method returns a single character from the zero-based index position passed as a parameter. Use this method instead of substring() when only one character is needed.

Following is an example of using the charAt() method:

```
var myString = "Hello World!!";

document.write( myString.charAt( 1 ) + "<br>" );
document.write( myString.charAt( 6 ) + "<br>" );
document.write( myString.charAt( 12 ) + "<br>" );
```

The output from this code segment would be

e, W, !

charCodeAt(index)

The charCodeAt(index) method returns the Unicode value of a single character from the zero-based index position passed as a parameter.

Following is an example of the charAt() method:

```
var myString = "Hello World!!";

document.write( myString.charCodeAt( 1 ) + "<br>" );
document.write( myString.charCodeAt( 6 ) + "<br>" );
document.write( myString.charCodeAt( 12 ) + "<br>" );
```

The output from this code segment would be

101, 87, 33

concat(string2)

The concat(string2) method appends string2 onto the end of the original string. This method is identical to the string concatenation operator +.

fixed()

The fixed() method creates a string that would be displayed as if it were embedded in a <TT> tag.

Following is an example of the fixed() method:

```
var myString = "Fixed text";

document.write( myString.fixed() );
```

This code would be comparable to the HTML tag

```
<TT>Fixed text</TT>
```

fontcolor(color)

The `fontcolor()` method creates a string that would be displayed as if it were embedded in a <FONT> tag with the parameter assigned to the font property COLOR.

Following is an example of using the `fontcolor()` method:

```
var myString = "Colored text";
```

```
document.write( myString.fontcolor( "blue" ) );
```

This code would be comparable to the HTML tag

```
<FONT COLOR="blue">Colored text</FONT>
```

fontsize(size)

The `fontsize(size)` method creates a string that would be displayed as if it were embedded in a <FONT> tag with the parameter assigned to the font property SIZE.

Following is an example of using the `fontsize()` method:

```
var myString = "Resized text";
```

```
document.write( myString.fontsize( 4 ) );
```

This code would be comparable to the HTML tag

```
<FONT SIZE=4>Resized text</FONT>
```

fromCharCode(num1, num2, ..., numN)

The `fromCharCode(num1,num2, ..., numN)` method is a static String method that creates a string containing one or more characters whose Unicode values are passed as parameters.

The following example of the `fromCharCode()` method:

```
document.write( String.fromCharCode( 101, 87, 33 ) + "<br>" );
```

would produce the following three characters as output:

eW!

indexOf(searchString, startIndex)

The `indexOf(searchString, startIndex)` method returns the index of the first occurrence of `searchString` starting from `startIndex` within the original string. The second parameter is optional and will default to zero.

Following is an example of using the indexOf() method:

```
var myString = "How many chucks could a woodchuck chuck?";
```

```
document.write( myString.indexOf( "chuck" ) + "<br>" );
document.write( myString.indexOf( "chuck", 10 ) + "<br>" );
```

The output from this code segment would be

> 9 and 28

italics()

The italics() method creates a string that would be displayed as if it were embedded in a <I> tag.

Following is an example of using the italics() method:

```
var myString = "Italicized text";
```

```
document.write( myString.italics() );
```

This code would be comparable to the HTML tag

```
<I>Italicized text</I>
```

lastIndexOf(searchString, startIndex)

The lastIndexOf(searchString, startIndex) method is similar to the String.indexOf method except it starts searching from the end of the string instead of the beginning. The second parameter is optional and will default to the last character in the string.

Following is an example of using the lastIndexOf() method:

```
var myString = "How much wood would a woodchuck chuck?";
```

```
document.write( myString.lastIndexOf( "chuck" ) + "<br>" );
document.write( myString.lastIndexOf ( "chuck", 10 ) + "<br>" );
```

The output from this code segment would be

> 34 and 9

link(url)

The link(url) method creates a string that would be displayed as if it were embedded in a <A> tag with the parameter assigned to the anchor property HREF.

Following is an example of the `link()` method:

```
var myString = "Linked text";
```

```
document.write( myString.link( "someURL" ) );
```

This code would be comparable to the HTML tag

```
<A HREF="someURL">Linked text</A>
```

match(regex)

The `match(regex)` method returns an array of strings that match the criteria set by the regular expression passed as a parameter.

replace(regex, newString)

The `replace(regex, newString)` method returns the new string that results after all matches of `regex` within the original string are replaced with the second parameter.

search(regex)

The `search(regex)` method returns a zero-based index of the first match between the regular expression and the string. This method is similar to the `String.indedOf` method, except it uses regular expressions.

slice(startIndex, endIndex)

The `slice(startIndex, endIndex)` method returns a subset of the string starting from `startIndex` and ending with `endIndex`. If `endIndex` is omitted, the last element of the string is taken to be `endIndex`. The total number of characters in the subset string is equal to `endIndex` - `startIndex`.

Following is an example of using the `slice()` method:

```
var myString = "How much wood would a woodchuck chuck?";
```

```
document.write( myString.slice( 6, 12 ) + "<br>" );
```

The output from this code segment would be

> ny chu

small()

The `small()` method creates a string that would be displayed as if it were embedded in a `<SMALL>` tag.

Following is an example of the `small()` method:

```
var myString = "Shrunken text";


document.write( myString.small() );
```

This code would be comparable to the HTML tag

```
<SMALL>Shrunken text</SMALL>
```

split(delimiter)

The `split(delimiter)` method returns an array object containing the results of tokenizing the original string, using the parameter as a delimiter.

Following is an example of the `split()` method:

```
var myString = "How,much,wood,would,a,woodchuck,chuck?";
var myArray = myString.split( "," );


for( i = 0 ; i < myArray.length ; i++ )
{
   document.write( myArray[i] + "<br>" );
}
```

The output from this code segment would be

> How
>
> much
>
> wood
>
> would
>
> a
>
> woodchuck
>
> chuck?

strike()

The strike() method creates a string that would be displayed as if it were embedded in a `<STRIKE>` tag.

Following is an example of the `strike()` method:

```
var myString = "Stricken text";


document.write( myString.strike() );
```

This code would be comparable to the HTML tag

```
<STRIKE>Stricken text</STRIKE>
```

sub()

The `sub()` method creates a string that would be displayed as if it were embedded in a `<SUB>` tag.

Following is an example of the `sub()` method:

```
var myString = "Sub text";

document.write( myString.sub() );
```

This code would be comparable to the HTML tag

```
<SUB>Sub text</SUB>
```

substr(startIndex, length)

The `substr(startIndex, length)` method returns a substring of the original string that starts at the zero-based index of `startIndex` and is no longer than the specified length. If the second parameter is omitted, the substring will end with the end of the original string.

Following is an example of using the `substr()` method:

```
var myString = "How much wood would a woodchuck chuck?";

document.write( myString.substr( 6, 6 ) + "<br>" );
```

The output from this code segment would be

     ch woo

substring(startIndex, endIndex)

The `substring(startIndex, endIndex)` returns a subset of the string starting from `startIndex` and ending with `endIndex`. The total number of characters in the subset string is equal to `endIndex - startIndex`.

An example of using the `substring()` method:

```
var myString = "How much wood could a woodchuck chuck?";

document.write( myString.substring( 6, 12 ) + "<br>" );
```

The output from this code segment would be

     ch woo

sup()

The sup() method creates a string that would be displayed as if it were embedded in a <SUP> tag.

Following is an example of the sup() method:

```
var myString = "Super text";
```

```
document.write( myString.sup() );
```

This code would be comparable to the HTML tag

```
<SUP>Super text</SUP>
```

toLowerCase()

The toLowerCase() method returns a copy of the original string in all lowercase letters. Non-alphabetic characters are not affected.

Following is an example of the toLowerCase() method:

```
var myString = "Hello World!!";
```

```
document.write( myString.toLowerCase() + "<br>" );
```

The output from this code segment would be

hello world!!

toUpperCase()

The toUpperCase() method returns a copy of the original string in all uppercase letters. Non-alphabetic characters are not affected.

Following is an example of the toUpperCase() method:

```
var myString = "Hello World!!";
```

```
document.write( myString.toUpperCase() + "<br>" );
```

The output from this code segment would be

HELLO WORLD!!

Summary

Hopefully you now see now why arrays and strings are so useful. Both are considered objects by the JavaScript interpreter, but they are specialized in ways that other objects are not. Arrays are used to hold similar data in a meaningful way. Arrays are the only objects that use the bracket operator (`[ ]`) to reference elements. Strings can be represented as literals, as in `"Hello World!!"`, or as objects, each of which have many properties and methods that can be used on them.

Chapter 4

A *function* is a collection of one or more script statements that can be made to run at any point during the life of a program. The true power of JavaScript lies in the ability it gives you to write and use user-defined functions. Functions allow you to write very compact, easy-to-understand, and reusable code. Without functions, you'd only be able to write very simple, very lengthy programs. In Chapter 3, I presented many examples of functions without giving you much explanation as to how they work. In this chapter, you'll explore, and I'll explain, every aspect of user-defined functions, as well as JavaScript's built-in, or top-level, functions.

Defining Functions

Declaring functions is just like declaring data of any other type. Here is the syntax:

```
function <identifier>( <parameter list> )
{
   <statements>
}
```

The `function` keyword is followed by an identifier that is the name of the function. The identifier is followed by a comma-separated parameter list enclosed in parentheses. The function body, which can consist of any legal JavaScript statements, is enclosed in curly braces. Unlike with the `if` and `for` statements, the curly braces surrounding the function body are required. Following are a couple of examples of functions that you have seen in previous chapters:

```
function getColor()
{
  var color;
  if( rowNumber > 2 )
    rowNumber = 1;

  if( rowNumber == 1 )
    color = "gray";
  else
    color = "white";

  rowNumber++;
  return( color );
}
```

This function, named `getColor`, takes zero parameters. It performs several calculations in its body and then returns a color name. The `return` statement in this function is common to many functions. When the `return` statement is reached, the function is exited and the value used as a parameter to the `return` statement is passed back to the portion of the program that called the function. If no `return` statement is included in the body of the function, execution is returned to the calling statement as soon as the last statement in the body of the function is done executing. For example, the following statement:

```
document.write( getColor() );
```

will print either the string `"gray"` or `"white"`, depending on the results of the calculations performed within the function body. In another previous example,

```
function toBinary( n )
{
  var answer = "";
  while( n != 0 )
  {
    answer = Math.abs(n % 2) + answer;
    n = parseInt( n / 2 );
  }
  if( answer.length == 0 ) answer = "0";
  return( answer );
}
```

the function `toBinary()` takes a single parameter, which it assumes is an integer, and returns the binary representation of that number. In the following, final example:

```
function insertAt( index, value )
{
  var part1 = this.slice( 0, index );
  var part2 = this.slice( index );
  part1.push( value );
  return( part1.concat( part2 ) );
}
```

the function `insertAt()` takes two parameters. It assumes that the first parameter is an integer number and that the second can be any valid JavaScript value. This function inserts the specified value into a preexisting array (`this`) and returns the results.

As you can see, functions can perform a variety of roles and can perform a vast number of operations.

Recursive Functions

Recursive functions are used very often in computer science. A *recursive* function is a function that, during the course of executing the statements in its body, makes a call to itself. The logic behind recursive functions is often very complex, but the functions themselves are generally quite simple.

It is important to remember than any function written with a recursive algorithm can also be written with sequential functions. There is a trade-off for using recursive functions instead of sequential functions, however. Recursive functions tend to be faster and require less code, but they require more complex logic and quite a bit more memory to run. Following is an example of a binary sort routine for strings:

```html
<html>

<head>
  <title>
    JavaScript Professional Projects - Recursive Functions
  </title>

  <script language="JavaScript">
  <!--
    var months = new Array( "January", "February", "March",
                            "April", "June", "July",
                            "August", "September", "October",
                            "November", "December" );

    function display()
    {
      for( i = 0 ; i < this.length ; i++ )
      {
        document.write( this[i] + "<br>" );
      }
    }
    Array.prototype.display = display;

    function sort( s )
    {
      if( s.length == 1 ) return;
      else
      {
        var a = new Array( parseInt( s.length / 2 ) );
        var b = new Array( s.length - a.length );

        for( i = 0 ; i < a.length ; i++ ) a[i] = s[i];
        for( i = 0 ; i < b.length ; i++ ) b[i] = s[i+a.length];
        sort( a ); sort( b );

        var ai = 0, bi = 0, i = 0;
        while( ai < a.length || bi < b.length )
        {
```

```
          if( bi >= b.length ) s[i++] = a[ai++];
          else if( ai >= a.length ) s[i++] = b[bi++];
          else if( a[ai].compareTo( b[bi] ) <= 0 ) s[i++] = a[ai++];
          else if( a[ai].compareTo( b[bi] ) > 0 ) s[i++] = b[bi++];
        }
      }
    }


    // <0 - this first
    // =0 - same
    // >0 - s first
    function compareTo( s )
    {
      var len1 = this.length;
      var len2 = s.length;
      var n = ( len1 < len2 ? len1 : len2 );

      for( i = 0 ; i < n ; i++ )
      {
        var a = this.charCodeAt( i );
        var b = s.charCodeAt( i )
        if( a != b )
        {
          return( a - b );
        }
      }
      return( len1 - len2 );
    }
    String.prototype.compareTo = compareTo;
  // -->
  </script>

</head>

<body>

  <center>
    <font size=6>JavaScript Professional Projects</font><br>
```

```
        <font size=4>Chapter 4: Recursive Functions</font>
    </center>

    <br><br>

    <table border=1 cellspacing="2" cellpadding="20">
      <tr>
        <td width=150><b>Unsorted</b></td>
        <td width="150"><b>Sorted</b></td>
      </tr>
      <tr>
        <td>
          <script language="JavaScript">
          <!--
            months.display();
          -->
          </script>
        </td>
        <td>
          <script language="JavaScript">
          <!--
            sort( months );
            months.display();
          -->
          </script>
        </td>
      </tr>
    </table>

  </body>

</html>
```

This example makes use of three programmer defined functions. The first function, which extends the Array object's functionality by the use of its `prototype` property, provides a quick and easy way to display the contents of an array object. Here it is:

```
function display()
{
```

```
  for( i = 0 ; i < this.length ; i++ )
  {
    document.write( this[i] + "<br>" );
  }
}
Array.prototype.display = display;
```

This function simply iterates through each element in the array (referred to by `this`) and prints it on its own line.

The third function also extends the functionality of a built-in object type, this time String objects:

```
function compareTo( s )
{
  var len1 = this.length;
  var len2 = s.length;
  var n = ( len1 < len2 ? len1 : len2 );

  for( i = 0 ; i < n ; i++ )
  {
    var a = this.charCodeAt( i );
    var b = s.charCodeAt( i )
    if( a != b )
    {
      return( a - b );
    }
  }
  return( len1 - len2 );
}
String.prototype.compareTo = compareTo;
```

This function compares two strings lexicographically. The comparison is based on the Unicode value of each character in the strings. If there is a difference in either of the strings, a return value that demonstrates that difference is generated. If the function returns a value less than zero, then `this` occurs lexicographically before `'s'`; a return value of zero means the strings are identical, and a return value that is greater than zero means `'s'` occurs lexicographically before `this`. The `compareTo()` function is very important when it comes to the recursive binary `sort` function:

```
function sort( s )
{
```

```
if( s.length == 1 ) return;
else
{
    var a = new Array( parseInt( s.length / 2 ) );
    var b = new Array( s.length - a.length );

    for( i = 0 ; i < a.length ; i++ ) a[i] = s[i];
    for( i = 0 ; i < b.length ; i++ ) b[i] = s[i+a.length];

    sort( a );
    sort( b );

    var ai = 0, bi = 0, i = 0;
    while( ai < a.length || bi < b.length )
    {
        if( bi >= b.length ) s[i++] = a[ai++];
        else if( ai >= a.length ) s[i++] = b[bi++];
        else if( a[ai].compareTo( b[bi] ) <= 0 ) s[i++] = a[ai++];
        else if( a[ai].compareTo( b[bi] ) > 0 ) s[i++] = b[bi++];
    }
}
}
```

There are two important parts to this function: the base case and the actual body. The base case in this example is

```
if( s.length == 1 ) return;
```

Every recursive function must have a base case. In this binary sort function, the base case is when the length of the array is equal to one. You might be wondering how that could occur—that will be explained shortly.

The second part of the recursive function, the body (which is inside the else block), in this case divides the array into roughly equal halves, calls itself with the array halves as arguments, and then reinserts the array halves back into the original array in alphabetical order.

When designing recursive algorithms, it is helpful to think of them as loops. Just as with loops, your recursive functions can sometimes become infinite. The recursive base case is similar to the condition statement in repetition structures—it must always provide a way for the process to end. In many cases, the recursive base case is as simple as the example above, providing no additional functionality, only a return statement.

Invoking Functions

The most important thing to know about using functions is how to make them work. Making a call to or invoking a function can be done anywhere within a Web page. Only three conditions need to be met for a function call to succeed. First, the function must have been previously defined in the program. Second, the correct number of parameters must be passed to it. Lastly, the correct object must be present—you cannot call the string object's split function without a string object. (For some functions, the last stipulation does not apply, as you will soon see.)

Use the following general syntax to invoke functions:

```
<function name>( <parameter list> );
```

When invoking a function, always follow the function name with a set of parentheses containing an optional parameter list. If the function returns a value, it can be set as the value of a variable, like this:

```
var binaryString = toBinary( 789 );
```

This statement (using the aforementioned `toBinary()` function) will cause the variable `binaryString` to have the value `"1100010101"`.

JavaScript Top-Level Functions

There are many top-level functions—also known as *global functions*—that can be used anywhere in a JavaScript Program. The following subsections describe those functions.

escape(string)

The top-level function `escape()` encodes a string parameter, so that it may be portable. A string is considered portable if can be transmitted across any network to any computer that recognizes ASCII characters.

In the encoding process, all characters with ASCII values larger than 69 are converted to their hexadecimal escape sequence.

Following is an example of the `escape()`:

```
var myString = "!#$%^&";


document.write( escape( myString ) );
```

The output from this code segment would be

%21%23%24%25%5E%26.

eval(string)

The top-level function `eval()` evaluates, and, if possible, executes a string containing JavaScript code that is passed as a parameter. The `eval` function can also be used to evaluate mathematical expressions.

Following is an example of the `eval()` function:

```
document.write( eval( "( 9 + 5 ) * 2" ) );
```

The output from this code segment would be

28.

isFinite(number)

The top-level function `isFinite()` determines whether a number is finite and, therefore, a legal number. If the parameter is a legal number, the function returns `true`; otherwise, it returns `false`.

Following is an example of the `isFinite()` function:

```
document.write( isFinite( 1001 ) );
```

The output from this code segment would be

True

isNaN(string)

The top-level function `isNaN()` determines whether the string passed as a parameter is not a number. If the string is not a number, the function returns `true`; otherwise it returns `false`.

Following is an example of the isNaN() function:

```
document.write( isNaN( "Hello World!!" ) + ", " );
```

```
document.write( isNaN( 42 ) );
```

The output from this code segment would be

true, false.

number(object)

The top-level function `number()` attempts to convert an object to its numerical representation. If the function succeeds, the numerical value is returned; otherwise, the value `NaN` is returned.

Following is an example of the `number()` function:

```
document.write( number( "Hello World!!" ) + ", " );

document.write( isNaN( "42" ) );
```

The output from this code segment would be

NaN, 42 (the number value).

parseFloat(string)

The top-level function `parseFloat()` attempts to convert a string parameter into a floating-point number. The number must start at the beginning of the string for the function to succeed. Any non-numeric characters following the number are discarded. If the function succeeds, the floating-point number is returned; otherwise the value `NaN` is returned.

Following is an example of the `parseFloat()` function:

```
document.write( parseFloat( "3.14" ) + ", " );

document.write( parseFloat( "3.14string" ) + ", " );

document.write( isNaN( "string" ) );
```

The output from this code segment would be

3.14, 3.14, NaN.

parseInt(string, radix)

The top-level function `parseInt()` attempts to convert a string parameter into an integer number. The number must start at the beginning of the string for the function to succeed. Any non-numeric characters following the number are discarded. If the function succeeds, the integer number is returned; otherwise, the value `NaN` is returned.

An optional parameter radix allows you to specify the number base from which to convert the number. The parameter may be anything from 2 to 36. A radix of 10 (decimal) is the default value.

Following is an example of the `parseInt()` function:

```
document.write( parseInt( "42" ) + ", " );

document.write( parseInt( "42string" ) + ", " );

document.write( isNaN( "string" ) );
```

The output from this code segment would be

42, 42, NaN.

string(object)

The top-level function `string()` converts an object parameter into its string representation.

Following is an example of the `string()` function:

```
var myBool = new Boolean( 0 );

document.write( string( myBool ) );
```

The output from this code segment would be

false.

taint()

The top-level function `taint()` is deprecated. This means that it is still technically part of the JavaScript language, but should no longer be used.

unescape()

The top-level function `unescape()` performs the opposite operation from that of the top-level function `escape`. The `unescape` function searches for hexadecimal escape sequences and replaces them with their character equivalents.

Following is an example of the `unescape()` function:

```
var myString = "%21%23%24%25%5E%26";

document.write( unscape( myString ) );
```

The output from this code segment would be

!#$%^&.

untaint()

The top-level function `untaint(0` is deprecated.

◢ **TIP**

Remember that JavaScript's top-level functions do not need to be defined anywhere in your program in order for you to use them.

Functions Scope

The statements within a function body have access to all global variables defined somewhere else in the document. The variables defined within a function body, however, can only be used inside the function itself. As soon as the function returns control to the calling statement, all variables declared within it are deleted and their memory freed.

The function itself has a global scope in the window in which it was defined. In the event that you need to call a function defined on a different frame, you will need to precede its name with the name of the frame, as follows:

```
parent.<frame name>.<function name>( <parameter list> );
```

Not preceding the non-local function with its frame name will cause the function to be undefined by the interpreter and will generate an error.

Functions as Data

Because a function is considered an object by the JavaScript interpreter, it can be assigned as the value of a variable. You have seen examples of this before, when extending the functionality of built-in JavaScript objects such as Array and String objects. The following example will look familiar; it has been presented several times already:

```
function display()
{
  for( i = 0 ; i < this.length ; i++ )
  {
    document.write( this[i] + "<br>" );
  }
}
Array.prototype.display = display;
```

This function extends the functionality of Array objects declared anywhere on the window in which the function is defined. The new object's method can then be used just like any other built in-method for that object type.

```
var myArray = new Array( 12, 42, 1001, 10 );

myArray.display();
```

will produce the following output:

    12

    42

1001

10

As you can see, the ability to use functions as data is a great advantage. Using functions will shorten the length of your programs and make them easier to follow.

Function-Specific Properties

Because functions are essentially objects, they have several built-in properties that are quite useful for retrieving information about a function.

arguments

The arguments property returns an array containing the values of each argument that was passed to the function, in the order in which they were passed.

Following is an example of using the arguments property:

```
function myFunction( param0, param1, param2 )
{
  for( i = 0 ; i < myFunction.arguments.length ; i++ )
  {
    document.write( myFunction.arguments[i] + "<br>" );
  }
}
```

The output of this code segment would be the values of each parameter that was passed to the myFunction function.

arity

The arity property returns an integer whose value is the number of parameters defined for the function.

Following is an example of using the arity property:

```
function myFunction( param0, param1, param2 )
{
  for( i = 0 ; i < myFunction.arity ; i++ )
  {
    document.write( myFunction.arguments[i] + "<br>" );
  }
}
```

The output of this code segment would be the values of each parameter that was passed to the myFunction function.

caller

The `caller` property returns a reference to the function that invoked the current function.

Following is an example of using the `caller` property:

```
function myFunction()
{
  if( myFunction.caller == someFunction )
  {
    <statements>
  }
}
```

length

The `length` property returns an integer whose value is the number of parameters defined for the function. (Netscape Navigator always returns a value of zero—refer to the `arity` property section presented previously.)

Following is an example of using the `length` property:

```
function myFunction( param0, param1, param2 )
{
  for( i = 0 ; i < myFunction.length ; i++ )
  {
    document.write( myFunction.arguments[i] + "<br>" );
  }
}
```

The output of this code segment would be the values of each parameter that was passed to the `myFunction` function.

prototype

The `prototype` property is a static property of the function object. Use the `prototype` property to assign new properties and methods to the function object for the current document.

To add an additional method to the function object, all you'd need to do is write the corresponding function:

```
function print()
{
  document.write( "Parameters: " + this.arity + "  Caller: " +
                  this.caller + "  String value: " +
```

```
                    this.toString() + "<br>" );
}
```

Then simply add it to the `prototype` property of the static function object:

```
Function.prototype.print = print;
```

Then, whenever a new instance of the function object is created, a new method, `print()`, will be available to it:

```
function myFunction( param0, param1, param2 )
{
  ...
}


myFunction.print();
```

When the `print()` method is called, the information for the function will be output.

Function Methods

The methods presented in the following subsections are part of every object, including function objects.

tostring()

The `tostring()` method returns the function's value as a string object. This method is generally not useful because the JavaScript interpreter converts all objects to their string representation before outputting them.

Following is an example of using the `toString()` method:

```
function myFunction()
{
  ...
}
document.write( myFunction.toString() );
```

The last statement would be equivalent to

```
document.write( myFunction );
```

They both output the string representation of the function object.

valueOf()

The valueOf() function returns a reference to the function object.

Following is an example of using the valueOf() method:

```
var funcRef = someFunction.valueOf();
```

This will set the value of funcRef equal to a reference to the someFunction function.

Example Functions

The following sub-sections describe and explain useful user-defined functions that have been written in JavaScript and used throughout this book.

Alternating Table Row Colors

The following function can be used to create HTML tables that have alternating row colors (the default colors are white and gray):

```
var rowNumber = 1;
function getColor()
{
  var color;
  if( rowNumber > 2 )
  {
    rowNumber = 1;
  }

  if( rowNumber == 1 ) color = "gray";
  else                 color = "white";

  rowNumber++;
  return( color );
}
```

This function would be very useful if you wanted to display a large amount of data in a table.

The following is an example of using the getColor() function that shows just how easy it is to create an HTML table with alternating row colors:

```
<html>
```

```
<head>
  <title>
    JavaScript Professional Projects - Functin Example
  </title>

  <script language="JavaScript">
<!--
    var rowNumber = 1;
    function getColor()
    {
      var color;
      if( rowNumber > 2 )
      {
        rowNumber = 1;
      }

      if( rowNumber == 1 ) color = "gray";
      else                 color = "white";

      rowNumber++;
      return( color );
    }
// -->
  </script>

</head>

<body>

  <table width="85%" border="1">
    <script language="JavaScript">
<!--
      for( i = 0 ; i < 25 ; i++ )
      {
        document.write( "<tr bgcolor='" + getColor() + "'>" );
        document.write( "<td>Row #" + i + "</td>" );
        document.write( "</tr>" );
      }
```

```
    // -->
    </script>
  </table>

</body>

</html>
```

This code example creates an HTML table with 25 rows and alternating colors.

The getColor() function could be simplified slightly by using the ternary operator, like this:

```
var rowNumber = 0;
function getColor()
{
   return( rowNumber++ % 2 == 0 ? "gray" : "white" );
}
```

Using the ternary operator would reduce the number of characters required for download, but would decrease the readability of the program.

Determining Number Postfixes

The following very simple function will return the proper numeral postfix for any number:

```
function getEnding( number )
{
  if( number > 10 && number < 20 ) return( "th" );

  switch( number % 10 )
  {
  case 0: case 4: case 5:
  case 6: case 7: case 8:
  case 9:
    return( "th" );
  case 1:
    return( "st" );
  case 2:
    return( "nd" );
  case 3:
    return( "rd" );
  }
}
```

This function would be very useful if you wanted to display a calendar with multiple days on it. Creating a calendar is the focus of Chapter 15

linked List – insertAt and linked List - removeAt

The linked list - `insertAt( index, value )` function was presented in Chapter 2, and is one of two functions that the Array object requires in order to be used as a fully functional linked list.

```
function insertAt( index, value )
{
  var part1 = this.slice( 0, index );
  var part2 = this.slice( index );
  part1.push( value );
  return( part1.concat( part2 ) );
}
Array.prototype.insertAt = insertAt;
```

This function, in combination with the linked list – `removeAt`, would provide all the functionality needed to use a regular array as a linked list.

The `linked list - removeAt` function is the second function the Array object requires in order to be used as a fully functional linked list.

```
function removeAt( index )
{
  var part1 = this.slice( 0, index );
  var part2 = this.slice( index );
  part1.pop();
  return( part1.concat( part2 ) );
}
Array.prototype.removeAt = removeAt;
```

This function, in combination with the `linked list - insertAt` function, would provide all the functionality needed to use a regular array as a linked list.

Linked List Example

An example of using the linked list functions follows:

```
<html>

  <head>
    <title>
```

```
      JavaScript Professional Projects - Example Function
  </title>

  <script language="JavaScript">
  <!--
    function insertAt( index, value )
    {
      var part1 = this.slice( 0, index );
      var part2 = this.slice( index );
      part1.push( value );
      return( part1.concat( part2 ) );
    }
    Array.prototype.insertAt = insertAt;

    function removeAt( index )
    {
      var part1 = this.slice( 0, index );
      var part2 = this.slice( index );
      part1.pop();
      return( part1.concat( part2 ) );
    }
    Array.prototype.removeAt = removeAt;
  // -->
  </script>

</head>

<body>

  <p>
    <b>Before:</b><br>
    <script language="JavaScript">
    <!--
      var numbers = new Array( 8888, 3561, 0, 4133, 5555, 62, 1 );
      document.write( numbers.join( "<br>" ) );
    // -->
    </script>
    <br><br>
```

```
<b>After:</b><br>
<script language="JavaScript">
<!--
    numbers = numbers.removeAt( 5 );
    numbers = numbers.insertAt( 2, 666 );
    document.write( numbers.join( "<br>" ) );
// -->
</script>
</p>


</body>

</html>
```

Comparing Strings

This function compares two strings lexicographically and returns a value specifying which string should come first alphabetically.

```
function compareTo( s )
{
  var len1 = this.length;
  var len2 = s.length;
  var n = ( len1 < len2 ? len1 : len2 );

  for( i = 0 ; i < n ; i++ )
  {
    var a = this.charCodeAt( i );
    var b = s.charCodeAt( i )
    if( a != b )
    {
      return( a - b );
    }
  }
  return( len1 - len2 );
}
String.prototype.compareTo = compareTo;
```

The comparison is based on the Unicode value of each character in the strings. If there is a difference in either of the strings, a return value that demonstrates that difference is generated. If the function returns a value less than zero and a return value that is greater than zero, then this occurs lexicographically before 's'.

Binary Sort for Strings

The sort() function recursively sorts an array of strings into alphabetical order. It makes extensive use of the compareTo() function above.

```
function sort( s )
{
  if( s.length == 1 ) return;
  else
  {
    var a = new Array( parseInt( s.length / 2 ) );
    var b = new Array( s.length - a.length );

    for( i = 0 ; i < a.length ; i++ ) a[i] = s[i];
    for( i = 0 ; i < b.length ; i++ ) b[i] = s[i+a.length];

    sort( a );
    sort( b );

    var ai = 0, bi = 0, i = 0;
    while( ai < a.length || bi < b.length )
    {
      if( bi >= b.length ) s[i++] = a[ai++];
      else if( ai >= a.length ) s[i++] = b[bi++];
      else if( a[ai].compareTo( b[bi] ) <= 0 ) s[i++] = a[ai++];
      else if( a[ai].compareTo( b[bi] ) > 0 ) s[i++] = b[bi++];
    }
  }
}
```

This is an extremely useful function, not only for sorting strings, but also for sorting the items in a list form element.

Following is an example of using this function with an array of strings:

```
<head>
  <title>
    JavaScript Professional Projects - Example Function
  </title>

  <script language="JavaScript">
  <!--
    var months = new Array( "January", "February", "March",
                            "April", "June", "July",
                            "August", "September", "October",
                            "November", "December" );

    function display()
    {
      for( i = 0 ; i < this.length ; i++ )
      {
        document.write( this[i] + "<br>" );
      }
    }
    Array.prototype.display = display;

    function sort( s )
    {
      if( s.length == 1 ) return;
      else
      {
        var a = new Array( parseInt( s.length / 2 ) );
        var b = new Array( s.length - a.length );

        for( i = 0 ; i < a.length ; i++ ) a[i] = s[i];
        for( i = 0 ; i < b.length ; i++ ) b[i] = s[i+a.length];
        sort( a ); sort( b );

        var ai = 0, bi = 0, i = 0;
        while( ai < a.length || bi < b.length )
        {
          if( bi >= b.length ) s[i++] = a[ai++];
          else if( ai >= a.length ) s[i++] = b[bi++];
```

```
        else if( a[ai].compareTo( b[bi] ) <= 0 ) s[i++] = a[ai++];
        else if( a[ai].compareTo( b[bi] ) > 0 ) s[i++] = b[bi++];
      }
    }
  }

  function compareTo( s )
  {
    var len1 = this.length;
    var len2 = s.length;
    var n = ( len1 < len2 ? len1 : len2 );

    for( i = 0 ; i < n ; i++ )
    {
      var a = this.charCodeAt( i );
      var b = s.charCodeAt( i )
      if( a != b )
      {
        return( a - b );
      }
    }
    return( len1 - len2 );
  }
  String.prototype.compareTo = compareTo;
// -->
</script>

</head>

<body>

  <table border=1 cellspacing="2" cellpadding="20">
    <tr>
      <td width=150><b>Unsorted</b></td>
      <td width="150"><b>Sorted</b></td>
    </tr>
    <tr>
      <td>
```

```
<script language="JavaScript">
<!--
  months.display();
-->
</script>
 </td>
<td>
<script language="JavaScript">
<!--
  sort( months );
  months.display();
-->
</script>
 </td>
</tr>
</table>

</body>
</html>
```

Sorting HTML Select Boxes

The sortSelect() function sorts the contents of an HTML select box by using the compareTo() function presented previously.

```
function sortSelect( select )
{
  var a = new Array();
  for( i = 0; i < select.options.length ; i++ )
  {
    a[a.length] = new Option( select.options[i].text,
                              select.options[i].value,
                              select.options[i].defaultSelected,
                              select.options[i].selected ) ;
  }

  a = a.sort(
    function( s, t )
```

```
    {
       return( s.text.compareTo( t.text ) );
    }
 );


 for( i = 0; i < a.length ; i++ )
 {
    select.options[i] = new Option( a[i].text,
                                    a[i].value,
                                    a[i].defaultSelected,
                                    a[i].selected );

 }
}
```

An example of using this function is presented in the next section.

Swap Selected Items in Select Boxes

The swapSelects() function moves a selected item in one select box into another select box, then sorts both lists using the sortSelect() function.

```
function swapSelects( fromSelect, toSelect )
{
  var toSelect_Length = toSelect.options.length;
  while( fromSelect.selectedIndex > -1 )
  {
    var index = fromSelect.selectedIndex;

    toSelect.options[toSelect_Length] = new Option(
      fromSelect.options[index].text );
    toSelect.options[toSelect_Length].value =
      fromSelect.options[index].value;
    fromSelect.options[index] = null;

    toSelect_Length++;
  }
  sortSelect( fromSelect );
  sortSelect( toSelect );
}
```

Here is an example of using both the swapSelect() and sortSelect() functions:

```
<html>
  <head>
    <title>
      JavaScript Professional Projects - Working with Forms
    </title>

    <style type="text/css">
    <!--
      .sameSize{ width: 125; }
    -->
    </style>

    <script language="JavaScript">
    <!--
      var months = new Array( "January", "February", "March",
                              "April", "May", "June", "July",
                              "August", "September", "October",
                              "November", "December" );

      function swapSelects( fromSelect, toSelect )
      {
        var toSelect_Length = toSelect.options.length;
        while( fromSelect.selectedIndex > -1 )
        {
          var index = fromSelect.selectedIndex;

          toSelect.options[toSelect_Length] = new Option(
            fromSelect.options[index].text );
          toSelect.options[toSelect_Length].value =
            fromSelect.options[index].value;
          fromSelect.options[index] = null;

          toSelect_Length++;
        }
        sortSelect( fromSelect );
        sortSelect( toSelect );
      }
```

```javascript
function compareTo( s )
{
  var len1 = this.length;
  var len2 = s.length;
  var n = ( len1 < len2 ? len1 : len2 );

  for( i = 0 ; i < n ; i++ )
  {
    var a = this.charCodeAt( i );
    var b = s.charCodeAt( i )
    if( a != b )
    {
      return( a - b );
    }
  }
  return( len1 - len2 );
}
String.prototype.compareTo = compareTo;

function sortSelect( select )
{
  var a = new Array();
  for( i = 0; i < select.options.length ; i++ )
  {
    a[a.length] = new Option( select.options[i].text,
                              select.options[i].value,
                              select.options[i].defaultSelected,
                              select.options[i].selected ) ;
  }

  a = a.sort(
    function( s, t )
    {
      return( s.text.compareTo( t.text ) );
    }
  );

  for( i = 0; i < a.length ; i++ )
```

```
                {
            select.options[i] = new Option( a[i].text,
                                             a[i].value,
                                             a[i].defaultSelected,
                                             a[i].selected );
            }
        }
    // -->
    </script>

</head>

<body>

  <center>
    <font size=6>JavaScript Professional Projects</font><br>
    <font size=4>Chapter 8: Working with Forms</font>
  </center>

  <br><br>
  <br><br>


  <form name="theForm">
    <table cellspacing="6">
      <tr>
        <td>
          <select size="12" name="ListA" multiple width="125">
            <script language="JavaScript">
            <!--
              for( i = 0 ; i < months.length ; i++ )
              {
                document.write( "<option>" + months[i] +
                                "</option>" );
              }
              sortSelect( document.theForm.ListA );
            // -->
            </script>
```

```
      </select>
    </td>

    <td>
      <input type="button" value="=====&gt;"
        onClick="JavaScript: swapSelects( document.theForm.ListA,
                                  document.theForm.ListB );">
      <br><br>
      <input type="button" value="&lt;====="
        onClick="JavaScript: swapSelects( document.theForm.ListB,
                                  document.theForm.ListA );">
    </td>

    <td>
      <select size="12" name="ListB" multiple
              width="125"></select>
      <script language="JavaScript">
      <!--
        if( navigator.appName != "Netscape" )
        {
          document.theForm.ListA.style.width = 125;
          document.theForm.ListB.style.width = 125;
        }
      // -->
      </script>
    </td>
  </tr>
 </table>
 </form>

 </body>
</html>
```

Inserting Options into a Select Box

The insertOption() function inserts an additional option into a preexisting HTML select box and then sorts the contents of the select box. This function uses the sortSelect() function presented previously.

```
function insertOption( select, text )
{
  select.options[select.options.length] =
    new Option( text, text, false, false );
  sortSelect( select );
}
```

Here is an example of using the insertOption() and sortSelect() functions:

```
<html>
  <head>
    <title>
      JavaScript Professional Projects - Dynamic Forms
    </title>

    <style type="text/css">
    <!--
      .sameSize{ width: 125; }
    -->
    </style>

    <script language="JavaScript">
    <!--
      function insertOption( select, text )
      {
        select.options[select.options.length] =
          new Option( text, text, false, false );
        sortSelect( select );
      }

      function compareTo( s )
      {
        var len1 = this.length;
        var len2 = s.length;
        var n = ( len1 < len2 ? len1 : len2 );

        for( i = 0 ; i < n ; i++ )
        {
          var a = this.toUpperCase().charCodeAt( i );
```

```
    var b = s.toUpperCase().charCodeAt( i )
    if( a != b )
    {
      return( a - b );
    }
  }
  return( len1 - len2 );
}
String.prototype.compareTo = compareTo;


function sortSelect( select )
{
  var a = new Array();
  for( i = 0; i < select.options.length ; i++ )
  {
    a[a.length] = new Option( select.options[i].text,
                              select.options[i].value,
                              select.options[i].defaultSelected,
                              select.options[i].selected ) ;
  }

  a = a.sort(
    function( s, t )
    {
      return( s.text.compareTo( t.text ) );
    }
  );

  for( i = 0; i < a.length ; i++ )
  {
    select.options[i] = new Option( a[i].text,
                                    a[i].value,
                                    a[i].defaultSelected,
                                    a[i].selected );
  }
}
// -->
```

```
    </script>

  </head>

  <body>

    <center>
      <font size=6>JavaScript Professional Projects</font><br>
      <font size=4>Chapter 8: Dynamic Foms</font>
    </center>

    <br><br>
    <br><br>

    <form name="theForm" onSubmit="return( false );">
      <table cellpadding="3">
        <tr>
          <td valign="bottom">
            <input type="text" name="theText" size="20">
               
            <input type="button" value="Insert"
              onClick="JavaScript:
                insertOption( document.theForm.theSelect,
                              document.theForm.theText.value );
                document.theForm.theText.value = '';">
          </td>
          <td>
                  
            <select size="10" name="theSelect"
                    class="sameSize" width=125></select>
          </td>
        </tr>
      </table>
    </form>

  </body>
</html>
```

Saving Form Data to the Cookie File

The saveForm() function saves the entire content of a form to the cookie file so that it can be reloaded at a later time.

```
function saveForm( form )
{
  for( i = 0 ; i < form.elements.length ; i++ )
  {
    with( form.elements[i] )
    {
      if( type != "submit" && type != "button" && type != "reset" )
        document.cookie = form.name + "." + name + "=" + value;
    }
  }
}
```

Retrieving Cookies Values

The getCookieValue() function searches the cookie file for a name=value pair with the given name and returns the corresponding value.

```
function getCookieValue( name )
{
  var c = document.cookie;
  var begin = c.indexOf( name );
  if( begin < 0 ) return( "" );
  begin += name.length + 1;
  var end = c.indexOf( ";", begin );
  if( end == -1 ) end = c.length;
  return( c.slice( begin, end ) );
}
```

Loading Form Data from the Cookie File

The loadForm() function is the opposite of the saveForm() function; it loads the form data that was previously stored in the cookie file. This function uses the getCookieValue() function that was presented above.

```
function loadForm( form )
{
  for( i = 0 ; i < form.elements.length ; i++ )
```

```
    {
      with( form.elements[i] )
       {
         if( type != "submit" && type != "button" && type != "reset" )
           value = getCookieValue( form.name + "." + name );
       }
     }
  }
```
Here is an example of using the saveForm(), loadForm() and getCookieValue() functions:
```
<html>
  <head>
    <title>
      JavaScript Professional Projects - Reading Cookies
    </title>

    <script language="JavaScript">
    <!--
      var now = new Date();
      now.setMonth( now.getMonth() + 1 );
      document.cookie = "expires=" + now.toGMTString();

      function saveForm( form )
      {
        for( i = 0 ; i < form.elements.length ; i++ )
        {
          with( form.elements[i] )
          {
            if( type != "submit" && type != "button" && type != "reset" )
              document.cookie = form.name + "." + name + "=" + value;
          }
        }
      }

      function loadForm( form )
      {
        for( i = 0 ; i < form.elements.length ; i++ )
        {
          with( form.elements[i] )
```

```
            {
                if( type != "submit" && type != "button" && type != "reset" )
                    value = getCookieValue( form.name + "." + name );
            }
        }
    }

    function getCookieValue( index )
    {
        var c = document.cookie;
        var begin = c.indexOf( index + "=" ) + index.length + 1;
        var end = c.indexOf( ";", begin );
        if( end == -1 ) end = c.length;
        return( c.slice( begin, end ) );
    }
    -->
    </script>

</head>

<body onLoad="JavaScript: loadForm( document.mailingForm );">

    <center>
        <font size=6>JavaScript Professional Projects</font><br>
        <font size=4>Chapter 11: Reading Cookies</font>
    </center>

    <br><br>
    <br><br>

    <table cellspacing="4" cellpadding="4" width="65%">
        <tr>
            <td>

                <form name="mailingForm" onSubmit="JavaScript: saveForm( this );">
                    <b><font size="5">Mailing Address<br></font></b>
                    <br>
                    <b>Last name, First name:</b><br>
```

```
        <input type="text" name="firstLine" size="36"><br>
        <b>Street/Address:</b><br>
        <input type="text" name="secondLine" size="36"><br>
        <b>City State, Zip code:</b><br>
        <input type="text" name="thirdLine" size="36">  
        <input type="submit" value="Submit">
    </form>

    </td>
  </tr>
</table>

</body>
</html>
```

Summary

Functions are what make a language truly powerful. With the ability to create user-defined functions, you have the power to perform complex operations with a single function call. Additionally, the use of functions will make your programs shorter, easier to read, and enable you to reuse code much more efficiently. I encourage you to look at the example functions in the previous section. Feel free to use them and modify them in order to make your Web sites as useful as possible.

Chapter 5

The benefits of using an object-oriented language like JavaScript are many. In general, programming problems are generally easier to conquer using an object-oriented approach because the problem is divided into sub-problems, each of which is solved by a separate object, which in turn all work together to solve the bigger problem. Additionally, using an object-oriented approach means that you will not have to solve the same problem more than once, as objects are reusable.

The three basic concepts on which object-oriented languages are built are encapsulation, inheritance, and polymorphism. An object-oriented language should provide you, the programmer, with easy tools with which to execute these three concepts.

Encapsulation means making an object's internal workings invisible to the programmer. Instead of being a drawback, this invisibility is, in fact, a benefit. When the code that is used to perform operations within an object is hidden, the author of the object's code has the ability to change how the object performs operations at any time without adversely affecting every program that was written using that object. For an example, Array objects contain a method called `sort()` that will sort all of the elements in an array. Imagine for a moment that this method was written using a slow, linear `sort` algorithm. If the designer of the Array object decided later on down the line to switch to the quicker, binary `sort` algorithm that was presented in Chapter 4, he could simply replace the old algorithm with the new one. Because both algorithms perform the same operation, the programmer who then uses the Array object would never know the switch ever took place. This allows the built-in functions of a language to be improved upon without compromising preexisting programs written in it.

Inheritance is one of the most important aspects of object-oriented programming. Inheritance allows a program to reuse preexisting object types without rewriting their functionality from scratch. For an example, let's examine the Array object type. If you wanted to have the functionality of a linked list, but did not have the `Array.prototype` property or did not want to use it, you could create a new class called `List` that extended the `Array` class. The new `List` class would have all of the functionality of the original `Array` class, but then you could add more functionality into it automatically.

Polymorphism is the most complicated of the three must-haves for an object-oriented language. The basis of this idea states that every class should be able to handle different data types. For example, if you write a `Shape` class that has a single method, `draw()`, and then create two more classes, `Square` and `Circle`, which implement the `draw()` method, invoking the `draw()` method on any `Shape` class (be it a `Square` or `Circle` object) should cause the operations needed to draw the proper shape to be executed.

Object Properties

Objects are not only another data type. Instances of objects have methods and properties that are part of their definition. Object properties can be any of the three primitive data types, or any of the abstract data types, such as another object. Object properties are usually variables that are used internally in the object's methods, but can also be globally visible variables that are used throughout the page.

The syntax for adding a property to an object is

```
<object name>.<property name> = <property value>;
```

The object's name is followed by a dot and then the property name. At this point, the object's property can be used just like any other variable—to assign values to or read values from memory. Following is a simple example to demonstrate what I mean:

```
var myCar = new Car();
```

```
myCar.year = 2005;
```

In this case, the instance of the object type Car, myCar, has a property named year that is being assigned the value 2005. An object's property is a local variable and can vary between object instances.

Object Methods

The true power of user-defined objects lies in your ability to write custom methods for them. An object's methods can perform any operations that a normal function can, and more. In fact, method declarations are identical to function declarations (which were discussed in Chapter 4). Methods are useful for everything from displaying the contents of the object to the screen to performing complex mathematical operations on a group of local properties and parameters. Native JavaScript objects have a property named prototype through which you can assign custom methods and properties. You have already seen several examples of custom methods in Chapters 3 and 4; refer to those chapters for a description of how to add custom methods and properties to native objects.

The usefulness of linked lists in computer science has been mentioned in previous chapters without actually producing a working definition of linked lists. What follows is a working example of a JavaScript linked list class that encapsulates the native Array class. This example demonstrates two very important concepts: how to create custom objects and how encapsulation works.

```
<html>
  <head>
    <title>
      JavaScript Professional Projects - Linked Lists
    </title>

    <script language="JavaScript">
    <!--
      function pop()
      {
        return( this.data.pop() );
      }
```

```
function push( value )
{
  this.data.push( value );
}

function insertAt( index, value )
{
  var part1 = this.data.slice( 0, index );
  var part2 = this.data.slice( index );
  part1.push( value );
  this.data = part1.concat( part2 );
}

function removeAt( index )
{
  var part1 = this.data.slice( 0, index );
  var part2 = this.data.slice( index );
  part1.pop();
  this.data = part1.concat( part2 );
}

function size()
{
  return( this.data.length );
}

function display()
{
  document.write( "<table border=1 cellpadding=5 cellspacing=2
                      width=50%>" +
                 "  <tr>" +
                 "    <td>" +
                 "      <b><code>Linked List - Size = " +
                              this.size() + "</code></b>" +
                 "    </td>" +
                 "  </tr><tr>" +
                 "    <td>" );
```

```
      if( this.size() == 0 ) document.write( "No data" );
      document.write( this.data.join( "</td></tr><tr><td>" ) );
      document.write( "</td></tr></table>" );
    }


    function List()
    {
      this.data = new Array( 0 );
      this.pop = pop;
      this.push = push;
      this.size = size;
      this.display = display;
      this.insertAt = insertAt;
      this.removeAt = removeAt;
    }
  // -->
  </script>


</head>

<body>

  <center>
    <font size=6>JavaScript Professional Projects</font><br>
    <font size=4>Chapter 5: Linked Lists </font>
  </center>


  <br><br>


  <script language="JavaScript">
  <!--
    var linkedList = new List();
    linkedList.display();


    document.write( "<br><br>" );


    for( i = 0 ; i < 5 ; i++ )
    {
```

```
        linkedList.push( Math.random() );
    }

    linkedList.display();

    document.write( "<br><br>" );

    for( i = 0 ; i < 5 ; i++ )
    {
        linkedList.insertAt( 3, Math.random() );
    }

    linkedList.display();
// -->
</script>

</body>
</html>
```

In this example, the user-defined class List encapsulates the native class Array. The new class contains a property of type Array. The user-defined methods make use of the Array property by calling its built-in functions. This all goes on behind the scenes without the user of the new class knowing, or needing to know, exactly how it was implemented.

The pop() and push() methods of the List class each make a call to the built-in method of the Array object data to insert or remove an item from the list:

```
function pop()
{
    return( this.data.pop() );
}

function push( value )
{
    this.data.push( value );
}
```

The methods insertAt() and removeAt() have been discussed extensively in previous chapters. They insert or remove a value anywhere in the list. Even these methods, which have no parallel method in the Array object, make extensive use of the Array object's built-in methods. The size() and display() methods create a shortcut for using the list data that would otherwise have made this example much longer. The `size()` method simply returns the size of the data `Array` property of the list. The `display()` method cleanly displays the entire contents of the list in an HTML table.

There are two other very simple dynamic data types that can be created in a similar way. A `Stack` is essentially a linked list in which you can only add and remove values from the top. An implementation of a `Stack` class would be

```
function pop()
{
  return( this.data.pop() );
}


function push( value )
{
  this.data.push( value );
}


function size()
{
  return( this.data.length );
}


function display()
{
  document.write( "<table border=1 cellpadding=5 cellspacing=2
                        width=50%>" +
                " <tr>" +
                "   <td>" +
                "     <b><code>Stack - Size = " +
                                this.size() + "</code></b>" +
                "   </td>" +
                " </tr><tr>" +
                "   <td>" );

  if( this.size() == 0 ) document.write( "No data" );
  document.write( this.data.join( "</td></tr><tr><td>" ) );
  document.write( "</td></tr></table>" );
}
```

```
function Stack()
{
  this.data = new Array( 0 );
  this.pop = pop;
  this.push = push;
  this.size = size;
  this.display = display;
}
```

The other useful dynamic data type is a queue. Queues allow you to add values to one end of the linked list and remove them from the other. An implementation of the Queue class would be

```
function dequeue()
{
  return( this.data.pop() );
}


function enqueue( value )
{
  this.data.unshift( value );
}


function size()
{
  return( this.data.length );
}


function display()
{
  document.write( "<table border=1 cellpadding=5 cellspacing=2
                       width=50%>" +
              "  <tr>" +
              "    <td>" +
              "      <b><code>Queue - Size = " +
                            this.size() + "</code></b>" +
              "    </td>" +
              "  </tr><tr>" +
              "    <td>" );
```

```
    if( this.size() == 0 ) document.write( "No data" );
    document.write( this.data.join( "</td></tr><tr><td>" ) );
    document.write( "</td></tr></table>" );
}


function Queue()
{
  this.data = new Array( 0 );
  this.dequeue = dequeue;
  this.enqueue = enqueue;
  this.size = size;
  this.display = display;
}
```

All three dynamic data types—linked lists, stacks, and queues—are very handy tools to have. The dynamic quality of these classes creates less of a memory drain when compared to static arrays.

Object Constructors

When creating custom classes, the constructor method must always be present. The constructor method *constructs*, or initializes, an instance of a class. In the linked list example above, the constructor

```
function List()
{
  this.data = new Array( 0 );
  this.pop = pop;
  this.push = push;
  this.size = size;
  this.display = display;
  this.insertAt = insertAt;
  this.removeAt = removeAt;
}
```

has the same name as the class it is used to construct—in this case List. Constructors are generally used to initialize local properties such as

```
var data = new Array();
```

This property will be available to all other methods of the initialized object just like any other object property. The only difference between constructors and other methods and functions is that a constructor should never return a value.

JavaScript Native Objects

Like every object-oriented programming language, JavaScript has several built-in or *native* objects that you, as a programmer, have access to. These objects are accessible anywhere in your program and will work the same way in any browser running in any operating system. That's not to say that each object behaves identically in any environment because that is not the case. Different browsers have implemented the JavaScript native objects in different ways. The object will run in the same way, producing similar, but not identical, output. This is yet another example of how encapsulation—hiding the internal workings of objects from the programmer—is very beneficial. Objects in different browsers have different internal workings, but they still accomplish the same tasks.

The following subsections list and describe all of the JavaScript objects and their properties and methods.

Boolean Object

A `Boolean` object represents any value that is evaluated to be either `true` or `false`. `Boolean` objects generally are not used because the browser automatically creates them for you when a `true`/`false` value is encountered. There are three ways to create a `Boolean` object:

```
var myBoolean = new Boolean();
var myBoolean = new Boolean( <boolean value> );
var myBoolean = <boolean value>;
```

The Boolean Property

There is only one `Boolean` property, `prototype`. `prototype` is a static property of the `Boolean` object. Use the `prototype` property to assign new properties and methods to the `Boolean` object in the current document.

Boolean Methods

The `Boolean` objects have two methods, `toString()` and `valueOf()`. These two methods are inherited from the JavaScript base object `Object` and are part of every JavaScript object's definition.

- ◆ **toString()**. Returns either `"true"` or `"false"` depending on the `Boolean` object's value.
- ◆ **valueOf()**. Returns the boolean value of the `Boolean` object—either `true` or `false`.

Date Objects

An instance of a `Date` object is a snapshot of the date and time at which the object was created. A `Date` object's value is an integer value representing the number of milliseconds since zero hours at January 1, 1970. Negative values represent dates before that time, and positive values represent dates after that time. Following are several different ways to create a `Date` object:

```
var now = new Date();
var myDate = new Date( "month dd, yyyy, hh:mm:ss" );
var myDate = new Date( "month dd, yyyy" );
var myDate = new Date( yy, mm, dd, hh, mm, ss );
var myDate = new Date( yy, mm, dd );
var myDate = new Date( milliseconds );
```

The first method, `var now = new Date();`, creates a snapshot of the current date and time, while the subsequent ways create a date object with the specified date and time.

The Date Property

There is one `Date` property, `prototype`. `prototype` is a static property of the `Date` object. Use the `prototype` property to assign new properties and methods to the `Date` object in the current document.

Date Methods

The `Date` objects have many very useful methods for manipulating the value of the `Date` object. Here is a complete list and description of each.

- ◆ **getDate()**. Returns an integer value representing the day of the month value of a `Date` object. Values are in the range of 1 to 31.

- ◆ **getDay()**. Returns an integer value representing the day value of a `Date` object. Values are in the range of 0 to 6—Sunday = 0 and Saturday = 6.

- ◆ **getFullYear()**. Returns an integer value representing the year value of a `Date` object. Netscape Navigator will not return a negative value, but Internet Explorer will.

- ◆ **getHours()**. Returns an integer value representing the hours value of a `Date` object. Values are in the range of 0 to 23.

- ◆ **getMilliseconds()**. Returns an integer value representing the milliseconds value of a `Date` object.

- ◆ **getMinutes()**. Returns an integer value representing the minutes value of a `Date` object. Values are in the range of 0 to 59.

- ◆ **getMonths()**. Returns an integer value representing the months value of a `Date` object. Values are in the range of 0 to 11.

- ◆ **getSeconds()**. Returns an integer value representing the seconds value of a `Date` object. Values are in the range of 0 to 59.

- **getTime()**. Returns an integer value representing the number of milliseconds since January 1, 1970 specified by the Date object.

- **getTimezoneOffset()**. Returns the number of minutes that differ between GMT and client computer's clock. The zones to the west of GMT return a positive value while the zones to the east of GMT return a negative value. Return values are in the range of -720 to 720.

- **getUTCDate()**. Returns the day of the month value of the UTC time stored internally by the browser in the range 1 to 31.

- **getUTCDay()**. Returns the day value of the UTC time stored internally by the browser in the range 0 to 6 – Sunday = 0 and Saturday = 6.

- **getUTCFullYear()**. Returns the year value of the UTC time stored internally by the browser.

- **getUTCHours()**. Returns the hours value of the UTC time stored internally by the browser in the range 0 to 23.

- **getUTCMilliseconds()**. Returns the milliseconds value of the UTC time stored internally by the browser in the range 0 to 999.

- **getUTCMinutes()**. Returns the minutes value of the UTC time stored internally by the browser in the range 0 to 59.

- **getUTCMonth()**. Returns the day value of the UTC time stored internally by the browser in the range 0 to 11.

- **getUTCSeconds()**. Returns the seconds value of the UTC time stored internally by the browser in the range 0 to 59.

- **getYear()**. Returns an integer specifying the last two digits of the year value of the Date object in the range 0 to 99 for years 1900 to 1999. This method behaves identically to the getFullYear() method with Date objects that have values after the year 2000.

- **parse(dateString)**. A static method that returns the number of milliseconds since January 1, 1970 to the date specified in the dateString parameter.

- **setDate(dateInt)**. Sets the day of the month value for the original Date object. The operand must be in the range 1 to 31.

- **setFullYear(yearInt)**. Sets the year value for the original Date object.

- **setHours(hourInt)**. Sets the hours value for the original Date object. The operand must be in the range 1 to 23.

- **setMilliseconds(milliInt)**. Sets the day of the month value for the original Date object. The operand must be in the range 0 to 999.

- **setMinutes(minInt)**. Sets the minutes value for the original Date object. The operand must be in the range 0 to 59.

- **setMonth(monthInt)**. Sets the month value for the original Date object. The operand must be in the range 0 to 11.

- **setSeconds(secInt)**. Sets the seconds value for the original `Date` object. The operand must be in the range 0 to 59.

- **setTime(timeInt)**. Sets the `Date` object to the number of milliseconds since January 1, 1970.

- **setUTCDate(dateInt)**. Sets the day of the month value for the UTC time stored internally in the browser. The operand must be in the range 1 to 31.

- **setUTCFullYear(yearInt)**. Sets the year value for the UTC time stored internally in the browser.

- **setUTCHours(monthInt)**. Sets the hours value for the UTC time stored internally in the browser. The operand must be in the range 0 to 23.

- **setUTCMilliseconds(milliInt)**. Sets the milliseconds value for the UTC time stored internally in the browser. The operand must be in the range 0 to 999.

- **setUTCMinutes(minInt)**. Sets the minutes value for the UTC time stored internally in the browser. The operand must be in the range 0 to 59.

- **setUTCMonth(monthInt)**. Sets the month value for the UTC time stored internally in the browser. The operand must be in the range 0 to 11.

- **setUTCSeconds(secInt)**. Sets the seconds value for the UTC time stored internally in the browser. The operand must be in the range 0 to 59.

- **setYear(yearInt)**. Sets the year value of the original `Date` object. Use `setFullYear()` if your browser version allows it.

- **toGMTString()**. Returns a string representation of the original `Date` object in the format:

  ```
  dayAbbrev, dd mmm yyyy hh:mm:ss
  ```

  Following is an example:

  Mon 16 Feb 2003 03:37:06

- **toLocaleString()**. Returns a string value of the original `Date` object in the format that may be localized for the particular country.

- **toString()**. A static method used to convert the current date time to a string.

- **toUTCString()**. Returns a string version of the UTC value of a Date object in the format:

  ```
  dayAbbrev, dd mmm yyyy hh:mm:ss
  ```

  Following is an example:

  Mon 16 Feb 2003 03:37:06

- **UTC(yyyy, mm, dd, hh, mm, ss, msec)**. A static method that returns a numeric version (not a `Date` object) of the date as stored internally by the browser. The return value is the number of milliseconds from January 1, 1970, to the specified date operands.

The Document Object

The Document object provides access to the HTML elements on a Web page. The Document object serves as the parent element for every HTML element on a page. Each window has a unique Document object.

Document Properties

- **alinkcolor**. Gets and sets the default color of all active links on the page.
- **anchors**. An array containing all anchors within the page. Use this property in the following way:

  ```
  document.anchors["anchorID"];
  ```

- **applets**. An array containing all applets within the page. Use this property in the following way:

  ```
  document.applets["appletID"];
  ```

- **bgColor**. Gets and sets the document's background color.
- **cookies**. Returns a report on all visible and unexpired cookies for the page. Use this property in the following way:

  ```
  document.cookies[= <expression>];
  ```

- **domain**. Gets or sets the domain name from which the page originated.
- **embeds**. An array containing all embeded tags within the page. Use this property in the following way:

  ```
  document.embeds["embedID"];
  ```

- **fgColor**. Gets or sets the documents foreground color.
- **"formname"**. Used to reference a specific form on the page.
- **forms**. An array containing all forms within the page. Use this property in the following way:

  ```
  document.forms["formID"];
  ```

- **images**. An array containing all images within the page. Use this property in the following way:

  ```
  document.images["imageID"];
  ```

- **lastModified**. Returns the date on which the page was last modified.
- **linkColor**. Gets or sets the default color for links on the page.
- **links**. An array containing all links within the page. Use this property in the following way:

  ```
  document.links["linkID"];
  ```

◆ **plugins**. An array containing all plugins within the page. Use this property in the following way:

```
document.plugins["pluginID"];
```

The plugins property is used with Netscape Navigator only.

◆ **referrer**. Returns the URL for the page that referred the visitor to your page.

◆ **title**. Returns the title of the page.

◆ **URL**. Returns the page's full URL.

◆ **VlinkColor**. Gets or sets the default color for all visited links on the page.

Document Methods

The Document object has many methods that are useful for performing an operation to an entire Web page. The following is a list of each method and its description:

◆ **captureEvent(event)**. Instructs the document to capture and handle all events of a certain type.

◆ **close()**. Closes an output stream previously opened with document.open() and flushes the buffer to the screen.

◆ **getSelection()**. Returns the contents of selected text on the document. Netscape only.

◆ **handleEvent(event)**. Calls the handler for the specified event's type.

◆ **open(mimeType, replace)**. Opens a stream to capture the output from the document.write() and document.writeln() methods.

◆ **releaseEvent(event)**. Instructs the document that the specified event type is to be captured further down the event hierarchy.

◆ **write(string)**. Writes the specified string onto the document.

◆ **writeln(string)**. Writes the specified string onto the document followed by a new line character.

Document Event Handlers

Like all Web page elements, the Document object has many event handlers that you can use to capture and use events. Each event handler is listed and described here.

◆ **onClick**. Captures the document's mouse click events. Syntax:

```
document.onClick = "<statements>";
```

◆ **onDblClick**. Captures the document's double mouse click event. Syntax:

```
document.onDblClick = "<statements>";
```

◆ **onKeyDown**. Captures the document's key-depress events. Syntax:

```
document.keyDown = "<statements>";
```

- ◆ **OnKeyPress**. Captures the document's mouse-press events. Syntax:

  ```
  document.onKeyPress = "<statements>";
  ```

- ◆ **onKeyUp**. Captures the document's key up events. Syntax:

  ```
  document.onKeyUp = "<statements>";
  ```

- ◆ **onMouseDown**. Captures the document's mouse down events. Syntax:

  ```
  document.onClick = "<statements>";
  ```

- ◆ **onMouseUp**. Captures the document's mouse up events. Syntax:

  ```
  document.onMouseUp = "<statements>";
  ```

Event Objects

An `Event` object is created automatically every time a Web page user presses a key or clicks his mouse button. `Event` objects can be captured and handled by event handlers.

Event Properties

Each `Event` object has several properties that you can use to identify the source and type of the event. Following is a complete list of their names and a description of each.

- ◆ **data**. Returns an array that contains the URL of any dropped objects as stings. Netscape only.
- ◆ **height**. The height of the window or frame that contains the element that initialized the event. Netscape only.
- ◆ **layerX/layerY**. Synonyms for the x/y properties of the event object. Netscape only.
- ◆ **modifiers**. Captures the document's mouse clicks. Netscape only. Syntax:

  ```
  document.onClick = "<statements>";
  ```

- ◆ **pageX** and **pageY**. These properties return the point at which the cursor was when the event occurred in relation to the page. Netscape only.
- ◆ **screenX/screenY**. These properties return the point at which the cursor was when the event occurred in relation to the screen. Netscape only.
- ◆ **target**. This property contains a reference to the object to which the event was originally sent. Netscape only.
- ◆ **type**. This property returns a string containing the vent type, click, key down, etc.
- ◆ **which**. This property returns the mouse button or key that was pressed. For the mouse, 1 = left button, 2 = middle button, and 3 = right button. For keys, this property is the ASCII value of the key. Netscape only.

- ◆ **width**. The width of the window or frame that contains the element that initialized the event. Netscape only.
- ◆ **x/y**. The horizontal/vertical position of the cursor at the time of the event in pixels relative to the layer that initialized the event.

The Math Object

The Math object is made up of several static methods used to perform mathematical operations for which there are no operators.

Math Properties

The Math object has many useful properties. Most of the properties of the Math object are constants that you might use in mathematical formulas.

- ◆ **E**. Euler's Constant: 2.718281828459045
- ◆ **LN2**. Natural logarithm of 2: 0.6931471805599453
- ◆ **LN10**. Natural logarithm of 10: 02.302585092994046
- ◆ **LOG2E**. Log base -2 of E: 0.6931471805599453
- ◆ **LOG10E**. Log base -10 of E: 0.4342944819032518
- ◆ **PI**3.141592653589793
- ◆ **SQRT1_2**. The square root of 0.5: 0.7071067811865476
- ◆ **SQRT2**. The square root of 2: 1.4142135623730951

Math Methods

The Math object also has many methods that are useful in mathematical formulas. The Math object is a static object, which means that you do not need to create an instance in order to call the methods. Each method may be called in the following way:

```
Math.<method name>( <arguments> );
```

- ◆ **abs(number)**. Returns the absolute value of number.
- ◆ **acos(number)**. Returns the arc cosine of number in radians.
- ◆ **asin(number)**. Returns the arc sine of number in radians.
- ◆ **atan(number)**. Returns the arc tangent of number in radians.
- ◆ **atan2(x,y)**. Returns the arctangent of the quotient of its two operands.
- ◆ **ceil(number)**. Returns the next highest integer from number.
- ◆ **cos(number)**. Returns the cosine of number in radians.
- ◆ **exp(number)**. Returns the value E raised to the power of number.
- ◆ **floor(number)**. Returns the next lowest integer from number.
- ◆ **long(number)**. Returns the logarithm (base e) of number.

- `max(n1, n2)`. Returns the larger of its two parameters.
- `min(n1, n2)`. Returns the lesser of its two parameters.
- `pow(n1, n2)`. Returns the first parameter raised to the power of the second parameter.
- `random()`. Returns a pseudo-random number between 0 and 1. This method does not work in Netscape version 2.
- `round(number)`. Rounds a decimal number to its nearest integer value and returns it.
- `sin(number)`. Returns the sine of number in radians.
- `sqrt(number)`. Returns the square root of number.
- `tan(number)`. Returns the tangent of number in radians.

The Number Object

The `Number` object represents numerical date, either integers or floating-point numbers. In general, you do not need to worry about `Number` objects because the browser automatically converts number literals to instances of the number class.

Number Properties

The `Number` object contains several constant values that are often used for comparison. Here is a list of each property and its description.

- `MAX_VALUE`. The largest possible value a number in JavaScript can have 1.7976931348623157E+308
- `MIN_VALUE`. The smallest possible value a number in JavaScript can have 5E-324
- `NaN`. Equal to a value that is not a number.
- `NEGATIVE_INFINITY`. A value that is less than MIN_VALUE.
- `POSOTIVE_INFINITY`. A value that is greater than MAX_VALUE.
- `prototype`. A static property of the `Number` object. Use the `prototype` property to assign new properties and methods to the `Number` object in the current document.

Number Methods

The Number object contains only the default methods that are part of every object's definition.

- `toString()`. Returns the string representation of the number's value.
- `valueOf()`. Returns the number's value.

The Object object

The `Object` object is the base class for all other classes. Every property and method in this class also appears in all other classes. There is only one way to create an instance of an `Object` object:

```
var myObject = new Object();
```

The following subsections list and describe the Object class properties and methods.

Object Properties

There is only one Object class property, prototype. prototype is a static property of the Object class. Use the prototype property to assign new properties and methods to the Object class in the current document.

Object Class Methods

Objects only contain two methods, toString() and valueOf(). Each Object that extends this class will contain these two methods.

- **toString()**. Returns the string representation of the object.
- **valueOf()**. Returns the object's value.

The Screen Object

The Screen object is most useful when trying to create a cross-platform Web page because it contains several properties that contain platform-specific information on the display screen's size and color depth.

Screen Properties

The following properties of the Screen object allow a programmer to access platform-specific detail about the screen size and color depth of the client's computer.

- **availHeight**. This property returns the height of the screen in pixels. The height of any components of the operating system's interface, such as the Windows Taskbar, is subtracted automatically.
- **availWidth**. This property returns the width of the screen in pixels. The width of any components of the operating system's interface, such as the Windows Taskbar, is subtracted automatically.
- **colorDepth**. This property represents the color depth of a color table, if one is in use. If no color table is being used, this property is the Screen.pixelDepth property.
- **height**. This property returns the height of the screen in pixels.
- **pixelDepth**. This property returns the color resolution of the display screen in bits per pixel.
- **width**. This property returns the width of the screen in pixels.

The Window Object

The Window object is the top-level object in the JavaScript client hierarchy. Every browser window and frame has a window object. The Window object contains properties and methods describing and modifying the browser window and also contains a reference to the Document object contained in the browser.

Window Properties

The properties contained in the Window object can be used to identify the state of the browser window. Many of these properties are read-only, but others can be modified.

- ◆ **closed**. This property is used to determine if the window has been closed. If the window has been closed, this property is true; otherwise, it is false. This property is read-only.

- ◆ **defaultStatus**. This property is used to change the default message that is used in the status bar.

- ◆ **document**. A reference to the Document object contained within the window. This property is read-only.

- ◆ **frames**. This property is an array containing all the named frames in the window. This property is read-only.

- ◆ **history**. A reference to the History object for this window. This property is read-only.

- ◆ **innerHeight/innerWidth**. The dimensions of the display are in pixels. Netscape only. This property is read-only.

- ◆ **length**. Identical to the value window.frames.length and represents the number of frames in the window. This property is read-only.

- ◆ **location**. The current URL for the window.

- ◆ **locationbar**. This property references the area of the browser into which the user types the URL. Setting the locationbar.visible boolean property will show/hide this portion of the browser. Netscape only.

- ◆ **menubar**. This property references the area of the browser that contains the menus. Setting the menubar.visible boolean property will show/hide this portion of the browser. Netscape only.

- ◆ **name**. This property is used to get or set the name of the window.

- ◆ **opener**. This property references the window that opened the current window. You can use window.opener.close() to close the window that opened the current one. This property is read-only.

- ◆ **outerheight/ outerwidth**. The dimensions of the entire window in pixels.

- ◆ **pageXOffset/pageYOffset**. The coordinates of the top-left corner of the window in relation to the desktop.

- ◆ **parent**. This property references the parent of the current window. The parent is the window or frame that contains the current frame. This property is read-only.

- ◆ **personalbar**. This property references the area of the browser that contains the user's custom links. Setting the personalbar.visible boolean property will show/hide this portion of the browser.

- ◆ **scrollbars**. This property references the windows vertical and horizontal scroll bars. Setting the scrollbars.visible boolean property will show/hide this portion of the browser.

- ◆ **status**. This property sets the message in the status bar for the current window.
- ◆ **statusbar**. This property references the status bar portion of the window. Setting the **statusbar.visible** boolean property will show/hide this portion of the browser.
- ◆ **toolbar**. This property references the tool bar portion of the window. Setting the **toolbar.visible** boolean property will show/hide this portion of the browser.

Window Methods

The **Window** object contains several static methods that can be called without first creating an instance of the **Window** object. To call one of the following methods, use the following syntax:

```
Window.<method name>( <arguments> );
```
  or
```
<method name>( <arguments> );
```

- ◆ **alert(string)**. Opens an alert dialog with the specified message.
- ◆ **back()**. This method provides the same functionality as hitting the back button on the browser.
- ◆ **blur()**. This method removes the focus from the **Window** object.
- ◆ **captureEvent(eventType)**. This method makes the window capture all events of the specified type.
- ◆ **clearInterval(intervalID)**. This method cancels a timeout previously set with the **setInterval()** method.
- ◆ **clearTimeout(intervalID)**. This method cancels a timeout previously set with the **setTimeout()** method.
- ◆ **close()**. Used to close a window previously opened with the **open()** method.
- ◆ **confirt(string)**. This method opens a confirm dialog with the specified message and two buttons: OK, which returns true when pressed, and Cancel, which returns false when pressed.
- ◆ **disableExternalCapture()**. This method disables the capturing of events previously set with the **enableExternalCapturing()** method.
- ◆ **enableExternalCapture()**. This method allows the window to capture events occurring in a document loaded from a different server.
- ◆ **find(string, caseSensitive, backward)**. Opens the find dialog for the browser. The first argument is the string to search for and the last two are boolean values. All three arguments are optional, but if you specify either **caseSensitive** or **backward**, you must provide a value for the others.
- ◆ **focus()**. This method gives focus to the window.
- ◆ **forward()**. This method provides the same functionality as hitting the Forward button on the browser.

- ◆ `handleEvent( eventID)`. This method calls the handler for the specified event.
- ◆ `home()`. This method provides the same functionality as hitting the home button on the browser.
- ◆ `moveBy(horizontal, vertical)`. This method moves the window the specified number of pixels from its current position.
- ◆ `moveTo(xPos, yPos)`. This method moves the window to specified x,y position on the screen.
- ◆ `open(URL, name, features)`. This method opens a new window with the specified URL, name, and features. The features include `directories`, `height`, `location`, `menubar`, `resizable`, `scrollbars`, `status`, `toolbar`, and `width`, each of which may be assigned the value yes or no.

  The following is an example:

  ```
  window.open( "http://www.somewhere.com",
  "myWindow", "width=400, height=400," +
  "resizable=no, toolbar=no" );
  ```

- ◆ `print()`. This method opens the print dialog for the browser.
- ◆ `prompt(message, default)`. This method opens a prompt dialog with the specified answer and an optional default answer.
- ◆ `releaseEvents( eventType)`. This method releases any events of the specified type and sends them further down the event hierarchy.
- ◆ `resizeBy( horizontal, vertical)`. This method resizes the window by the specified amount.
- ◆ `routEvent( eventType)`. This method releases the specified event type back to the original target object or a sub-object of the window (a document).
- ◆ `scroll()`. This method is deprecated; use `scrollTo()`.
- ◆ `scrollBy(horizontal, vertical)`. This method scrolls the window by the specified amount in each horizontal and vertical direction.
- ◆ `scrollTo(xPos, yPos)`. This method scrolls the contents of the window. The x,y position located in the window's document becomes the top-left corner of the visible area.
- ◆ `setInterval( expression/function, milliseconds)`. This method is used to evaluate an expression or call a function at the specified interval.
- ◆ `setTimeout( expression/function, milliseconds)`. This method is used to evaluate an expression or call a function once, after the specified delay.
- ◆ `stop()`. This method provides the same functionality as hitting the Stop button on the browser.

Window Event Handlers

The `Window` object contains several event handlers that can capture events anywhere on the browser. The following is a list of their names and descriptions of each.

- **onBlur**. This event handler executes the specified JavaScript code on the occurrence of the `Blur` event:

  ```
  window.onBlur="JavaScript Statements"
  ```

- **onDragDrop**. This event handler executes the specified JavaScript code on the occurrence of the `DragDrop` event:

  ```
  window.onDragDrop="JavaScript Statements"
  ```

- **onError**. This event handler executes the specified JavaScript code on the occurrence of the `Error` event:

  ```
  window.onError="JavaScript Statements"
  ```

- **onFocus**. This event handler executes the specified JavaScript code on the occurrence of the `Focus` event:

  ```
  window.onFocus="JavaScript Statements"
  ```

- **onLoad**. This event handler executes the specified JavaScript code on the occurrence of the `Load` event:

  ```
  window.onLoad="JavaScript Statements"
  ```

- **onMove**. This event handler executes the specified JavaScript code on the occurrence of the `Move` event:

  ```
  window.onMove="JavaScript Statements"
  ```

- **onResize**. This event handler executes the specified JavaScript code on the occurrence of the `Resize` event:

  ```
  window.onResize="JavaScript Statements"
  ```

- **onUnload**. This event handler executes the specified JavaScript code on the occurrence of the `Unload` event:

  ```
  window.onUnload="JavaScript Statements"
  ```

These classes were created for the programmer's convenience. I encourage you to use them as often as possible in order to avoid reinventing the wheel, and to make all of your Web applications run in a similar fashion.

Inheritance and Polymorphism

As mentioned at the beginning of the chapter, inheritance allows a program to reuse preexisting object types without rewriting their functionality from scratch. By way of example let's examine the Array object type. If you wanted to have the functionality of a linked list, but did not have the Array.prototype property or did not want to use it, you could create a new class called List that extended the Array class. The new List class would have all the functionality of the original Array class, but you could add more functionality into it automatically.

Inheritance in JavaScript is slightly different than in other languages. Following is a classic example used in many computer science classes:

```
Employee.prototype = new Person();
Employee.prototype.constructor = Employee;
Employee.superclass = Person.prototype;


// Employee constructor
function Employee()
{
   ...

}
```

In this example, the Employee class extends the functionality of the Person class. Person is considered to be the super class and Employee is considered the subclass. In the first line, the prototype property of the Employee class is being assigned to an instance of the Person class. This provides an instance of Employee with all the functionality of the Person class. Unfortunately, this statement overrides the constructor for the Employee class, so the second line is to make sure the proper constructor is executed when an Employee object is created. The third line provides a way for the JavaScript interpreter to understand the class hierarchy by specifying which class is a subclass and which is the super class.

When inheriting properties and methods from a super class, there may come a point at which you need to perform some similar function but don't know the exact type of the object you are working with. A classic case is the shape example. To begin with, a super class called Shape is declared. Shape has a single method paint(). Later, two subclasses of Shape are created, Circle and Square. Both subclasses inherit the method paint() from the Shape class, but both override it to provide specific support for their data. The Circle.paint() method provides a way to draw a circle to the screen, while the Square.paint() provides code to draw a square. If you were using a lot of these shape objects, you might store them in an array such as the following:

```
var shapeArray = new Array( n );


shapeArray = new Circle();
shapeArray = new Square();

   ...
```

Later on in your code, if you wanted to draw this array of shapes to the screen but did not keep track of the order in which you stored them, you would not need to worry. Since the super class, `Shape`, has the method `paint()` both subclasses will also have the method. As long as you know your array is full of some type of `Shape` object, you can call `paint()` and have it perform the proper operations that will draw the subclass's actual shape. This results in a method that has been implemented differently in multiple subclasses in order to provide class specific functionality. This is called polymorphism.

Summary

An object-oriented language is required to have three tools: encapsulation, inheritance, and polymorphism. JavaScript contains these three tools, making it an object-oriented language. JavaScript provides the programmer with many built-in, or native, objects. Each object generally has a collection of properties and methods. Properties are nothing more than variables stored within the object. A property can be either a primitive data type or an instance of another object. Methods are functions that are linked to the objects themselves. Usually you will need to create an instance of an object before you can call its methods, but there are some objects (`Window` and `Document`) that have static methods that can be called at any time. There is a special method called a *constructor* that is used to instantiate each instance of a method.

Chapter 6

One of the most useful things JavaScript has brought to the world of static Web pages is the ability to generate, capture, and use a wide variety of events. These events—ranging from key presses to mouse movements—brought dynamism to Web pages that could only be dreamed of before.

The events in JavaScript can be divided into two groups. The first group consists of events that happen automatically, such as `onBeforeUnload`, `onError`, `onLoad`, and `onUnload`, just to name a few. The other group contains events that are userdriven, such as `onClick`, `onDblClick`, `onHelp`, `onKeyDown`, and `onMouseOver`.

JavaScript Basic Events

This section covers the group of JavaScript events that happen automatically, called *basic events*. Basic events are events that occur without any input from the user. Events such as onLoad and onUnload are very useful for running scripts every time a Web page loads or is unloaded because they are generated by the browser and are guaranteed to run at a predictable time. The following is a list of basic events that are generated by the browser at certain times while a Web page is being used.

- **onAfterUpdate**. This event is triggered when the transfer of data from a databound document to a data source has finished updating. Internet Explorer only.

- **onBeforeUnload**. This event is triggered prior to a page being uploaded. Internet Explorer only.

- **onBeforeUpdate**. This event is triggered before the transfer of data from a databound document to a data source begins updating. Internet Explorer only.

- **onDateAvailable**. This event is triggered periodically as asynchronous data has arrived for an object such as an Applet. Internet Explorer only.

- **onDatasetChanged**. This event is triggered as the data source content of an object such as an applet changes or the initial data becomes available. Internet Explorer only.

- **onDatasetComplete**. This event is triggered when all data from the data source object is available to an object such as an applet. Internet Explorer only.

- **onError**. This event is triggered when an error occurs in a script or other external data.

- **onErrorUpdate**. This event is triggered when an error occurs during the transfer of data from a databound object to a data source. Internet Explorer only.

- **onFilterChange**. This event is triggered as a filter changes the state of an element or as a transition completes. Internet Explorer only.

- **onFinish**. This event is triggered at the end of MARQUEE looping. Internet Explorer only.

- **onLoad**. This event is triggered when the document or other external object has completed downloading to the browser.

- **onReadyStateChange**. This event is triggered when the state of an object changes. Internet Explorer only.

- **onStart**. This event is triggered at the beginning of MARQUEE looping. Internet Explorer only.

- **onUnload**. This event is triggered as the document is about to be unloaded from the browser.

The basic events listed here all occur without visitor input and usually without the visitor even knowing that they're occurring.

Basic Event Example

Following is a very basic example that demonstrates the use of three of the basic events listed in the previous section:

```html
<html>
  <head>
    <title>
      JavaScript Professional Projects - Basic Events
    </title>
  </head>

  <body
    onBeforeUnload="JavaScript: alert('onBeforeUnload event');"
    onLoad        ="JavaScript: alert('onLoad event');"
    onUnload      ="JavaScript: alert('onUnload event');">

    <center>
      <font size=6>JavaScript Professional Projects</font><br>
      <font size=4>Chapter 3: Basic Events</font>
    </center>

    <br><br>
    <br><br>

    <a href="http://www.yahoo.com/">Some other page.</a>

  </body>
</html>
```

This example binds three events to the <body> tag of the document (event binding is discussed later in this chapter). As soon as the page is visible in the browser, the onLoad event is triggered and displays a dialog box displaying the text onLoad event. If you were to switch to a different Web page, the onBeforeUnload event would be triggered immediately and would display another dialog box with the text onBeforeUnload. Just before the original document is replaced by the new one, the onUnload event is triggered, displaying the message onUnload event. While useful for illustration purposes, this example drastically oversimplifies the usefulness of these events. In the chapters to come you will be presented with several instances where these events are of practical use.

Using these basic JavaScript events affords you great power, but also leaves room for abuse. Many less reputable Web sites do try to trap a visitor within their site using code very similar to the following

```
<body
  onBeforeUnload="JavaScript: local=window.location;"
  onUnload       ="JavaScript: window.location=local;">
```

This example would prevent the visitor of a site from leaving the page that it was used on. Not even the Forward and Back buttons would allow the visitor to move to a different page. Needless to say, this would be very annoying to your Web site's visitors.

JavaScript User-Created Events

Virtually everything a visitor does when he visits a site generates an event—from clicking with the mouse to selecting text on a Web page. This allows you to use JavaScript as an event-driven language. Because the basic events presented in the previous section run automatically, they could be considered sequential events. The events presented in this section only happen because of something the user does in the Web site. The names and descriptions of all user-created events are as follows:

- **OnAbort**. This event is triggered when the user interrupts the transfer of data to the browser, such as by pressing the Stop button.
- **onBlur**. This event is triggered when an element loses focus, either because the user clicked outside of the element's bounds or because he or she hit the Tab key.
- **onBounce**. This event is triggered when then contents of a MARQUEE element has reached the edge of the page.
- **onChange**. This event is triggered when an element loses focus after the contents of the element have changed. An example of this is changing the contents of a text field on a form then clicking the Submit button.
- **onClick**. This event is triggered when the user presses and releases the mouse button or keyboard equivalent.
- **onDblclick**. This event is triggered when the user double-clicks a mouse button.
- **onDragDrop**. This event is triggered when the user drags a desktop icon into the browser window.
- **onDragStart**. This event is triggered when the user begins selecting elements on the page.
- **onFocus**. This event is triggered when an element gains focus.
- **onHelp**. This event is triggered when the user presses the F1 key or chooses Help from the browser window.
- **onKeyDown**. This event is triggered when the user begins pressing a key on the keyboard.
- **onKeyPress**. This event is triggered when the user presses and releases a key on the keyboard.
- **onKeyUp**. This event is triggered when the user releases a key on the keyboard.

- ◆ **onMouseDown**. This event is triggered when the user begins pressing a mouse button.
- ◆ **onMouseMove**. This event is triggered when the user moves the mouse cursor.
- ◆ **onMouseOut**: This event is triggered when the user takes the mouse cursor outside of the browser or element bounds.
- ◆ **onMouseOver**. This event is triggered when the user positions the mouse cursor over an element.
- ◆ **onMouseUp**. This event is triggered when the user releases a mouse button.
- ◆ **onMove**. This event is triggered when the user moves the browser window.
- ◆ **onReset**. This event is triggered when the user clicks the Reset button.
- ◆ **onResize**. This event is triggered when the user resizes the browser window.
- ◆ **onRowEnter**. This event is triggered when the data in a databound object has changed in the current row.
- ◆ **onRowExit**. This event is triggered when the data in a databound object is about to change in the current row.
- ◆ **onScroll**. This event is triggered when the user adjusts an element's scroll bar.
- ◆ **onSelect**. This event is triggered when the user selects text in either an INPUT or TEXTAREA element.
- ◆ **onSelectStart** This event is triggered when the user is beginning to select an element.
- ◆ **onSubmit**. This event is triggered when the user clicks the Submit button on a form.

User-Created Event Examples

Take a look at the example below, which captures two of the most commonly used events. This example captures both key presses and mouse button events.

```
<html>
  <head>
    <title>
      JavaScript Professional Projects - User Created Events
    </title>
  </head>

  <body
    onKeyDown="JavaScript: alert( 'Key Down' );"
    onMouseDown="JavaScript: alert( 'Mouse Down' );">

    <center>
      <font size=6>JavaScript Professional Projects</font><br>
      <font size=4>Chapter 3: User Created Events</font>
```

```
        </center>

      </body>
    </html>
```

Each time the user of this Web page clicks with the mouse or types a key an alert box is created that tells the type of event.

The example below performs all the operations you would expect from a simple calculator. It demonstrates the use of some of the user-defined events:

```
<html>

  <head>
    <title>Numeric Calculator</title>

    <style   type="text/css">
    <!--
      input{ font-family: monospace; }
    -->
    </style>

    <script language="JavaScript">
    <!--
      window.onerror = handleError;

      function handleError()
      {
        document.CalcForm.Display.value = "Error";
      }

      function append( c )
      {
        document.CalcForm.Display.value =
            document.CalcForm.Display.value + c;
      }

      function calculate( expression )
      {
        var answer = eval( expression );
```

```
      if( answer != undefined )
      {
        return( answer );
      }
      else
      {
        return( "Error" );
      }
    }
  // -->
  </script>
</head>

<body>
  <center>
    <font size=6>JavaScript Professional Projects</font><br>
    <font size=4>Chapter 6: User Created Events</font>
  </center>

  <br><br>

  <form name="CalcForm">
    <table style="border-collapse: collapse" bordercolor="#111111"
          cellpadding="2" border="1">
      <tr>
        <td colspan="4"><center>
          <input name="Display" size="30">
        </center></td>
      </tr>
      <tr>
        <td bordercolor="#FFFFFF">
          <input type="button" value=" 7 "
                onClick="javascript: append( '7' );">
        </td>
        <td bordercolor="#FFFFFF">
          <input type="button" value=" 8 "
                onClick="javascript: append( '8' );">
        </td>
```

```
<td bordercolor="#FFFFFF">
  <input type="button" value=" 9 "
         onClick="javascript: append( '9' );">
</td>
<td align="right" bordercolor="#FFFFFF">
  <input type="button" value="  +  "
         onClick="javascript: append( '+' );">
</td>
</tr>
<tr>
<td bordercolor="#FFFFFF">
  <input type="button" value=" 4 "
         onClick="javascript: append( '4' );">
</td>
<td bordercolor="#FFFFFF">
  <input type="button" value=" 5 "
         onClick="javascript: append( '5' );">
</td>
<td bordercolor="#FFFFFF">
  <input type="button" value=" 6 "
         onClick="javascript: append( '6' );">
</td>
<td align="right" bordercolor="#FFFFFF">
  <input type="button" value="  -  "
         onClick="javascript: append( '-' );">
</td>
</tr>
<tr>
<td bordercolor="#FFFFFF">
  <input type="button" value=" 1 "
         onClick="javascript: append( '1' );">
</td>
<td bordercolor="#FFFFFF">
  <input type="button" value=" 2 "
         onClick="javascript: append( '2' );">
</td>
<td bordercolor="#FFFFFF">
```

```
    <input type="button" value=" 3 "
            onClick="javascript: append( '3' );">
  </td>
  <td align="right" bordercolor="#FFFFFF">
    <input type="button" value="  *  "
            onClick="javascript: append( '*' );">
  </td>
</tr>
<tr>
  <td bordercolor="#FFFFFF">
    <input type="button" value=" 0 "
            onClick="javascript: append( '0' )">
  </td>
  <td bordercolor="#FFFFFF">
    <input type="button" value=" - "
            onClick="javascript: append( '-' );">
  </td>
  <td bordercolor="#FFFFFF">
    <input type="button" value=" . "
            onClick="javascript: append( '.' );">
  </td>
  <td align="right" bordercolor="#FFFFFF">
    <input type="button" value="  /  "
            onClick="javascript: append( '/' );">
  </td>
</tr>
<tr>
  <td bordercolor="#FFFFFF">
    <input type="button" value=" ( "
            onClick="javascript: append( '(' );">
  </td>
  <td bordercolor="#FFFFFF">
    <input type="button" value=" ) "
            onClick="javascript: append( ')' );">
  </td>
  <td bordercolor="#FFFFFF">
    <input type="button" value=" C "
      onClick="javascript: document.CalcForm.Display.value=''">
```

```
          </td>
          <td align="right" bordercolor="#FFFFFF">
            <input type="button" value="  =  "
                    onClick="javascript:document.CalcForm.Display.value=
                             calculate( document.CalcForm.Display.value );">
          </td>
        </tr>
      </table>
    </form>
  </body>

</html>
```

This example makes use of the onClick event for each of the buttons and also the onError event to correct any errors that occur.

Modifier Keys

Modifier keys are special-purpose keys—such as Atl, Ctrl, and Shift—that may or may not alter the behavior of an event. Most commonly, the Alt key is used to access a program's menus, the Ctrl key is used to perform common tasks such as copying and pasting, and the Shift key is used to enter capital letters instead of lowercase letters. You can use modifier keys on your Web pages in a similar way.

The following is an example that visually displays the modifier keys that are pressed when an event occurs:

```
<html>
  <head>
    <title>
      JavaScript Professional Projects - Modifier Keys
    </title>

    <style type="text/css">
    <!--
      .modKeys{ position: relative;
                clip:rect( 0, 80, 18, 0 );
                background-color: white; }
    -->
    </style>
```

```
<script language="JavaScript">
<!--
  var isNav = navigator.appName == "Netscape";

  function getModifiers( event )
  {
    var alt = ( isNav ? event.modifiers & Event.ALT_MASK :
                        window.event.altKey );
    var ctr = ( isNav ? event.modifiers & Event.CONTROL_MASK :
                        window.event.ctrlKey );
    var sft = ( isNav ? event.modifiers & Event.SHIFT_MASK :
                        window.event.shiftKey );

    setColor( "key1", ( alt ? "gray" : "white" ) );
    setColor( "key2", ( ctr ? "gray" : "white" ) );
    setColor( "key3", ( sft ? "gray" : "white" ) );
  }

  function setColor( object, color )
  {
    var obj = eval( "document." + ( !isNav ? "all." : "" ) +
                    object + ( !isNav ? ".style" : "" ) );

    if( isNav )
      obj.bgColor = color;
    else
      obj.backgroundColor = color;
  }
// -->
</script>
</head>

<body>

<center>
  <font size=6>JavaScript Professional Projects</font><br>
  <font size=4>Chapter 6: Modifier Keys</font>
</center>
```

```html
<br><br>

<table border="1" cellpadding="0" cellspacing="0" width="50%">
  <tr>
    <td width="75%" colspan="3">
      <b><font face="Courier" size="5">
          Modifier Keys:
      </font></b>
    </td>
  </tr>
  <tr>
    <td width=80 height=20 align=center ID=key1 class=modKeys>
      <font face="Courier" size="5">Alt</font>
    </td>
    <td width=80 height=20 align=center ID=key2 class=modKeys>
      <font face="Courier" size="5">Control</font>
    </td>
    <td width=80 height=20 align=center ID=key3 class=modKeys>
      <font face="Courier" size="5">Shift</font>
    </td>
  </tr>
</table>

<p>
  <font size="4">
    While holding one or more modifier keys, click
    <a href="JavaScript: void(0);"
       onMouseDown="JavaScript: getModifiers( event );">here</a>
    to find out which ones you are using.
  </font>
</p>

  </body>
</html>
```

As you can see, the event model is different for each browser. The implementation in the Internet Explorer browser is fairly straightforward—you get the boolean value representing the state of the modifier key by the window.event property, followed by the modifier key. With Netscape, however, you need to use the bitwise operator and (&) to get the same information.

The following is an example of how to get all modifier key flags out of the event object:

```
var altPressed = event.modifiers & Event.ALT_MASK;
var ctrlPressed = event.modifiers & Event.CONTROL_MASK;
var shiftPressed = event.modifiers & Event.SHIFT_MASK;
var metaPressed = event.modifiers & Event.META_MASK;
```

It is important to keep these differences in mind when you're designing for both browser types.

Binding Events to Elements

There are two ways to bind an event to an element so that it can be used: by using tag attributes or assigning an event handler to an object property. Event handler as tag attribute is the type of event handler you will use most often. Event handlers as tag attributes are useful for capturing events generated by HTML elements. Event handlers as object properties are only used with objects such as the built-in JavaScript window and document objects.

Event Handlers as Tag Attributes

The most common, and easiest, way to bind an event to an element is through the element's tag attributes. The examples earlier in this chapter mostly used this type of event binding. In the calculator example, the Equal key, (=), had the following event binding:

```
<input type="button" value="  =  "
        onClick="JavaScript: document.CalcForm.Display.value=
                calculate( document.CalcForm.Display.value );">
```

This means that every time this button (onClick) is pressed, the code that is assigned to the onClick parameter is executed.

It is important that you specify the language that you are using so that the interpreter knows how to execute the code. You do this by preceding the JavaScript code with "JavaScript:"

The keyword this comes into play again when using events. In the following example, this is referencing the element in which the event handler is located—the input tag:

```
<html>
  <head>
    <title>
      JavaScript Professional Projects -
        Event Binding via Tag Attributes
    </title>

    <script language="JavaScript">
```

```
<!--
  function upper( field )
  {
    field.value = field.value.toUpperCase();
  }
// -->
</script>
</head>

<body>

  <center>
    <font size=6>JavaScript Professional Projects</font><br>
    <font size=4>Chapter 6: Event Binding via Tag Attributes</font>
  </center>

  <br><br>

  <form>
    <b>Input text here:  </b>
    <input type="text" size="20" onKeyUp="JavaScript: upper(this);">
  </form>

</body>
</html>
```

This example makes use of the onClick event to convert the contents of a text field into upper-case letters by passing a reference to itself to the function upper().

Event Handlers as Object Properties

In Navigator 3 and Internet Explorer 4 and later, there is another way to bind event handlers—by binding it to an object property. For every event handler that an object supports, there is a property with the same name in all lowercase letters. You can bind the event handler to the object by using the assignment operator (=), just like you would for any other kind of object property.

```
<html>
  <head>
    <title>
      JavaScript Professional Projects - Binding Events
```

```
    </title>

    <script language="JavaScript">
    <!--
      function load()
      {
        alert("onLoad event");
      }

      function unload()
      {
        alert("onUnload event")
      }

      window.onload   = load;
      window.onunload = unload;
    // -->
    </script>
</head>

<body>

  <center>
    <font size=6>JavaScript Professional Projects</font><br>
    <font size=4>Chapter 3: Binding Events</font>
  </center>

  <br><br>
  <br><br>

  <a href="http://www.yahoo.com/">Some other page.</a>

  </body>
</html>
```

You can create an event handler function just as you would any other function. To make it an event handler for an object, simply assign it to the appropriate object property, as in the example above. This technique skirts the problem older browsers have with event binding as tag attributes. Tag attributes are not recognized as valid HTML in older browsers. One disadvantage of this approach is that parameters cannot be passed to the event handler functions.

Event Handler Return Values

One big advantage of using event handlers as tag attributes is that the return value from the handler function can often be used to modify the default actions of the browser. Here is an example to demonstrate this concept:

```
<html>
  <head>
    <title>
      JavaScript Professional Projects - Event Handler Return Values
    </title>

    <script language="JavaScript">
    <!--
      function changeBGColor( color )
      {
        document.bgColor = color;
        return( false );
      }
    // -->
    </script>
  </head>

  <body>

    <center>
      <font size=6>JavaScript Professional Projects</font><br>
      <font size=4>Chapter 6: Event Handler Return Values</font>
    </center>

    <br><br>
    <br><br>

    Make the background
      <a href="unknown_page.html"
         onClick="return( changeBGColor( 'red' ) );">red</a>!
```

```
<br><br>

Make the background
  <a href="unknown_page.html"
    onClick="return( changeBGColor( 'blue' ) );">blue</a>!

<br><br>

Make the background
  <a href="unknown_page.html"
    onClick="return( changeBGColor( 'green' ) );">green</a>!

<br><br>

Make the background
  <a href="unknown_page.html"
    onClick="return( changeBGColor( 'yellow' ) );">yellow</a>!

<br><br>

Make the background
  <a href="unknown_page.html"
    onClick="return( changeBGColor( 'purple' ) );">purple</a>!

<br><br>

Make the background
  <a href="unknown_page.html"
    onClick="return( changeBGColor( 'white' ) );">white</a>!

  </body>
</html>
```

The event handlers are always called before the HTML commands are executed. In the example above, the link href="unknown_page.html" does not exist, but that really doesn't matter. Because the event handler function returns the value false, the Web page interprets that as an error and does not follow the link at all. This trick becomes especially useful when validating forms:

```
<form method="POST" onSubmit="return( validate( this ) );">
```

This form will only submit if the event handler function `validate` (which checks the validity of each form element) returns a `true` value.

Event Propagation

The propagation of events through the object hierarchy is very important to understand. If an event is fired for a specific object that does not have an event handler for it, where does the event go? Unfortunately, like many things, event propagation differs between Netscape and Internet Explorer. Netscape uses a top-down technique of event propagation where an event starts at the document level and passes through each layer of HTML code on its way to the source. An event can be captured at any one of these layers. Internet Explorer uses an event propagation approach that is the complete opposite of Netscape. In Internet Explorer, an event starts at the source and bubbles up through the different HTML layers. Just like Netscape, the even can be captured and handled at any one of these layers.

Netscape Navigator Event Propagation

When an event is fired in a Netscape browser, the event travels through each of the objects in the object hierarchy—`window`, `document`, `layer`—before it reaches the element that was the target of the event. Without any instructions to the contrary, these objects simply pass the event down the hierarchy. If you wish to capture the events at any one of these object levels, you need to use the `captureEvent()` method for any of the `window`, `document`, or `layer` objects.

The `captureEvent()` method requires one parameter that will tell the corresponding object which type of event to capture. This parameter can be one of several static properties of the Event object:

Event.ABORT	Event.BLUR	Event.CHANGE	Event.CLICK
Event.DBLCLICK	Event.DRAGDROP	Event.ERROR	Event.FOCUS
Event.KEYDOWN	Event.KEYPRESS	Event.KEYUP	Event.LOAD
Event.MOUSEDOWN	Event.MOUSEMOVE	Event.MOUSEOUT	Event.MOUSEOVER
Event.MOUSEUP	Event.MOVE	Event.RESET	Event.RESIZE
Event.SCROLL	Event.SELECT	Event.SUBMIT	Event.UNLOAD

You can specify several event types to be captured with one call to the `captureEvent()` method by using the bitwise operator or (¦). For example, if you wanted to capture several of the mouse events, you could use the following call to the `captureEvent()` method:

```
captureEvent( Event.MOUSEDOWN ¦ Event.MOUSEUP ¦ Event.CLICK ¦
                    Event.MOUSEOVER ¦ Event.MOUSEOUT );
```

After specifying which event to capture, you still need to write handler functions for each event. You tell the object which handler function goes with which event by setting the object's event handler properties, like this:

```
document.mouseover = imageRollOver;
document.mouseout = imageRollBack;
```

When an event handler function is called, it is automatically passed the event object as a parameter. The function can then query information about the event, such as where the mouse was at the time, what modifier keys were used, and what the intended target for the event was.

```
function imageRollOver( event )
{
  <statements>
}


function imageRollBack( event )
{
  <statements>
}
```

A Navigator event supports the following Navigator-specific properties:

- **Data**. Returns a string array that contains the URL of any dropped objects. Netscape only.

- **layerX/layerY**. Synonyms for the x/y properties of the event object.

- **Modifiers**. Captures the document's mouse clicks. Syntax is:

    ```
    document.onClick="<statements>"
    ```

- **pageX/pageY**. These properties return the point at which the cursor was when the event occurred in relation to the page.

- **screenX/screenY**. These properties return the point at which the cursor was when the event occurred in relation to the screen.

- **target**. This property contains a reference to the object to which the event was originally sent.

- **Type**. This property returns a string containing the vent type, click, key down, etc.

- **Which**. This property returns which mouse button or key was pressed. For the mouse, 1 = left button, 2 = middle button, and 3 = right button. For keys, this property is the ASCII value of the key.

Some events may not have information in each property; whether they do or not depends on what type of events they are. To make sure the event handlers for the top-level objects—window, document, and layer—work immediately when the page loads, it would be a good idea to put the code to capture them in the onLoad event handler for the object, like this:

```
document.onload = loading;
```

```
function loading( event )
{
  document.onclick = clicked;
  document.ondblclick = dblClicked;
}

function clicked( event )
{
  <statements>
}

function dblClicked( event )
{
  <statements>
}
```

This will ensure that the event handlers are set up before any events of that type can occur.

It is often necessary, after capturing an event, to send the event to a different object for handling. There are two separate ways to do this. The routeEvent() method of the window and document objects allows an event to be transferred to its intended target. The routeEvent() method requires that the event object be passed to the event handler function as a parameter. The second way to pass an event to a different object is by the object's handleEvent() method. Every object that has event handler capabilities has the handleEvent() method. The handleEvent() method takes one parameter, the event object passed to the event handler function.

Sometime in the execution of the code on your page, it may be necessary to release events that were previously captured. All top-level objects in the Navigator hierarchy have the method releaseEvents(), which will turn off event capturing for that object. Just like the captureEvents() method, the releaseEvents() method requires one parameter that will specify which event or events are to be released.

Internet Explorer Event Bubbling

Internet Explorer handles events in the opposite way that Netscape Navigator does. Events in Internet Explorer bubble up from the root element (the target of the event) through the element hierarchy. The element hierarchy is different from Netscape's object hierarchy in that it is comprised of HTML elements instead of JavaScript objects. For example, in this simple HTML document:

```
<HTML>
  <BODY>
    <FORM>
```

```
     <INPUT TYPE="text">
   </FORM>
 </BODY>
</HTML>
```

any events that are generated for the text field, such as the user typing into it or clicking on it, are passed up the element hierarchy if not captured at the text field itself. The event could go through the INPUT element, and, if there is not a suitable event handler, propagate up through the FORM and BODY elements, each of which will get a chance to capture the event.

Event bubbling is automatic in Internet Explorer, and for the most part, you will not need to worry about it. If, however, you need to turn off this feature, you can do so with the following command:

```
window.event.cancelBubble = true;
```

This statement can be used to cancel any given event anywhere in the element hierarchy. Only one event can bubble through the hierarchy at a time, so this command can be used on a per-event basis.

Drag and Drop

One very common ability that you can enjoy with most native applications is *drag and drop*. The ability to perform drag-and-drop operations in a Web page is quite a bit more complicated. This example will help you to understand Internet Explorer's event propogation.

```
<html>
  <head>
    <title>
      JavaScript Professional Projects - Drag and Drop
    </title>

    <style type="text/css">
    <!--
      #imageA{ position: absolute; left: 450; top = 250; z-index: 1; }
      #imageB{ position: absolute; left: 10; top = 150; z-index: 0; }
    -->
    </style>

    <script language="JavaScript">
    <!--
      var clicked;
```

```javascript
function onLoad()
{
  document.onmousedown = mouseDown;
}

function mouseDown()
{
  if( clicked == null )
  {
    if( clicked = getClickedImage( event ) )
    {
      document.onmousemove = mouseMove;
      clicked.style.zIndex += 2;
    }
  }
  else
  {
    document.onmousemove = null;
    clicked = null;
  }
}

function mouseMove()
{
  with( clicked.style )
  {
    positionImage( clicked, window.event.x, window.event.y );
  }
}

function getClickedImage( event )
{
  var obj = window.event.srcElement.parentElement;
  if( obj.tagName == "DIV" )
    return( window.event.srcElement.parentElement );
  else
    return( null );
```

```
      }

      function positionImage( image, xPos, yPos )
      {
        image.style.left = xPos;
        image.style.top  = yPos;
      }
    // -->
    </script>

  </head>

  <body onLoad="JavaScript: onLoad();">

    <center>
      <font size=6>JavaScript Professional Projects</font><br>
      <font size=4>Chapter 6: Drag and Drop</font>
    </center>

    <br><br>
    Click on an image to move it. 
    Click again to release it.<br><br>

    <div ID="imageB">
      <img border="0" src="myImage1.jpg">
    </div>
    <div ID="imageA">
      <img border="0" src="myImage2.jpg">
    </div>


  </body>
</html>
```

In this example, all events are forwarded to the document object of the Web page. From there, the mouse events are used to move one of two images around on the screen. Unfortunately, this example will only work in Internet Explorer browsers, due to Netscape's inability to access HTML elements directly.

JavaScript Timers

One very powerful aspect of JavaScript is the ability to set a delay before performing an action. For example, if a user is taking an online quiz that requires him to finish within a given amount of time, you can use a JavaScript timer to warn him when he was nearing the end of his allotted time.

The following very simple example demonstrates the use of two independent timers:

```
<html>
  <head>
    <title>
      JavaScript Professional Projects - Timers
    </title>

    <script language="JavaScript">
    <!--
      var timeout1, timeout2;

      function onLoad()
      {
        var command = "alert( 'You have only 10 seconds left!' );";
        timeout1 = window.setTimeout( command, 20000 );
        timeout2 = window.setTimeout( "timesUp();", 30000 );
      }


      function timesUp()
      {
        alert( "Time is up!" );
        document.theForm.theButton.disabled = true;
      }


      function checkAnswer()
      {
        window.clearTimeout( timeout1 );
        window.clearTimeout( timeout2 );

        if( document.theForm.theAnswer.value == "3x2+10x" )
        {
```

```
              alert( "That is correct!" );
          }
          else
          {
            alert( "Sorry, the correct answer is:  3x2+10x" );
          }
      }
    // -->
    </script>

</head>

<body onLoad="JavaScript: onLoad();">

  <center>
    <font size=6>JavaScript Professional Projects</font><br>
    <font size=4>Chapter 8: Timers</font>
  </center>

  <br><br>
  <br>
  You have 30 seconds to answer the following question: <br>
  <br>

  <form name="theForm" onSubmit="JavaScript: checkAnswer();">
    What is the differential of the following function: 
    <font face="Courier">x<sup>3</sup>+5x<sup>2</sup>+</font>9 ?
            
            
    <input type="text" name="theAnswer" size="20"><br>
    <br>
    <input type="submit" value="Submit" name="theButton">
  </form>

</body>
</html>
```

The first timer,

```
var command = "alert( 'You have only 10 seconds left!' );";
timeout1 = window.setTimeout( command, 20000 );
```

is set to go off 20 seconds (20,000 milliseconds) after the page loads. This warns the user via an alert dialog that he has only 10 more seconds to complete the quiz.

Ten seconds after the first alert dialog is closed, the second timer,

```
timeout2 = window.setTimeout( "timesUp();", 30000 );
```

goes off and disables the Submit button on the form. The first timer runs a single line of JavaScript, which is given as a parameter. The second timer calls a function; this is called a *function callback*. Both calls to the window object's method, setTimer(), return a handle to the timeout object, which can be used to cancel the timeout prematurely. If the user submits an answer before the timers have run their course, the separate calls to window.clearTimeout(),

```
window.clearTimeout( timeout1 );
window.clearTimeout( timeout2 );
```

will cancel the timers. If these two method calls were not included, the user would still get the timeout messages after submitting the form.

It is important to note that all timers in Internet Explorer are paused when the first alert dialog is popped up. If the user decided not to close this dialog, he would have as long as he needed (plus ten seconds) to complete the quiz. Most users will not know this—especially if no running clock is visible—but it still must be taken into consideration.

Sometimes it is useful to display an onscreen clock, so that the user knows exactly how much time has passed. Doing so is very simple with JavaScript timers:

```
<html>
  <head>
    <title>
      JavaScript Professional Projects - Timers
    </title>

    <script language="JavaScript">
<!--
      var timeout, currentTime = 30;
      function adjustTime()
      {
        window.defaultStatus = "Time left = 0:" +
          ( currentTime < 10 ? "0" : "" ) + currentTime;
```

```javascript
    if( currentTime == 10 )
    {
      alert( "You have only 10 seconds left!" );
    }
    else if( currentTime == 0 )
    {
      alert( "Time is up!" );
      document.theForm.theButton.disabled = true;
      return;
    }

    currentTime = currentTime - 1;
    timeout = window.setTimeout( "adjustTime();", 1000 );
  }

  function checkAnswer()
  {
    if( !document.theForm.theButton.disabled )
    {
      window.clearTimeout( timeout );

      if( document.theForm.theAnswer.value == "3x2+10x" )
      {
        alert( "That is correct!" );
      }
      else
      {
        alert( "Sorry, the correct answer is:  3x2+10x" );
      }
    }
  }
// -->
</script>

</head>

<body onLoad="JavaScript: adjustTime();">
```

```
<center>
  <font size=6>JavaScript Professional Projects</font><br>
  <font size=4>Chapter 8: Timers</font>
</center>

<br><br>
<br>
You have 30 seconds to answer the following question: <br>
<br>

<form name="theForm" onSubmit="JavaScript: checkAnswer();">
  What is the differential of the following function: 
  <font face="Courier">x<sup>3</sup>+5x<sup>2</sup>+</font>9 ?
          
          
  <input type="text" name="theAnswer" size="20"><br>
  <br>
  <input type="submit" value="Submit" name="theButton">
</form>


  </body>
</html>
```

This example performs the same function as the previous example, but it displays a timer in the window's status bar that counts down the amount of time left to answer the question.

It might also be handy to show the current time onscreen, so that the user of a Web application can know the correct time. This would be useful when time-sensitive activities are being performed.

Here's how to display the local machine's clock time in the browser:

```
<html>
  <head>
    <title>
      JavaScript Professional Projects - Timers and Time
    </title>

    <script language="JavaScript">
    <!--
      function displayTime()
```

```
      {
        var now = new Date();
        var h = now.getHours();
        var m = now.getMinutes();
        var s = now.getSeconds();

        with( document.theForm )
        {
          hours.value = h % 12;
          minutes.value = ( m < 10 ? "0" : "" ) + m;
          seconds.value = ( s < 10 ? "0" : "" ) + s;
          range.value = ( h >= 12 ? "PM" : "AM" );
        }

        window.setTimeout( "displayTime();", 1000 );
      }
    // -->
    </script>

</head>

<body onLoad="JavaScript: displayTime();">

  <center>
     <font size=6>JavaScript Professional Projects</font><br>
     <font size=4>Chapter 8: Timers and Time</font>
  </center>

  <br><br>
  <br><br>

  <form name="theForm">
    <table>
      <tr>
        <td><input name="hours" size="2"></div></td>
        <td><b><font size="5">:</font></b></td>
        <td><input name="minutes" size="2"></div></td>
        <td><b><font size="5">:</font></b></td>
```

```
        <td><input name="seconds" size="2"></div></td>
        <td><input name="range" size="2"></div></td>
      </tr>
    </table>
  </form>

  </body>
</html>
```

You can, of course, query a server for the time and display that in the browser instead.

Creating a One-Shot Timer

The quiz example above used a timer that executed only once. Such a timer is called a *one-shot timer*. To create a one-shot timer, you can use the following syntax:

```
window.setTimeout( "<statement>", millisecondDelay );
```

This method call will cause the statement or statements as the first parameter (they must be enclosed in quotation marks) to execute after the specified delay.

Creating a Multi-Shot Timer

Creating a multi-shot timer is just as easy as creating a one-shot timer. The only difference is that one of the statements that are passed as the first parameter needs to contain either another `setTimeout()` call or a call to a function that makes a `setTimeout()` call. In the example above, the following function:

```
function displayTime()
{
  var now = new Date();
  var h = now.getHours();
  var m = now.getMinutes();
  var s = now.getSeconds();

  with( document.theForm )
  {
    hours.value = h % 12;
    minutes.value = ( m < 10 ? "0" : "" ) + m;
    seconds.value = ( s < 10 ? "0" : "" ) + s;
    range.value = ( h >= 12 ? "PM" : "AM" );
  }
```

```
    window.setTimeout( "displayTime();", 1000 );
}
```

is called when the page loads and contains the statement

```
window.setTimeout( "displayTime();", 1000 );
```

which creates a callback to the same function. This process will loop the entire time the page is being displayed.

Summary

Everything that happens while a Web page is loaded creates an event. Most of these events can be captured and used. Event propagation for Netscape and Internet Explorer is vastly different. Netscape uses a top-down propagation technique while Internet Explorer uses a bubbling effect to propagate events. Timers are used to create either one-shot or cyclic events.

Chapter 7

The Document
Object Model

Document objects (not to be confused with JavaScript objects) are scriptable entities that you can use to add a dynamic feel to your Web page. Every HTML element on a Web page has a corresponding document object. As you've seen before, an object is made up of its properties, methods, and event handlers. One of the biggest problems when it comes to working with objects in the Document Object Model (DOM) is the different way in which each browser converts HTML tags into document objects. In JavaScript's current state, there are innumerable different objects, each of which has varying degrees of support in a given browser or operating system.

The first part of this chapter will show you many of the most useful objects in the DOM (an entire listing is outside the scope of this chapter and even this book). This is by no means a complete list of HTML elements that are part of the DOM. Many of the ones that were left out were either not very useful or behaved in obviously the same manner as elements that were listed.

In the second part of the chapter, I'll explain the uses and problems associated with the DOM.

DOM HTML Elements

In the first part of this chapter, I will try to present you with as many DOM objects as possible. As I stated earlier, this is by no means the entire list of objects that make up the DOM. The objects that I have listed here are some of the most useful or have similar functionality as others in the DOM. If you'd like a more complete list of objects in the DOM, I encourage you to visit the World Wide Web Consortium's Web site at http://www.w3.org/DOM.

Common DOM Properties

These properties, methods, and collections represent the common denominator for all objects in the document object model. Almost all of the objects in the DOM support these properties, methods, and collections to a greater or lesser degree. None of these properties, methods, or collections is supported by Netscape however.

- **className**. This property is used to associate an element with a style sheet set of rules grouped together under a class name. Setting this property can provide a shortcut for adjusting many element attributes at once.
- **document**. This property is a reference to the document object that contains the current element.
- **id**. A unique identifier for the current element. This property is used to assemble references to the element. If more than one element in a document contains the same id, an array is created to hold them all.
- **innerHTML**. This property references all the text and HTML tags between the current element's start and end tags. This property can be changed only after the page has fully loaded. This property is not supported by many versions of the Macintosh Internet Explorer.
- **innerText**. This property references all the text between the current element's start and end tags. This property can be changed only after the page has fully loaded. This property is not supported by many versions of the Macintosh Internet Explorer.
- **isTextEdit**. A boolean value representing whether or not the current element can be used to create a TextRange. Only BODY, BUTTON, INPUT, and TEXTAREA elements can have TextRanges. You can create a TextRange with the createTextRange() method.
- **lang**. The language being used for the element's parameter and property values.
- **language**. The scripting language being used within the element, *i.e.*, "JavaScript" or "VBScript."
- **offsetHeight, offsetWidth**. These properties represent the height and width of the element. In Windows versions of Internet Explorer, margins, borders, and other padding are taken into account when calculating these values. These browsers include the padding into this property not once but twice. If no padding is used, both offsetHeight and offsetWidth are accurate on the Windows and Macintosh platforms.

◆ **offsetLeft, offsetTop**. These properties represent the left and top offsets for the current element in relation to its parent element. Internet Explorer implements these properties very unreliably across operating systems.

◆ **offsetParent**. This property is a reference to the current element's parent element, which is used to generate the coordinate system. For most elements this is the BODY object.

◆ **outerHTML**. All text and HTML tags between and including the current element's start and end tags. This property can be changed only after the page has fully loaded. outerHTML is not supported by many versions of the Macintosh Internet Explorer.

◆ **outerText**. All text, but no HTML tags, of the current element. This property can be changed only after the page has fully loaded. outerText is not supported by many versions of the Macintosh Internet Explorer.

◆ **parentElement**. This property is a reference to the current element's parent element.

◆ **parentTextEdit**. This property is a reference to the next-outermost HTML element that allows a TextRange object to be created with it.

◆ **sourceIndex**. This property is a zero-based index for this element in the document.all collection.

◆ **style**. This property allows the reading and writing of style sheet properties to and from the element.

◆ **tagName**. This property is the name of the tag used to create the current element in all capital letters.

◆ **title**. Internet Explorer renders the value of this property as the tool tip text for the element.

Common DOM Methods

Like all useful objects, the objects in the DOM have many built-in methods that you can use to modify their behavior or the way they look.

◆ **click()**. Simulates a mouse click by the user on the current element.

◆ **contains(element)**. Determines whether the current element contains the specified element.

◆ **getAttribute(attributeName, caseSensitive)**. Returns the value of the request attribute owned by the element. caseSensitive is a boolean value that determines whether the capitalization of the attribute is important.

◆ **insertAdjacentHTML(where, HTML)**. Inserts the given HTML (or text) either BeforeBegin, AfterBegin, BeforeEnd, or AfterEnd of the current element.

◆ **insertAdjacentText (where, text)**. Inserts the given text either BeforeBegin, AfterBegin, BeforeEnd, or AfterEnd of the current element. If HTML tags are included in the text, they are output literally.

- ◆ removeAttribute(attributeName, caseSensitive). Removes the desired attribute from the current element. caseSensitive is a boolean value that determines whether the capitalization of the attribute is important.
- ◆ scrollIntoView(showAtTop). Scrolls the document containing the current element so that the element is brought into view and, optionally, shown at the top of the view space.
- ◆ setAttribute(attributeName, value, caseSenstive). Sets the named attribute with the specified value in the current element. caseSensitive is a boolean value that determines whether the capitalization of the attribute is important.

Common DOM Collections

The following collections are also part of the definition of every object in the DOM:

- ◆ All[]. An array containing all HTML elements contained within the current element.
- ◆ children[]. An array containing all the first-level HTML elements contained within the current element. All the elements on the document that consider the current element their parent are included in this collection.
- ◆ filters[]. An array containing all filter objects contained by the current element.

The <A> Object

Each <A> object is both a member of the document object's link[] and anchor[] collections regardless of if it's an anchor, link, or both. Internet Explorer also lets you reference these objects as a member of the document.all[] collection.

<A>Properties

Each of the following properties is supported by the <A> object, as are the properties common to every object in the DOM.

- ◆ accessKey. A single keyboard character that either brings focus to the element or, as with the case of the anchor tag, follows a link. An access key, determined by the browser or operating system, is generally required.
- ◆ dataFld. A case-sensitive identifier for a remote data source column. The dataSrc property must also be set.
- ◆ dataSrc. A case-sensitive identifier for the data source to be associated with the element.
- ◆ hash. The part of the URL following the pound (#) symbol that refers to an anchor object in a document.
- ◆ host. The name of the host of the destination document specified by the link. Optionally, the host name can be followed by a colon and the port number.

- **hostname.** The name of the host of the destination document specified by the link.
- **href.** The URL assigned to the element's HREF attribute.
- **Methods.** This property could be used to change the appearance of the anchor tag based on its destination, but Internet Explorer does not appear to do anything with this information.
- **mimeType.** Returns the MIME type of the destination document in plain English, for example: JPEG Image.
- **name.** This property is the value assigned to the anchor's NAME attribute.
- **nameProp.** Returns just the file name of the URL specified by the tag's HREF attribute.
- **pathname.** Returns just the path name of the URL specified by the tag's HREF attribute, including the initial forward slash.
- **port.** The port number of the host of the destination document specified by the link.
- **protocol.** The protocol used by the element's HREF attribute. For example: http:, file:, ftp:, or mailto:.
- **protocolLong.** A verbose description of the protocol used by the element's HREF attribute.
- **recordNumer.** An integer specifying the record within the data set that created the element.
- **rel.** This property currently does nothing.
- **rev.** This property currently does nothing.
- **search.** The part of the URL starting with the question mark.
- **tabIndex.** This property indicates which position this element has in the tab order of the document.
- **target.** The name of the window or frame that will receive the new URL as a result of clicking on this link. self is the default value, but can also be one of the following default values: parent, top, or blank.
- **urn.** The destination document as a Uniform Resource Name.

<A> Methods

Each of the following methods is supported by the <A> object, as are the methods common to every object in the DOM.

- **blur().** Removes focus from the current element and fires an onBlur event.
- **focus().** Gives the focus to the current element.

<A> Event Handlers

Table 7.1 lists the events that the <A> object can capture. The first column lists the name of the event, and the next two columns list the earliest browser version to support the event.

Table 7.1 <A> Event Handlers

Event Handler	Netscape	Internet Explorer
onblur		4
onclick	2	3
ondblclick	4	4
onfocus		4
onhelp		4
onkeydown		4
onkeypress		4
onkeyup		4
onmousedown	4	4
onmousemove		4
onmouseout	3	4
onmouseover	2	3
onmouseup	4	4
onselectstart		4

The <ACRONYM>, <CITE>, <CODE>, <DFN>, <EM>, <KBD>, <SAMP>, <STRONG>, and <VAR> Objects

Each of these HTML elements supports the event handlers listed in Table 7.2, as well as their common properties and methods.

Table 7.2 Event Handlers

Event Handler	Netscape	Internet Explorer
onblur		4
onclick		4
ondblclick		4
onfocus		4
onhelp		4
onkeydown		4
onkeypress		4
onkeyup		4
onmousedown		4
onmousemove		4
onmouseout		4
onmouseover		4
onmouseup		4
onselectstart		4

The <APPLET> Object

Each <APPLET> object can be referenced directly through the document object such as
`document.<appletName>`.

<APPLET> Properties

Each of the following properties is supported by the <APPLET> object, as are the properties
common to every object in the DOM:

- **accessKey**. A single keyboard character that either brings focus to the element or,
  as with the case of the anchor tag, follows a link. An access key, determined by the
  browser or operating system, is generally required.
- **align**. This property defines the alignment of the element within its container
  element.
- **altHTML**. A HTML message to be displayed if the applet fails to be loaded.
- **code**. This property contains the name of the Java applet class file.

- **codeBase**. This property contains the path to the directory where the Java applet can be found.
- **DataFld**. A case-sensitive identifier for a remote data source column. The **dataSrc** property must also be set.
- **dataSrc**. A case-sensitive identifier for the data source to be associated with the element.
- **width, height**. The size of the applet element.
- **hspace, vspace**. The number of pixels that surround the applet horizontally and vertically.
- **name**. This property holds the unique identifier for the applet.
- **src**. This property holds the URL to the Java class file.
- **tabIndex**. This property indicates which position this element has in the tab order of the document.

<APPLET> Methods

Each of the following methods is supported by the <APPLET> object, as are the methods common to every object in the DOM:

- **blur()**. Removes focus from the current element and fires an **onBlur** event.
- **focus()**. Gives the focus to the current element.

<APPLET> Event Handlers

Table 7.3 lists the events that the <APPLET> object can capture. The first column lists the name of the event, and the next two columns list the earliest browser version to support the event.

Table 7.3 <APPLET> Event Handlers

Event Handler	Netscape	Internet Explorer
onafterupdate		4
onbeforeupdate		4
onblur		4
onclick		3
ondataavailable		4
ondatasetchanged		4
ondatasetcomplete		4
ondblclick		4

Event Handler	Netscape	Internet Explorer
onerrorupdate		4
onfocus		4
onhelp		4
ohkeydown		4
onkeypress		4
onkeyup		4
onload		4
onmousedown		4
onmousemove		4
onmouseout		4
onmouseover		3
onmouseup		4
onreadystatechange		4
onresize		4
onrowenter		4
onrowexit		4

The <AREA> Object

The <AREA> object is used to create a clickable image map. Both Internet Explorer and Netscape consider an <AREA> object to be part of the document object's link[] array.

<AREA> Properties

Each of the following properties is supported by the <AREA> object, as are the properties common to every object in the DOM:

- **alt**. The value of this property is displayed as the tool tip text for the element.
- **areas**. A collection of <AREA> elements sorted in source code order.
- **cords**. A comma-separated string of coordinates that defines the outline of the area.
- **hash**. The part of the URL following the pound (#) symbol that refers to an anchor object in a document.

- ◆ **host**. The name of the host of the destination document specified by the link. Optionally, the host name can be followed by a colon and the port number.
- ◆ **hostname**. The name of the host of the destination document specified by the link.
- ◆ **href**. The URL assigned to the element's HREF attribute.

<AREA> Methods

Each of the following methods is supported by the <AREA> object, as are the methods common to every object in the DOM:

blur(). Removes focus from the current element and fires an onBlur event.

focus(). Gives the focus to the current element.

<AREA> Event Handlers

Table 7.4 lists the events that the <AREA> object can capture. The first column lists the name of the event, and the next two columns list the earliest browser version to support the event.

Table 7.4 <AREA> Event Handlers

Event Handler	Netscape	Internet Explorer
ondatasetchanged		4
ondatasetcomplete		4
ondblclick		4
onerrorupdate		4
onfocus		4
onhelp		4
ohkeydown		4
onkeypress		4
onkeyup		4
onload		4
onmousedown		4
onmousemove		4
onmouseout	3	4
onmouseover	3	3

Event Handler	Netscape	Internet Explorer
onmouseup		4
onreadystatechange		4
onresize		4
onrowenter		4
onrowexit		4

The <B>, <BIG>, <I>, <S>, <SMALL>, <STRIKE>, <TT>, and <U> Objects

Each of these HTML elements supports the event handlers listed in Table 7.5, as well as their common properties and methods.

Table 7.5 Event Handlers

Event Handler	Netscape	Internet Explorer
onclick		4
ondblclick		4
ondragstart		4
onfilterchange		4
onhelp		4
onkeydown		4
onkeypress		4
onkeyup		4
onmousedown		4
onmousemove		4
onmouseout		4
onmouseover		4
onmouseup		4
onselectstart		4

The <BGSOUND> Object

The <BGSOUND> object is not part of any collection, but you can still reference it in Internet Explorer with document.all.<id>. The innerHTML and innerText properties of this object do not apply because it has no closing tag.

<BGSOUND> Properties

Each of the following properties is supported by the <BGSOUND> object, as are the properties common to every object in the DOM:

♦ **balance**. This value represents how the audio is divided between the left and right speakers. This property cannot be set with code. This property contains a value between -10,000 and 10,000. A negative value means more sound is going to the left speaker, and a positive value means more sound is going to the right speaker.

♦ **loop**. The number of times to play the sound. A value of -1 means the sound is looped indefinitely.

♦ **src**. URL of the sound file to be played

♦ **volume**. The volume of the sound being played. A value of 0 means full volume. Negative values to -10,000 are less than full volume.

<BGSOUND> Methods

The blur() method, which removes focus from the current element and fires an onBlur event, is supported by the <BGSOUND> object, as are the methods common to every object in the DOM.

The <BODY> Object

The <BODY> object is different from the document object in that a <BODY> object refers to just the element and its nested elements. You can reference the <BODY> object in Internet Explorer with the document.body shortcut.

<BODY> Properties

Each of the following properties is supported by the <BODY> object, as are the properties common to every object in the DOM:

♦ **accessKey**. A single keyboard character that either brings focus to the element of, as with the case of the anchor tag, follows a link. An access key, determined by the browser or operating system, is generally required.

♦ **aLink**. The color that hypertext links become as they are clicked.

♦ **background**. The URL for the background image for the document.

♦ **bgColor**. The background color for the document.

- **bgProperties**. This property determines whether the background image scrolls or appears to be fixed. **bgProperties** can have one of two values: scroll or fixed.

- **bottomMargin**. An integer specifying the number of pixels between the bottom of the visible document and the scroll bar at the bottom of the browser. This value must be zero or greater.

- **clientHeight, clientWidth**. The size of the document's contents.

- **clientLeft, clientTop**. The offset from the top-left corner of the browser display area.

- **leftMargin**. An integer specifying the number of pixels between the left of the visible document and the left side of the browser. This value must be zero or greater.

- **link**. The color of hypertext links that have not been visited.

- **noWrap**. A boolean value telling the browser to wrap the document content when needed. If this property is set to true, the document will not wrap.

- **recordNumber**. Returns an integer representing the record that generated the element.

- **rightMargin**. An integer specifying the number of pixels between the right of the visible document and the scroll bar on the side of the browser. This value must be zero or greater.

- **scroll**. A boolean value telling the browser whether or not to display scroll bars.

- **scrollHeight, scrollWidth**. This property is ambiguous—Microsoft's description of how it is implemented in Internet Explorer and the way in which it is implemented in Netscape do not agree. Therefore, these properties should not be used unless necessary. These two properties represent the visible area of an element that may or may not be covered by scroll bars.

- **scrollLeft, scrollTop**. The number of pixels that, due to user scrolling, have been hidden on the top or left of the document.

- **text**. The default color for text on the document.

- **topMargin**. An integer specifying the number of pixels between the top of the visible document and the top of the browser. This value must be zero or greater.

- **vLink**. The color of hypertext links that have been visited recently.

<BODY> Methods

The **createTextRange()**, which creates a TextRange object from the source code of the current element, is supported by the <BODY> object, as are the methods common to every object in the DOM.

<BODY> Event Handlers

Table 7.6 lists the events that the <BODY> object can capture. The first column lists the name of the event, and the next two columns list the earliest browser version to support the event.

Table 7.6 <BODY> Event Handlers

Event Handler	Netscape	Internet Explorer
onafterupdate		4
onbeforeunload		4
onbeforeupdate		4
onblur	3	4
onclick		4
ondblclick		4
ondragdrop	4	
onfocus	3	4
onhelp		4
onkeydown		4
onkeypress		4
onkeyup		4
onload	2	3
onmousedown		4
onmousemove		4
onmouseout		4
onmouseover		3
onmouseup		4
onmove	4	
onresize	4	
onrowenter		4
onrowexit		4
onscroll		4
onselect		4
onselectstart		4
onunload	2	3

The <DIV> Object

The <DIV> object can be referenced in Internet Explorer by document.all.<id>. In the Windows version of Internet Explorer 4.x, the client and scroll properties are not available unless the <DIV> object has its position attribute set to absolute.

<DIV> Properties

Each of the following properties is supported by the <DIV> object, as are the properties common to every object in the DOM:

♦ **align.** The horizontal alignment of the elements within the DIV tag. This property can have one of three values: center, left, or right.

♦ **clientHeight, clientWidth.** The size of the element's content.

♦ **dataFld.** Associates a remote data source column name to the DIV element's content.

♦ **dataFormatAs.** Tells the browser how to interpret the data from the remote data source. This property can have one of two values, text or HTML.

♦ **dataSrc.** Used to bind a remote data source to the element. This property will contain the name of the remove ODBC source, such as an Oracle or SQL database.

♦ **scrollHeight, scrollWidth.** These two properties represent the visible area of an element that may or may not be covered by scroll bars. They are ambiguous— Microsoft's description of how they are implemented in Internet Explorer and the way in which they are implemented in Netscape do not agree. Therefore, these properties should not be used unless necessary.

♦ **scrollLeft, scrollTop.** The number of pixels that, due to user scrolling, have been hidden on the top or left of the document.

<DIV> Methods

Each of the following methods is supported by the <DIV> object, as are the methods common to every object in the DOM:

♦ **blur().** Removes focus from the current element and fires an onBlur event.

♦ **focus().** Gives the focus to the current element.

<DIV> Event Handlers

Table 7.7 lists the events that the <DIV> object can capture. The first column lists the name of the event, and the next two columns list the earliest browser version to support the event.

Table 7.7 <DIV> Event Handlers

Event Handler	Netscape	Internet Explorer
onafterupdate		4
onbeforeupdate		4
onblur	3	4
onclick		4
ondblclick		4
ondragstart		4
onfocus	3	4
onhelp		4
onkeydown		4
onkeypress		4
onkeyup		4
onload	2	3
onmousedown		4
onmousemove		4
onmouseout		4
onmouseover		3
onmouseup		4
onresize		4
onrowenter		4
onrowexit		4
onscroll		4
onselectstart		4

The <EMBED> Object

The <EMBED> object can be referenced by document.<elementName> in Netscape Navigator or by document.all.<id> in Internet Explorer.

<EMBED> Properties

Each of the following properties is supported by the <EMBED> object, as are the properties common to every object in the DOM:

- ◆ **accessKey**. A single keyboard character that either brings focus to the element or, as with the case of the anchor tag, follows a link. An access key, determined by the browser or operating system, is generally required.
- ◆ **clientHeight, clientWidth**. The size of the document's content
- ◆ **clientLeft, clientTop**. The offset from the top-left corner of the browser display area.
- ◆ **hidden**. A boolean value specifying if the control panel for the embedded data is visible.
- ◆ **name**. This property is used by both Internet Explorer and Netscape to reference the element. With Netscape, however, this property is read-only.
- ◆ **palette**. Returns the value of the PALETTE attribute that was used with the EMBED element.
- ◆ **pluginspage**. The URL at which the required plug-in can be downloaded so that the embedded data can be displayed.
- ◆ **readyState**. Returns the current status of the download process for embedded data. When this property changes, an onReadyStateChange event is fired.
- ◆ **src**. A URL where the file containing the embedded data can be retrieved.
- ◆ **tabIndex**. This property indicates which position this element has in the tab order of the document.
- ◆ **units**. The unit of measurement for the height and width of the embedded data area. This property can have one of three values: pixels, px, or em.

<EMBED> Methods

Each of the following methods is supported by the <EMBED> object, as are the methods common to every object in the DOM:

- ◆ **blur()**. Removes focus from the current element and fires an onBlur event.
- ◆ **focus()**. Gives the focus to the current element.

The <IMG> Object

The <IMG> object was one of the first objects to be used to create dynamic effects on Web pages. Each <IMG> object is in the document object's images[] collection or can be referenced by document.<imageName>.

<IMG> Properties

Each of the following properties is supported by the <IMG> object, as are the properties common to every object in the DOM:

- **align**. Specifies how the image is aligned relative to the surrounding text. This property can have one of nine values: absbottom, absmiddle, baseline, bottom, right, left, none, texttop, or top.

- **alt**. The text that is displayed if the image fails to load or is in the process of being downloaded.

- **border**. The thickness of the image border in pixels.

- **complete**. A boolean value that is used to determine if the image has completely downloaded or not.

- **dataFld**. Associates a remote data source column name to the DIV element's content.

- **dataSrc**. Used to bind a remote data source to the element. This property will contain the name of the remove ODBC source, such as an Oracle or SQL database.

- **dynsrc**. The URL of the video clip to be played through the IMG element.

- **height, width**. The size of the image when it is displayed on the browser.

- **href**. The URL of the image to be displayed. Identical to the src property.

- **hspace, vspace**. The horizontal and vertical padding for the image.

- **isMap**. Used to determine if the image is using a server-side image map.

- **loop**. How many times the video specified with the dynsrc property is looped. The value of -1 means the video will loop indefinitely.

- **lowsrc**. The URL to the lower-resolution image that will be displayed if the image specified by the src property takes a long time to load.

- **name**. An identifier used to reference the image via scripts.

- **protocol**. This property does not appear to work properly. Instead of returning the value file:, it returns File Protocol.

- **readyState**. Returns the current status of the download process for the image. When this property changes, a onReadyStateChange event is fired.

- **useMap**. The URL to the MAP element that is used to create hot spots and links on this image.

- **x, y**. The coordinates of the image in relation to the document. Netscape only.

<IMG> Methods

Each of the following methods is supported by the <IMG> object, as are the methods common to every object in the DOM:

- **blur()**. Removes focus from the current element and fires an onBlur event.

- **focus()**. Gives the focus to the current element.

<IMG> Event Handlers

Table 7.8 lists the events that the <IMG> object can capture. The first column lists the name of the event, and the next two columns list the earliest browser version to support the event.

Table 7.8 <IMG> Event Handlers

Event Handler	Netscape	Internet Explorer
onabort	3	4
onafterupdate		4
onbeforeupdate		4
onblur	3	4
onclick		4
ondblclick		4
ondragstart		4
onerror	3	4
onfocus	3	4
onhelp		4
onkeydown		4
onkeypress		4
onkeyup		4
onload	2	3
onmousedown		4
onmousemove		4
onmouseout		4
onmouseover		3
onmouseup		4
onresize		4
onrowenter		4
onrowexit		4
onscroll		4
onselectstart		4

The <OBJECT> Object

Using the <OBJECT> object is an updated way of embedding external data into a Web page. You can reference an <OBJECT> object with `document.all.<id>` in Internet Explorer.

<OBJECT> Properties

Each of the following properties is supported by the <OBJECT> object, as are the properties common to every object in the DOM:

- **accessKey**. A single keyboard character that either brings focus to the element or, as with the case of the anchor tag, follows a link. An access key, determined by the browser or operating system, is generally required.

- **align**. Specifies how the image is aligned relative to the surrounding text. This property can have one of nine values: `absbottom`, `absmiddle`, `baseline`, `bottom`, `right`, `left`, `none`, `texttop`, or `top`.

- **altHTML**. Alternate HTML to display if the object fails to load.

- **classid** The URL of the object's implementation.

- **code**. The name of the Java .class file.

- **codeBase**. This property contains the path to the directory where the Java applet can be found.

- **codeType**. The MIME type of the object referenced by the object's `classid` property. A list of all common MIME types can be found at:

  ftp://ftp.isi.edu/in-notes/iana/assignments/media-types/

- **data**. The URL for the file that contains the data for this object element.

- **dataFld**. A case-sensitive identifier for a remote data source column. The `dataSrc` property must also be set.

- **dataSrc**. A case-sensitive identifier for the data source to be associated with the element.

- **form**. A reference to the FORM element that contains the current object element, if there is one.

- **width, height**. The size of the applet element.

- **hspace, vspace**. The number of pixels that surround the applet horizontally and vertically.

- **name**. This property holds the unique identifier for the object.

- **object**. This property tells the interpreter to get the property of the HTML object element instead of the internal JavaScript object's property.

- **readyState**. Returns the current status of the download process for the object's content. When this property changes, a `onReadyStateChange` event is fired.

- **tabIndex**. This property indicates which position this element has in the tab order of the document.

- **type**. The MIME type of the object's external data.

<OBJECT> Event Handlers

Table 7.9 lists the events that the <OBJECT> object can capture. The first column lists the name of the event, and the next two columns list the earliest browser version to support the event.

Table 7.9 <OBJECT> Event Handlers

Event Handler	Netscape	Internet Explorer
onafterupdate		4
onbeforeupdate		4
onblur	3	4
onclick		4
ondblclick		4
ondragstart		4
onhelp		4
onkeydown		4
onkeypress		4
onkeyup		4
onmousedown		4
onmousemove		4
onmouseout		4
onmouseover		3
onmouseup		4
onreadystatechange		4
onresize		4
onrowenter		4
onrowexit		4
onselectstart		4

The <SELECT> Object

The <SELECT> object is a form element that contains OPTION elements. The properties innerHTML and innerText are not available in the Macintosh version of Internet Explorer 4. A <SELECT> object can be referenced one of two ways: document.<formName>.<elementName> or document.form[i].element[i].

<SELECT> Properties

Each of the following properties is supported by the <SELECT> object, as are the properties common to every object in the DOM:

- **accessKey**. A single keyboard character that either brings focus to the element or, as with the case of the anchor tag, follows a link. An access key, determined by the browser or operating system, is generally required.

- **dataFld**. A case-sensitive identifier for a remote data source column. The dataSrc property must also be set.

- **dataSrc**. A case-sensitive identifier for the data source to be associated with the element.

- **disabled**. A boolean flag indicating whether the element is disabled. If this property is set to true, no events will be generated for this event and its GUI representation will appear grayed-out.

- **form**. A reference to the FORM element that contains the current select element, if there is one.

- **length**. The number of option objects nested inside the select object.

- **multiple**. A flag that determines if multiple selection is possible with this select object.

- **form**. A reference to the FORM element that contains the current Object element, if there is one.

- **name**. This property holds the unique identifier for the Select object.

- **options[]**. An array holding all the Option objects contained by the Select object.

- **recordNumber**. An integer representing the record within the dataset that generated the element.

- **selectedIndex**. The first selected option in the Select object.

- **tabIndex**. This property indicates which position this element has in the tab order of the document.

- **type**. The type of element. This property can have one of many values: button, checkbox, file, hidden, image, password, radio, reset, select-multiple, select-one, submit, text, or textarea.

- **value**. This property is the value of the selected Option object within the Select object.

<SELECT> Methods

Each of the following methods is supported by the <SELECT> object, as are the methods common to every object in the DOM:

- ◆ **blur()**. Removes focus from the current element and fires an onBlur event.
- ◆ **focus()**. Gives the focus to the current element.

<SELECT> Event Handlers

Table 7.10 lists the events that the <SELECT> object can capture. The first column lists the name of the event, and the next two columns list the earliest browser version to support the event.

Table 7.10 <SELECT> Event Handlers

Event Handler	Netscape	Internet Explorer
onafterupdate		4
onbeforeupdate		4
onblur	3	4
onchange	2	3
onclick		4
ondblclick		4
ondragstart		4
onfocus	2	3
onhelp		4
onkeydown		4
onkeypress		4
onkeyup		4
onmousedown		4
onmousemove		4
onmouseout		4
onmouseover		3
onmouseup		4
onrowenter		4
onrowexit		4
onselectstart		4

The <TEXTAREA> Object

The <TEXTAREA> object is a form element that allows a user to input multiple lines of text for submission to a server. The innerHTML property for this object is not available in the Macintosh version of Internet Explorer 4. A <TEXTAREA> object can be referenced one of two ways: document.<formName>.<elementName> or document.form[i].element[i].

<TEXTAREA> Options

Each of the following properties is supported by the <TEXTAREA> object, as are the properties common to every object in the DOM:

◆ **accessKey**. A single keyboard character that either brings focus to the element or, as with the case of the anchor tag, follows a link. An access key, determined by the browser or operating system, is generally required.

◆ **clientHeight, clientWidth**. The size of the document's content.

◆ **clientLeft, clientTop**. The offset from the top-left corner of the browser display area.

◆ **cols**. The width of the editable area on the text area. This value represents the number of mono-spaced characters that can fit on one row of the text area.

◆ **dataFld**. A case-sensitive identifier for a remote data source column. The dataSrc property must also be set.

◆ **dataSrc**. A case-sensitive identifier for the data source to be associated with the element.

◆ **defaultValue**. The default text displayed within the text area that is displayed when the page first loads.

◆ **disabled**. A boolean flag indicating if the element is disabled. If this property is set to true not events will be generated for this event and its GUI representation will appear grayed-out.

◆ **form**. A reference to the FORM element that contains the current Object element, if there is one.

◆ **name**. This property holds the unique identifier for the Select object.

◆ **readOnly**. A flag representing whether or not the text within the text area can be changed.

◆ **rows**. The number of rows in the text area.

◆ **scrollHeight, scrollWidth**. These two properties represent the visible area of an element that may or may not be covered by scroll bars. They are ambiguous—Microsoft's description of how they are implemented in Internet Explorer and the way in which they are implemented in Netscape do not agree. Therefore, these properties should not be used unless necessary.

◆ **scrollLeft, scrollTop**. The number of pixels that, due to user scrolling, have been hidden on the top or left of the document.

◆ **tabIndex**. This property indicates which position this element has in the tab order of the document.

◆ **type**. The type of element. This property can have one of many values: `button`, `checkbox`, `file`, `hidden`, `image`, `password`, `radio`, `reset`, `select-multiple`, `select-one`, `submit`, `text`, or `textarea`.

◆ **value**. This property is the value of the selected `Option` object within the `Select` object.

◆ **wrap**. The type of word wrapping that the text area submits to the server. This property can have one of three values: `physical`, `off`, or `virtual`.

<TEXTAREA> Methods

Each of the following methods is supported by the `<TEXTAREA>` object, as are the methods common to every object in the DOM:

◆ **blur()**. Removes focus from the current element and fires an `onBlur` event.

◆ **createTextRange()**. Creates a `TextRange` object from the source code of the current element.

◆ **focus()**. Gives the focus to the current element.

◆ **handleEvent(event)**. Instructs the object to process the give event.

◆ **select()**. Selects all the text contained within the text area.

<TEXTAREA> Event Handlers

Table 7.11 lists the events that the `<TEXTAREA>` object can capture. The first column lists the name of the event, and the next two columns list the earliest browser version to support the event.

Table 7.11 <TEXTAREA> Event Handlers

Event Handler	Netscape	Internet Explorer
onafterupdate		4
onbeforeupdate		4
onblur	3	4
onchange	2	3
onclick		4
ondblclick		4
ondragstart		4
onfocus	2	3

(continues)

Table 7.11 <TEXTAREA> Event Handlers *(continued)*

Event Handler	Netscape	Internet Explorer
onhelp		4
onkeydown		4
onkeypress		4
onkeyup		4
onmousedown		4
onmousemove		4
onmouseout		4
onmouseover		3
onmouseup		4
onresize		4
onrowenter		4
onrowexit		4
onscroll		3
onselect	2	3
onselectstart		4

Using the DOM

There is virtually no limit to what you can do with the Document Object Model. DOM uses include everything from simple mouseover image rotations to complex mouseover menus. Instead of trying to present every facet of using the DOM in a dry, formal discussion, I will present several examples and explain the problems and issues that occurred while writing them.

Mouseover Image Rotation

The most commonly used example of the DOM at work is the popular mouseover image rotation. Here is a partial example of how this is done:

```
<img src="image1.jpg"
     onMouseOver="JavaScript: this.src='image2.jpg';"
     onMouseOut="JavaScript: this.src='image1.jpg';">
```

When the image element is first loaded, image1.jpg is displayed. As the user moves his mouse cursor over the image element, the image changes to image2.jpg. When the user moves his mouse cursor off of the image, the original image1.jpg is displayed again. This simple example can be expanded to include the onMouseDown event, like this:

```
<img src="image1.jpg"
     onMouseOver="JavaScript: this.src='image2.jpg';"
     onMouseOut="JavaScript: this.src='image1.jpg';"
     onMouseDown="JavaScript: this.src='image3.jpg';">
```

This will not only give the user visual feedback when he moves the mouse cursor over or out of the image, but will also create an interesting effect when he clicks on the image—especially if the image is used as a hyperlink. This example is very simple to implement. You won't have any trouble with this technique as long as the browser can interpret all three mouse events.

Mouseover Menus

The mouseover menu is a very popular feature that is used with great success on many Web applications. *Mouseover menus* are the menus, including File, Edit, View, Help, and others, found on the menu bar on any popular application.

Compared to the image rollover example above, this mouseover menu example is quite a bit more complex. Because of the limitations of the Netscape browser, this example can only be easily implemented for Internet Explorer. The techniques used in the example can be used in both browsers, however.

The first step to creating a mouseover menu is to create a function that will position HTML elements anywhere on the document:

```
function openMenuAbsolute( element, xPos, yPos )
{
  element.style.left = xPos;
  element.style.top = yPos;
}
```

The openMenuAbsolute() function will position any element at the given coordinates on the document. Once this function is established, you can begin to create the menu bar. For simplicity's sake, this example will mimic Internet Explorer's menu bar but not its functionality. The HTML to make the actual bar that contains the menus would be something like this:

```
<center>
  <table border="1" width="75%">
    <tr>
      <td width="17%">
```

```
        <a href="JavaScript: void 0;" onMouseOver="JavaScript:">
          File
        </a>
      </td>
      <td width="17%">
        <a href="JavaScript: void 0;" onMouseOver="JavaScript:">
          Edit
        </a>
      </td>
      <td width="17%">
        <a href="JavaScript: void 0;" onMouseOver="JavaScript:">
          View
        </a>
      </td>
      <td width="17%">
        <a href="JavaScript: void 0;" onMouseOver="JavaScript:">
          Favorites
        </a>
      </td>
      <td width="17%">
        <a href="JavaScript: void 0;" onMouseOver="JavaScript:">
          Tools
        </a>
      </td>
      <td width="17%">
        <a href="JavaScript: void 0;" onMouseOver="JavaScript:">
          Help
        </a>
      </td>
    </tr>
  </table>
</center>
```

The event handlers for each menu will be filled in later.

Now that the menu bar has been created, the actual menus must be designed. The menus will be created in two parts. The first part is a style sheet class from which the menus will inherit, and the second part is the actual menu element.

Here's the first part, the style sheet class:

```css
.menu {
        visibility: hidden;
        position: absolute;
        padding: 4px;
        background-color: "#D0D0D0";
        border-style: solid;
        border-width: 2px;
        border-color: black;
        font-family: "Courier New";
        font-size: 10;
        left: -1000; top: -1000;
    }
```

This style sheet class is called menu and sets several important aspects of its object. First of all, the menu objects will be initially hidden. They will also be absolutely positioned at coordinates -1000, -1000—this is necessary because even when absolutely positioned elements are hidden, they still may make it necessary for the browser to create scroll bars. The other attributes are just look-and-feel properties.

And now for the second part. The HTML DIV tag lends itself perfectly to this example. Here is the File menu fully written out:

```html
<div class="menu" ID="File" style="width: 235;" level="0">
  <a href="JavaScript: void 0;"
     onMouseOver="JavaScript:
       openMenuAbsolute( document.all.File_New,
                         document.all.File.offsetLeft +
                         document.all.File.clientWidth - 1,
                         document.all.File.offsetTop
                       );">
    New
  </a><br>

  <a href="JavaScript: void 0;"
     onMouseOver="JavaScript: hideLevel( 1 );">
    Open...
  </a><br>
```

```
<a href="JavaScript: void 0;"
   onMouseOver="JavaScript: hideLevel( 1 );">
  Edit with Microsoft Front Page
</a></br>

<a href="JavaScript: void 0;"
   onMouseOver="JavaScript: hideLevel( 1 );">
  Save
</a><br>

<a href="JavaScript: void 0;"
   onMouseOver="JavaScript: hideLevel( 1 );">
  Save as...
</a><br>

<hr>

<a href="JavaScript: void 0;"
   onMouseOver="JavaScript: hideLevel( 1 );">
  Print...
</a><br>

<hr>

<a href="JavaScript: void 0;"
   onMouseOver="JavaScript:
      openMenuAbsolute( document.all.File_New,
                        document.all.File.offsetLeft +
                        document.all.File.clientWidth - 1,
                        document.all.File.offsetTop + 125
                      );">
  Send
</a><br>

<a href="JavaScript: void 0;"
   onMouseOver="javascrip: hideLevel( 1 );">
  Import and Export...
</a><br>
```

```
<hr>

<a href="JavaScript: void 0;"
   onMouseOver="javascrip: hideLevel( 1 );">
  Properties
</a><br>

<a href="JavaScript: void 0;"
   onMouseOver="javascrip: hideLevel( 1 );">
  Close
</a><br>
</div>
```

Two things make this DIV element interesting. The first is that it has a new property name, level, which has a value of 0. This property is used so that no two menus with the same level value can be open at one time. Secondly, each item in the menu has an onMouseOver event handler. Most of the event handlers make a call to the function hideLevel(), which will be explained later. The New and Send menu items, however, make a call to the openMenuAbsolute() function, which was explained previously.

Notice that on your Internet Explorer menu, New and Send each open a submenu. The HTML menus you create here will do the same thing. First, though, there needs to be a way to hide menus that should not be visible. The following function does just that:

```
function hideLevel( level )
{
  // Get all the <DIV> tags on the document
  var divTags = document.all.tags( "div" );
  // Loop through the array of <DIV> tags
  for( i = 0 ; i < divTags.length ; i++ )
  {
    // If the <DIV> is a menu and its level is greater
    // or equal to 'level' then hide it
    if( divTags[i].className == "menu" &&
        divTags[i].level >= level )
    {
      // Hid the menu
      divTags[i].style.visibility = "hidden";
      // Even when a menu is hidden, it might still
      // cause the scroll bars to be abnormally positioned
      // so I move the menu off the screen
```

```
      divTags[i].style.left = -1000;
      divTags[i].style.top = -1000;

   }

  }

}
```

The `hideLevel()` function requests an array that contains a reference to every DIV element on the page, loops through each element in the array to see if it's a menu, and hides it if the level is bigger than the specified value.

One more item is required for this example to be fully functional: a function that will open a menu relative to another HTML element. Here is one possible implementation of such a function:

```
function openMenuRelative( divMenu, parent, position )
{
  xPos = 0; yPos = 0;
  // I subtract 4 because of the menu's border
  // ( 2 * border-width in pixels )
  if( position == "TOP" )
    yPos = 0 - divMenu.clientHeight - 4;
  else if( position == "BOTTOM" )
    yPos = parent.clientHeight;
  // I subtract 4 because of the menu's border
  // ( 2 * border-width in pixels )
  else if( position == "LEFT" )
    xPos = 0 - divMenu.clientWidth - 4;
  else if( position == "RIGHT" )
    xPos = parent.clientWidth;
  do
  {
    // For some reason <CENTER> tags mess up the
    // x,y coordinates so I ignore them
    if( parent.tagName != "CENTER" )
    {
      xPos += parent.offsetLeft;
      yPos += parent.offsetTop;

      // The border-width of any element that has
      // a border is factored into the elements actual size
      // Running this part of the code will make
```

```
       // the menu cover up the border
       if( parent.border != null )
       {
         xPos -= parent.border * 2;
         yPos -= parent.border * 2;
       }
     }
     // Move to the next highest element
     parent = parent.parentElement;
   }
   while( parent != null );
   // Open the menu with the relative x,y coordinate
   openMenuAbsolute( divMenu, xPos, yPos );
}
```

This function takes a DIV element that is being used as a menu, the element that the menu will be opened relative to, and the relative position to open the menu. The last parameter can have one of four values—"BOTTOM", "TOP", "LEFT" or "RIGHT". This example will use only the "BOTTOM" position.

All that is left to complete this mouseover menu example is to create the page with all of the given functions and menus. This example contains only the first three Internet Explorer menus in order to conserve space:

```
<html>

  <head>
    <title>
      JavaScriptt Professional Projects - Mouse Over Menus
    </title>

    <style type="text/css">
    <!--
      a        {
                 color: blue;
                 text-decoration: none;
                 font-size: 12;
                 font-family: "Courier New";
               }
```

```
a:hover {

        color: blue;

        text-decoration: underline;

        font-size: 12;

        font-family: "Courier New";

    }


.menu    {

        visibility: hidden;

        position: absolute;

        padding: 4px;

        background-color: "#D0D0D0";

        border-style: solid;

        border-width: 2px;

        border-color: black;

        font-family: "Courier New";

        font-size: 10;

        left: -1000; top: -1000;

    }
-->
</style>

<script language="javascript">
  function openMenuAbsolute( divMenu, xPos, yPos )
  {
    hideLevel( divMenu.level );
    divMenu.style.left = xPos;
    divMenu.style.top = yPos;
    divMenu.style.visibility = "visible";
  }


  function openMenuRelative( divMenu, parent, position )
  {
    xPos = 0; yPos = 0;
    // I subtract 4 because of the menu's border
    // ( 2 * border-width in pixels )
    if( position == "TOP" )
      yPos = 0 - divMenu.clientHeight - 4;
```

```
    else if( position == "BOTTOM" )
      yPos = parent.clientHeight;
    // I subtract 4 because of the menu's border
    // ( 2 * border-width in pixels )
    else if( position == "LEFT" )
      xPos = 0 - divMenu.clientWidth - 4;
    else if( position == "RIGHT" )
      xPos = parent.clientWidth;
    do
    {
      // For some reason <CENTER> tags mess up the
      // x,y coordinates so I ignore them
      if( parent.tagName != "CENTER" )
      {
        xPos += parent.offsetLeft;
        yPos += parent.offsetTop;

        // The border-width of any element that has a
        // border is factored into the element's actual size
        // Running this part of the code will make
        // the menu cover up the border
        if( parent.border != null )
        {
          xPos -= parent.border * 2;
          yPos -= parent.border * 2;
        }
      }
      // Move to the next highest element
      parent = parent.parentElement;
    }
    while( parent != null );
    // Open the menu with the relative x,y coordinate
    openMenuAbsolute( divMenu, xPos, yPos );
}

function hideLevel( level )
{
```

```
    // Get all the <DIV> tags on the document
    divTags = document.all.tags( "div" );
    // Loop through the array of <DIV> tags
    for( i = 0 ; i < divTags.length ; i++ )
    {
      // If the <DIV> is a menu and its level is greater
      // or equal to 'level' then hide it
      if( divTags[i].className == "menu" &&
          divTags[i].level >= level )
      {
        // Hid the menu
        divTags[i].style.visibility = "hidden";
        // Even when a menu is hidden, it might still
        // cause the scroll bars to be abnomaly positioned
        // so I move the menu off the screen
        divTags[i].style.left = -1000;
        divTags[i].style.top = -1000;
      }
    }
  }
  </script>
</head>

<body onMouseUp="JavaScript: hideLevel( 0 );"
      onResize="JavaScriptt: hideLevel( 0 );">

  <center>
    <font size=6>JavaScriptt Professional Projects</font><br>
    <font size=4>Chapter 7: Mouse Over Menus</font>

    <br><br>
    <br><br>

    <table border="1" width="75%">
      <tr>
        <td width="17%">
          <a onMouseOver="JavaScript:
```

```
                    openMenuRelative( document.all.File,
                                      this.parentElement,
                                      'BOTTOM' );">
            File
          </a>
        </td>
        <td width="17%">
          <a onMouseOver="JavaScript:
                openMenuRelative( document.all.Edit,
                                  this.parentElement,
                                  'BOTTOM' );">
            Edit
          </a>
        </td>
        <td width="17%">
          <a onMouseOver="JavaScript:
                openMenuRelative( document.all.View,
                                  this.parentElement,
                                  'BOTTOM' );">
            View
          </a>
        </td>
        <td width="17%"><a>Favorites</a></td>
        <td width="17%"><a>Tools</a></td>
        <td width="17%"><a>Help</a></td>
      </tr>
    </table>
</center>

<div class="menu" ID="File" style="width: 235;" level="0">
  <a href="JavaScript: void 0;"
     onMouseOver="JavaScript:
        openMenuAbsolute( document.all.File_New,
                          document.all.File.offsetLeft +
                          document.all.File.clientWidth - 1,
                          document.all.File.offsetTop );">
```

```
    New
</a><br>

<a href="JavaScript: void 0;"
    onMouseOver="JavaScript: hideLevel( 1 );">
  Open...
</a><br>
<a href="JavaScript: void 0;"
    onMouseOver="JavaScript: hideLevel( 1 );">
  Edit with Microsoft Front Page
</a></br>

<a href="JavaScript: void 0;"
    onMouseOver="JavaScript: hideLevel( 1 );">
  Save
</a><br>

<a href="JavaScript: void 0;"
    onMouseOver="JavaScript: hideLevel( 1 );">
  Save as...
</a><br>

<hr>

<a href="JavaScript: void 0;"
    onMouseOver="JavaScript: hideLevel( 1 );">
  Print...
</a><br>

<hr>

<a href="JavaScript: void 0;"
    onMouseOver="JavaScript:
      openMenuAbsolute( document.all.File_New,
                        document.all.File.offsetLeft +
                        document.all.File.clientWidth - 1,
                        document.all.File.offsetTop + 125 );">
```

```
   Send
 </a><br>


 <a href="JavaScript: void 0;"
    onMouseOver="JavaScript: hideLevel( 1 );">
   Import and Export...
 </a><br>


 <hr>


 <a href="JavaScript: void 0;"
    onMouseOver="JavaScript: hideLevel( 1 );">
   Properties
  </a><br>


 <a href="JavaScript: void 0;"
    onMouseOver="JavaScript: hideLevel( 1 );">
   Close
 </a><br>
</div>


<div class="menu" ID="Edit" style="width: 185;" level="0">
  <a href="JavaScript: void 0;">
    Cut
  </a><br>
  <a href="JavaScript: void 0;">Copy</a><br>
  <a href="JavaScript: void 0;">Paste</a><br>
  <hr>
  <a href="JavaScript: void 0;">Select All...</a><br>
  <hr>
  <a href="JavaScript: void 0;">Find (on This Page)</a><br>
</div>


<div class="menu" ID="View" style="width: 155;" level="0">
  <a href="JavaScript: void 0;"
     onMouseOver="JavaScript:
       openMenuAbsolute( document.all.View_Toolbars,
```

```
                              document.all.View.offsetLeft +
                              document.all.View.clientWidth - 1,
                              document.all.View.offsetTop );">
     Toolbars
  </a><br>

  <input type="checkbox" name="C1" value="ON">
  <font color="#0000FF" size="2">Status Bar</font><br>

  <a href="JavaScript: void 0;"
     onMouseOver="JavaScript:
        openMenuAbsolute( document.all.View_ExplorerBar,
                              document.all.View.offsetLeft +
                              document.all.View.clientWidth - 1,
                              document.all.View.offsetTop + 43 );">
     Explorer Bar
  </a><br>

  <hr>

  <a href="JavaScript: void 0;"
     onMouseOver="JavaScript:
        openMenuAbsolute( document.all.View_GoTo,
                              document.all.View.offsetLeft +
                              document.all.View.clientWidth - 1,
                              document.all.View.offsetTop + 70 );">
     Go To
  </a><br>

  <a href="JavaScript: void 0;"
     onMouseOver="JavaScript: hideLevel( 1 );">
     Stop
  </a><br>

  <a href="JavaScript: void 0;"
     onMouseOver="JavaScript: hideLevel( 1 );">
     Refresh
  </a><br>
```

```html
    <hr>

    <a href="JavaScript: void 0;"
       onMouseOver="JavaScript: hideLevel( 1 );">
      Text Size
    </a><br>

    <a href="JavaScript: void 0;"
       onMouseOver="JavaScript: hideLevel( 1 );">
      Encoding
    </a><br>

    <hr>

    <a href="JavaScript: void 0;"
       onMouseOver="JavaScript: hideLevel( 1 );">
      Source
    </a><br>

    <a href="JavaScript: void 0;"
       onMouseOver="JavaScript: hideLevel( 1 );">
      Scrip Debugger
    </a><br>

    <a href="JavaScript: void 0;"
       onMouseOver="JavaScript: hideLevel( 1 );">
      Full Screen
    </a>
</div>

<div class="menu" ID="File_New" style="width: 115;" level="1">
  <a href="JavaScript: void 0;">Window</a><br>
  <hr>
  <a href="JavaScript: void 0;">Message</a><br>
  <a href="JavaScript: void 0;">Post</a><br>
  <a href="JavaScript: void 0;">Contact</a><br>
  <a href="JavaScript: void 0;">Internet Call</a><br>
</div>
```

```html
<div class="menu" ID="File_Send" style="width: 150;" level="1">
  <a href="JavaScript: void 0;">Page by E-mail</a><br>
  <a href="JavaScript: void 0;">Link by E-mail</a><br>
  <a href="JavaScript: void 0;">Shortcut to Desktop</a><br>
</div>

<div class="menu" ID="View_Toolbars" style="width: 150;" level="1">
  <a href="JavaScript: void 0;">Standard Buttons</a><br>
  <a href="JavaScript: void 0;">Address Bar</a><br>
  <a href="JavaScript: void 0;">Links</a><br>
  <a href="JavaScript: void 0;">Radio</a>
  <hr>
  <a href="JavaScript: void 0;">Customize</a>
</div>

<div class="menu" ID="View_ExplorerBar"
     style="width: 150;" level="1">
  <a href="JavaScript: void 0;">Search</a><br>
  <a href="JavaScript: void 0;">Favorites</a><br>
  <a href="JavaScript: void 0;">History</a><br>
  <a href="JavaScript: void 0;">Folders</a>
  <hr>
  <a href="JavaScript: void 0;">Tip of the Day</a><br>
  <a href="JavaScript: void 0;">Discuss</a>
</div>

<div class="menu" ID="View_GoTo" style="width: 150;" level="1">
  <a href="JavaScript: void 0;">Back</a><br>
  <a href="JavaScript: void 0;">Forward</a>
  <hr>
  <a href="JavaScript: void 0;">Home Page</a>
  <hr>
</div>

</body>

</html>
```

Summary

Through the use of the Document Object Model (DOM) you can add a large range of dynamic effects to your Web page. Every HTML element on your Web page corresponds to an object in the DOM and can be referenced within your code (as long as you are using Internet Explorer). Many aspects of the DOM cannot be used if you are writing your Web page for Netscape Navigator, which severely limits your capabilities. Even with Netscape Navigator's limitations, however, you can still add some basic and very effective dynamic effects.

Chapter 8

Handling and Validating Forms

One of the best features of JavaScript is its ability to handle forms. Before the introduction of JavaScript, form validation required that the contents of a form be sent back to the originating server, checked, and if there were errors in the form data, sent back to the client for corrections. This was not only complicated, but very time-consuming. When JavaScript was introduced, form validation became a one-step process—the client would fill out the form, and before the form data was submitted to the server, it was validated with JavaScript scripts located on the Web page itself. This made JavaScript-enabled Web pages not only faster but more user-friendly. Some of the Javascript techniques that can be used with forms are dynamic form creation, form validation prior to submission, and data manipulation within form elements. Each of these techniques will be described in this chapter.

Defining Dynamic Forms

With JavaScript, a Web page designer is no longer limited to the static elements that are part of HTML. With a JavaScript-enabled Web page, you can request specific data on a per-user basis. For example, if you are running an online store, you might want to know an account number from clients working for a business, but you would not want to ask for this information from a home shopper. With JavaScript, you can hide or disable the appropriate form fields for each of your visitors.

Adding Form Elements Depending on Visitor Form Selections

There are two ways to customize a form for the user. The first way is to build the form, with the proper elements already in place, while the page is loading. You can do so by using input either from a previous page, in the form of cookies (covered in Chapter 11), or by using previous form information passed through the page URL.

You have probably seen Web sites with pages that have been created using a server-side language such as ASP or PHP. Even though these sites appear to contain multiple pages, more often than not, they are made up of only one document. The programmer of such a site makes it appear as though the site is very large by passing parameter variables through the URL. A good example of this is the excellent search engine Google.com:

```
http://www.google.com/search?hl=en&ie=UTF-8&oe=UTF-8&q=JavaScript
```

There are several variables that have been stored in Google's URL. URL parameters that occur after the first question mark in the URL are separated by ampersands and are variable/value pairs. The Google example has four variables and corresponding values:

```
hl=en
ie=UTF-8
oe=UTF-8
q=JavaScript
```

The last variable corresponds to an example query I performed. In a server-side language such as ASP or PHP, these URL fields are automatically generated for the programmer in the form of variables, but with JavaScript they are not. This is important for JavaScript programmers because forms submit information through the URL in the same way. To get the information out of the URL, you simply need to parse it with the built-in String object methods.

The following example prompts the user to enter his age when the page first loads:

```
<html>
  <head>
    <title>
      JavaScript Professional Projects - Dynamic Forms
    </title>
```

```
<script language="JavaScript">
<!--
  var visitorAge = -1;
  function getParams()
  {
    var urlquery   = location.href.split( "?" );
    var variable   = ( urlquery[1] ? urlquery[1].split( "=" ) : 0);
    visitorAge = ( variable ? variable[1] : -1 );
  }
// -->
</script>

</head>

<body>

<center>
  <font size=6>JavaScript Professional Projects</font><br>
  <font size=4>Chapter 9: Dynamic Forms</font>
</center>

<br><br>
<br><br>

<form>
  <script language="JavaScript">
  <!--
    getParams();
    if( visitorAge >= 12 )
    {
      document.write( "Welcome to my page." );
    }
    else if( visitorAge == -1 )
    {
      document.write(
        "Please tell me your age:  " +
        "<input type='text' name='age'size='5'></input><br><br>" +
        "<input type='submit' value='Continue'></input>"
```

```
        );
    }
    else
    {
        document.write( "Sorry, you must be at least 12 years old" +
                            " to access this site." );
    }
    -->
    </script>
</form>


</body>
</html>
```

After submitting the form, the page is reloaded with the form element name=value pairs in the URL. When the page reloads, the value of the first parameter is saved. If the value is less than 12, the page shows a message indicating that there is an age requirement. This would be, of course, a very insecure way to perform age checking, but the example does show how to get variables out of the URL.

Changing Selection List and Other Form Input Properties

One of the very useful features that JavaScript brings to your Web page is the ability to manipulate data that is already in the forms. For instance, if you were creating a form with which you planned to survey your Web site's visitors on their experience at the site, you might include something like, "Which products most interested you at this site? Select all that apply" and then a list all of the product lines sold on your Web site. You could list each product as a check box and require the visitor to click on each item that interested him or her. Unfortunately, if you have more than ten products this could get tedious. One alternative would be to place each item in a select box on your form and allow the user to select each item that interested him or her. Of course, if you used this approach, you would want to present the list in an ordered way so as to make answering the question as easy as possible. Before JavaScript, this would have been nearly impossible without hard-coding the list order into the HTML source. With JavaScript, you can now add items into the select box in any order and worry about sorting afterwards.

This example has two select boxes in a form. The first select box contains the names of each month in the year and the second select box is empty. Two buttons allow you to move items to and from the first select box into the second. After each move, both select boxes are sorted.

```
<html>
  <head>
    <title>
      JavaScript Professional Projects - Working with Forms
```

```
</title>

<style type="text/css">
<!--
  .sameSize{ width: 125; }
-->
</style>

<script language="JavaScript">
<!--
  var months = new Array( "January", "February", "March",
                          "April", "May", "June", "July",
                          "August", "September", "October",
                          "November", "December" );

  function swapSelects( fromSelect, toSelect )
  {
    var toSelect_Length = toSelect.options.length;
    while( fromSelect.selectedIndex > -1 )
    {
      var index = fromSelect.selectedIndex;

      toSelect.options[toSelect_Length] = new Option(
        fromSelect.options[index].text );
      toSelect.options[toSelect_Length].value =
        fromSelect.options[index].value;
      fromSelect.options[index] = null;

      toSelect_Length++;
    }
    sortSelect( fromSelect );
    sortSelect( toSelect );
  }

  function compareTo( s )
  {
    var len1 = this.length;
    var len2 = s.length;
```

```javascript
    var n = ( len1 < len2 ? len1 : len2 );

    for( i = 0 ; i < n ; i++ )
    {
      var a = this.charCodeAt( i );
      var b = s.charCodeAt( i )
      if( a != b )
      {
        return( a - b );
      }
    }
    return( len1 - len2 );
}
String.prototype.compareTo = compareTo;

function sortSelect( select )
{
  var a = new Array();
  for( i = 0; i < select.options.length ; i++ )
  {
    a[a.length] = new Option( select.options[i].text,
                              select.options[i].value,
                              select.options[i].defaultSelected,
                              select.options[i].selected ) ;
  }

  a = a.sort(
    function( s, t )
    {
      return( s.text.compareTo( t.text ) );
    }
  );

  for( i = 0; i < a.length ; i++ )
  {
    select.options[i] = new Option( a[i].text,
                                    a[i].value,
                                    a[i].defaultSelected,
                                    a[i].selected );
  }
```

```
      }
    }
  // -->
  </script>

</head>

<body>

  <center>
    <font size=6>JavaScript Professional Projects</font><br>
    <font size=4>Chapter 8: Working with Forms</font>
  </center>

  <br><br>
  <br><br>


  <form name="theForm">
    <table cellspacing="6">
      <tr>
        <td>
          <select size="12" name="ListA" multiple width="125">
            <script language="JavaScript">
            <!--
              for( i = 0 ; i < months.length ; i++ )
              {
                document.write( "<option>" + months[i] +
                              "</option>" );
              }
              sortSelect( document.theForm.ListA );
            // -->
            </script>
          </select>
        </td>

        <td>
          <input type="button" value="=====&gt;"
```

```
            onClick="JavaScript: swapSelects( document.theForm.ListA,
                                        document.theForm.ListB );">
        <br><br>
        <input type="button" value="&lt;=====" 
          onClick="JavaScript: swapSelects( document.theForm.ListB,
                                      document.theForm.ListA );">
      </td>

      <td>
        <select size="12" name="ListB" multiple
              width="125"></select>
        <script language="JavaScript">
        <!--
          if( navigator.appName != "Netscape" )
          {
            document.theForm.ListA.style.width = 125;
            document.theForm.ListB.style.width = 125;
          }
        // -->
        </script>
      </td>
    </tr>
  </table>
</form>

  </body>
</html>
```

This small example contains two very useful bits of code. The first function, swapSelects(),

```
function swapSelects( fromSelect, toSelect )
{
  var toSelect_Length = toSelect.options.length;
  while( fromSelect.selectedIndex > -1 )
  {
    var index = fromSelect.selectedIndex;

    toSelect.options[toSelect_Length] = new Option(
      fromSelect.options[index].text );
```

```
  toSelect.options[toSelect_Length].value =
    fromSelect.options[index].value;
  fromSelect.options[index] = null;

  toSelect_Length++;
}


sortSelect( fromSelect );
sortSelect( toSelect );
}
```

will take all of the selected elements out of `fromSelect` and put them into `toSelect`.

At the end of the `swapSelect()` function, both select boxes are sorted with the following function, `sortSelect()`:

```
function sortSelect( select )
{
  var a = new Array();
  for( i = 0; i < select.options.length ; i++ )
  {
    a[a.length] = new Option( select.options[i].text,
                              select.options[i].value,
                              select.options[i].defaultSelected,
                              select.options[i].selected ) ;
  }


  a = a.sort(
    function( s, t )
    {
      return( s.text.compareTo( t.text ) );
    }
  );


  for( i = 0; i < a.length ; i++ )
  {
    select.options[i] = new Option( a[i].text,
                                    a[i].value,
                                    a[i].defaultSelected,
                                    a[i].selected );
```

```
  }
}
```

The `sortSelect()` function uses a custom version of the `compareTo()` function presented in Chapter 3 to sort the options in the select box.

It is also very useful to be able to insert a new item into a single select box, particularly when building a dynamic list of any sort. Here is a basic example that takes input from the user from a text box and inserts it into a select box:

```html
<html>
  <head>
    <title>
      JavaScript Professional Projects - Dynamic Forms
    </title>

    <style type="text/css">
    <!--
      .sameSize{ width: 125; }
    -->
    </style>

    <script language="JavaScript">
    <!--
      function insertOption( select, text )
      {
        select.options[select.options.length] =
          new Option( text, text, false, false );
        sortSelect( select );
      }

      function compareTo( s )
      {
        var len1 = this.length;
        var len2 = s.length;
        var n = ( len1 < len2 ? len1 : len2 );

        for( i = 0 ; i < n ; i++ )
        {
          var a = this.toUpperCase().charCodeAt( i );
```

```
      var b = s.toUpperCase().charCodeAt( i )
      if( a != b )
      {
        return( a - b );
      }
    }
    return( len1 - len2 );
  }
String.prototype.compareTo = compareTo;

function sortSelect( select )
{
  var a = new Array();
  for( i = 0; i < select.options.length ; i++ )
  {
    a[a.length] = new Option( select.options[i].text,
                              select.options[i].value,
                              select.options[i].defaultSelected,
                              select.options[i].selected ) ;
  }

  a = a.sort(
    function( s, t )
    {
      return( s.text.compareTo( t.text ) );
    }
  );

  for( i = 0; i < a.length ; i++ )
  {
    select.options[i] = new Option( a[i].text,
                                    a[i].value,
                                    a[i].defaultSelected,
                                    a[i].selected );
  }
}
// -->
</script>
```

```
  </head>

  <body>

    <center>
      <font size=6>JavaScript Professional Projects</font><br>
      <font size=4>Chapter 8: Dynamic Foms</font>
    </center>

    <br><br>
    <br><br>

    <form name="theForm" onSubmit="return( false );">
      <table cellpadding="3">
        <tr>
          <td valign="bottom">
            <input type="text" name="theText" size="20">
               
            <input type="button" value="Insert"
              onClick="JavaScript:
                  insertOption( document.theForm.theSelect,
                                document.theForm.theText.value );
                  document.theForm.theText.value = '';">
          </td>
          <td>
                  
            <select size="10" name="theSelect"
                    class="sameSize" width=125></select>
          </td>
        </tr>
      </table>
    </form>

  </body>
</html>
```

The text in the text box can be accessed through the text box's value property, as you can see above. All form elements have this property, but on some it is not always straightforward. For example, with select boxes, the value property is the value of the first option that is selected. All options, of course, have a value property, but you must iterate through the select box's options array to access them. The value property of a button is the text that is shown on the button.

Handling Events During Data Entry

The goal of a form designer should be to make filling out a form as easy as possible for the user. Every action a user takes when filling out a form creates an event. Sometimes those events—such as button presses and keyboard events—can be used to aid the user in form completion, and others—like mouse movement events—generally cannot be used to fill out forms. The proper use of events within a form will make visitors' experiences at your site easier and more pleasant by requiring them to type less.

The following example automatically fills out the Billing Address section of the form from the Mailing Address when the user requests it:

```html
<html>
  <head>
    <title>
      JavaScript Professional Projects - Working with Forms
    </title>

    <script language="JavaScript">
    <!--
      function copyForm()
      {
        document.billingForm.firstLine.value =
          document.mailingForm.firstLine.value;
        document.billingForm.secondLine.value =
          document.mailingForm.secondLine.value;
        document.billingForm.thirdLine.value =
          document.mailingForm.thirdLine.value;
      }
    // -->
    </script>

  </head>

  <body>
```

```
<center>
  <font size=6>JavaScript Professional Projects</font><br>
  <font size=4>Chapter 8: Working with Forms</font>
</center>


<br><br>
<br><br>


<table cellspacing="4" cellpadding="4" width="65%">
  <tr>
    <td>


      <form name="mailingForm">
        <b><font size="5">Mailing Address<br>
        </font></b><br>
        <br>
        <b>Last name, First name:</b><br>
        <input type="text" name="firstLine" size="36"><br>
        <b>Street/Address:</b><br>
        <input type="text" name="secondLine" size="36"><br>
        <b>City State, Zip code:</b><br>
        <input type="text" name="thirdLine" size="36">
      </form>


    </td>
    <td>


      <form name="billingForm">
        <b><font size="5">Billing Address<br>
        </font></b>
        <input type="checkbox" onClick="JavaScript: copyForm();"
               value="ON">Same as mailing address?<br>
        <br>
        <b>Last name, First name:</b><br>
        <input type="text" name="firstLine" size="36"><br>
        <b>Street/Address:</b><br>
        <input type="text" name="secondLine" size="36"><br>
```

```
            <b>City State, Zip code:</b><br>
            <input type="text" name="thirdLine" size="36">
          </form>


        </td>
      </tr>
    </table>


  </body>
</html>
```

This very simple example cuts the amount of time needed to fill out the form in half.

Two events are used very often with forms: the onReset event and the onSubmit event. The onReset event should clear all the elements in the form so that the user can start filling it out from scratch. The onSubmit event handler is generally used for form validation.

Reset Events

The reset feature of forms is very easy to implement. If the user makes a mistake, such as typing in the wrong address, he or she will not want to go back to each form field and remove the previous entries. The Reset button should reset the form to the way it was when the Web page was first loaded.

The following example clears all the value properties of form elements that are not buttons:

```
<html>
  <head>
    <title>
      JavaScript Professional Projects - Form Events
    </title>

    <script language="JavaScript">
    <!--
      function resetForm( form )
      {
        for( i = 0 ; i < form.elements.length ; i++ )
        {
          with( form.elements[i] )
          {
            if( type != "button" &&
                type != "reset" &&
```

```
                    type != "submit" )
              form.elements[i].value = "";
          }
        }
      }
    // -->
    </script>

</head>

<body>

  <center>
    <font size=6>JavaScript Professional Projects</font><br>
    <font size=4>Chapter 8: Form Events</font>
  </center>

  <br><br>
  <br><br>

  <table cellspacing="4" cellpadding="4" width="65%">
    <tr>
      <td>
        <form name="mailingForm"
             onReset="JavaScript: resetForm( this );">
          <b><font size="5">Mailing Address<br>
          </font></b><br>
          <br>
          <b>Last name, First name:</b><br>
          <input type="text" name="firstLine" size="36"><br>
          <b>Street/Address:</b><br>
          <input type="text" name="secondLine" size="36"><br>
          <b>City State, Zip code:</b><br>
          <input type="text" name="thirdLine" size="36">  
          <input type="reset" value="Reset" name="B1">
        </form>
      </td>
    </tr>
```

```
    </table>

  </body>
</html>
```

This example loops through each field in the form and if the field is not a button, clears the data that has been input to it.

Submit Events

Form validation is a slightly more complicated way to reset events. Form validation occurs after the visitor has entered data into the form and before it is submitted to the server. The function of form validation is to make sure that all form fields have data and that the data that has been entered into the form correctly.

Here is a simple example that checks to make sure that data has been entered into the form before it is submitted:

```
<html>
  <head>
    <title>
      JavaScript Professional Projects - Form Events
    </title>

    <script language="JavaScript">
    <!--
      function validate()
      {
        if( isNaN( document.theForm.theText.value ) )
        {
          alert( "Please input a Number!" );
          document.theForm.theText.value = "";
          return( false );
        }
        else return( true );
      }
    // -->
    </script>

  </head>

  <body>
```

```
<center>
  <font size=6>JavaScript Professional Projects</font><br>
  <font size=4>Chapter 8: Form Events</font>
</center>

<br><br>
<br><br>

<form name="theForm" onSubmit="JavaScript: return( validate() );">
  Input a number<br>
  <input type="text" name="theText" size="20">   
  <input type="submit" value="Insert">
</form>

</body>
</html>
```

Form validation will be explained in more detail later in this chapter.

Select Events

There are, of course, other events that can be used with forms—mainly selection events. A select event occurs when the visitor clicks on any of the contents of a form field. Selecting text in a text box or text area or choosing an option in a drop-down list will create a selection event. Most of the selection events that you'll deal with when programming in JavaScript will come from the select box form elements, so that is what I'll focus on here.

Following is an example that allows a user to change the current page by selecting an option from a drop-down list:

```
<html>
  <head>
    <title>
      JavaScript Professional Projects - Form Events
    </title>

    <script language="JavaScript">
    <!--
      function validate()
      {
```

```
        if( isNaN( document.theForm.theText.value ) )
        {
          alert( "Please input a Number!" );
          document.theForm.theText.value = "";
          return( false );
        }
        else return( true );
      }
    // -->
    </script>

  </head>

  <body>

    <center>
      <font size=6>JavaScript Professional Projects</font><br>
      <font size=4>Chapter 8: Form Events</font>
    </center>

    <br><br>
    <br><br>

    <form name="theForm">
      Select a search engine to use: 
      <select size="1" name="Menu"
        onChange="JavaScript: window.location=
          this.options[this.options.selectedIndex].value;">
        <option value="http://www.google.com/">Google</option>
        <option value="http://www.yahoo.com/">Yahoo</option>
        <option value="http://www.dogpile.com/ ">Dogpile</option>
        <option value="http://www.altavista.com/">Altavista</option>
      </select>
    </form>

  </body>
</html>
```

This example redirects the page to the location selected in the drop-down box. This technique is very popular, even though there are much better ways to accomplish the same thing (namely, by using normal anchor tags or by using DHTML). However, the example does effectively illustrate how to use selection events.

Form Validation Prior to Submission

At long last we arrive at what is considered one of the biggest advantages of using JavaScript: the ability to validate forms before they are sent to the originating server. This topic has been mentioned throughout the book but as yet has been explained very little.

Form validation used to occur at the server, after the client had entered all necessary data and then pressed the Submit button. If some of the data that had been entered by the client had been in the wrong form or was simply missing, the server would have to send all the data back to the client and request that the form be resubmitted with correct information. This process used to be long and tedious because of slow transfer speeds, but with the introduction of JavaScript, all validation of form data could be done on the client's computer without any input needed from the server.

Form validation generally performs two functions. First of all, the form must be checked to make sure data was entered into each form field that required it. Secondly, the data that is entered must be checked for correct form and value. The first part is usually trivial—just loop through each field in the form and check for data. It is the second part of form validation that required the most thought. Everything you have learned thus far will play a part in the validation process.

The most common type of form on the Web right now is used to get billing information for an online transaction. Here is an example of such a form with just a basic validation function:

```
<html>
  <head>
    <title>
      JavaScript Professional Projects - Form Validation
    </title>

    <script language="JavaScript">
    <!--
      function validate()
      {
        var good = true;

        with( document.theForm )
        {
```

```
        if( names.value == "" ||
            names.value.indexOf( "," ) < 1 )
        {
          alert( "Please provide your first and" +
                 " last name separated by a comma." );
          good = false;
        }
        if( address.value == "" )
        {
          alert( "Please provide an address." );
          good = false;
        }
        if( city.value == "" )
        {
          alert( "Please provide a city." );
          good = false;
        }
        if( state.value == "" )
        {
          alert( "Please provide a state." );
          good = false;
        }
        if( zip.value == "" ||
            isNaN( zip.value ) ||
            zip.value.length != 5 )
        {
          alert( "Please provide a zip in the format #####." );
          good = false;
        }
      }
      return( good );
    }
  // -->
  </script>

</head>

<body>
```

```
<center>
    <font size=6>JavaScript Professional Projects</font><br>
    <font size=4>Chapter 8: Form Validation</font>
</center>


<br><br>
<br><br>


<table cellspacing="4" cellpadding="4" width="65%">
    <tr>
        <td>
            <form name="theForm"
                    onSubmit="JavaScript: return( validate() );">
                <b><font size="5">Mailing Address</font></b><br>
                <br>
                <b>Last name, First name:</b><br>
                <input type="text" name="names" size="36"><br>
                <b>Street/Address:</b><br>
                <input type="text" name="address" size="36"><br>
                <b>City:</b><br>
                <input type="text" name="city" size="36"><br>
                <b>State:<br>
                </b><input type="text" name="state" size="36"><br>
                <b>Zip code:</b><br>
                <input type="text" name="zip" size="36">  
                <input type="submit" value="Submit"></form>
        </td>
    </tr>
</table>


    </body>
</html>
```

This example performs a very basic form validation by checking each form element's value to make sure it conforms to the desired information type. One downfall and annoying feature of this validation function is that it creates an error message for every error that occurs in the page. If the user accidentally hits the Submit button and this form was much longer, he or she would spend the next couple of minutes repeatedly hitting the alert dialog's OK button.

Thankfully, there is a better way to report errors than this:

```html
<html>
  <head>
    <title>
      JavaScript Professional Projects - Form Validation
    </title>

    <script language="JavaScript">
<!--
    function validate()
    {
      try
      {
        with( document.theForm )
        {
          if( names.value == "" ||
              names.value.indexOf( "," ) < 1 )
          {
            throw "Please provide your first and" +
                    " last name separated by a comma.";
          }
          if( address.value == "" )
          {
            throw "Please provide an address.";
          }
          if( city.value == "" )
          {
            throw "Please provide a city.";
          }
          if( state.value == "" )
          {
            throw "Please provide a state.";
          }
          if( zip.value == "" ||
              isNaN( zip.value ) ||
              zip.value.length != 5 )
          {
```

```
              throw "Please provide a zip in the format #####.";
            }
          }
        }
        catch( error )
        {
          alert( error );
          return( false );
        }
        return( true );
      }
    // -->
    </script>

</head>

<body>

  <center>
    <font size=6>JavaScript Professional Projects</font><br>
    <font size=4>Chapter 8: Form Validation</font>
  </center>

  <br><br>
  <br><br>

  <table cellspacing="4" cellpadding="4" width="65%">
    <tr>
      <td>
        <form name="theForm"
              onSubmit="JavaScript: return( validate() );">
          <b><font size="5">Mailing Address</font></b><br>
          <br>
          <b>Last name, First name:</b><br>
          <input type="text" name="names" size="36"><br>
          <b>Street/Address:</b><br>
          <input type="text" name="address" size="36"><br>
          <b>City:</b><br>
```

```
        <input type="text" name="city" size="36"><br>
        <b>State:<br>
        </b><input type="text" name="state" size="36"><br>
        <b>Zip code:</b><br>
        <input type="text" name="zip" size="36">  
        <input type="submit" value="Submit"></form>
      </td>
    </tr>
  </table>


</body>
</html>
```

Instead of using a flag variable like the previous example, this example uses JavaScript's built-in error catching feature to make sure that only one error message is shown at a time. Unfortunately, this means that for very long forms the user will have to repeatedly hit the Submit button to fix each error. Although this is preferable to getting a cascade of error messages, it still isn't the best approach.

Luckily, there is a way to provide information for each error without presenting the user with multiple alert dialog boxes or forcing him to click on the Submit button repeatedly. Here it is:

```
<html>
  <head>
    <title>
      JavaScript Professional Projects - Form Validation
    </title>

    <style type="text/css">
    <!--
      .message{ position: absolute; visibility: hidden; }
    -->
    </style>

    <script language="JavaScript">
    <!--
      function validate()
      {
        var good = false;
        if( navigator.appName == "Netscape" )
        {
```

```
with( document.theForm )
{
  if( names.value == "" ||
      names.value.indexOf( "," ) < 1 )
  {
    alert( "Please provide your first and" +
           " last name separated by a comma." );
    good = false;
  }
  else if( address.value == "" )
  {
    alert( "Please provide an address." );
    good = false;
  }
  else if( city.value == "" )
  {
    alert( "Please provide a city." );
    good = false;
  }
  else if( state.value == "" )
  {
    alert( "Please provide a state." );
    good = false;
  }
  else if( zip.value == "" ||
      isNaN( zip.value ) ||
      zip.value.length != 5 )
  {
    alert( "Please provide a zip in the format #####." );
    good = false;
  }
 }
}
else
{
  with( document.theForm )
  {
    if( names.value == "" || names.value.indexOf( "," ) < 1 )
```

```
{
  with( document.all.namesMessage.style )
  {
    position = "relative";
    visibility = "visible";
  }
  good = false;
}
else
{
  with( document.all.namesMessage.style )
  {
    position = "absolute";
    visibility = "hidden";
  }
}
if( address.value == "" )
{
  with( document.all.addressMessage.style )
  {
    position = "relative";
    visibility = "visible";
  }
  good = false;
}
else
{
  with( document.all.addressMessage.style )
  {
    position = "absolute";
    visibility = "hidden";
  }
}
if( city.value == "" )
{
  with( document.all.cityMessage.style )
  {
    position = "relative";
```

```
            visibility = "visible";
        }
        good = false;
    }
    else
    {
        with( document.all.cityMessage.style )
        {
            position = "absolute";
            visibility = "hidden";
        }
    }
    if( state.value == "" )
    {
        with( document.all.stateMessage.style )
        {
            position = "relative";
            visibility = "visible";
        }
        good = false;
    }
    else
    {
        with( document.all.stateMessage.style )
        {
            position = "absolute";
            visibility = "hidden";
        }
    }
    if( zip.value == "" ||
        isNaN( zip.value ) ||
        zip.value.length != 5 )
    {
        with( document.all.zipMessage.style )
        {
            position = "relative";
            visibility = "visible";
        }
```

```
              good = false;
            }
            else
            {
              with( document.all.zipMessage.style )
              {
                position = "absolute";
                visibility = "hidden";
              }
            }
          }
        }
      return( good );
    }
  // -->
  </script>

</head>

<body>

  <center>
    <font size=6>JavaScript Professional Projects</font><br>
    <font size=4>Chapter 8: Form Validation</font>
  </center>

  <br><br>
  <br><br>

  <table cellspacing="4" cellpadding="4" width="65%">
    <tr>
      <td>
        <form name="theForm"
              onSubmit="JavaScript: return( validate );">
          <b><font size="5">Mailing Address</font></b><br>
          <br>
          <b>Last name, First name:</b><br>
          <div id="namesMessage" class="message">
```

```
                  <font color=red>Please provide your first and last name
                                  separated by a comma.</font>
            </div>
            <input type="text" name="names" size="36"><br>

            <b>Street/Address:</b><br>
            <div id="addressMessage" class="message">
              <font color=red>Please provide an address.</font>
            </div>
            <input type="text" name="address" size="36"><br>

            <b>City:</b><br>
            <div id="cityMessage" class="message">
              <font color=red>Please provide a city.</font>
            </div>
            <input type="text" name="city" size="36"><br>

            <b>State:</b><br>
            <div id="stateMessage" class="message">
              <font color=red>Please provide a state.</font>
            </div>
            <input type="text" name="state" size="36"><br>

            <b>Zip code:</b><br>
            <div id="zipMessage" class="message">
              <font color=red>Please provide an zip
                              in the format #####.</font>
            </div>
            <input type="text" name="zip" size="36">  
            <input type="submit" value="Submit"></form>
        </td>
      </tr>
    </table>

  </body>
</html>
```

This example hides DIV elements with error messages in them above each form field. If the user tries to submit incorrect data, the DIV elements will be shown for each form field containing the erroneous data. This technique not only provides feedback for each error, but it does so right on the screen. The drawback to this method is that it only works effectively in Internet Explorer, so if you're doing error checking outside of a controlled environment like an intranet, you may wish to use one of the alternative ways to report the errors described above.

The above example, in order to fully demonstrate the concept, was really longer than it needed to be. The function validate() could have been written like this:

```
function validate()
{
  var good = false;
  if( navigator.appName == "Netscape" )
  {
    with( document.theForm )
    {
      if( !( good = !(names.value == "" ||
          names.value.indexOf( "," ) < 1)) )
        alert( "Please provide your first and" +
                " last name separated by a comma." );
      else if( !(good = !(address.value == "")) )
        alert( "Please provide an address." );
      else if( !( good = !(city.value == "")) )
        alert( "Please provide a city." );
      else if( !( good = !(state.value == "")) )
        alert( "Please provide a state." );
      else if( !( good = !(zip.value == "" ||
                            isNaN( zip.value ) ||
                            zip.value.length != 5)) )
        alert( "Please provide a zip in the format #####." );
    }
  }
  else
  {
    with( document.theForm )
    {
      var flag = names.value == "" ||
                 names.value.indexOf( "," ) < 1;
```

```
with( document.all.namesMessage.style )
{
  position = ( flag ? "relative" : "absolute" );
  visibility = ( flag ? "visible" : "hidden" );
}
if( !flag ) good = false;

flag = address.value == "";
with( document.all.addressMessage.style )
{
  position = ( flag ? "relative" : "absolute" );
  visibility = ( flag ? "visible" : "hidden" );
}
if( !flag ) good = false;

flag = city.value == "";
with( document.all.cityMessage.style )
{
  position = ( flag ? "relative" : "absolute" );
  visibility = ( flag ? "visible" : "hidden" );
}
if( !flag ) good = false;

flag = state.value == "";
with( document.all.stateMessage.style )
{
  position = ( flag ? "relative" : "absolute" );
  visibility = ( flag ? "visible" : "hidden" );
}
if( !flag ) good = false;

flag = zip.value == "" ||
    isNaN( zip.value ) ||
    zip.value.length != 5;
with( document.all.zipMessage.style )
{
  position = ( flag ? "relative" : "absolute" );
  visibility = ( flag ? "visible" : "hidden" );
```

```
      }
      if( !flag ) good = false;
    }
  }
  return( good );
```

This example is a much shorter (albeit harder-to-read) version of the previous example. If you're worried about download time for your page, then use the second version instead of the first, as it reduces the number of characters needed to download from 1627 to 1410.

There are far too many ways to validate a form to present in the limited space of this book. I encourage you to visit professional Web sites that use forms in order to find new and better techniques of form validation.

Enabling and Disabling Form Fields

You may at some point in time find it necessary to disable a form field. The most common time to disable a form field is after the form has been submitted but before the user's view changes. Disabling the Submit button at this time will make it impossible for the user to submit the same information twice. Enabling and disabling forms is a simple feat to accomplish in Internet Explorer. Here is an example:

```html
<html>
  <head>
    <title>
      JavaScript Professional Projects - Form Validation
    </title>

    <script language="JavaScript">
    <!--
      function disable( element )
      {
        element.disabled = true;
      }
    // -->
    </script>

  </head>

  <body>
```

```
<center>
  <font size=6>JavaScript Professional Projects</font><br>
  <font size=4>Chapter 8: Form Validation</font>
</center>


<br><br>
<br><br>


<table cellspacing="4" cellpadding="4" width="65%">
  <tr>
    <td>
      <form name="theForm"
            onSubmit="JavaScript: disable( this.theButton );
                              return( false );">
        <b><font size="5">Mailing Address</font></b><br>
        <br>
        <b>Last name, First name:</b><br>
        <input type="text" name="names" size="36"><br>

        <b>Street/Address:</b><br>
        <input type="text" name="address" size="36"><br>

        <b>City:</b><br>
        <input type="text" name="city" size="36"><br>

        <b>State:</b><br>
        <input type="text" name="state" size="36"><br>

        <b>Zip code:</b><br>
        <input type="text" name="zip" size="36">  
        <input type="submit" value="Submit" name="theButton">
      </form>
    </td>
  </tr>
</table>

  </body>
</html>
```

As you can see from the example, disabling a form element with Internet Explorer is as simple as setting its disabled property to true:

```
element.disabled = true;
```

This will cause the Submit button to no longer accept any events and, consequently, not allow the form to be submitted more than once. Unfortunately, the example submits the form long before you can actually see the disabled button, which is why return(false) is used in the form's onSubmit event handler to halt the submission. To enable a disabled form element, all you need to do is set the element's disabled property to false.

You can accomplish the same basic functionality in Netscape, as follows:

```html
<html>
  <head>
    <title>
      JavaScript Professional Projects - Form Validation
    </title>

    <script language="JavaScript">
    <!--
      function disable( element )
      {
        element.disabled = true;
      }
    // -->
    </script>

  </head>

  <body>

    <center>
      <font size=6>JavaScript Professional Projects</font><br>
      <font size=4>Chapter 8: Form Validation</font>
    </center>

    <br><br>
    <br><br>
```

```
<table cellspacing="4" cellpadding="4" width="65%">
  <tr>
    <td>
      <form name="theForm"
            onSubmit="JavaScript: disable( this.theButton );
                          return( !this.theButton.disabled );">
        <b><font size="5">Mailing Address</font></b><br>
        <br>
        <b>Last name, First name:</b><br>
        <input type="text" name="names" size="36"><br>

        <b>Street/Address:</b><br>
        <input type="text" name="address" size="36"><br>

        <b>City:</b><br>
        <input type="text" name="city" size="36"><br>

        <b>State:</b><br>
        <input type="text" name="state" size="36"><br>

        <b>Zip code:</b><br>
        <input type="text" name="zip" size="36">  
        <input type="submit" value="Submit" name="theButton">
      </form>
    </td>
  </tr>
</table>

  </body>
</html>
```

This example checks the disabled parameter of the button element and determines whether the form should submit:

```
return( !this.theButton.disabled );
```

Buttons are not the only form elements that take advantage of the disabled property. You can disable any visual field that is part of a form, including all `input` and `select` fields.

Summary

Working with forms is a very important part of designing an efficient working Web site. JavaScript makes your job easier by providing many events and objects that work directly with form fields. Form validation used to be a long and tedious function, but after the introduction of JavaScript, it became much easier. The power of JavaScript's form validation is in its ability to do the validation on the client's computer. Efficient use of the techniques throughout this book will make form validation easy and useful.

Chapter 9

One unique feature that JavaScript possesses is the ability to communicate between different windows and frames. These communications can take the form of *function calls*—statements that change the look and feel of a separate window or frame or even form submissions. The ability to communicate between different windows and frames will allow you to preserve data even after a window has been closed or to open a new window that will help the user fill out a form.

Using data on other windows is a simple enough matter. Once you have a handle to the window (returned by the window.open() method), you can use it just like any other object in the JavaScript language. In this chapter, you will learn how to create new windows and modify how they look using their move and resize features, access data on the new child window, access data on a child's parent window, and share data between frames.

Creating, Resizing, Moving, and Closing Windows

The first technique you will need to master before you can confidently share information between different windows is how to pragmatically create a new window. Thankfully, there is a relatively simple method for creating windows that is part of the window class. The open() method allows you to create a custom window with only one call. Here's the syntax for calling the open() method:

```
window.open( <url>, <name>, <features> );
```

All three parameters are string values. The first parameter is the URL that will be loaded into the new window. The second parameter is used to reference the window later in the code and has nothing to do with how the window looks. The last parameter is optional and is a comma-separated list of features that alter the look and feel of the new window. Table 9.1 lists and describes the features that can be applied to a window that you open.

Table 9.1 Window Features

Feature	Platform	Description
alwaysLowered	Netscape only	When set to **yes**, the new window will always float below the others.
alwaysRaised	Netscape only	When set to **yes**, the new window will always float above the others.
channelmode	IE only	When set to **yes**, the new window will always appear in channel mode.
dependent	Netscape only	When set to **yes**, the new window is a child window of the original. The new window will be closed when the parent is and will not show up in the task bar.
directories	both	When set to **yes**, the new window has the standard directory buttons.
fullscreen	IE only	When set to **yes**, the new window will appear in full-screen mode.
height	both	Specifies the height of the new window.
hotkeys	Netscape only	When set to **yes**, the new window has all hotkeys disabled except security and quit hotkeys in a window without a menu bar.

Feature	Platform	Description
innerHeight	Netscape only	Specifies the inner height of the new window. The inner height is the height of the internal document.
innerWidth	Netscape only	Specifies the inner width of the new window. The inner width is the width of the internal document.
left	IE only	Specifies the pixel offset of the left side of the screen.
location	both	When set to **yes**, a standard location field is created in the new browser.
menubar	both	When set to **yes**, a standard menu bar is created in the new browser containing File, View, Help, etc.
outerHeight	Netscape only	Specifies the outer height of the new window.
outerWidth	Netscape only	Specifies the outer width of the new window.
resizable	both	When set to **use**, the new window allows the user to resize it.
screenX	Netscape only	Specifies the pixel offset in the horizontal direction of the screen.
screenY	Netscape only	Specifies the pixel offset in the vertical direction of the screen.
scrollbars	both	When set to **yes**, the standard scroll bars are displayed on the new window.
status	both	When set to **yes**, the standard status bar at the bottom of the browser will be created.
titlebar	Netscape only	When set to **yes**, the new window will have the standard title bar.
toolbar	both	When set to **yes**, the new window will have the standard tool bar containing Forward, Backward, Home, etc.
top	IE only	Specifies the pixel offset from the top of the screen.
width	both	Specifies the width of the new window.
z-lock	Netscape only	When set to **yes**, the new window will not be allowed to rise above other windows when given focus.

Following is an example of using several of the features listed in Table 9.1:

```
window.open( "http://google.com/", "search",
             "height=300,width=350,toolbar=yes" );
```

This statement would open a separate window with the Google search engine displayed. The new window would be 300×350 pixels and contain a tool bar, but nothing else. The open method also returns a handle to the newly created window that you can use to communicate with the new window. You can both resize and move the handle to the new window, as described in the next subsection.

Resizing and Moving Windows

Although not the most important techniques you can perform with a window in a practical Web application, resizing and moving a newly created window comes in handy when you want to have absolute control over the size and location of your new window.

To resize a window, use one of the two built-in window methods, resizeBy() or resizeTo().

The syntax for resizeBy() is as follows:

```
<window handle>.resizeBy( dx, dy );
```

and the syntax for the resizeTo() method is as follows:

```
<window handle>.resizeTo( outerWidth, outerHeight );
```

The resizeTo() method is perhaps more useful because you do not need to keep track of the window's current size, but both methods are very straightforward.

Here is an example of using the resizeBy() method:

```
myWindow = window.open( "http://google.com/", "search",
                        "height=300,width=350,toolbar=yes" );


myWindow.resizeBy( 25, 50 );
```

At the end of this example, the new window will have a width of 375 and a height of 350.

Using the resizeTo() method is equally simple; here is an example:

```
myWindow = window.open( "http://google.com/", "search",
                        "height=300,width=350,toolbar=yes" );


myWindow.resizeTo( 375, 350 );
```

At the end of this example, the new window will once again have a width of 375 and a height of 350.

It is important to remember that every window has a handle to it—even the parent window. Without a handle to a window, you would not be able to change its look and feel or to use it to communicate with other windows. You can reference the handle to the window on which the code is located by using the self reference. For example:

```
self.resizeTo( 375, 350 );
```

This statement will resize the current window. The self reference can be used with any window look-and-feel methods such as resizeTo() and moveBy().

You can move a window in the same way in which you resize it. Here is the syntax for both move methods in the window class:

```
<window handle>.moveBy( dx, dy );
```

and

```
<window handle>.moveTo( xPos, yPos );
```

Both of these methods have a one-to-one correlation to the resize methods mentioned above. The first method, moveBy(), moves a window a certain distance from its current position on the screen. The moveTo() method moves a window to a specific point on the client's screen.

Closing Windows

Once you have created a window, you can, of course, close it. Once again, you use the built-in close() method of the window object.

Here is the syntax for the close() method:

```
<window handle>.close();
```

And once again, here is a simple example:

```
myWindow = window.open( "http://google.com/", "search",
                        "height=300,width=350,toolbar=yes" );


myWindow.close();
```

This example will open a new window, but then close it immediately.

```
<html>
  <head>
    <title>
        JavaScript Professional Projects - Creating, Moving,
                                Resizing and Closing Windows
```

```
        </title>

    </head>

<body>

  <center>
    <font size=6>JavaScript Professional Projects</font><br>
    <font size=4>Chapter 9: Creating, Moving,
                        Resizing and Closing Windows</font>
  </center>

  <br><br>
  <br><br>


  <p>Click this button to open a separate window:  </p>
  <form>
    <input type="button" value="Open"
      onClick="JavaScript: window.open(window.location,'_blank');">
  </form>

  <p>Click the button to close this window:</p>
  <form>
    <input type="button" value="Close"
      onClick="JavaScript:  self.close();">
  </form>

  </body>
</html>
```

This example opens a window that contains two buttons. When the first button is clicked, a new window is opened containing the same document. When the second button is closed, the current window is closed.

Working with the Popup Object

The pop-up window is a special type of overlapping window object that is used for dialog boxes, message boxes, and other temporary windows. Pop-up windows are very useful for creating menus or advanced tool tip text because they can be shown and hidden at will. That they can be customized and moved around on a Web page makes them ideal for displaying tips, notes, or context menus. The only limitation inherent to popup objects is that they must always stay on the document for which they were created. In other words, they cannot exist outside of their parent windows.

Popup Properties

There are two properties that are part of the Popup object's definition.

- ◆ **document**. A reference to the document contained on this Popup object.
- ◆ **isOpen**. A boolean value representing whether the Popup is currently open or not.

Popup Methods

The following two methods are part of the Popup object's definition.

- ◆ **hide()**. Hides a visible Popup object.
- ◆ **show (xPos, yPos, width, height, obj)**. Reveals a hidden Popup object in the specified x,y position and the specified width and height. If the `obj` parameter is included, it is the object to which the position is relative. If the `obj` parameter is not included, the Popup will be positioned relative to the desktop.

You can create a Popup object by using the built-in method `createPopup()` in the window class. Here is the syntax for the `createPopup()` method:

```
var myPopup = window.createPopup();
```

This statement will return a Popup object that you can then use like any other window. The Popup's document object will initially be blank, but you can add HTML to it using the `document.body.innerHTML` property. Following is an example of doing just that:

```
<html>
  <head>
    <title>
      JavaScript Professional Projects - Working with Popup Windows
    </title>

    <script language="JavaScript">
    <!--
      var thePopup = window.createPopup();

      with( thePopup.document.body )
      {
        bgColor = "lightgreen";
```

```
            innerHTML = "<center>" +
                        "<font size=6>JavaScript Professional " +
                            "Projects</font><br>"+
                        "<font size=4>Chapter 9: A Popup Window</font>" +
                        "</center>";
        }
    -->
    </script>

</head>

<body>

  <center>
    <font size=6>JavaScript Professional Projects</font><br>
    <font size=4>Chapter 9: Working with Popup Windows</font>
  </center>

  <br><br>
  <br><br>


  <p>Click this button to show the popup window:  </p>
  <form>
    <input type="button" value="Show"
      onClick="JavaScript:  thePopup.show( 150, 150, 450, 350 );">
  </form>

  <p>Click the button to hide the popup window:</p>
  <form>
    <input type="button" value="Hide"
      onClick="JavaScript:  thePopup.hide();">
  </form>

  </body>
</html>
```

This example creates a pop-up window when a button is pressed and hides it when another button is pressed.

Working with Frame, Frameset, and Iframe Objects

A *frame* is a fractional part of a window. Frames usually come in groups and are all contained in a frameset object. Each frame is considered a separate window to the browser, and a different HTML document can be loaded into each. An *iframe* is a frame that occurs within the natural flow of the rest of the page. An iframe can also have a completely different HTML document than the rest of the page.

Frames and iframes can be considered separate windows when you are writing your code. This, of course, might cause some confusion because even though a Web page can have multiple frames and iframes, they are technically all contained on the same window. Following is the syntax for referencing a frame object in Internet Explorer:

```
WindowHandle.document.all.frameID
```

The windowHandle is the handle to the window that contains the frame. This value can be one of the values returned from window.open(), as mentioned above, or can be parent or top (the parent and top properties will be discussed later in this chapter).

Referencing an iframe object is slightly easier than referencing frames because there is no ambiguity about the window it is contained on. Here is the syntax for Internet Explorer:

```
Document.all.frameID
```

Netscape browsers don't allow you to directly access frames in this way. You can, however, access frames through the frames[] collection in both browsers. Here is the syntax for doing so:

```
windowHandle.frames[i]
```

This technique provides cross-platform compliance, but does not provide the control that Internet Explorer alone provides. There is generally no need to reference a frameset object, but if the need arises, the frameset object can be referenced just like any other HTML element—by its ID property.

Understanding the Difference between Parent and Top Frames

The window property parent is a reference to the window that defined the frameset. Use the parent reference when you need to access functions, variables, or elements in another frame. For example:

```
parent.frames[0].document.form[0].theTextArea.value = "New Text";
```

If you have several frames that are nested inside each other, you can use the parent of the parent property:

```
parent.parent.frames[0];
```

The window property `top`, on the other hand, always refers to the window object that contains the frame. Scripts contained in frames can access variables and functions loaded in the topmost position of the window by referencing the `top` attribute.

Accessing Code between Windows and Frames

Because JavaScript allows a programmer to create additional windows and frames, it must also provide a way to access variables and functions from any point in the window or frame hierarchy. The next three sections describe how to access data on child or parent windows and how to access data on frames.

Accessing Variables and Functions on Child Windows

It is very simple for a parent window to access the variables and code on a child window. When you use the `window.open()` method, a handle is returned that allows you to access the newly created window. This handle is useful for many tasks, including resizing, moving, closing, and accessing data on the new window.

Here is the syntax for accessing variables and functions on a child window:

```
windowHandle.variableName;
```

The child window function access syntax is as follows:

```
windowHandle.functionName( <parameter list> );
```

To illustrate the simplicity of this concept, here is a short example:

```
<html>

  <head>
    <title>JavaScript Professional Projects -
                Accessing data on other windows</title>
  </head>

  <body>
```

```
<center>
  <font size=6>JavaScript Professional Projects</font><br>
  <font size=4>Chapter 9: Accessing data on other windows</font>
</center>


<br><br>
<br><br>


The value of 'theVariable' on the other page is <b>
<script language="JavaScript">
<!--
  var otherPage = window.open( "other.html", "other" );

  document.write( otherPage.theVariable );
// -->
</script>
</b>.


  </body>

</html>
```

And here is the code that makes up "other.html":

```
<html>

  <head>
    <script language="JavaScript">
    <!--
      var theVariable = 42;
    // -->
    </script>

  </head>

<body>
  <code>
    In this window, the value of 'theVariable' is <b>
    <script language="JavaScript">
```

```
    <!--
      document.write( theVariable );
    // -->
    </script>
    </b>.
  </code>
</body>

</html>
```

As you can see, it is very easy to access data on a child window.

Accessing Variables and Functions on Parent Windows

It is equally easy to access data on the parent window from the child window. The window.opener property is a pointer to the window that created the child window. The example above could be rewritten as:

```
<html>

  <head>
    <title>JavaScript Professional Projects -
              Accessing data on other windows</title>

    <script language="JavaScript">
    <!--
      var theVariable = 42;
    // -->
    </script>
  </head>

  <body>

    <center>
      <font size=6>JavaScript Professional Projects</font><br>
      <font size=4>Chapter 9: Accessing data on other windows</font>
    </center>
```

```
  <br><br>
  <br><br>

  The value of 'theVariable' on this page is <b>
  <script language="JavaScript">
  <!--
    var otherPage = window.open( "other.html", "other" );

    document.write( theVariable );
  // -->
  </script>
  </b>.

</body>

</html>
```

And here is the code that makes up "other.html":

```
<html>

  <head>

  </head>

  <body>
    <code>
      The value of 'theVariable' on the parent window is <b>
      <script language="JavaScript">
      <!--
        document.write( opener.theVariable );
      // -->
      </script>
      </b>.
    </code>
  </body>

</html>
```

Accessing Variables and Functions on Frames

Data on frames can be accessed by referencing the correct frame in the `document.frames[]` collection. Here is the syntax for doing so:

```
parent.frames[i].<variableName>
```

Frame function access syntax is as follows:

```
parent.frames[i].<functionName>( <parameter list> );
```

One operation that is very useful when working with frames is changing the document that is displayed within the frame. Because each frame is considered a window by the browser, you can change the document displayed in the frame by changing the value of its `location` property. Here is the syntax for doing so:

```
parent.frames[i].location = "new URL";
```

or

```
rent.frameID.location = "new URL";   (IE only)
```

It is important to remember that data on windows or frames may not be totally loaded by the time the parent window or frame tries to access it. To prevent premature access of data—and embarrassing JavaScript errors—you can take one of two actions. One action is to create a flag variable in the child window or frame that indicates the readiness of the data contained within. Here is a partial example to illustrate:

```
<html>
  <head>
    <script language="JavaScript">
    <!--
      var loaded = false;
    // -->
    </script>
  </head>

  <body onLoad="JavaScript: loaded = true;">
  ...
  </body>
</html>
```

Checking the variable `loaded` in the above example will indicate whether the data on the child window has fully loaded.

The second way to guarantee that the child has finished loading is with the use of a callback function. Here is another simple example to demonstrate:

```html
<html>
  <head>
  </head>

  <body onLoad="JavaScript: opener.childLoaded();">
  ...
  </body>
</html>
```

This example will call the function `childLoaded()` on the window that opened it as soon as all the data on the child window has finished loading.

Summary

Before JavaScript was introduced, a Web page was limited in its ability to create and communicate to other windows. With the introduction of JavaScript, Web pages had access to built-in functions that would allow a programmer to create, modify and communicate to other windows. This ability allowed the programmer to show a visitor more data, aid a visitor in filling out forms, and to create more efficient Web pages.

Chapter 10

As anyone in the technology field knows, much difference exists between products made by different companies—even when the products are supposed to perform the same function. A perfect example of this phenomenon is the differences between Internet Explorer and Netscape. A page written and tested for Internet Explorer may look nothing like it should in Netscape and vice versa. Only a small range of features is implemented identically by both of these browsers. But that's not the only problem you have to deal with when designing a Web page. Not only are the browsers themselves fundamentally different, but they also have several different versions, which each behave in a different manner. If you add in the fact that the underlying operating system can have one of several resolutions and color depths that affect the way a Web page is displayed, you may be tempted to give up the idea of ever creating a professional-looking and effective Web site. But don't give up yet—this chapter will show you how to avoid the pitfalls and traps that occur along the path of creating a multi-browser, multi-platform Web page.

Hiding Scripts from Older Browsers

Hiding the JavaScript from browsers that do not support it is one of the most fundamental steps in creating a JavaScript-enabled Web page that can run under all conditions. Netscape Version 1 and Internet Explorer Versions 1 and 2 do not support JavaScript-enabled Web pages, and they'll behave strangely when they encounter your JavaScript. To prevent this strange behavior, you can enclose your scripts in HTML comment tags. This technique has been used throughout this book and takes the following form:

```
<script language="JavaScript">
<!--
  <JavaScript statements>
// -->
</script>
```

Enclosing your scripts in HTML comment tags will prevent the non-JavaScript-enabled browsers from trying to interpret the JavaScript statements as HTML. The closing HTML comment line follows a JavaScript style comment so that the JavaScript interpreter will not try to interpret the comment as a statement.

The HTML <NOSCRIPT> tag is also useful in the event that the user's browser does not support your scripts. Inside the <NOSCRIPT> tag you can place a suitable HTML message that will only be displayed if the browser does not support the script or if the user has disabled the browser's script functionality.

Following is an example of using the <NOSCRIPT> tag:

```
<html>

  <head>
    <title>
      JavaScript Professional Projects - Hiding Scripts from
                                            Older Browsers
    </title>
  </head>

  <body>

    <center>
      <font size=6>JavaScript Professional Projects</font><br>
      <font size=4>Chapter 10: Hiding Scripts from
                                Older Browsers</font>
```

```
</center>

<br><br>
<br><br>

<script language="JavaScript">
<!--
   document.write( "Congratulations, your browser" +
                        "supports JavaScript!" );
// -->
</script>
<noscript>
   I'm sorry, your browser does not support my scripts.<br>
   Please download a newer browser or
   enable scripts for your browser.
</noscript>

</body>

</html>
```

The <NOSCRIPT> tags do not need to follow the <SCRIPT> tags—they can be placed anywhere within the body of the page. It is a good idea to always use <NOSCRIPT> tags when you are writing JavaScript-enabled pages, so that the user will be aware of any problems that might occur with his or her browser.

Creating a Multi-Browser Compatible Web Page

It is important to understand the differences between different browsers in order to handle each in the way it expects. First of all, though, you need to know which browser your Web page is running in. To get information about the browser your Web page is currently running in, use the built-in navigator object.

Navigator Properties

There are several Navigator-only properties that you can use in your Web page. The following is a list of the names and descriptions of each:

- ◆ **appCodeName.** This property is a string that contains the code name of the browser, "Netscape" for Netscape and "Microsoft Internet Explorer" for Internet Explorer.

- ◆ `appVersion`. This property is a string that contains the version of the browser as well as other useful information such as its language and compatibility.
- ◆ `language`. This property contains the two-letter abbreviation for the language that is used by the browser. Netscape only.
- ◆ `mimTypes[]`. This property is an array that contains all MIME types supported by the client. Netscape only.
- ◆ `platform[]`. This property is a string that contains the platform for which the browser was compiled—`"Win32"` for 32-bit Windows operating systems.
- ◆ `plugins[]`. This property is an array containing all the plug-ins that have been installed on the client. Netscape only.
- ◆ `userAgent[]`. This property is a string that contains the code name and version of the browser. This value is sent to the originating server to identify the client.

Navigator Methods

In addition to Navigator-specific properties, there are several Navigator-specific methods. Here is a list of their names and descriptions:

- ◆ `javaEnabled()`. This method determines if JavaScript is enabled in the client. If JavaScript is enabled, this method returns `true`; otherwise, it returns `false`.
- ◆ `plugings.refresh`. This method makes newly installed plug-ins available and populates the `plugins` array with all new plug-in names. Netscape only.
- ◆ `preference(name,value)`. This method allows a signed script to get and set some Netscape preferences. If the second parameter is omitted, this method will return the value of the specified preference; otherwise, it sets the value. Netscape only.
- ◆ `taintEnabled()`. This method returns `true` if data tainting is enabled and `false` otherwise.

Handling Differences in Event Models among Browsers

When an event is fired in a Netscape browser, the event travels through each of the objects in the object hierarchy—`window`, `document`, `layer`—before it reaches the element that was the target of the event. Without any instructions to the contrary, these objects simply pass the event down the hierarchy. If you wish to capture the events at the `window`, `document`, or `layer` objects, you must use the `captureEvent()` method.

You can specify several event types to be captured with one call to the `captureEvent()` method by using the bitwise operator or (¦). For example, if you wanted to capture several of the mouse events, you could use the following call to the `captureEvent()` method:

```
captureEvent( Event.MOUSEDOWN ¦ Event.MOUSEUP ¦ Event.CLICK ¦
              Event.MOUSEOVER ¦ Event.MOUSEOUT );
```

After specifying which event to capture, you still need to write handler functions for each event. You tell the object which handler function goes with which event by setting the object's event handler properties:

```
document.mouseover = imageRollOver;
document.mouseout = imageRollBack;
```

When an event handler function is called, it is automatically passed the event object as a parameter. The function can then query information about the event, such as where the mouse was at the time, what modifier keys were used, and what the intended target for the event was.

```
function imageRollOver( event )
{
    <statements>
}


function imageRollBack( event )
{
    <statements>
}
```

Some events may not have information in each property. To make sure the event handlers for window, document, and layer work immediately when the page loads, it would be a good idea to put the code to capture them in the onLoad event handler for the object:

```
document.onload = loading;


function loading( event )
{
    document.onclick = clicked;
    document.ondblclick = dblClicked;
}


function clicked( event )
{
    <statements>
}


function dblClicked( event )
{
    <statements>
}
```

This will ensure that the event handlers are set up before any events of that type can occur.

It is often necessary, after capturing an event, to send the event to a different object for handling. There are two separate ways to do this. The routeEvent() method of the window and document objects allow an event to be transferred to its intended target. The routeEvent() method requires that the event object be passed to the event-handler function as a parameter. The second way to pass an event to a different object is by the object's handleEvent() method. Every object that has event-handler capabilities has the handleEvent() method. The handleEvent() method takes one parameter, the event object passed to the event-handler function.

Some time during the execution of the code on your page, it may be necessary to release events that were previously being captured. All top-level objects in the Navigator hierarchy have the releaseEvents()method, which will turn off event-capturing for that object. Just like the captureEvents() method, the releaseEvents() method requires one parameter that will specify which event or events are to be released.

Internet Explorer handles events in the opposite way that Netscape does. Events in Internet Explorer bubble up from the root element (the target of the event) through the element hierarchy. The element hierarchy is different from Netscape's object hierarchy in that it is comprised of HTML elements rather than JavaScript objects. For example, in the following simple HTML document:

```
<HTML>
  <BODY>
    <FORM>
      <INPUT TYPE="text">
    </FORM>
  </BODY>
</HTML>
```

any events that are generated for the text field, such as the user typing into it or clicking on it, are passed up the element hierarchy if not captured at the text field itself. The event could go through the INPUT element, and if there is no suitable event handler, the event will propagate up through the FORM and BODY elements, each of which will get a change to capture it.

Event bubbling is automatic in Internet Explorer and, for the most part, you will not need to worry about it. Sometimes it is necessary to turn this feature off. For example, if you are using an onClick event handler on the document object of your Web page and at the same time capturing onClick events of specific buttons in a form, you would not want the onClick events caused by the buttons that don't have an event handler to propagate to the document object. If you find that you need to turn off this feature, you can do so with the following command:

```
window.event.cancelBubble = true;
```

This statement can be used to cancel any given event anywhere in the element hierarchy. Only one event can bubble through the hierarchy at a time, so this command can be used on a per-event basis.

Here is a partial example of using bubbling and non-bubbling events together:

```
var isNav = navigator.appName == "Netscape";
function onLoad()
{
  if( isNav )
  {
    captureEvent( Event.MOUSEDOWN | Event.MOUSEUP );
  }
  document.onmousedown = mouseDown();
  document.onmouseup   = mouseUp();
}


function mouseDown()
{
  if( isNav )
  {
    captureEvent( Event.MOUSEMOVE );
  }
  document.mousemove = mouseMove();
}


function mouseMove()
{
  ...
}


function mouseUp()
{
  if( isNav )
  {
    releaseEvent( Event.MOUSEMOVE );
  }
  document.mousemove = null;
}
```

As you can see, it is not that difficult to handle both types of event propagation.

Handling Screen Resolution Issues

Browser differences are only half the problem you'll encounter when attempting to create a universally viewable Web page. The conditions in which the browser is running, operating system and screen resolution to name a couple, also create problems. Luckily, there is a built-in JavaScript object, Screen, which will help you with this. The Screen object contains information on the display screen's size and color depth.

Screen Properties

There are several properties that are built into the Screen object in order for you to more effectively use it. Here is a complete list of their names and descriptions of each:

◆ `availHeight`. This property returns the height of the screen in pixels. The height of any components of the operating system's interface—such as those of the Windows Taskbar—are subtracted automatically.

◆ `availWidth`. This property returns the width of the screen in pixels. The width of any components of the operating system's interface—such as those of the Windows Taskbar—are subtracted automatically.

◆ `colorDepth`. This property represents the color depth of a color table, if one is in use. If no color table is being used, this property is the `Screen.pixelDepth` property.

◆ `height`. This property returns the height of the screen in pixels.

◆ `pixelDepth`. This property returns the color resolution of the display screen in bits per pixel.

◆ `width`. This property returns the width of the screen in pixels.

Even though the Screen object is available to return information about the client's screen, it is not a good idea to give the user a message informing him that he's not viewing your Web page under ideal conditions. It's your responsibility as the programmer to make your Web pages work with as many screen variations as possible.

Working with Different Screen Settings

How to get all of your content on the page and how your images will look when they are displayed are two of the most important issues you'll encounter when dealing with different screen settings.

Getting all of your content onto a page is relatively easy because HTML has built-in features that can be used to create content that fits on any resolution. The best way to make sure that all of a page's content fits in any screen resolution is to enclose the entire content in a table (which may or not have a border) and set its `width` property to 600 pixels.

```
<html>

    <head>
```

```
  <title>
    JavaScript Professional Projects - Containing Content
  </title>
</head>

<body>

  <table width="600"><tr><td>
    <center>
      <font size=6>JavaScript Professional Projects</font><br>
      <font size=4>Chapter 10: Containing Content</font>
    </center>

    <br><br>
    <br><br>

    <code>
      If you place all your page's content into a table that has a
      defined width of 600 pixels, it will all fit into a browser
      that is being used under any screen resolution <b>and</b> it
      will look exactly the same under any of the many screen
      resolutions.
    </code>

  </td></tr></table>
  </body>

</html>
```

Because the smallest standard screen resolution is 640×480 pixels, your Web page will fit into any browser running under any of the many screen resolutions. Not only will all your content fit on the page, but it will also look exactly the same under any condition. The only adverse side effect of using this technique occurs when the user is viewing your Web page in a browser window that is not maximized. If this is the case, some of the content of your page will be hidden, and the user will have to use the scroll bar to view it. Fortunately, with your knowledge of the window and screen objects, this side effect can easily be avoided. Here's how:

```
<html>

  <head>
```

```
<title>
  JavaScript Professional Projects - Resizing Small Windows
</title>

<script language="JavaScript">
<!--
  function onLoad()
  {
    self.moveTo( 0, 0 );
    self.resizeTo( screen.availWidth, screen.availHeight );
  }
// -->
</script>

</head>

<body onLoad="JavaScript: onLoad();">

  <table width="600"><tr><td>
    <center>
      <font size=6>JavaScript Professional Projects</font><br>
      <font size=4>Chapter 10: Resizing Small Windows </font>
    </center>

    <br><br>
    <br><br>

    <code>
      If you place all your page's content into a table that has a
      defined width of 600 pixels, it will all fit into a browser
      that is being used under any screen resolution <b>and</b> it
      will look exactly the same under any of the many screen
      resolutions.
    </code>

  </td></tr></table>
  </body>

</html>
```

This example resizes the window as soon as it loads to make sure it is big enough to hold all of the horizontal content without scroll bars. As most users will become annoyed by having their windows resized unnecessarily, it's a good idea to put a check in the onLoad() function above, so that the window will only resize if it is necessary in order to show all of the content:

```
function onLoad()
{
  if( self.innerWidth < 600 )
  {
    self.moveTo( 0, 0 );
    self.resizeTo( screen.availWidth, screen.availHeight );
  }
}
```

As a last resort, you can always display a message for the user if he is using a screen resolution that you feel your content or images just cannot accommodate. Here is a modified onLoad() function again that does just that:

```
function onLoad()
{
  if( self.innerWidth < 600 )
  {
    self.moveTo( 0, 0 );
    self.resizeTo( screen.availWidth, screen.availHeight );
  }

  if( self.innerWidth < 600 )
  {
    alert( "This Web page was designed to be viewed using a" +
           " screen resolution of 640x480 or larger." );
  }
}
```

This function attempts to resize the window, but if it's still not large enough, a message is displayed explaining the problem.

Another important thing to remember when writing a Web page for different screen resolutions is that images will appear larger on smaller resolutions. Fortunately, the width and height properties of the HTML <IMG> tag allow you to dynamically set the size of the image. Here is a typical image tag that dynamically sizes the image to the screen:

```
<img src="image.jpg"
    width="JavaScript: getWidth( 150 )"
    height="JavaScript: getHeight( 200 )">
```

That statement, in combination with the following two functions:

```
function getWidth( width )
{
  return( width * screen.width / 1024 );
}


function getHeight( height )
{
  return( height * screen.height / 768 );
}
```

will dynamically resize the image so that it will look the same on any screen resolution. These two functions—getWidth() and getHeight()—assume that the image was designed for screen resolution 1024×768, but you can change that by changing the resolution width and height in the return statements.

Handling Screen Color Depth Issues

Just as with screen resolutions, there are several different color depths with which your Web page might be viewed. Color resolution is simply the number of colors that can be used to display your page's content. Table 10.1 lists some common color depths.

Table 10.1 Common Color Depths

Bit Depth	Color Depth Name	Number of Colors
1 bit	Black-and-White	2 colors
4 bit	Grayscale	16 colors
8 bit	256 Colors	256 colors
16 bit	High Color	65,536 colors
24 bit	True Color	16,777,216 colors
32 bit	True Color	16,777,216 colors

Luckily, only bit depths of 8-bit or higher are commonly used. This simplifies the problem of creating a universal Web page from six color combinations to only four. The differences between bit depths are drastic. A Web page created and designed under 32-bit conditions may look absolutely terrible under 8-bit conditions. A Web page designed under 8-bit conditions, however, will look exactly the same under 32-bit conditions. The only drawback to designing all of your Web pages for 8-bit platforms is that you'll be missing out on a lot of very wonderful color combinations.

So how do you design a Web page that uses all available colors, but still looks good when viewed with low bit depths? By using the same technique used above with dynamically resizing images, that's how. This time around though, you're not changing the size of the image that's loaded; instead, you're changing the actual image that is loaded. Once again, here is a sample HTML <IMG> tag that uses this technique:

```
<img src="JavaScript: getImage( 'image' );">
```

That statement, in combination with the following function:

```
function getImage( image )
{
  return( image + screen.colorDepth + ".jpg" );
}
```

will load an image in the form: image8.jpg or image32.jpg. The image name is followed by the bit depth and the file extension. Using this form will ensure that only an image created for a certain bit depth is displayed.

When you're dealing with HTML element colors, there is no easy shortcut that will work for all color depths. There are, however, 16 colors that work on screens with any color depth. Table 10.2 lists them and their hexadecimal values.

Table 10.2 Color Constants

Color Name	Hexadecimal Value
Aqua	#00FFFF
Black	#000000
Blue	#0000FF
Fuchsia	#FF00FF
Gray	#808080
Green	#008000
Lime	#00FF00

(continues)

Table 10.2 Color Constants *(continued)*

Color Name	Hexadecimal Value
Maroon	#800000
Navy	#000080
Olive	#808000
Purple	#800080
Red	#FF0000
Silver	#C0C0C0
Teal	#008080
White	#FFFFFF
Yellow	#FFFF00

These values are case-insensitive and can be used instead of their hexadecimal literals like this:

```
<body bgColor="Fuchsia">
```

Using these color constants ensures that your Web page will look the same no matter what conditions it is being viewed under.

Summary

The conditions under which your Web page will be run are many and varied. As the programmer, you are required to allow for as many as you can in order to get your message to as many people as you can. Three main differences you will encounter in the Web page running environment are: different browsers, varying screen resolutions, and the many bit depths. Fortunately, there are very simple techniques to overcome each of these obstacles.

Chapter 11

With many natively compiled programs, you have the ability to read, write, and change files on the computers on which the programs run. Natively compiled programs have nearly unlimited access to any file anywhere on your hard drive. This is generally not a problem because these types of programs are usually written by professionals in well-known software companies whose reputations are on the line. But that's not the case with Web pages. Anybody who has Internet access and a simple text editor has the ability to create potentially dangerous or destructive programs. An unsuspecting Web surfer could visit such a site designed by a malicious person and end up with all of the information on his or her hard drive completely corrupted. Or worse yet, the person who created the site could steal sensitive information from the visitor and use it against him.

For this reason, most programming languages that are used on Web pages, JavaScript included, do not allow you to use files that are stored on a client's machine. The browser that a Web page visitor uses will also have strict rules built into it that prevent the nightmare situations mentioned above. There is one way, however, to store on a client's computer semi-permanent data that can be accessed pragmatically, and that is by using cookies.

JavaScript and Cookies

A *cookie*, in its simplest form, is a text file. Cookies can be used to identify a user, store personal information about a Web site visitor, or modify the way a Web page looks and feels based on a user's preference. This information can be used on subsequent visits to your Web page to greet the visitor in his own language, fill out long forms automatically, or resume his visit where he left off the previous time. Cookies are also very easy to store and read compared to other types of files. Unlike other types of files, a cookie file has a size limit of 4 kilobytes or 4096 characters.

Because reading and writing files with Web pages can be such a dangerous operation, the browser takes care of all of the low-level I/O required to read and write to the cookie file. The benefits of this are twofold. First of all, the common Web surfer will not need to fear malicious code that could damage his or her computer. Secondly, the programmer does not have to worry about the complexities of creating file streams—reading and writing data and then remembering to close the file stream when I/O is complete. To write a string to the cookie file, all you need to do is assign a value to the `document.cookie` parameter. The browser will do the rest.

Here is an example of writing a value to the cookie file taken from a form field:

```html
<html>
  <head>
    <title>
      JavaScript Professional Projects - Writing Cookies
    </title>

    <script language="JavaScript">
    <!--
      var now = new Date();
      now.setMonth( now.getMonth() + 1 );
      document.cookie = "expires=" + now.toGMTString();
    -->
    </script>

  </head>

  <body>

    <center>
      <font size=6>JavaScript Professional Projects</font><br>
      <font size=4>Chapter 11: Writing Cookies</font>
    </center>


    <br><br>
```

```
    <br><br>

    <form onSubmit="JavaScript: document.cookie = this.Name.value;">
      Please tell me your name:
      <input type="text" name="Name" size="20">
      <input type="submit" value=" Ok "></p>
    </form>


  </body>
</html>
```

This example sets the cookie parameter of the document object equal to the value in the text box. The value assigned to this parameter can be of any form. When you want to store more than one item in the cookie file, it is a good idea to use a delimiter, such as a comma or semi-colon, so that each item can be accessed via the String object's `split()` method. Here is an example of doing just that:

```
<html>
  <head>
    <title>
      JavaScript Professional Projects - Writing Cookies
    </title>

    <script language="JavaScript">
    <!--
      var now = new Date();
      now.setMonth( now.getMonth() + 1 );
      document.cookie = "expires=" + now.toGMTString();

      function getFormData( form )
      {
        var answer = "";
        answer += form.Name.value + ",";
        answer += form.Age.value + ",";
        answer += form.Color.value;
        return( answer );
      }
    // -->
    </script>
  </head>
```

```
<body>

  <center>
    <font size=6>JavaScript Professional Projects</font><br>
    <font size=4>Chapter 11: Writing Cookies</font>
  </center>

  <br><br>
  <br><br>

  <form onSubmit="JavaScript: document.cookie = getFormData( this );">
    Please tell me your name:
    <input type="text" name="Name" size="20"><br>
    How old are you:
    <input type="text" name="Age" size="10"><br>
    What is your favorite color:
    <input type="text" name="Color" size="10"><br>
    <input type="submit" value=" Ok "></p>
  </form>

  </body>
</html>
```

This example takes the values from each form field and stores them in the cookie file. A comma separates each field value so that they can be easily split up next time the page loads.

It is often a good idea to store the value's name along with the value itself. This will be useful if the number and order of values is not known before the page loads. For example, the previous example could be rewritten as follows:

```
<html>
  <head>
    <title>
      JavaScript Professional Projects - Writing Cookies
    </title>

    <script language="JavaScript">
    <!--
      var now = new Date();
      now.setMonth( now.getMonth() + 1 );
      document.cookie = "expires=" + now.toGMTString();
```

```
      function getFormData( form )
      {
        for( i = 0 ; i < form.elements.length ; i++ )
        {
          with( form.elements[i] )
          {
            if( type != "submit" && type != "button" )
              document.cookie = name + "=" + value;
          }
        }
      }
    // -->
    </script>
  </head>

<body>

  <center>
    <font size=6>JavaScript Professional Projects</font><br>
    <font size=4>Chapter 11: Writing Cookies</font>
  </center>

  <br><br>
  <br><br>

  <form onSubmit="JavaScript: getFormData( this );">
    Please tell me your name:
    <input type="text" name="Name" size="20"><br>
    How old are you:
    <input type="text" name="Age" size="10"><br>
    What is your favorite color:
    <input type="text" name="Color" size="10"><br>
    <input type="submit" value=" Ok "></p>
  </form>

  </body>
</html>
```

This example saves all information contained in the form in a name = value pair. With this approach, it would be easy for your Web page to fill in the form automatically the next time the visitor visited or to get just one value out of the cookie file without searching the entire thing.

Reading Cookies

Because the document.cookie parameter is essentially a string object, the reading of cookies is very simple. Again, all of the low-level I/O operations required to read the cookie file are taken care of by the browser. The only task left to the programmer is parsing the cookie values. If there is only one value in the cookie file, as with the first example in the previous section, it is relatively easy to retrieve it:

```html
<html>
  <head>
    <title>
      JavaScript Professional Projects - Reading Cookies
    </title>

    <script language="JavaScript">
    <!--
      var now = new Date();
      now.setMonth( now.getMonth() + 1 );
      document.cookie = "expires=" + now.toGMTString();

      function getName()
      {
        if( document.cookie != "" )
        {
          document.write( "<font size='5'>Welcome back " +
                        document.cookie + "!</font>" );
        }
      }
    // -->
    </script>
  </head>

<body>

  <center>
    <font size=6>JavaScript Professional Projects</font><br>
```

```
    <font size=4>Chapter 11: Reading Cookies</font>
  </center>

  <br><br>
  <br><br>

  <script language="JavaScript">
  <!--
    getName();
  // -->
  </script>

  <form onSubmit="JavaScript: document.cookie = this.Name.value;">
    Please tell me your name:
    <input type="text" name="Name" size="20">
    <input type="submit" value=" Ok "></p>
  </form>

</body>
</html>
```

This example will display a welcome message if the visitor has entered his name previously; otherwise, the page displays as usual. This example is useful only if you are storing a single value in the cookie file. Unfortunately, a single value is not always enough for a good Web site.

Another way to store values in a cookie file is to separate each value by a comma. This makes retrieving data from the file very simple. The following example shows how it is done:

```
<head>
  <title>
    JavaScript Professional Projects - Reading Cookies
  </title>

  <script language="JavaScript">
  <!--
    var now = new Date();
    now.setMonth( now.getMonth() + 1 );
    document.cookie = "expires=" + now.toGMTString();

    function getFormData( form )
```

```
  {
    var answer = "";
    answer += form.Name.value + ",";
    answer += form.Age.value + ",";
    answer += form.Color.value;
    return( answer );
  }

  function getCookieValue( index )
  {
    var value = document.cookie.split( "," )[index];
    return( value == undefined ? "" : value );
  }
  // -->
  </script>
</head>

<body>

  <center>
    <font size=6>JavaScript Professional Projects</font><br>
    <font size=4>Chapter 11: Reading Cookies</font>
  </center>

  <br><br>
  <br><br>

  <form name="theForm"
        onSubmit="JavaScript: document.cookie = getFormData( this );">
    Please tell me your name:
    <input type="text" name="Name" size="20"><br>
    How old are you:
    <input type="text" name="Age" size="10"><br>
    What is your favorite color:
    <input type="text" name="Color" size="10"><br>
    <input type="submit" value=" Ok "><p></p>
  </form>
```

```
<script language="JavaScript">
<!--
  document.theForm.Name.value = getCookieValue( 0 );
  document.theForm.Age.value = getCookieValue( 1 );
  document.theForm.Color.value = getCookieValue( 2 );
-->
</script>


  </body>
</html>
```

This example demonstrates how to split the cookie string into its respective parts. Using the String class's `split()` method, the previously stored values can be broken down into an array, which you can then use in any way you see fit. The example above uses the array for a very short amount of time before discarding it. This reduces the amount of code required—and therefore the download time—but makes the program run slower once downloaded.

The only drawback to this approach is that each value in the cookie file must be read back in the same order that it was entered. If you are working with a team to create a page, this can become a hassle. There is, however, one last way to store values in the cookie file that will let you store and retrieve them in any order, and that is by storing the information you need in a name=value pair. So, instead of storing data in a comma-separated list, the previous example could have stored the form data like this:

```
function getFormData( form )
{
  document.cookie = "Name=" + form.Name.value;
  document.cookie = "Age=" + form.Age.value;
  document.cookie = "Color=" + form.Color.value;
}
```

As you might have guessed, this creates extra complexity while reading the data back from the cookie file. The previous page could be rewritten using this technique as follows:

```
  <head>
<title>
  JavaScript Professional Projects · Reading Cookies
</title>

<script language="JavaScript">
<!--
  var now = new Date();
```

```
      now.setMonth( now.getMonth() + 1 );
      document.cookie = "expires=" + now.toGMTString();

      function getFormData( form )
      {
        document.cookie = "Name=" + form.Name.value;
        document.cookie = "Age=" + form.Age.value;
        document.cookie = "Color=" + form.Color.value;
      }

      function getCookieValue( name )
      {
        var c = document.cookie;
        var begin = c.indexOf( name );
        if( begin < 0 ) return( "" );
        begin += name.length + 1;
        var end = c.indexOf( ";", begin );
        if( end == -1 ) end = c.length;
        return( c.slice( begin, end ) );
      }
    // -->
    </script>
</head>

<body>

  <center>
    <font size=6>JavaScript Professional Projects</font><br>
    <font size=4>Chapter 11: Reading Cookies</font>
  </center>

  <br><br>
  <br><br>

  <form name="theForm"
      onSubmit="JavaScript: document.cookie = getFormData( this );">
    Please tell me your name:
    <input type="text" name="Name" size="20"><br>
```

```
    How old are you:
    <input type="text" name="Age" size="10"><br>
    What is your favorite color:
    <input type="text" name="Color" size="10"><br>
    <input type="submit" value=" Ok "><p></p>
  </form>

  <script language="JavaScript">
  <!--
    document.theForm.Name.value = getCookieValue( "Name" );
    document.theForm.Age.value = getCookieValue( "Age" );
    document.theForm.Color.value = getCookieValue( "Color" );
  -->
  </script>


  </body>
</html>
```

This technique allows you to write and read cookie values in any order and without having to parse the entire cookie file. It is usually more work than it's worth if you only need to remember one or two pieces of information, but it makes things much easier if you need to save a lot of data, such as the entire contents of a form.

One example of where saving form data in a cookie file would be beneficial to your visitor would be when entering shipping or billing information. This process can be long and repetitive for the visitor, but can be significantly shortened if the Web page remembers his or her information from page to page. The following example, which is of a form that actually remembers the visitor's address from the last time it was entered and automatically fills out the form, is adapted from an example presented in Chapter 8 on Forms:

```
<html>
  <head>
    <title>
      JavaScript Professional Projects - Reading Cookies
    </title>

    <script language="JavaScript">
    <!--
      var now = new Date();
      now.setMonth( now.getMonth() + 1 );
      document.cookie = "expires=" + now.toGMTString();
```

```
function saveForm( form )
{
  for( i = 0 ; i < form.elements.length ; i++ )
  {
    with( form.elements[i] )
    {
      if( type != "submit" && type != "button" && type != "reset" )
        document.cookie = name + "=" + value;
    }
  }
}

function loadForm( form )
{
  for( i = 0 ; i < form.elements.length ; i++ )
  {
    with( form.elements[i] )
    {
      if( type != "submit" && type != "button" && type != "reset" )
        value = getCookieValue( name );
    }
  }
}

function getCookieValue( index )
{
  var c = document.cookie;
  var begin = c.indexOf( index + "=" ) + index.length + 1;
  var end = c.indexOf( ";", begin );
  if( end == -1 ) end = c.length;
  return( c.slice( begin, end ) );
}
-->
</script>

</head>
```

```html
<body onLoad="JavaScript: loadForm( document.mailingForm );">

  <center>
    <font size=6>JavaScript Professional Projects</font><br>
    <font size=4>Chapter 11: Reading Cookies</font>
  </center>

  <br><br>
  <br><br>

  <table cellspacing="4" cellpadding="4" width="65%">
    <tr>
      <td>

        <form name="mailingForm" onSubmit="JavaScript: saveForm( this );">
          <b><font size="5">Mailing Address<br></font></b>
          <br>
          <b>Last name, First name:</b><br>
          <input type="text" name="firstLine" size="36"><br>
          <b>Street/Address:</b><br>
          <input type="text" name="secondLine" size="36"><br>
          <b>City State, Zip code:</b><br>
          <input type="text" name="thirdLine" size="36">  
          <input type="submit" value="Submit">
        </form>

      </td>
    </tr>
  </table>

  </body>
</html>
```

Because commas may be part of the data in this example, the plus symbol (+) was used as a delimiter between name=value pairs. This simple application makes a visitor's visit much more enjoyable, which in turn makes them want to use your site again.

Using Cookies

There are many uses for the cookie file beyond automatically filling out forms for a visitor. Some of its uses include visit counters, remembering user-specific details such as color scheme and language preferences, customization of your Web site, and much more. All this data and more can be stored in a single cookie file in such a way that it can be easily accessed, updated, and applied at a later date. The proper use of the cookie file will make the visitors to your Web site feel welcome and at home. If you greet them with a customized start page containing their name and a list of their commonly used links, they will be more willing to return the next time.

One very popular way to use the cookie file is to count the number of times a specific person has visited your site. Although this example is not useful in terms of Web design, it does illustrate how to alter a preexisting value in a cookie file:

```html
<html>
  <head>
    <title>
      JavaScript Professional Projects - Using Cookies
    </title>

    <script language="JavaScript">
    <!--
      var now = new Date();
      now.setMonth( now.getMonth() + 1 );
      document.cookie = "expires=" + now.getGMTString();

      function getCookieValue( name )
      {
        var c = document.cookie;
        var begin = c.indexOf( name );
        if( begin < 0 ) return( "" );
        begin += name.length + 1;
        var end = c.indexOf( ";", begin );
        if( end == -1 ) end = c.length;
        return( c.slice( begin, end ) );
      }

      function updateVisitCount()
      {
        var count = getCookieValue( "visits" );
        if( count == "" )
```

```
      {
        document.cookie = "visits=" + 1;
      }
      else
      {
        document.cookie = "visits=" + (parseInt(count)+1);
      }
    }
  -->
  </script>

</head>

<body onLoad="JavaScript: updateVisitCount();">

  <center>
    <font size=6>JavaScript Professional Projects</font><br>
    <font size=4>Chapter 11: Using Cookies</font>
  </center>

  <br><br>
  <br><br>

  Welcome, you have visited this site
  <script language="JavaScript">
  <!--
    var count = getCookieValue( "visits" );
    document.write( count == "" ? "0" : count );
  -->
  </script>
  times!

  </body>
</html>
```

As you can see, all that you need to do to change a value in a cookie file is to assign the name=value pair to the cookie file a second time.

One important variable in the cookie file that must be replaced very often is the `expires` variable. This cookie variable holds the date on which the client computer should delete the cookie file. The `expires` value should be in the format that is returned by the Date class's `getGMTString()` method. You may have noticed the following three lines:

```
var now = new Date();
now.setMonth( now.getMonth() + 1 );
document.cookie = "expires=" + now.getGMTString();
```

in the examples in this chapter. They tell the client computer to delete the cookie file one month after the current date. Every time a person visits a site with that code, the `expires` variable will be updated. When a client has not visited the site in a month, the cookie file for that site is deleted. If the `expires` value is set to a date before the current browser date, or is left out altogether, the cookie file will be deleted as soon as the visitor closes his browser window.

Two other generic cookie variables help to hide the data from other Web sites. The `path` variable, if set, will limit access to the cookie file to only the pages within the given path on the Web server. Similarly, the `domain` variable, if set, will restrict the cookie file's access to only the pages in the given domain.

Allowing a user to customize your Web site's color scheme is another popular use for the cookie file. For instance, a user might not like the various colors used on your Web page for one reason or another and may want to change it.

Here is a simple example of how to customize your site for your visitor's color preferences (among other things!):

```html
<html>
  <head>
    <title>
      JavaScript Professional Projects - Using Cookies
    </title>

    <script language="JavaScript">
    <!--
      var now = new Date();
      now.setMonth( now.getMonth() + 1 );
      document.cookie = "expires=" + now.toGMTString();

      function saveForm( form )
      {
        for( i = 0 ; i < form.elements.length ; i++ )
        {
          if( form.elements[i].value != "" && form.elements[i].name != "" )
```

```
        {
            document.cookie = form.name + "." + form.elements[i].name + "=" +
                form.elements[i].value;
        }
    }
}


function loadForm( form )
{
    for( i = 0 ; i < form.elements.length ; i++ )
    {
        if( form.elements[i].name != "" )
        {
            form.elements[i].value =
                getCookieValue( form.name + "." + form.elements[i].name );
        }
    }
}


function getCookieValue( name )
{
    var c = document.cookie;
    var begin = c.indexOf( name );
    if( begin < 0 ) return( "" );
    begin += name.length + 1;
    var end = c.indexOf( ";", begin );
    if( end == -1 ) end = c.length;
    return( c.slice( begin, end ) );
}


function updateVisitCount()
{
    var count = getCookieValue( "visits" );
    if( count == "" )
    {
        document.cookie = "visits=" + 1;
    }
    else
```

```
        {
          document.cookie = "visits=" + (parseInt(count)+1);
        }
    }

    function setCustoms()
    {
      var bg = getCookieValue( "custom.bgColor" );
      var fg = getCookieValue( "custom.fgColor" );
      if( bg != "" ) document.bgColor = bg;
      if( fg != "" ) document.fgColor = fg;
    }
  // -->
  </script>
</head>

<body onLoad="JavaScript: loadForm( document.mailingForm );
                         loadForm( document.custom );
                         updateVisitCount();
                         setCustoms();">

  <center>
    <font size=6>JavaScript Professional Projects</font><br>
    <font size=4>Chapter 11: Using Cookies</font>
  </center>

  <br><br>
  <br><br>

  Welcome, you have visited this site
  <script language="JavaScript">
  <!--
    var count = getCookieValue( "visits" );
    document.write( count == "" ? "0" : count );
  -->
  </script>
  times!<br><br>
```

```html
<table cellspacing="4" cellpadding="4" width="85%">
  <tr>
    <td>

      <form name="mailingForm" onSubmit="JavaScript: saveForm( this );">
        <b><font size="5">Mailing Address<br></font></b>
        <br>
        <b>Last name, First name:</b><br>
        <input type="text" name="firstLine" size="36"><br>
        <b>Street/Address:</b><br>
        <input type="text" name="secondLine" size="36"><br>
        <b>City State, Zip code:</b><br>
        <input type="text" name="thirdLine" size="36">  
        <input type="submit" value="Submit">
      </form>

    </td>
    <td>

      <form name="custom" onSubmit="JavaScript: saveForm( this );">
        <table>
          <tr>
            <td><b><font size="5">Customize<br>
            <br></font></b></td>
          <tr>
            <td><b>Background Color:    </b></td>
            <td><input type="text" name="bgColor" size="15"></td>
          </tr>
          <tr>
            <td><b>Foreground Color:</b></td>
            <td><input type="text" name="fgColor" size="15"></td>
            <td>  <input type="submit" value="Submit"></td>
          </tr>
        </table>
      </form>

    </td>
  </tr>
```

```
  </table>

  </body>
</html>
```

This example uses cookies to perform three different operations. The first simply counts the number of times a person has visited the page. The second automatically fills not one, but two forms with information that has been entered by the visitor previously. The third operation the cookie file above performs is to customize the background and foreground colors on the page.

The following function stores data in the cookie file, in this case the mailing address of the visitor:

```
function setCustoms()
{
  var bg = getCookieValue( "custom.bgColor" );
  var fg = getCookieValue( "custom.fgColor" );
  if( bg != "" ) document.bgColor = bg;
  if( fg != "" ) document.fgColor = fg;
}
```

reads values from the cookie file, which had previously been saved from a form, and changes the colors of the page accordingly. You'll notice the addition of the form name followed by a period and the field name being used as the name part of the `name=value` pair. This is used to be able to distinguish elements on the separate forms apart. It was not really necessary in this example because none of the elements have the same name, but could be useful later on as you learn how to use a single cookie file for multiple Web pages.

One very useful feature of cookie files is that Web pages can share the data stored in them. For example, if a Web page stores data in the cookie file, as follows:

```
<html>
  <head>
    <title>
      JavaScript Professional Projects - Using Cookies
    </title>

    <script language="JavaScript">
    <!--
      var now = new Date();
      now.setMonth( now.getMonth() + 1 );
      document.cookie = "expires=" + now.toGMTString();

      function saveForm( form )
```

```
        {
          for( i = 0 ; i < form.elements.length ; i++ )
          {
            if( form.elements[i].value != "" && form.elements[i].name != "" )
            {
              document.cookie = form.name + "." + form.elements[i].name + "=" +
                form.elements[i].value;
            }
          }
        }

        function loadForm( form )
        {
          for( i = 0 ; i < form.elements.length ; i++ )
          {
            if( form.elements[i].name != "" )
            {
              form.elements[i].value =
                getCookieValue( form.name + "." + form.elements[i].name );
            }
          }
        }

        function getCookieValue( name )
        {
          var c = document.cookie;
          var begin = c.indexOf( name );
          if( begin < 0 ) return( "" );
          begin += name.length + 1;
          var end = c.indexOf( ";", begin );
          if( end == -1 ) end = c.length;
          return( c.slice( begin, end ) );
        }
    // -->
    </script>
</head>

<body onLoad="JavaScript: loadForm( document.mailingForm );">
```

```
<center>
  <font size=6>JavaScript Professional Projects</font><br>
  <font size=4>Chapter 11: Using Cookies</font>
</center>

<br><br>
<br><br>

<table cellspacing="4" cellpadding="4" width="85%">
  <tr>
    <td>

      <form method="POST" action="Display.html" name="mailingForm"
            onSubmit="JavaScript: saveForm( this );">
        <b><font size="5">Mailing Address<br></font></b>
        <br>
        <b>Last name, First name:</b><br>
        <input type="text" name="firstLine" size="36"><br>
        <b>Street/Address:</b><br>
        <input type="text" name="secondLine" size="36"><br>
        <b>City State, Zip code:</b><br>
        <input type="text" name="thirdLine" size="36">  
        <input type="submit" value="Submit">
      </form>

    </td>
  </tr>
</table>

  </body>
</html>
```

Then a second page, named `Display.html`, could read the data and display it:

```
<html>
  <head>
    <title>
      JavaScript Professional Projects - Using Cookies
    </title>
```

```
<script language="JavaScript">
<!--
   var now = new Date();
   now.setMonth( now.getMonth() + 1 );
   document.cookie = "expires=" + now.toGMTString();

   function getCookieValue( name )
   {
     var c = document.cookie;
     var begin = c.indexOf( name );
     if( begin < 0 ) return( "" );
     begin += name.length + 1;
     var end = c.indexOf( ";", begin );
     if( end == -1 ) end = c.length;
     return( c.slice( begin, end ) );
   }
 // -->
 </script>
</head>

<body>

  <center>
    <font size=6>JavaScript Professional Projects</font><br>
    <font size=4>Chapter 11: Using Cookies</font>
  </center>

  <br><br>
  <br><br>

  This is the mailing address you have entered.<br>
  Please check to make sure it is correct.

  <br><br>

    </div>
```

```
<table border="1" cellspacing="5" cellpadding="5"><tr><td>
  <b>
  <script language="JavaScript">
  <!--
    document.write( getCookieValue( "mailingForm.firstLine" ) + "<br>" );
    document.write( getCookieValue( "mailingForm.secondLine" ) + "<br>" );
    document.write( getCookieValue( "mailingForm.thirdLine" ) );
  // -->
  </script>
  </b>
   </td></tr></table>


</body>


</html>
```

`Display.html` can read the data and display it because nothing in the cookie file tells `Display.html` that it can't use the data therein. You can restrict access to data in the cookie file by setting the `path` and `domain` values in the cookie. These values default to the directory or domain in which the Web page resides. This makes it so that only pages in the same directory/domain or deeper can view the cookie data of the page that creates it.

Understanding Cookie Limitations

There are two fundamental limitations to the cookie file itself. First of all, it can only be 4 kilobytes or 4096 characters long. That is approximately equal to the number of characters in a full page of text (12-point serif font) including the spaces. Secondly, the semicolon (;) and equal sign (=) are reserved characters in the cookie file and should not be used in either the name or value of the `name=value` pair.

Another cookie limitation concerns the browser itself: Settings within the browser may not allow your Web page to create cookies at all. It is very simple to tell whether cookies are enabled in the client's browser—simply set a cookie and try to read it back. If you are unable to read back the value you set in the cookie file, then cookies are not enabled.

Here's an example of how to check whether cookies are enabled in the client's browser:

```
<html>
  <head>
    <title>
      JavaScript Professional Projects - Using Cookies
    </title>
```

```
<script language="JavaScript">
<!--
  function cookiesEnabled()
  {
    document.cookie = "Enabled=True";
    return( getCookieValue( "Enabled" ) == "True" );
  }

  function getCookieValue( name )
  {
    var c = document.cookie;
    var begin = c.indexOf( name );
    if( begin < 0 ) return( "" );
    begin += name.length + 1;
    var end = c.indexOf( ";", begin );
    if( end == -1 ) end = c.length;
    return( c.slice( begin, end ) );
  }
// -->
  </script>
</head>

<body>

  <center>
    <font size=6>JavaScript Professional Projects</font><br>
    <font size=4>Chapter 11: Detecting if Cookies
                        are Enabled</font></center>

  <br><br>
  <br><br>

  <script language="JavaScript">
<!--
  if( cookiesEnabled() )
  {
    document.write( "<b>Congratulations, cookies are" +
                    " enabled in your browser.</b>" );
```

```
    }
    else
    {
      document.write( "<b>Sorry, cookies are not" +
                      " enabled in your browser.</b>" );
    }
  // -->
  </script>

  </body>
</html>
```

Upon discovering that the client does not have cookies enabled, you can either redirect him to a cookie-less page or instruct him on how to enable cookies.

Summary

The use of a cookie file is simple and often very beneficial. Cookies can be stored and retrieved in many different ways. The data that you store in the cookie file can be used to remember who a visitor is, what his preferences are, and to automatically fill out lengthy forms for him. The proper use of cookies can make your Web site a comfortable and welcome place.

Chapter 12

Ensuring
JavaScript
Security

Like many common software systems, JavaScript has a history of security problems. Many of these problems could allow a person with malevolent intent to steal sensitive information from a visitor. The number and type of such holes in security vary among browsers and operating system versions. Most JavaScript security holes have been caught and fixed, but new ones are being discovered all the time. For a list of current security holes check out your browser's and operating system's Web pages. As a Web site author, it is your responsibility to keep up-to-date on the current status of known security holes in the applications you create.

Signing Scripts

In Chapter 11, I explained that JavaScript does not provide the ability to directly access files on the client computer. This can be a very large hurdle to overcome if you're trying to upload a file to a server from the client computer. Fortunately, file uploading is one of many functional enhancements that signed scripts provide. *Signed scripts* are specially packaged scripts that have been verified and signed to be correct and non-threatening. These scripts have additional rights on the client computer that allow a programmer to do many things that he wouldn't otherwise be able to.

With the introduction of Netscape 4.0, a new security model was put in place that would allow digitally signed scripts to bypass some of the restrictions that had previously been placed on them. A signed script can request expanded privileges from the visitor and, with the visitor's permission, gain access to restricted data. A signed script requests these additional permissions through LiveConnect, which allows your JavaScript code to communicate with the Java Capabilities API. The security model allows JavaScript to access certain classes in Java in order to extend its functionality while still maintaining tight security for the client.

A *digital signature* is a fingerprint of the original programmer, and it allows the security model of the browser to detect where (or from whom) it originated. A script signer can be a person or an organization. By signing a script, you acknowledge yourself as the author and accept responsibility for the program's actions. A signed script contains a cryptographic checksum, which is just a special value that ensures the signed script has not been changed. When a digital signature is detected, you are assured that the code has not been tampered with since the programmer signed it.

Once you finish writing a script, you can use the Netscape Signing Tool to digitally sign it. Signing a script does the following:

- Unambiguously assigns ownership of the script to a person or organization.
- Allows an HTML page to use multiple signed scripts.
- Places the signed script into a Java Archive (JAR) file.
- Places the source of the script in the JAR file.

Once a user confirms the origin of the script and is assured that it has not been tampered with since its signing, he or she can then decide whether to grant the privileges requested by the script based on the validated identity of the certificate owner and validated integrity of the script.

Using the Netscape Signing Tool

The latest version of the Netscape Signing Tool can be downloaded for free from http://developer.netscape.com/software/signedobj/jarpack.html. In order to use the signing tool, you first need to acquire an object-signing certificate. There are two ways to do obtain this certificate—you can use the tool itself to create one for you, or you can purchase a certificate from a third-party company that specializes in object signing such as VeriSign (www.verisign.com). A certificate created by using the tool itself is only to be used for testing purposes, according to the Netscape Web site. In order to use signed scripts in a production environment, you will need to get a certificate from either an independent certificate authority that can authenticate your identity (and will charge you a fee) or from certificate-authority server software running on your corporate intranet or extranet.

Creating a Test Object-Signing Certificate

Once you've downloaded the Netscape Signing Tool, you'll be ready to create an object-signing certificate for testing purposes. In order to create a certificate, you will need to locate the files key3.db and cert7.db in your Netscape directory. Once you have found these two files, you'll need to back them up somewhere safe, in case you accidentally damage the databases.

To generate a certificate, use the Netscape Signing Tool command, which is as follows:

```
signtool -G <certificate name> -d <path to key3.db and cert7.db>
```

The -G option lets you specify the name of the certificate you are creating. The -d must be used to specify the directory in which the key and certificate databases are located. If the databases are located in the same directory as the signing tool, you can use the option -d. An actual example of a command that would sign a script could be as follows:

```
signtool -G MyCert -d C:\Program Files\NETSCAPE\USERS\jdow\
```

This command will create a certificate named MyCert in the certificate database of user jdow on a Windows NT machine. After running the command, the program will ask you for your identification data, which will then be digitally included in the signed scripts you create with the certificate.

Signing a file

Once you have acquired an object-signing certificate, either through a third party or by using the signing tool, you are ready to start signing files.

Follow these simple steps to create a signed script:

1. Create an empty directory and put some script files into it. Files can include JavaScript files or entire HTML files.
2. Specify the name of your object-signing certificate and sign the directory. Use the following command (as one line):

   ```
   signtool -d <path to certificate database> -k <certificate name>
              -Z <jar file name> <directory with script files>
   ```

3. Type the password to your private-key database.
4. Test the archive you just created using the following command:

   ```
   signtool -v <jar file name>
   ```

You can use the Netscape Signing Tool from within a Windows script file. Here is an example script file that is provided on the Netscape Web site:

```
REM Expand the jar file into a new directory
unzip -qq myjar.jar -d signjar
del myjar.jar
rem Sign everything in the new directory and recompress
signtool -k MySignCert -Z myjar.jar signdir
```

This script unpacks a JAR file containing script files, signs them, and then repacks them into the JAR file.

The aspects of the Netscape Signing Tool covered here are only a fraction of what the Signing Tool can do. I encourage you to visit Netscape's documentation of their Signing Tool at http://developer.netscape.com/docs/manuals/cms/41/adm_gide/app_sign.htm.

Using Signed Scripts

All inline scripts, event handler scripts, or JavaScript files that are signed require a SCRIPT tag's ARCHIVE attribute whose value is the name of the JAR file that contains the digitally signed scripts.

For example, to sign an inline script, you would use the following syntax:

```
<script archive="MySignedArchive.jar" ID="a">
<!--
   ...
// -->
</script>
```

To import functionality from a JavaScript file that is signed, you would use the following syntax:

```
<script archive="MySignedArchive.jar" src="MyScriptFile.js"> </script>
```

Event handlers do not need to directly specify an archive attribute, but they should always follow a script tag that does. For example:

```
<script archive="MySignedArchive.jar" ID="a">
<!--
   ...
// -->
</script>
```

```
<form onSubmit="JavaScript: formSubmit();" ID="b">
  ...
</form>
```

Unless you are using more than one archive file, you need only specify the attribute value in the first script tag. For example:

```
<script archive="MySignedArchive.jar" ID="a">
<!--
  document.write( "This is a signed script." );
// -->
</script>

<script ID="b">
<!--
  document.write( "This is also a signed script." );
// -->
</script>
```

Every signed inline and event handler script requires an ID attribute. The ID is a unique string that identifies the script to its signature in the JAR file. Each ID is unique to each JAR file— no two script tags can use the same JAR file and have the same ID. On the other hand, two script tags using different JAR files can have the same ID.

Using Expanded Privileges

Within a signed script are many very powerful features, or "privileges," that you can use to perform many operations in areas you normally would not have access to. First, though, you must ask for these privileges. Requesting an expanded privilege requires one line per privilege.

Here is an example that requests a privilege called UniversalSendMail:

```
netscape.security.PrivilegeManager.enablePrivilege("UniversalSendMail")
```

This line of code allows the author of the script to send e-mail on the visitor's behalf.

There are several privileges that you can request from the browser. Table 12.1 lists and describes some of these privileges.

Table 12.1 Netscape Signed Script Privileges

Privilege Name	Description
UniversalBrowserRead	Allows reading of privileged data from the browser
UniversalBrowserWrite	Allows modification of privileged data in a browser.
UniversalBrowserAccess	Allows both reading and modification of privileged data from the browser.
UniversalFileRead	Allows a script to read any files stored on hard disks or other storage media connected to your computer.
UniversalPreferencesRead	Allows the script to read preferences using the `navigator.preference` method.
UniversalPreferencesWrite	Allows the script to set preferences using the `navigator.preference` method.
UniversalSendMail	Allows the program to send mail in the user's name.

This is only a partial list of the privileges or targets that you can request. For a complete list, see http://developer.netscape.com/docs/manuals/signedobj/targets/index.html.

JavaScript Features Requiring Privileges

There are many features of the JavaScript language that may not be used unless they are part of a signed script. Table 12.2 lists the features that signed scripts give you and what privilege you need to request in order to use them.

Table 12.2 Privileged Features

Feature	Privilege
Set a file upload widget	UniversalFileRead
Submit a form to a mailto: or news: URL	UniversalSendMail
Use an about: URL other than about:blank	UniversalBrowserRead
Set any property of an event object	UniversalBrowserWrite
Get the value of the data property from a `DragDrop` event	UniversalBrowserRead
Get the value of any property of the history object	UniversalBrowserRead
Get or set the value of a preference from the navigator object using the preference method	UniversalPreferencesRead

Many functions of the window object, such as writing files to the hard drive, require `UniversalBrowserWrite`.

Summary

Like any software technology, JavaScript has the occasional problem. Sometimes a problem manifests itself as a security hole and must be fixed. It is your responsibility to keep up-to-date on the possible security issues your Web pages might have. In order to minimize the abuse of JavaScript security holes, all dangerous operations, such as reading and writing to the hard drive, have been removed. Sometimes it is necessary to use some of the features that have been removed from the language. In order to use these features, Netscape Navigator allows a programmer to sign scripts. A signed script requests extra rights from the visitor in order to do its task.

Chapter 13

Handling Errors and Debugging Scripts

No matter how much you plan, or how much foresight you have, it's inevitable: At some point you'll get an error. Errors can occur when a programmer tries to use a method with an object that doesn't support it, or tries to use an object variable that has not been initialized, or simply makes a typing mistake. There are literally hundreds of errors that can occur in any given program and often more than one way to interpret the messages that the errors generate. Learning where and how an error occurred takes quite a bit of skill and patience. Luckily, most modern Web browsers have built-in debuggers to help you find and fix errors in code. This chapter will discuss the basic makeup of error messages and present many steps you can go through in order to solve the errors you inevitably encounter.

Displaying Errors in Netscape Navigator

When a JavaScript error is encountered in a page opened in Netscape Navigator, a message is displayed in the browser's status bar as you can see in Figure 13.1. The message "JavaScript Error: Type 'javascript:' into Location for details" is only visible while the page is loading.

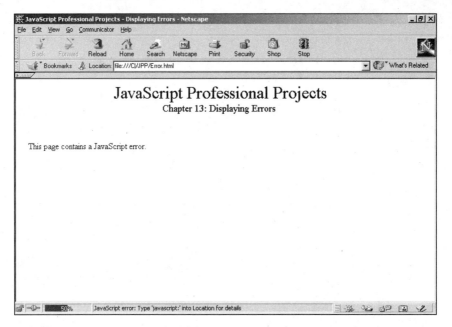

FIGURE 13.1 *Netscape error status*

After the page loads, the message is replaced with the status "done." Unfortunately, because the error message disappears so quickly means that you often won't notice if there is an error while loading because pages viewed from your local machine will load much too quickly. If you think that there might be an error occurring in one of your pages, type **javascript:** into the location bar (just to the right of Go to) to bring up the JavaScript Communicator Console, shown in Figure 13.2.

Once you've opened the Communicator Console, you will find that it is a very helpful tool. Not only will it give you details on each error that has occurred in your code, but it will also let you manually execute JavaScript statements. Manually executing JavaScript statements can be helpful if you need to check the value of a variable or close a child window that is misbehaving. Any valid JavaScript statement may be run in the Communicator Console.

Another way to locate the errors on a Web page—especially if it isn't your own—is to view the source of the Web page itself. To do so in Netscape, open the View menu and select Page Source. This will bring up a separate window containing the textual source of the current page as shown in Figure 13.3.

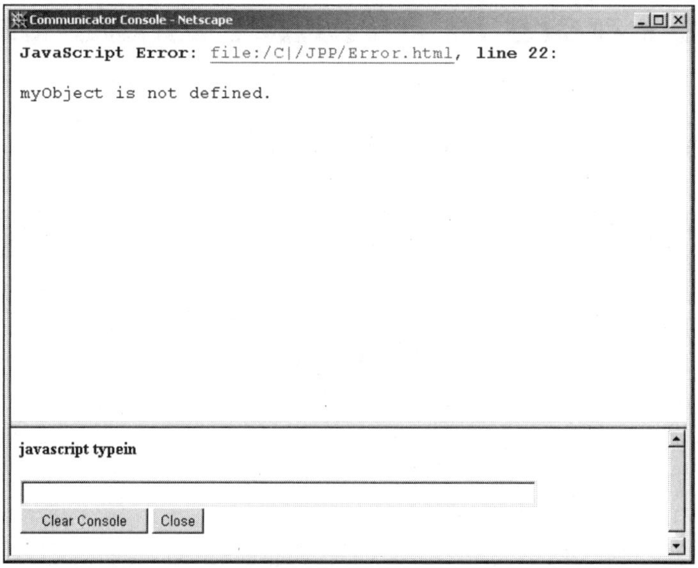

FIGURE 13.2 *Netscape's JavaScript Communicator Console*

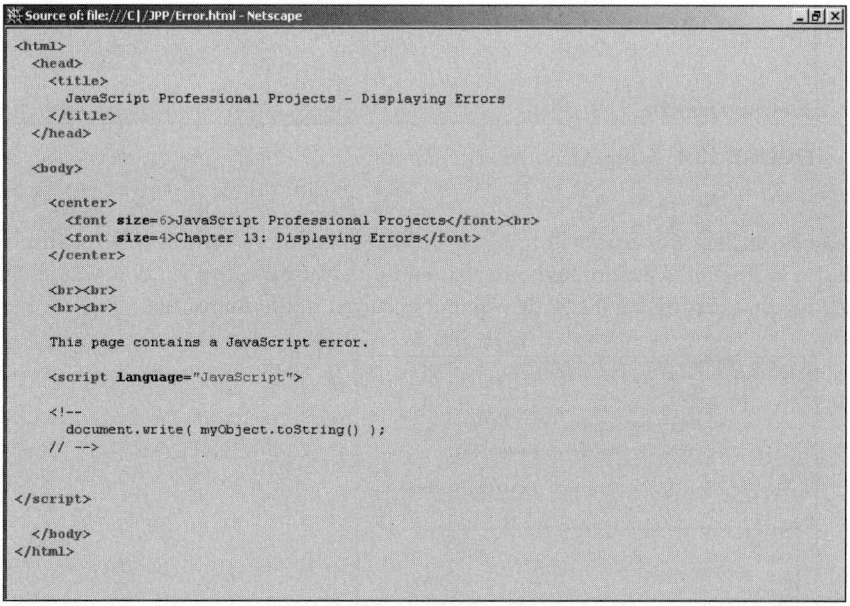

FIGURE 13.3 *Page Source in Netscape*

Displaying Errors in Internet Explorer

When an error occurs in Internet Explorer, it is quite a bit more obvious than in Netscape. A little yellow warning icon will appear in the lower left of the browser's status bar when any error occurs on the page. You can see the yellow icon in Figure 13.4.

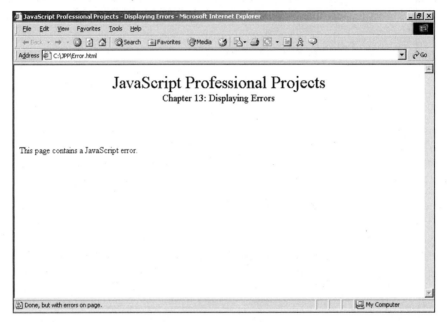

FIGURE 13.4 *Internet Explorer error status*

Double-clicking this icon will bring up Internet Explorer's version of error display, which is shown in Figure 13.5. Although not as friendly as Netscape, this window will tell you the type of error that occurred and exactly where it occurred in the source file.

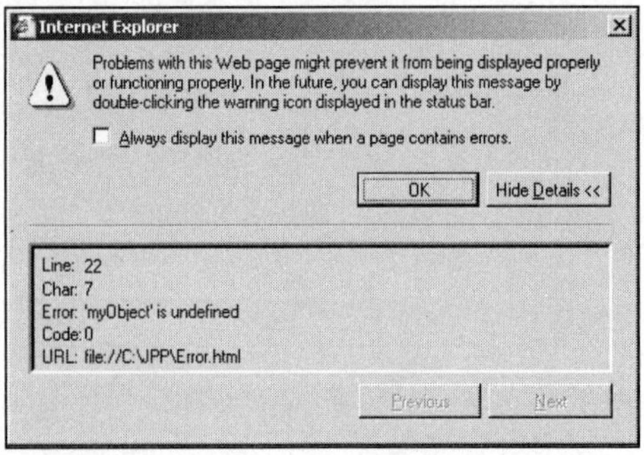

FIGURE 13.5 *Internet Explorer's JavaScript Communicator Console*

If the status bar is set to invisible, either in your code or because the client wanted it that way, you will need to make it visible again. To do that, open Internet Explorer's View menu and choose Status Bar.

Just as with Netscape, you can view the source of any Web page viewed in Internet Explorer. Once the page fully loads, you can open the View menu and select Source to open a Notepad window with the page's full source code.

Understanding Error Messages

Now that you know how to display error messages, you're probably wondering what the message means. People in the computer industry used to joke about error messages because these messages were generally (and sometimes still are) short, confusing, and oftentimes of no use whatsoever. It would not be uncommon for an early program writer to get an error similar to "Error #3810482," which contains no useful error message at all. Error messages have become more sophisticated and useful since they first began appearing, but they can still sometimes be quite confusing.

JavaScript error messages generally have three parts to them. If you look at Figures 13.2 and 13.5, you will notice that the figures both show the name of the file that caused the error, `C:\JPP\Error.html`; the line on which the error was detected, `22`; and the actual error message, `myObject is not defined`.

The first part of every error message, the path to the file that caused the error, is useful only if you are using a multiple-page Web site. If you're building a site that has multiple frames or that shares functions between pages, this error information will narrow your search for the cause of the error down to one page.

The second part of every error message is the line number on which the error was detected. Unfortunately, there is a big difference between which line *caused* the error and in which line the error was *detected*. In the running example so far, the line number is helpful because line 22 was the line in which I used an object instance `myObject` before the variable was actualy defined. This is not always the case. One notable exception of an error message giving the wrong line number is when you forget to end a string literal with a quotation mark. The interpreter will not normally catch the error on the line that is missing a quotation—it will catch it in the next `<script>` block of the Web page. As a rule of thumb, the error in question usually occurred on the line number that was given in the error message or shortly before it.

The last part of every error is a message defining the type of error that occurred. This part of the error message is usually self-explanatory, but it can occasionally be confusing if you aren't familiar with every aspect of the JavaScript language. If the message is helpful, then great, go fix the error. If the message is confusing, don't worry about it—the first two parts of the error message will usually provide enough information to fix the error.

Debugging is not an easy task. Nobody writes a program perfectly the first time through, which makes debugging a useful and necessary skill to acquire.

If you encounter an error that you are having difficulty fixing, try these simple steps to get you started:

- **Fix only one error at a time**. Oftentimes, several errors will be caused by a single error previously in the document. Fixing the first error first will usually solve the following ones.

- **Seek help**. Chances are that others in your field have already encountered the error you're working on. If so, they will generally be more than willing to help you solve the problem. If you're working on a project alone, use the Internet to find help with the problem. Searching for a specific error message on the Internet usually provides a large number of possible solutions on discussion boards and online databases.

- **Be patient**. Some errors just take time to figure out. If you find a particularly difficult bug and have worked on it for a long time to no avail, leave it for later. You can always work on a different part of your project or take a break. A fresh perspective may be all that is required.

Using Try-Catch Blocks

When there is a good chance that a program segment may cause an error, you may want to enclose the segment in a try-catch block. A try-catch block will *try* to execute all code between the curly braces. If an error is caused by the code in the block, the try-catch block will *catch* the error and allow you to either elegantly report the error to the user or totally suppress it.

Here is the try-catch block syntax:

```
try{ <statements> } catch( <identifier> ){ <statements> }
```

Statements in the try block will execute sequentially, just as usual. As soon as an error is generated, execution is rerouted to the catch block, where the error will be handled. After the catch block is executed, execution continues with the statement immediately after the catch block. Here is some pseudo code to demonstrate:

```
try
{
  no error.
  no error.
  an error!  control is passed to the catch block here.
  this will never execute.
}
catch( exception )
{
```

```
   error handling code is run here.
}
execution continues from here.
```

In general, it is not a good idea to let the visitor know when an error occurs—nobody wants to visit a Web site that generates errors. By using `try-catch` blocks, you can ensure that your Web site visitors never know when an error occurs.

```html
<html>
  <head>
    <title>
      JavaScript Professional Projects - Handling Errors
    </title>
  </head>

  <body>

    <center>
      <font size=6>JavaScript Professional Projects</font><br>
      <font size=4>Chapter 13: Handling Errors</font>
    </center>


    <br><br>
    <br><br>


    This page contains a JavaScript error
    which is caught by a try-catch block.

    <script language="JavaScript">
    <!--
      try
      {
        document.write( myObject.toString() );
      }
      catch( e )
      {
      }
    // -->
    </script>
```

```
    </body>
</html>
```

This example suppresses the example error used previously in the chapter. Try-catch blocks are also very useful when debugging your Web page and keeping it running.

The following example provides no error checking in the average() function:

```
<html>
  <head>
    <title>
      JavaScript Professional Projects - Handling Errors
    </title>

    <script language="JavaScript">
    <!--
      var theArray = new Array( 10, 99, 75, 42, 56, 2, 87, 15 );

      function displayArray( a )
      {
        for( i = 0 ; i < a.length ; i++ )
        {
          document.write( "<b>" + a[i] + "</b>" );
          if( i != a.length - 1 ) document.write( ", " );
        }
      }

      function average( a )
      {
        var total = 0;
        for( i = 0 ; i < a.length ; i++ )
        {
          total += a[i];
        }
        return( total / a.length );
      }
    // -->
    </script>
  </head>
```

```
<body>

  <center>
    <font size=6>JavaScript Professional Projects</font><br>
    <font size=4>Chapter 13: Handling Errors</font>
  </center>

  <br><br>
  <br><br>

  The average of the array
  <script language="JavaScript">
  <!--
    displayArray( theArray );
  // -->
  </script>
  is<b>
  <script language="JavaScript">
  <!--
    document.write( average( theArray ) );
  // -->
  </script></b>.

  </body>
</html>
```

At first glance, this situation might not seem like such a bad thing, but think about what would happen if an array of strings were passed to the function instead of an array of numbers. The average() function will return the value NaN, which is not helpful at all if you need to know the average of the array. The same is true if the array length is zero (a much more likely occurrence). Thankfully, there is a way to handle both these possibilities. Here is a modified version of the previous example:

```
<html>
  <head>
    <title>
      JavaScript Professional Projects - Handling Errors
    </title>
```

```
<script language="JavaScript">
<!--
  var theArray = new Array( 10, 99, 75, 42, 56, 2, 87, 15 );

  function displayArray( a )
  {
    for( i = 0 ; i < a.length ; i++ )
    {
      document.write( "<b>" + a[i] + "</b>" );
      if( i != a.length - 1 ) document.write( ", " );
    }
  }

  function average( a )
  {
    if( a.length == 0 ) throw( "Divide by zero error." );

    var total = 0;
    for( i = 0 ; i < a.length ; i++ )
    {
      if( isNaN( a[i] ) ) throw( "Number array expected." );
      total += a[i];
    }
    return( total / a.length );
  }
// -->
</script>
</head>

<body>

  <center>
    <font size=6>JavaScript Professional Projects</font><br>
    <font size=4>Chapter 13: Handling Errors</font>
  </center>

  <br><br>
  <br><br>
```

```
The average of the array
<script language="JavaScript">
<!--
    displayArray( theArray );
// -->
</script>
is<b>
<script language="JavaScript">
<!--
    try
    {
        document.write( average( theArray ) );
    }
    catch( e )
    {
        document.write( "ERROR: " + e );
    }
// -->
</script></b>.

    </body>
</html>
```

The modified `average()` function checks that two conditions exist before it calculates the average of the array. The first condition is that the array has some elements in it. If the array is empty, a new exception is thrown with the error message "Divide by zero error." I chose this error message because the last line of the function divides `total` by the length of the array and an empty array has a length of zero. The second condition the function requires before it will calculate the average is that each element in the array be a number. This condition is checked during each iteration of the `for` loop. If an element is not a number, a "Number array expected" error message is thrown.

Creating and throwing errors is only half of what you need to do to keep errors from reaching the client. Each time you use the `average()` function you must put it in a `try-catch` block to catch the possible errors. In the previous example, the function call was placed in the following `try-catch` block, like this:

```
try
{
    document.write( average( theArray ) );
}
```

```
catch( e )
{
  document.write( "ERROR: " + e );
}
```

This `try-catch` block catches any of the errors that may or may not be created by the `average()` function. If no error is created—a non-zero length array of numbers is used—the program will return the average of the array and then print it to the screen. If an error is created, the `try-catch` block captures it and echoes it to the screen instead of the results of the `average()` function.

If you don't want to put the function call inside of a `try-catch` block each time you use it, you could alternatively write the `average()` function as follows:

```
function average( a )
{
  var total = 0;
  try
  {
    if( a.length == 0 ) throw( "Divide by zero error." );
    for( i = 0 ; i < a.length ; i++ )
    {
      if( isNaN( a[i] ) ) throw( "Number array expected." );
      total += a[i];
    }
  }
  catch( e )
  {
    return( e );
  }
  return( total / a.length );
}
```

This version of the function performs exactly like the previous one, except that you no longer have to place the function call in a `try-catch` block. The only disadvantage of this method is that you can no longer control what happens when an error occurs in the `average()` function because it is coded into the function itself.

Exploiting the OnError() Method

One event handler that was not discussed in Chapter 6 is the `OnError()` event handler. The `OnError()` event handler can act like a global `try-catch` block for your entire Web page, and will capture any error that occurs. Here is a simple example to demonstrate:

```html
<html>
  <head>
    <title>
      JavaScript Professional Projects - The OnError Method
    </title>

    <script language="JavaScript">
    <!--
      function error()
      {
        alert( "An error occured." );
      }
      window.onerror = error;
    // -->
    </script>
  </head>

  <body>

    <center>
      <font size=6>JavaScript Professional Projects</font><br>
      <font size=4>Chapter 13: The OnError Method</font>
    </center>

    <br><br>
    <br><br>

    This page contains a JavaScript error
    which is caught by the OnError event handler.

    <script language="JavaScript">
    <!--
      document.write( myObject.toString() );
    // -->
    </script>

  </body>
</html>
```

This example captures all errors that occur in the page with the OnError event handler of the window object. This example uses an alert dialog to tell the user that an error occurred, but as I said before, telling the user about errors is generally not a good idea. The fact that errors are annoying, compounded with the fact that alert dialog boxes are also annoying, might make the visitor never want to visit your site again. If you had not expected the error to occur at all, it is usually a better idea to simply ignore it than bombarding the visitor with alert dialogs.

The OnError() event handler is also useful if you're worried about only one portion of your code causing errors. You can place the event handler

```
OnError="JavaScript: null;"
```

in a surrounding tag and it would block all errors that occur therein.

Finite Steps to Debugging

Debugging is a science. You make a hypothesis based on your previous experiments, then make predictions either for or against the hypothesis. Next you run the program, providing it with new and hypothetical input; then you observe its output and then either confirm or refute your original hypothesis. What follows is a short list of steps to follow to solve the bugs you invariably create in the process of program writing.

NOTE

The *real* first step is to not write buggy code in the first place. This may seem like a no-brainer, but is important to consider. When a good chess player plays a game he is constantly thinking at least five moves ahead. With 16 different pieces, that could be more than a million different moves. Of course, the chess player doesn't need to analyze every possible move because he knows that many of them would be bad. Experienced players no longer seem to even see the possible bad moves. The same principal applies to program writing. As you become more experienced, you will make fewer and fewer mistakes that result in bugs. Eventually, you will no longer even think about the common mistakes that beginning programmers make—it will become second nature to write non-buggy code.

The first thing to do when you do encounter a bug is to find out as much as you can about it. For this, the JavaScript interpreter is your most useful resource. Read the error message carefully; it will usually tell you exactly what the problem is. If you don't understand the error message, your second best resource is the Internet. Unlike in grade school, looking up an answer is not cheating in the computer industry.

After finding out as much as you can about the error, the next logical step is to fix it in your source code. If it is a simple bug, by all means dive right in. If you find yourself in the clutches of a beastly bug, you might think about backing up your source file before making drastic changes to it.

The last step in debugging is to test your changes. If everything works correctly, then great, you're done. If not, jump back up to step one and start again. You can't fix a program unless you understand how it works in the first place. The JavaScript interpreter will help you collect data, but it can't interpret it for you, and it certainly can't fix the problem. Only you can do that.

Summary

Debugging is a science. Nobody is born a natural debugger; it takes years of practice to become really good at it. This does not mean that you aren't perfectly equipped to fix the bugs in your own code. A little bit of practice, intuitive researching, and a hefty dose of patience is all you need to solve any bug you encounter.

PART II

Applying Your Skills: The Center Park School Project

Chapter 14

Now that you have an understanding of the JavaScript essentials, it's time to put your new knowledge to work. To demonstrate a more exciting (and practical) application of JavaScript, we are going to frame the project chapters around a fictitious secondary school we'll call Center Park. In an effort to remain current with the use of technology in education—as well as provide its students, teachers, and parents with valuable and easy-to-access information—the school administration has decided to develop a Web site for the school. Because of your renown JavaScript coding skills, you have been asked to lead the development of Center Park's new Web site.

This chapter, then, will serve as an introduction to the project and will "preview" the individual chapters of this part (each chapter will highlight a different functional perspective of the school's site).

Ready to see your new programming skills put to good use? Read on!

Planning the Center Park Web Site

As a good Web designer, the first thing with which you've asked the Center Park administrators to provide you is a list of required functionality, deadlines, and budget. They have produced the list of required functionality; it is now your job to design the site, via JavaScript, with the functionality they require.

Here is the list:

♦ **Dynamic calendars**. Students have asked to be able to view their homework assignments "at a glance," and to be able to do so in weekly and monthly increments; moreover, important dates for the operation of the school year (start/ending dates, vacations, meetings, etc.) need to be communicated via the site. The site will require several dynamic calendars so that users of the site can locate the information when they want and in the fashion (weekly, monthly) they want.

♦ **A test and survey feature**. Administrators of the school recently visited a sister school in another district and were impressed to see that school performing online testing. This feature has proven very useful as a method of assessment for advanced-standing students in continuing education, as well as (through some fairly simple modification of the code) a means of gathering information via online surveys. The Center Park administrators would like such a feature for their Web site.

♦ **An online store**. As with all things involving education, fund-raising is critical to ensuring that the important programs and initiatives of the school continue despite the omnipresent red pen of the local, state, and federal legislature. Center Park administrators have requested that the site feature some type of online store, at which orders for various fund-raising items can be placed at any time of day or night. To help further facilitate this online store, the administrators have also requested that basic financial calculators be included on the site so that visitors and members can perform quick price calculations.

♦ **Secure, members-only access**. Many of the features of the site, while open to the general public (*e.g.* the online store), will require secure access for current students and faculty only. In order to ensure that the information deemed confidential can remain as such, you will need to utilize some of the security features of JavaScript coding.

- **Rotating banner advertisements**. Not surprisingly, several organizations within the school (*e.g.* the sports teams, the band, and various student clubs) have asked for advertising space on the site so that visitors can be aware of their activities. Several of the rotating-banner ads will provide links to specific sections of the site, so being able to hyperlink within the ads will be a critical.

- **Bold, attractive appearance**. Finally, all of the above-mentioned functionality, as well as the general look and feel of the site, must be as eye-pleasing as possible. To that end, the site will also include various dynamic HTML (DHTML) effects, including highlighted navigation buttons on the home page. Figure 14.1 shows an example of such an effect in action.

FIGURE 14.1 *Highlighted navigation buttons on the home page draw attention to major site functionality.*

As you can see from this list, the finished site will include some fairly advanced JavaScript functionality. However, while the functionality will be quite advanced, it can be implemented relatively easily through the power of JavaScript and what it brings to otherwise static and unexciting Web pages.

DON'T FORGET TO PLAN!

While this book is not about Web site or IT planning in general, planning is a critical topic that deserves a mention here.

No matter what the size of your Web project—from a personal home page to a site such as that for the Center Park School—planning is an absolute requirement. When planning any Web project, be sure to consider (even in the most rudimentary fashion) the following issues:

◆ **The necessary work to be performed**. Not unlike the bulleted list shown earlier, this high-level concept planning defines the major functionality of the project and who will perform/coordinate/implement/administer/ and ultimately be responsible for the final project.

◆ **Special vendor requirements**. What existing electronic systems are already in place, and/or what existing or soon-to-be-implemented hardware/software must function with the site? Are you using special products or otherwise proprietary technology (*e.g.* Microsoft platform: ActiveX controls) that will have a serious impact on how the functionality of the completed site is accessed?

◆ **Design and documentation**. What if you get only halfway through the project and you get hit by the proverbial bus (or, in a less violent scenario, get called away to a different project)? Will those who follow you be able to pick up where you left off in order to complete the project? To ensure that the answer is yes, you should be careful to document your code and your general site design at every step of the way. Not only will proper code documentation help those who follow you, but it can be invaluable when you need to go back to troubleshoot or fix the inevitable bug.

◆ **Training**. While everything about your code and your site functionality makes perfect sense to you, it may be anything but intuitive to your end user. While the above-mentioned documentation will help with this, you should also consider some training sessions (as well as written training documentation) that will ensure that both your end users and those charged with administering your site understand your thinking and know how to take the best advantage of your programming acumen.

◆ **Scope Creep**. Avoiding the dreaded scope creep—allowing your project to go off in directions you didn't plan for—is an absolute must. More than likely, you will be constrained by two things of which there is never enough: time and money. That said, plan carefully and then stick to your plan!

JavaScript Functionality: Special Features of the Center Park Web Site

While we'll discuss each functional component of the Center Park Web site in the following chapters, we'd like to introduce these components now, so that you can get an idea of what the final project will look like. In each of the sections below, we will cross-reference the chapter(s) in which we discussed the specific JavaScript coding foundation from which the specific functional component is to be built.

◢ TIP

We've listed each of the Center Park functional components in the same order as they will appear in the following chapters. For example, the calendar functionality will be presented in Chapter 15, "Creating a JavaScript Calendar."

Functional Requirement: JavaScript Calendars

The question has been raised: Does anybody really know what time it is? The other question that always seems to need asking is, "What's today's date?" Let's face it: in today's harried world, time just slips away from us. That said, being able to quickly determine not only today's date but also dates in the future is critical for any type of planning. This type of functionality is often of high importance on a Web site, too, as visitors will need to schedule events or view planned events days, weeks, and yes, even years in advance.

For the Center Park site, calendar functionality is an important element. From allowing visitors to see planned events at the school to allowing teachers to make their lesson plans available to students, calendars are an absolute must. Figures 14.2, 14.3, and 14.4 all highlight some of the "pop-up calendar" functionality of the Center Park Web site. It should be apparent—even from a quick glance at these figures—how useful such calendar functionality can be to a well-designed, information-rich Web site.

Functional Requirement: Online Test and Surveys

Many schools (especially at the secondary and college level) are turning to online testing as a convenient, efficient way of assessing student progress. The Center Park administrators, in their quest to stay one step ahead of the technology curve, have asked that this online testing component be included in their new site, too.

Figures 14.4, 14.5, 14.6, and 14.7 illustrate the online testing component of the site.

FIGURE 14.2 *Visitors are able to see "at a glance" events for the school planned for the week, month, or year.*

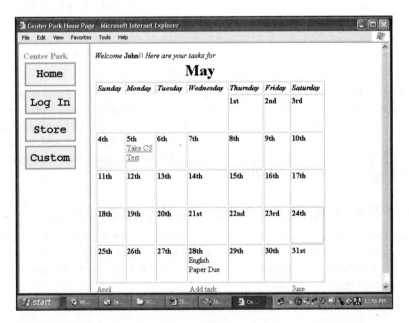

FIGURE 14.3 *Students are able to quickly view assignments for the week. Being able to view assignments online makes it impossible to say, "But I didn't know that paper was due today!"*

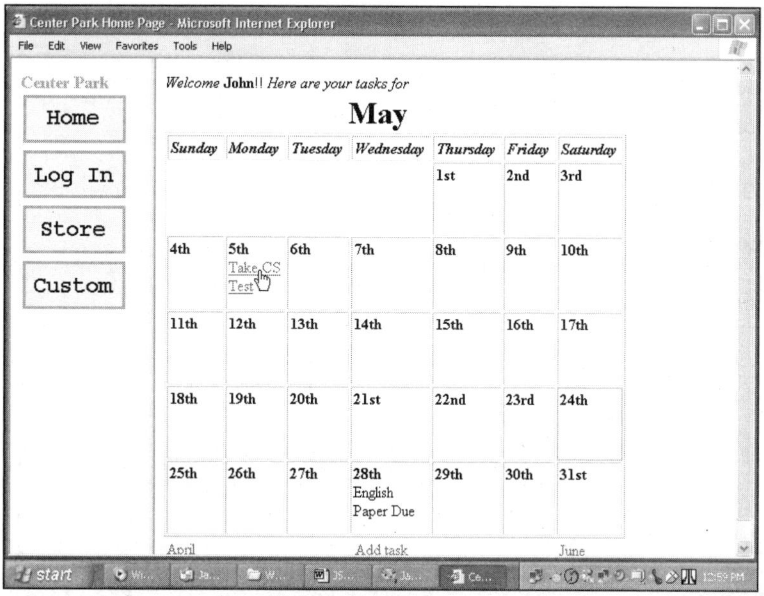

FIGURE 14.4 *Direct links to the exams are found within the monthly calendars; students simply click on the test link...*

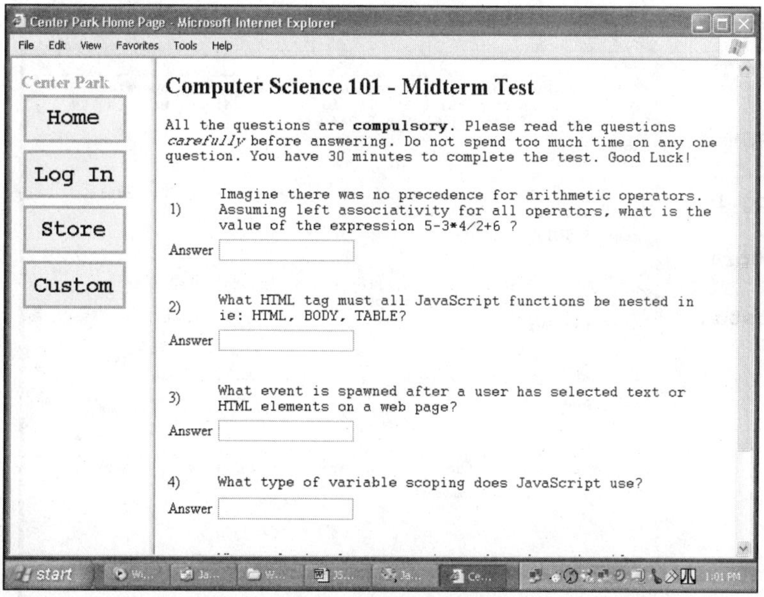

FIGURE 14.5 *...to be taken to the actual test form.*

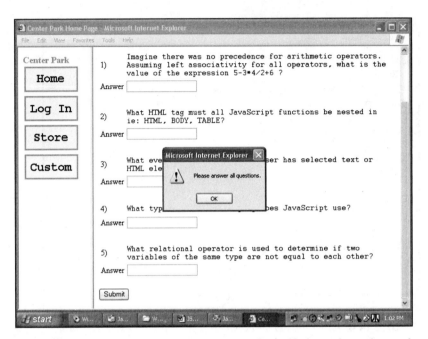

FIGURE 14.6 *Students must provide an answer of some kind to each question, or else the test will not be submitted.*

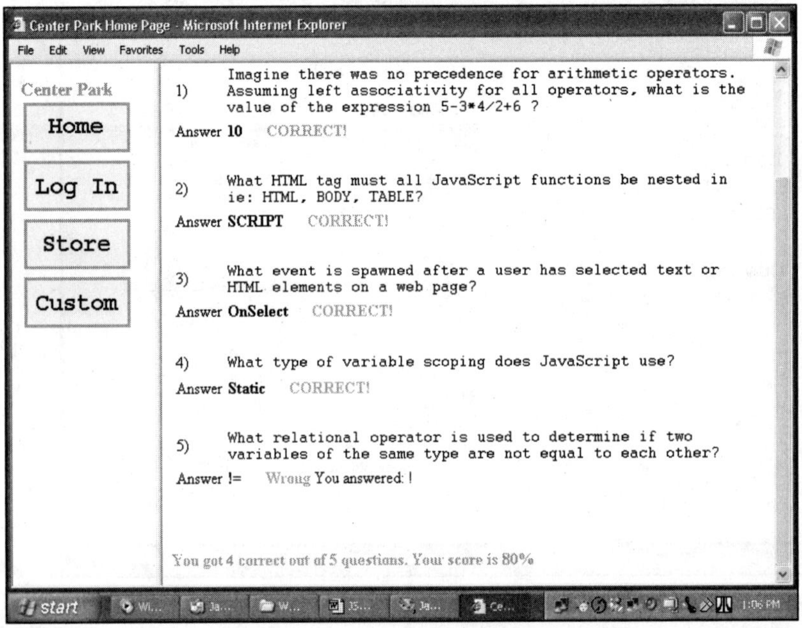

FIGURE 14.7 *Upon submission of the answers, the test is immediately scored and presented to the student.*

In addition to the online testing component, you will see that—with some relatively simple coding modification—the test functionality can be turned into a survey form. This has obvious implications for any site, but for the Center Park site school administrators might use such a survey to gather parent feedback, to solicit donations from the community at large…the list goes on.

Functional Requirement: Creating an Online Shopping Cart

Ah, the school bake sale…where would education be without it? But what if you could take Mrs. Riley's famous apple turnovers and sell them via the wonders of technology? As you can see in Figures 14.8, 14.9, and 14.10, the online shopping cart allows visitors to both view items for sale and see a running cost total of the items they've added to their online shopping cart.

Functional Requirement: "Members-Only" Security/Password Protection

Not all information presented on the Center Park Web site is intended for public consumption. Indeed, sensitive information such as faculty home addresses and telephone numbers, as well as budgetary and other administrative information, should probably not be accessible to everyone.

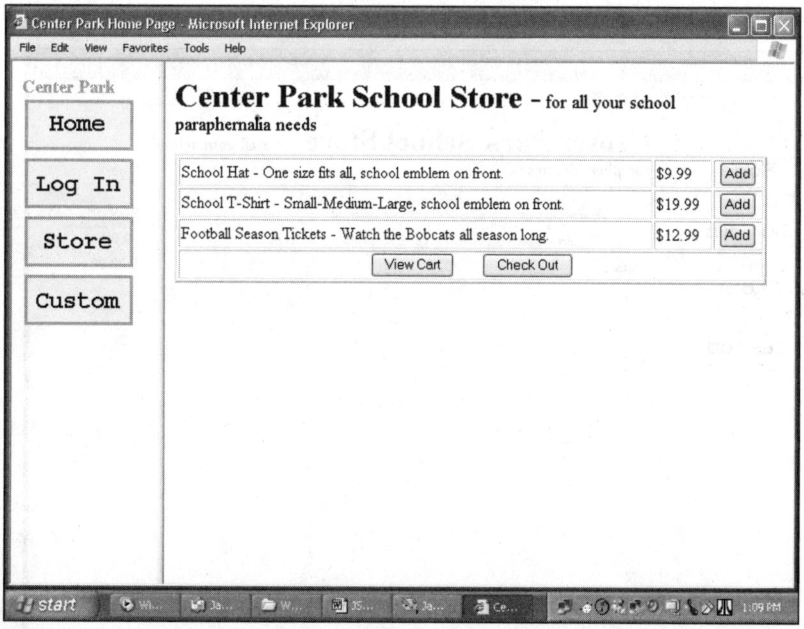

FIGURE 14.8 *The "Center Park Store" home page allows visitors to select an item of interest. Note that navigation links are present that quickly take the visitor to other areas of the site.*

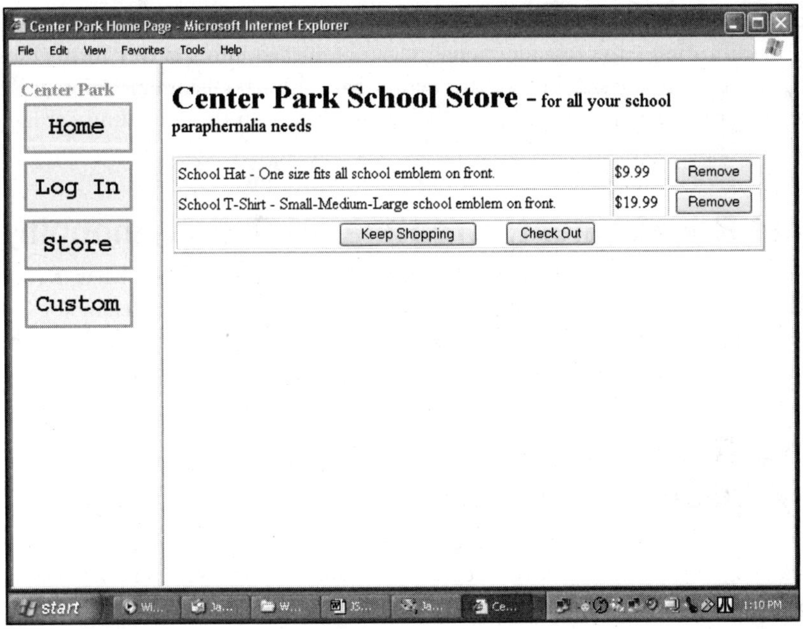

FIGURE 14.9 *Once an item is selected, it is automatically added to the online cart. Note that the total cost of the cart is also updated.*

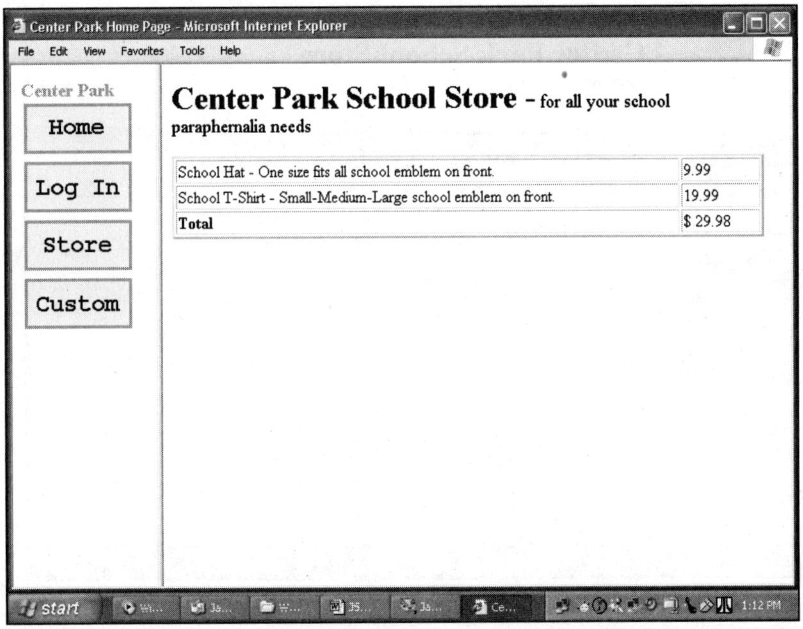

FIGURE 14.10 *Ready for check out. Note the list of all items ready for purchase as well as the total cost.*

Fortunately, your JavaScript coding skills will allow you to meet the security functional requirement of the site. Figure 14.11 illustrates the prompt presented to users who must enter an authorized password before being allowed to progress any further into this section of the site.

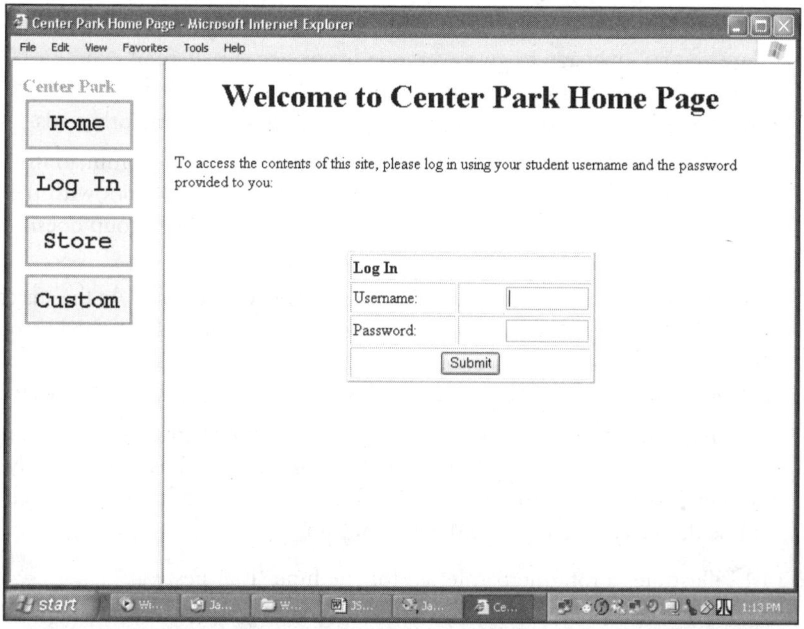

FIGURE 14.11   *Stop! Who goes there? If you don't have an authorized password, you're not going anywhere in this specific section of the Center Park Web site.*

Functional Requirement: Rotating Banner Advertisements

Undoubtedly you've been annoyed by them in your journeys throughout the Web. But rotating banner ads actually can serve a very useful purpose when they are enclosed within a private site or intranet.

Given that screen real estate is always limited—and that, quite often, several people/organizations are vying for that real estate—rotating banner ads can be just what the Web design doctor ordered. By combining both functionality (*i.e.* being able to hyperlink them to other sections of your site) and eye-catching design, a rotating banner ad can serve a multitude of purposes.

When a survey was put to Center Park students as to what functional requirements they'd like to see met in the Web site, one very common response was that they'd like to see advertising for various student group activities. In your planning meetings with the school administrators, you (rightly) suggested that rotating banner ads would be a perfect answer to this request, because:

- **Banner ads make good use of screen real estate.** If you gave space on a Web page to every organization, it would result in a very busy (and probably unreadable) page. However, by using rotating banner ads, you can take up only a fraction of screen real estate and still manage to give everyone his or her fair share of exposure. Moreover, the rotating ad probably gives an organization more bang for its buck, as during the time it is being displayed the ad has no competition from any other ads.

- **Each ad would be designed in a similar fashion.** The school administrators want to be fair to each group, and banner ads force the groups to work with the same specifications (such as size), thus helping to ensure that one group doesn't get more attention than any other.

- **Banner ads allow interested users to "click for more information."** As the ads can be hyperlinked, they can focus on quick, attention-grabbing tactics (*i.e.* good graphic design). Then, once a visitor's attention is captured, he or she can click within the ad to be taken to a page with more specific information about the event/function being advertised.

- **Rotating banner ads are easy to administer.** The groups interested in advertising submit their ads by a specific deadline; then the site administrators simply load them into a queue, set specific options (such as order of ads and time each ad will be displayed onscreen), and away they go.

Figure 14.12 illustrates a rotating banner ad for the June "Bug Festival."

FIGURE 14.12 *The rotating banner ad for the Bug Festival. Note the difference in this rotating graphic versus the graphic seen in Figure 14.2.*

Functional Requirement: Dynamic HTML (DHTML) Effects

A Web site can be packed with information, but—let's face it—the Web is a multimedia medium: If it doesn't look good, then the power of that information can be lost. The Center Park administrators are aware of this and want to make the site as eye-catching (yet not obnoxious) as possible. Moreover, they have visited other Web sites and know that good design can also enhance functionality of the site.

An example of good design is the bold navigation buttons on the site home page. Note how, in Figure 14.13, the menus add a visually appealing quality to the site, as well as provide a very real functional usability.

FIGURE 14.13 *When the mouse cursor is placed over the button, it changes colors to show it is highlighted. Also note the functionality of these buttons is duplicated in the right frame of the site (next to the rotating graphic, the links for "Log In", "Store" and "Customize").*

Summary

This chapter introduced and previewed all the JavaScript functionality that you will code in order to build the fictitious (but realistic) Center Park School Web site. As you progress through each of the following chapters, you will program this functionality sequentially, so that when you are done you should have a good idea of how different JavaScript functionality can build on itself in order to complete a powerful, functional Web site.

Chapter 15

Students of any age are notoriously unorganized. Think back to, for example, your bedroom in high school, or your dorm room in college. More than likely, "neat and tidy" is not a description that comes readily to mind. While a messy desk is often the sign of a busy and dedicated individual, these qualities can quickly fall by the wayside if you can't find what you're looking for, when you need it!

The administrators at the Center Park School were facing the same conceptual problem in trying to organize and disseminate information about the school to various audiences, including students, tutors, and parents. At Center Park, there are always multiple events occurring at any given time, from PTA meetings to sporting events, and the school administrators wanted to ensure that their Web site had the ability to organize and neatly present all this information so everyone knew what was going on and could plan accordingly.

However, in addition to general information, the school faculty were particularly interested in using the new Web site as a mechanism to organize student work, including homework assignments and tests. They envisioned "student-specific" calendars, so that as individual students logged in to the site they would see their own custom schedule. That way, the old excuse of "But, I didn't know the assignment was due then!" would cease to be plausible (if it ever was in the first place...)!

Listening to all of these requests, you—as JavaScript Web developer—quickly realized that dynamic calendars could quickly solve many of these issues. In addition to other well-designed information delivery features (such as rotating banner ads), the calendars would serve two vital functions: presenting information and—most importantly—organizing information.

This chapter will cover two different types of online calendars. The first type will be the kind of calendar that you may have already used in your e-mail client. The second type of calendar is one that will aid in the filling out of form fields. Both of these types of calendars are easy to implement, easy to use, and will make your Web site more attractive and user-friendly. And, as you will see, both fit neatly into the overall Central Park School Web site design.

Perpetual Calendar for Scheduling

The first type of calendar you'll implement in this chapter is a perpetual calendar, which is most often used for scheduling events. This type of calendar is most closely related to the calendar in your e-mail client or the one hanging on your wall. There are three basic features of a good online calendar that you should consider while implementing yours. The first feature of a good online calendar is a user-friendly and efficient display. The second feature is the ability to change the displayed month, and the last important feature of an online calendar is allowing the calendar to interact with critical data, so that information can be retrieved and displayed. Each of these aspects will be explained in full in this section.

Displaying the Calendar

Probably the most difficult part of creating an online calendar is creating the user interface. Fortunately, JavaScript includes many functions that will aid you in this task, and HTML has all of the elements that will allow you to display your calendar. I'll walk you through creating a calendar that will display the days of the current month in an HTML table. First I'll present the code and then I'll explain it in detail. In order to experience the changes that I make to the calendar throughout the chapter, I encourage you to save each example as a separate file. This example, for instance, is named Static_Calendar.html.

```
<html>

  <head>
    <title>Calendar</title>
```

```
<script language="JavaScript">
<!--
  var now = new Date();
  var month = new Date( fixYear( now.getYear() ), now.getMonth(), 1 );
  var months = new Array( "January", "February", "March", "April",
                          "May", "June", "July", "August", "September",
                          "October", "November", "December" );

  function fixYear( year )
  {
    return( year < 1000 ?  year + 1900 : year );
  }

  function getNumberDays( d )
  {
    switch( d.getMonth() + 1 )
    {
      case 1: case 3: case 5: case 7:
      case 8: case 10: case 12:
        return( 31 );
      case 4: case 6: case 9: case 11:
        return( 30 );
      case 2:
        return( 28 + ( d.getYear % 4 == 0 ? 1 : 0 ) );
    }
  }
// -->
  </script>
</head>

<body>
  <table border="1" cellpadding="2" width="75%">
    <tr>
      <td colspan="7" align="center">
        <font size="6"><b>
        <script language="JavaScript">
        <!--
```

```
        document.write( months[month.getMonth()] + " " +
                       fixYear( month.getYear() ) );
     // -->
     </script>
     </b></font>
   </td>
</tr>
<tr>
  <td width="14%"><b><i>Sunday</i></b></td>
  <td width="14%"><b><i>Monday</i></b></td>
  <td width="14%"><b><i>Tuesday</i></b></td>
  <td width="14%"><b><i>Wednesday</i></b></td>
  <td width="14%"><b><i>Thursday</i></b></td>
  <td width="14%"><b><i>Friday</i></b></td>
  <td width="14%"><b><i>Saturday</i></b></td>
</tr>
<tr>
  <script language="JavaScript">
  <!--
    var startDay = month.getDay();
    for( i = 0 ; i < startDay ; i++ )
    {
      document.write( "<td></td>" );
    }

    var numDays = getNumberDays( month );
    for( i = 0 ; i < numDays ; i++ )
    {
      if( ( i + startDay + 1 ) % 7 == 1 )
      {
        document.write( "</tr><tr>" );
      }
      document.write( "<td height='75' valign='top'><b>" +
                     (i+1) + "</b></td>" );
    }
  // -->
  </script>
</tr>
```

```
    </table>

  </body>

</html>
```

This example displays a very simple, very plain calendar, as shown in Figure 15.1. There are two basic parts to this example, the functions and the table.

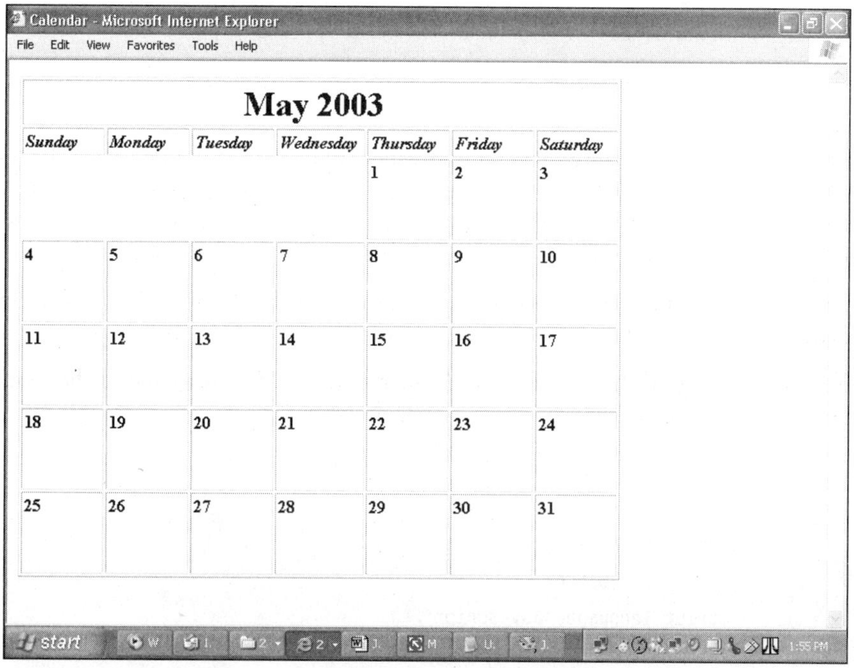

FIGURE 15.1 *A simple calendar that displays the current month in a table layout.*

The functions in this example may not seem absolutely necessary at first glance, but believe me, they are. Due to a lingering aspect of the Y2K bug, some browsers still only store the year of a JavaScript Date object as two digits. The fixYear() function,

```
function fixYear( year )
{
  return( year < 1000 ?  year + 1900 : year );
}
```

corrects the bug and allows the calendar to display correctly. The second function, getNumberDays():

```
function getNumberDays( d )
  {
```

```
switch( d.getMonth() + 1 )
{
  case 1: case 3: case 5: case 7:
  case 8: case 10: case 12:
    return( 31 );
  case 4: case 6: case 9: case 11:
    return( 30 );
  case 2:
    return( 28 + ( d.getYear % 4 == 0 ? 1 : 0 ) );
}
}
```

performs some functionality that you may expect to be part of the JavaScript Date object, but is not. This function will take a Date object as a parameter and return the number of days that are in the month specified by the Date object's `month` field. This value is used later on, when you'll build the calendar display so that the correct number of days are displayed.

The second basic part of the calendar example is the table itself. I'll walk you through each logical step that must be taken in order to display the calendar correctly.

First of all, you need the two different header rows, one for the name of the month and one for the names of the days.

```
<table border="1" cellpadding="2" width="75%">
  <tr>
    <td colspan="7" align="center">
      <font size="6"><b>
      <script language="JavaScript">
      <!--
        document.write( months[month.getMonth()] + " " +
                        fixYear( month.getYear() ) );
      // -->
      </script>
      </b></font>
     </td>
  </tr>
  <tr>
    <td width="14%"><b><i>Sunday</i></b></td>
    <td width="14%"><b><i>Monday</i></b></td>
    <td width="14%"><b><i>Tuesday</i></b></td>
    <td width="14%"><b><i>Wednesday</i></b></td>
    <td width="14%"><b><i>Thursday</i></b></td>
```

```
<td width="14%"><b><i>Friday</i></b></td>
    <td width="14%"><b><i>Saturday</i></b></td>
  </tr>
```

This part is fairly straightforward. The name of the month is generated from an array of month names that was declared earlier. The names of the days are simply hard-coded into the Web page. The next parts are trickier. Not every month starts with the first day as Sunday, so you'll have to find some way to pad the first week to make it line up with the previous month. Luckily, the JavaScript Date object will tell you what day of the week the date falls on, and if you set the Date object to be the first day of the month (as I did in the ninth line of the example), then you can easily find out how many days need to be padded in order for the calendar to display correctly.

```
<tr>
  <script language="JavaScript">
  <!--
    var startDay = month.getDay();
    for( i = 0 ; i < startDay ; i++ )
    {
      document.write( "<td></td>" );
    }
```

Because there are never more than six days padded at the beginning of the month, you don't need to worry about starting and ending additional rows in the table. For each day that needs to be padded, simply write an empty table cell.

The final part of displaying the calendar is adding in the days of the month. Since you already know that you're starting on the correct day of the week, you need only add the days in.

```
    var numDays = getNumberDays( month );
    for( i = 0 ; i < numDays ; i++ )
    {
      if( ( i + startDay + 1 ) % 7 == 1 )
      {
        document.write( "</tr><tr>" );
      }
      document.write( "<td height='75' valign='top'><b>" +
                           (i+1) + "</b></td>" );
    }
  // -->
  </script>
  </tr>
</table>
```

The one thing that is different about this code snippet is that you do have to worry about starting and ending rows. Whenever your counter (in this case i) reaches 1, or Sunday, simply write a closing row tag and an opening row tag before adding the next day.

Rotating the Calendar

A calendar is not very useful if all it does is display one month—even if it is the current month. People often need to schedule events months or even years in advance. With the setup that I have presented thus far, it is a very simple matter to add functionality to rotate the calendar, or move to another month or year.

In the previous examples, the entire calendar was dependant on one variable, the month Date object. If you wanted to display a different month or different year, all you would have to do is modify that variable. Of course, that's an easy thing to do if you are writing the program, but what you really want to do is allow the user to change the display. There are two ways to add this functionality. The first, by using URL parameters, will be presented next; and the second, by using cookies, will be presented later in the chapter.

The code needs to be modified in two places in order to allow the calendar to be rotated. The first place is in the script tag, in order to get the new parameters out of the URL and modify the month variable. The second place in which the program needs to be modified is in the body, in order to add links that will add the parameters into the URL and allow the calendar to rotate. I will discuss the second part first so that you'll know what the first part is working with.

Adding the links to rotate the calendar is not a straightforward matter. You'll need four links, two for the month rotation and two for the year rotation. One link out of each group will rotate forward and the other will rotate backward. Here is the source code that will cause the proper link rotation:

```
<table cellpadding="2" width="75%">
  <tr>
    <td>
      <script language="JavaScript">
      <!--
        var y = fixYear( month.getYear() );
        var m = fixMonth( month.getMonth() - 1 );
        document.write( "<a href='" + getLocation() + "?year=" + y +
                        "&month=" + m + "'>" + months[m] + "</a>" );
      // -->
      </script>
    </td>
    <td rowspan="2">
      <center><font size="6"><b>
      <script language="JavaScript">
```

```html
    <!--
      document.write( months[month.getMonth()] + " " +
                        fixYear( month.getYear() ) );
    // -->
    </script>
    </center></b></font>
  </td>
  <td align="right">
    <script language="JavaScript">
    <!--
      var y = fixYear( month.getYear() );
      var m = fixMonth( month.getMonth() + 1 );
      document.write( "<a href='" + getLocation() + "?year=" + y +
                        "&month=" + m + "'>" + months[m] + "</a>" );
    // -->
    </script>
  </td>
</tr>
<tr>
  <td>
    <script language="JavaScript">
    <!--
      var y = fixYear( month.getYear() - 1 );
      var m = fixMonth( month.getMonth() );
      document.write( "<a href='" + getLocation() + "?year=" + y +
                        "&month=" + m + "'>" + y + "</a>" );
    // -->
    </script>
  </td>
  <td align="right">
    <script language="JavaScript">
    <!--
      var y = fixYear( month.getYear() + 1 );
      var m = fixMonth( month.getMonth() );
      document.write( "<a href='" + getLocation() + "?year=" + y +
                        "&month=" + m + "'>" + y + "</a>" );
    // -->
    </script>
```

```
    </td>
  </tr>
</table>
```

In order to prevent the table from getting too cluttered, I placed the rotation links, along with the month header, in a separate table without a border. Each of the four links follows the same basic pattern.

```
<script language="JavaScript">
<!--
  var y = fixYear( month.getYear()+ <change> );
  var m = fixMonth( month.getMonth() + <change> );
  document.write( "<a href='" + getLocation() + "?year=" + y +
                     "&month=" + m + "'>" + months[m] + "</a>" );
// -->
</script>
```

Each link generates a year value and a month value based on the current year or month. Each value is modified depending on whether the rotation is for the year or month, or if the rotation is going forward or backward. After each new value is generated, an anchor tag with the desired parameters is written to the document. For clarity's sake, here is an actual example to rotate the month backward one month:

```
<script language="JavaScript">
<!--
  var y = fixYear( month.getYear() );
  var m = fixMonth( month.getMonth() - 1 );
  document.write( "<a href='" + getLocation() + "?year=" + y +
                     "&month=" + m + "'>" + months[m] + "</a>" );
// -->
</script>
```

You should notice that the year value is not modified in this example. That's because only one value should be rotated at time (in order to accurately track the current date). The `<change>` value of the month variable in this case is -1.

In order to display the changed calendar, you will need a way to get the parameters out of the URL string and modify the `month` variable. This change is short compared to the previous one.

```
var urlquery = location.href.split( "?" );
if( urlquery[1] )
{
  var params = urlquery[1].split( "&" );
```

```
      var y = ( params[0] ? params[0].split( "=" )[1] :
                              fixYear( now.getYear() ) );
      var m = ( params[1] ? params[1].split( "=" )[1] :
                              fixMonth( now.getMonth() ) );
      month = new Date( y, m, 1 );
    }
```

This code snippet should come after the variable month is declared. Although the code seems complex, the function that it performs is rather simple. If a parameter for the month and date rotation is in the URL string, it gets applied to the month variable. If no parameters are present, the month variable is unaffected and the current month and year will be displayed.

Here is a complete working example of the rotating calendar; its file name is Rotating_Calendar.html (you can check it out in Figure 15.2):

```
<html>

  <head>

    <title>Calendar</title>

    <script language="JavaScript">
    <!--
      var now = new Date();
      var month = new Date( fixYear( now.getYear() ), now.getMonth(), 1 );
      var months = new Array( "January", "February", "March", "April",
                              "May", "June", "July", "August", "September",
                              "October", "November", "December" );

      var urlquery = location.href.split( "?" );
      if( urlquery[1] )
      {
        var params = urlquery[1].split( "&" );
        var y = ( params[0] ? params[0].split( "=" )[1] :
                              fixYear( now.getYear() ) );
        var m = ( params[1] ? params[1].split( "=" )[1] :
                              fixMonth( now.getMonth() ) );
        month = new Date( y, m, 1 );
      }

      function getLocation()
```

```
{
  return( location.href.split( "?" )[0] );
}


function fixYear( year )
{
  return( year < 1000 ?  year + 1900 : year );
}


function fixMonth( month )
{
  return( month < 0 ? month + 12 : (month > 11 ? month - 12 : month) );
}


function getNumberDays( d )
{
  switch( d.getMonth() + 1 )
  {
    case 1: case 3: case 5: case 7:
    case 8: case 10: case 12:
      return( 31 );
    case 4: case 6: case 9: case 11:
      return( 30 );
    case 2:
      return( 28 + ( d.getYear % 4 == 0 ? 1 : 0 ) );
  }
}


function getEnding( number )
{
  if( number > 10 && number < 20 ) return( "th" );

  switch( number % 10 )
  {
    case 0: case 4: case 5:
    case 6: case 7: case 8:
    case 9:
```

```
        return( "th" );
      case 1:
        return( "st" );
      case 2:
        return( "nd" );
      case 3:
        return( "rd" );
    }
  }
// -->
</script>
</head>

<body>
  <table cellpadding="2" width="75%">
    <tr>
      <td>
        <script language="JavaScript">
        <!--
          var y = fixYear( month.getYear() );
          var m = fixMonth( month.getMonth() - 1 );
          document.write( "<a href='" + getLocation() + "?year=" + y +
                          "&month=" + m + "'>" + months[m] + "</a>" );
        // -->
        </script>
      </td>
      <td rowspan="2">
        <center><font size="6"><b>
        <script language="JavaScript">
        <!--
          document.write( months[month.getMonth()] + " " +
                          fixYear( month.getYear() ) );
        // -->
        </script>
        </center></b></font>
      </td>
      <td align="right">
```

```
<script language="JavaScript">
<!--
  var y = fixYear( month.getYear() );
  var m = fixMonth( month.getMonth() + 1 );
  document.write( "<a href='" + getLocation() + "?year=" + y +
                  "&month=" + m + "'>" + months[m] + "</a>" );
// -->
  </script>
  </td>
</tr>
<tr>
  <td>
    <script language="JavaScript">
    <!--
      var y = fixYear( month.getYear() - 1 );
      var m = fixMonth( month.getMonth() );
      document.write( "<a href='" + getLocation() + "?year=" + y +
                      "&month=" + m + "'>" + y + "</a>" );
    // -->
    </script>
  </td>
  <td align="right">
    <script language="JavaScript">
    <!--
      var y = fixYear( month.getYear() + 1 );
      var m = fixMonth( month.getMonth() );
      document.write( "<a href='" + getLocation() + "?year=" + y +
                      "&month=" + m + "'>" + y + "</a>" );
    // -->
    </script>
  </td>
</tr>
</table>

<br><br>
<br><br>
```

```
<table border="1" cellpadding="2" width="75%">
  <tr>
    <td width="14%"><b><i>Sunday</i></b></td>
    <td width="14%"><b><i>Monday</i></b></td>
    <td width="14%"><b><i>Tuesday</i></b></td>
    <td width="14%"><b><i>Wednesday</i></b></td>
    <td width="14%"><b><i>Thursday</i></b></td>
    <td width="14%"><b><i>Friday</i></b></td>
    <td width="14%"><b><i>Saturday</i></b></td>
  </tr>
  <tr>
    <script language="JavaScript">
    <!--
      var startDay = month.getDay();
      for( i = 0 ; i < startDay ; i++ )
      {
        document.write( "<td></td>" );
      }

      var numDays = getNumberDays( month );
      for( i = 0 ; i < numDays ; i++ )
      {
        if( ( i + startDay + 1 ) % 7 == 1 )
        {
          document.write( "</tr><tr>" );
        }
        document.write( "<td height='75' valign='top'b>" + (i+1) +
                        getEnding( i + 1 ) + "</b></td>" );
      }
    // -->
    </script>
  </tr>
</table>

</body>

</html>
```

One function that has not been presented yet, and that you may or may not find useful, is the getEnding() function. Here it is:

```
function getEnding( number )
{
  if( number > 10 && number < 20 ) return( "th" );

  switch( number % 10 )
  {
    case 0: case 4: case 5:
    case 6: case 7: case 8:
    case 9:
      return( "th" );
    case 1:
      return( "st" );
    case 2:
      return( "nd" );
    case 3:
      return( "rd" );
  }
}
```

This is a very simple function that will return the number suffix. For example, this function would return st if passed 21 or rd if passed 53. That way, you'd have 21st or 53rd.

Getting and Setting Calendar Events

Due to JavaScript's lack of file I/O and its inability to talk to a server to request data from a database, the getting and setting of calendar events cannot be written using only JavaScript. A server-side language, such as ASP or ASP.NET, is required to query a database for the events of a given month. Here is a very simple example of loading data from a server-side database with ASP:

```
<%@ LANGUAGE=VBSCRIPT %>
<%
  Dim Database_Connection
  Set Database_Connection = Server.CreateObject( "ADODB.Connection" )
  Database_Connection.Open( "DRIVER={SQL Server};" &
             "SERVER=MyServer;DATABASE=MyDatabase" )
```

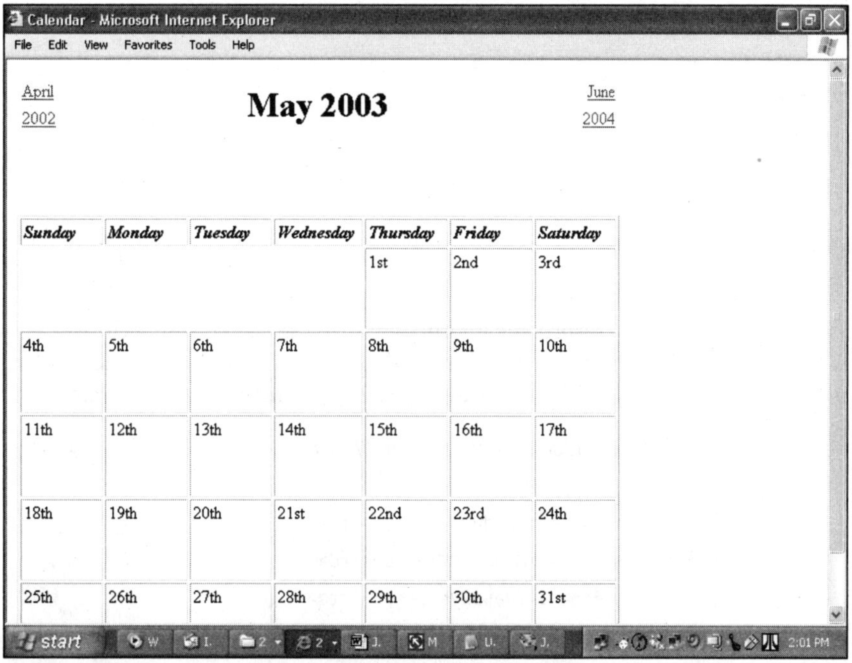

FIGURE 15.2 *An enhanced calendar, with more attractive date naming (note the addition of the "st" and "rd" to dates), as well as jump forward/back buttons to previous year and months.*

```
Dim SQL_Statement
Dim Record_Set
SQL_Statement = "Select * FROM Calendar_Events_Table"
Set Record_Set = Database_Connection.Execute( SQL_Statement )
%>


<html>
  <head>
    <title>Calendar Example</title>
    <script language="JavaScript">
    <!--
      // Other JavaScript functions

      var tasks = new Array( <% While NOT Record_Set.EOF %>
          <%=Response.write( "'Record_Set("task")', ") %>
        <% WEnd %> );
```

```
    // -->
    </script>
  </head>

  <body>
    <!-- Place calendar here -->
  </body>
</html>
```

What JavaScript *can* do is display the information that is given. For simplicity's sake, I will assume that the data generated by the server-side language is in the form of a JavaScript array, and that the array name is `tasks`. If this is the case, displaying the information is a simple matter.

```
<table border="1" cellpadding="2" width="75%">
  <tr>
    <td width="14%"><b><i>Sunday</i></b></td>
    <td width="14%"><b><i>Monday</i></b></td>
    <td width="14%"><b><i>Tuesday</i></b></td>
    <td width="14%"><b><i>Wednesday</i></b></td>
    <td width="14%"><b><i>Thursday</i></b></td>
    <td width="14%"><b><i>Friday</i></b></td>
    <td width="14%"><b><i>Saturday</i></b></td>
  </tr>
  <tr>
    <script language="JavaScript">
    <!--
      var startDay = month.getDay();
      for( i = 0 ; i < startDay ; i++ )
      {
        document.write( "<td></td>" );
      }

      var numDays = getNumberDays( month );
      for( i = 0 ; i < numDays ; i++ )
      {
        if( ( i + startDay + 1 ) % 7 == 1 )
        {
          document.write( "</tr><tr>" );
        }
```

```
            document.write( "<td height='75' valign='top'" );
            if( fixYear( now.getYear() ) == fixYear( month.getYear() ) &&
                now.getMonth() == month.getMonth() && now.getDate() == i + 1 )
                document.write( " bordercolor='red'" );
            document.write( "><b>" + (i+1) + getEnding( i+1 ) + "</b><br>" );
            if( tasks[i+1] ) document.write( tasks[i+1] );
            document.write( "</td>" );
        }
    // -->
    </script>
  </tr>
</table>
```

This example fills in the calendar events as it is building the calendar itself. The line

```
if( tasks[i+1] ) document.write( tasks[i+1] );
```

looks in the array of tasks, and if a task exists, writes it into the current table cell. It's really as simple as that.

Depending on your specific use for your table, it may be a good idea to mark which cell in the table represents the current day. This is easily taken care of in a couple of lines of code:

```
            document.write( "<td height='75' valign='top'" );
            if( fixYear( now.getYear() ) == fixYear( month.getYear() ) &&
                now.getMonth() == month.getMonth() && now.getDate() == i + 1 )
                document.write( " bordercolor='red'" );
            document.write( "><b>" + (i+1) + getEnding( i+1 ) + "</b><br>" );
            if( tasks[i+1] ) document.write( tasks[i+1] );
            document.write( "</td>" );
```

The if statements will make the border of the current cell red if the month and year that are being displayed are the current month and year. Here is a complete example that uses a rotating calendar and displays a couple of tasks in their corresponding days; its file name is Calendar.html:

```
<html>
  <head>
    <title></title>

    <script language="JavaScript">
    <!--
```

```
var now = new Date();
var months = new Array( "January", "February", "March", "April",
                        "May", "June", "July", "August", "September",
                        "October", "November", "December" );

var yString = getCookieValue( "year" );
var mString = getCookieValue( "month" );
var y = fixYear( yString ? parseInt( yString ) : now.getYear() );
var m = fixMonth( mString ? parseInt( mString ) : now.getMonth() );
var month = new Date( y, m, 1 );

function getCookieValue( name )
{
  var c = document.cookie;
  var begin = c.indexOf( name );
  if( begin < 0 ) return( "" );
  begin += name.length + 1;
  var end = c.indexOf( ";", begin );
  if( end == -1 ) end = c.length;
  return( c.slice( begin, end ) );
}

function fixYear( year )
{
  return( year < 1000 ?  year + 1900 : year );
}

function fixMonth( month )
{
  return( month < 0 ? month + 12 : (month > 11 ? month - 12 : month) );
}

function getNumberDays( d )
{
  switch( d.getMonth() + 1 )
  {
    case 1: case 3: case 5: case 7:
    case 8: case 10: case 12:
```

```
          return( 31 );
        case 4: case 6: case 9: case 11:
          return( 30 );
        case 2:
          return( 28 + ( d.getYear % 4 == 0 ? 1 : 0 ) );
      }
    }

    function getEnding( number )
    {
      if( number > 10 && number < 20 ) return( "th" );

      switch( number % 10 )
      {
        case 0: case 4: case 5:
        case 6: case 7: case 8:
        case 9:
          return( "th" );
        case 1:
          return( "st" );
        case 2:
          return( "nd" );
        case 3:
          return( "rd" );
      }
    }

    // These should be loaded from a server-side language such as ASP
    var tasks = new Array( 30 );
    tasks[5] = "<a href='Test.html'>Take CS Test</a>";
    tasks[28] = "English Paper Due";
  // -->
  </script>
</head>

<body onLoad="JavaScript: document.cookie='loggedin=true';">
  <i>Welcome</i><b>
  <script language="JavaScript">
```

```
<!--
  document.write( getCookieValue( "username" ) + "</b>!! " );
// -->
</script>
<i>Here are your tasks for</i>

<table width="75%">
  <tr><td align="center">
    <font size="6"><b>
      <script language="JavaScript">
      <!--
        document.write( months[m] );
      // -->
      </script>
    </b></font>
  </td></tr>
</table>

<table border="1" cellpadding="2" width="75%">
  <tr>
    <td width="14%"><b><i>Sunday</i></b></td>
    <td width="14%"><b><i>Monday</i></b></td>
    <td width="14%"><b><i>Tuesday</i></b></td>
    <td width="14%"><b><i>Wednesday</i></b></td>
    <td width="14%"><b><i>Thursday</i></b></td>
    <td width="14%"><b><i>Friday</i></b></td>
    <td width="14%"><b><i>Saturday</i></b></td>
  </tr>
  <tr>
    <script language="JavaScript">
    <!--
      var startDay = month.getDay();
      for( i = 0 ; i < startDay ; i++ )
      {
        document.write( "<td></td>" );
      }
```

```
      var numDays = getNumberDays( month );
      for( i = 0 ; i < numDays ; i++ )
      {
        if( ( i + startDay + 1 ) % 7 == 1 )
        {
          document.write( "</tr><tr>" );
        }
        document.write( "<td height='75' valign='top'" );
        if( fixYear( now.getYear() ) == fixYear( month.getYear() ) &&
            now.getMonth() == month.getMonth() && now.getDate() == i + 1 )
            document.write( " bordercolor='red'" );
            document.write( "><b>"+(i+1)+getEnding(i+1)+"</b><br>" );
        if( tasks[i+1] ) document.write( tasks[i+1] );
        document.write( "</td>" );
      }
    // -->
    </script>
  </tr>
</table>

<table width="75%">
  <tr>
    <td>
      <script language="JavaScript">
      <!--
        document.write( "<a href=\"" + document.location + "\" " );
        document.write( "onClick=\"JavaScript: document.cookie='month=" +
                        fixMonth(m-1) + "';\">" );
        document.write( months[fixMonth(m-1)] + "</a>" );
      // -->
      </script>
    </td>
    <td align="right">
      <script language="JavaScript">
      <!--
        document.write( "<a href=\"" + document.location + "\" " );
        document.write( "onClick=\"JavaScript: document.cookie='month=" +
```

```
                       fixMonth(m+1) + "';\">" );
            document.write( months[fixMonth(m+1)] + "</a>" );
         // -->
         </script>
        </td>
      </tr>
    </table>


    </body>
</html>
```

This example is part of the running Center Park Web site and is the screen a user will see just after logging in to the site (this will be explained fully in later chapters).

One noteworthy part of the previous example is the fact that it uses cookies instead of passing the month and year parameters through the URL string. Two links at the bottom of the page will allow the user to rotate the calendar. Here is the basic format for the two links:

```
<script language="JavaScript">
<!--
document.write( "<a href=\"" + document.location + "\" " );
document.write( "onClick=\"JavaScript: document.cookie='month=" +
                            fixMonth(m-1) + "';\">" );
document.write( months[fixMonth(m+<change>)] + "</a>" );
// -->
</script>
```

Although different from the previous method of passing the parameters through the URL string, the functionality is identical. The code needed to extract the parameters from the cookie file is as follows:

```
var yString = getCookieValue( "year" );
var mString = getCookieValue( "month" );
var y = fixYear( yString ? parseInt( yString ) : now.getYear() );
var m = fixMonth( mString ? parseInt( mString ) : now.getMonth() );
var month = new Date( y, m, 1 );
```

This method is nearly identical to the previous method of extracting the parameters from the URL string. Both methods work equally well; it is up to you to choose which one is best for your site.

See Figure 15.3 for an even more enhanced calendar.

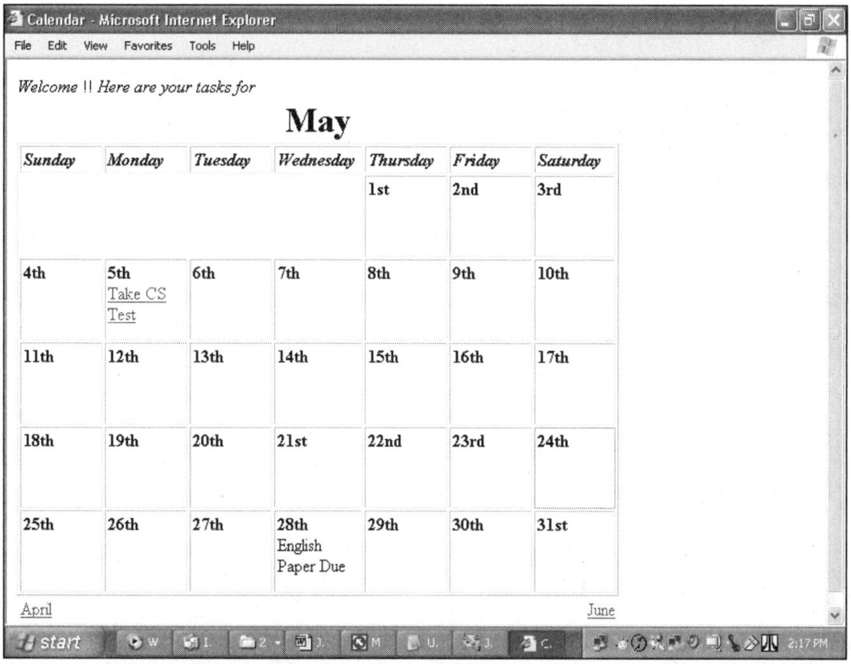

FIGURE 15.3 *Now the calendar includes a hyperlink to a student test, prior and next month navigation buttons at bottom, and today's date is highlighted in red (in this figure, the date of 5/24).*

Pop-Up Calendar for Form Completion

The pop-up calendar is a completely different type of calendar used on a Web site. Although it is quite different from the perpetual calendar, much of the code used to create it is nearly identical to the code you used for that calendar.

Here are some ways in which an online pop-up calendar is different from a perpetual calendar:

◆ A pop-up calendar is displayed in its own window.

◆ After a user selects a date, the pop-up window closes and fills in a field on the parent window.

◆ No events are can be displayed in the calendar.

Just like with the perpetual calendar, display and rotation are two basic functions of the pop-up calendar. Luckily, getting and setting events is not an issue with this type of calendar. This time around, though, you'll have to worry about inter-window communication between the calendar and its parent window.

Displaying the Pop-up Calendar

When I wrote "display" above, I meant creating the table and filling it with the calendar data. Using the parent window to pop up the calendar will be discussed in the section titled "Inter-Window Communications."

Calendar display should be familiar to you by now, so I will simply give you the source for the calendar and explain the very few different features of a pop-up calendar. The file name of this example is Simple_Popup_Calendar.html:

```html
<html>

  <head>
    <title>Date Chooser</title>

    <style type="text/css">
    <!--
      .mono{ font-family: monospace; }
    -->
    </style>

    <script language="JavaScript">
    <!--
      var now = new Date();
      var month = new Date( fixYear( now.getYear() ), now.getMonth(), 1 );
      var months = new Array( "January", "February", "March", "April",
                              "May", "June", "July", "August", "September",
                              "October", "November", "December" );

      function fixYear( year )
      {
        return( year < 1000 ?  year + 1900 : year );
      }

      function fixMonth( month )
      {
        return( month < 0 ? month + 12 : (month > 11 ? month - 12 : month) );
      }

      function getNumberDays( d )
```

```
  {
    switch( d.getMonth() + 1 )
    {
      case 1: case 3: case 5: case 7:
      case 8: case 10: case 12:
        return( 31 );
      case 4: case 6: case 9: case 11:
        return( 30 );
      case 2:
        return( 28 + ( d.getYear % 4 == 0 ? 1 : 0 ) );
    }
  }


  function getEnding( number )
  {
    if( number > 10 && number < 20 ) return( "th" );

    switch( number % 10 )
    {
      case 0: case 4: case 5:
      case 6: case 7: case 8:
      case 9:
        return( "th" );
      case 1:
        return( "st" );
      case 2:
        return( "nd" );
      case 3:
        return( "rd" );
    }
  }


  function onSelect()
  {
  }
// -->
</script>
```

```html
</head>

<body>

  <form name="theForm">
    <table border="1" width="75%" style="border-collapse: collapse">
      <tr>
        <td align="left" colspan=2>
           </td>
        <td colspan=3>
          <center>
            <b><script language="JavaScript">
            <!--
              document.write( months[fixMonth( month.getMonth() )] + " " +
                              fixYear( month.getYear() ) );
            // -->
            </script></b></center>
        </td>
        <td align="right" colspan=2>
           </td>
      </tr>
      <tr>
        <td width="14%"><b><i>Sun</i></b></td>
        <td width="14%"><b><i>Mon</i></b></td>
        <td width="14%"><b><i>Tue</i></b></td>
        <td width="14%"><b><i>Wed</i></b></td>
        <td width="14%"><b><i>Thu</i></b></td>
        <td width="14%"><b><i>Fri</i></b></td>
        <td width="14%"><b><i>Sat</i></b></td>
      </tr>
      <tr>
        <script language="JavaScript">
        <!--
          var startDay = month.getDay();
          for( i = 0 ; i < startDay ; i++ )
          {
            document.write( "<td></td>" );
          }
```

```
var numDays = getNumberDays( month );
for( i = 1 ; i < numDays + 1 ; i++ )
{
  if( ( i + startDay ) % 7 == 1 )
  {
    document.write( "</tr><tr>" );
  }
  document.write(
    "<td><center>" + input type='button' " +
    "onClick='JavaScript: document.theForm.date.value=\"" +
        fixMonth( month.getMonth() + 1 ) + "/" + i + "/" +
        fixYear( month.getYear() ) + "\"; onSelect();' " +
    "value='" + (i < 10 ? " " : "") + i + getEnding( i ) + "' " +
    "class='mono'>" + "</center></td>" );
}
// -->
</script>
    </tr>
  </table>
  <input type="hidden" name="date">
</form>
</body>

</html>
```

In this example, the size of the calendar is an issue. Because the calendar is going to be displaying in a separate pop-up window, it will most likely be smaller than a parent window. Because of this, I created a cascading style sheet class named .mono that is applied to each button in the calendar to make them the same size. Buttons are used in the table cells this time around because they produce events that are easier to capture. The onSelect() function and the hidden form field will be explained later in this section.

Rotating the Pop-up Calendar

There are two places in which the code needs to be modified in order to allow the calendar to be rotated. The first place is in the script tag, in order to get the new parameters out of the URL and modify the month variable. The second place the program needs to be modified is in the body, in order to add links that will add the parameters into the URL and allow the calendar to rotate. I will discuss the second part first so that you'll know what the first part is working with.

This time around, I will add text fields so that the user can simply type in the number of the month and date that they wish to view. This only modifies the first row of the calendar. Here is the modified code:

```
<tr>
  <td align="left" colspan=2>
    <b>Month:</b>
    <input type="text" name="Month" size="5">
    <script language="JavaScript">
    <!--
      document.theForm.Month.value = fixMonth( month.getMonth() + 1 );
    // -->
    </script>
  </td>
  <td colspan=3>
    <center>
      <b><script language="JavaScript">
      <!--
        document.write( months[fixMonth( month.getMonth() )] + " " +
                        fixYear( month.getYear() ) );
      // -->
      </script></b><br>
      <input type="submit" value="Submit">
    </center>
  </td>
  <td align="right" colspan=2>
    <b>Year:</b>
    <input type="text" name="Year" size="5">
    <script language="JavaScript">
    <!--
      document.theForm.Year.value = fixYear( month.getYear() );
    // -->
    </script>
  </td>
</tr>
```

The first cell in the row contains a text field for the month and the third cell contains a text field for the year. Both of these are controlled by a Submit button just under the Month heading. The month and year that are being displayed in the calendar are the default values of each of the text fields. When the Submit button is pressed, the page refreshes and changes the calendar. Because the names of the form fields are Month and Year, the exact same code that I used in the perpetual calendar can be used to retrieve them from the URL string:

```
var urlquery = location.href.split( "?" );
if( urlquery[1] )
{
  var params = urlquery[1].split( "&" );
  var m = ( params[0] ? params[0].split( "=" )[1] - 1 :
                        fixMonth( now.getMonth() ) );
  var y = ( params[1] ? params[1].split( "=" )[1] :
                        fixYear( now.getYear() ) );
  month = new Date( y, m, 1 );
}
```

Modifying the month variable will, just like before, change what is displayed in the calendar table.

Here is the complete source code for the rotating pop-up calendar; the file name of this code example is Rotating_Popup_Calendar.html:

```
<html>

  <head>
    <title>Date Chooser</title>

    <style type="text/css">
    <!--
      .mono{ font-family: monospace; }
    -->
    </style>

    <script language="JavaScript">
    <!--
      var now = new Date();
      var month = new Date( fixYear( now.getYear() ), now.getMonth(), 1 );
      var months = new Array( "January", "February", "March", "April",
                              "May", "June", "July", "August", "September",
                              "October", "November", "December" );
```

```
var urlquery = location.href.split( "?" );
if( urlquery[1] )
{
  var params = urlquery[1].split( "&" );
  var m = ( params[0] ? params[0].split( "=" )[1] - 1 :
                        fixMonth( now.getMonth() ) ) );
  var y = ( params[1] ? params[1].split( "=" )[1] :
                        fixYear( now.getYear() ) ) );
  month = new Date( y, m, 1 );
}


function fixYear( year )
{
  return( year < 1000 ?  year + 1900 : year );
}


function fixMonth( month )
{
  return( month < 0 ? month + 12 : (month > 11 ? month - 12 : month) );
}


function getNumberDays( d )
{
  switch( d.getMonth() + 1 )
  {
    case 1: case 3: case 5: case 7:
    case 8: case 10: case 12:
      return( 31 );
    case 4: case 6: case 9: case 11:
      return( 30 );
    case 2:
      return( 28 + ( d.getYear % 4 == 0 ? 1 : 0 ) );
  }
}


function getEnding( number )
{
```

```
    if( number > 10 && number < 20 ) return( "th" );

    switch( number % 10 )
    {
      case 0: case 4: case 5:
      case 6: case 7: case 8:
      case 9:
        return( "th" );
      case 1:
        return( "st" );
      case 2:
        return( "nd" );
      case 3:
        return( "rd" );
    }
  }

  function onSelect()
  {
  }
  // -->
  </script>
</head>

<body>

  <form name="theForm">
    <table border="1" width="75%" style="border-collapse: collapse">
      <tr>
        <td align="left" colspan=2>
          <b>Month:</b>
          <input type="text" name="Month" size="5">
          <script language="JavaScript">
          <!--
            document.theForm.Month.value = fixMonth( month.getMonth() + 1 );
          // -->
          </script>
```

```
    </td>
    <td colspan=3>
      <center>
        <b><script language="JavaScript">
        <!--
          document.write( months[fixMonth( month.getMonth() )] + " " +
                          fixYear( month.getYear() ) );
        // -->
        </script></b><br>
        <input type="submit" value="Submit">
      </center>
    </td>
    <td align="right" colspan=2>
      <b>Year:</b>
      <input type="text" name="Year" size="5">
      <script language="JavaScript">
      <!--
        document.theForm.Year.value = fixYear( month.getYear() );
      // -->
      </script>
    </td>
  </tr>
  <tr>
    <td width="14%"><b><i>Sun</i></b></td>
    <td width="14%"><b><i>Mon</i></b></td>
    <td width="14%"><b><i>Tue</i></b></td>
    <td width="14%"><b><i>Wed</i></b></td>
    <td width="14%"><b><i>Thu</i></b></td>
    <td width="14%"><b><i>Fri</i></b></td>
    <td width="14%"><b><i>Sat</i></b></td>
  </tr>
  <tr>
    <script language="JavaScript">
    <!--
      var startDay = month.getDay();
      for( i = 0 ; i < startDay ; i++ )
      {
        document.write( "<td></td>" );
```

```
                  }

                  var numDays = getNumberDays( month );
                  for( i = 1 ; i < numDays + 1 ; i++ )
                  {
                    if( ( i + startDay ) % 7 == 1 )
                    {
                      document.write( "</tr><tr>" );
                    }
                    document.write(
                      "<td><center><input type='button' " +
                      "onClick='JavaScript: document.theForm.date.value=\"" +
                          fixMonth( month.getMonth() + 1 ) + "/" + i + "/" +
                          fixYear( month.getYear() ) + "\"; onSelect();' " +
                      "value='" + (i < 10 ? " " : "") + i + getEnding( i ) + "' " +
                      "class='mono'>" + "</center></td>" );
                  }
                // -->
                </script>
              </tr>
            </table>
            <input type="hidden" name="date">
          </form>
        </body>

</html>
```

Inter-Window Communications

Now that the pop-up calendar has been designed, all that remains is to create it and have it automatically fill in a form field for the user. First you need a form to fill in, though. Here is a page that will be part of the Center Park site; the file name of this example is AddTask.html:

```
<html>

  <head>
    <title>Center Park - Add Task</title>

    <script language="JavaScript">
```

```
<!--
  var dateElement;
  function openDatePicker( target )
  {
    dateElement = target;
    var ieSize = "width=380,height=255";
    var navSize = "width=480,height=295";
    var isNav = navigator.appName == "Netscape";
    window.open( "PopupCalendar.html", "calendar",
              "menubar=no,resizable=no,scrollbars=no," +
              "status=yes,toolbar=no," +
              ( isNav ? navSize : ieSize ) );
  }

  function setDate( date )
  {
    dateElement.value = date;
  }

  function getCookieValue( name )
  {
    var c = document.cookie;
    var begin = c.indexOf( name );
    if( begin < 0 ) return( "" );
    begin += name.length + 1;
    var end = c.indexOf( ";", begin );
    if( end == -1 ) end = c.length;
    return( c.slice( begin, end ) );
  }
// -->
</script>
</head>

<body>
  <br>
  <br>
  <i>Center Park Task Scheduler for</i><b>
  <script language="JavaScript">
```

```
<!--
  document.write( getCookieValue( "username" ) );
// -->
</script></b>.


<br><br>
<br><br>


<form name="taskForm" onSubmit="JavaScript: return( false );">
  <center>
    <table border="1" width="75%">
      <tr>
        <td width="100%" colspan="2"><b>Schedule Task</b></td>
      </tr>
      <tr>
        <td width="50%">
          Date of task: 
          <input type="text" name="date" size="10">
          <input type="button" value="..."
            onClick="JavaScript: openDatePicker(document.taskForm.date);">
        </td>
        <td width="50%">
          Task description (HTML is ok):<br>
          <textarea rows="7" cols="35"></textarea>
        </td>
      </tr>
      <tr>
        <td align="center" colspan="2">
          <input type="submit" value="Submit" name="B1">
        </td>
      </tr>
    </table>
  </center>
</form>
</body>


</html>
```

One of these fields requires a date from the user. Because dates can be represented in so many different ways, and because parsing all the different ways into the format you want is so difficult, it is a good idea to create a way for the user to fill in the field automatically, which is the one and only purpose of the pop-up calendar. Two functions are required to automatically fill in the form field for the user. The openDatePicker() function, shown below, will create the pop-up window and display it:

```
var dateElement;
function openDatePicker( target )
{
  dateElement = target;
  var ieSize = "width=380,height=255";
  var navSize = "width=480,height=295";
  var isNav = navigator.appName == "Netscape";
  window.open( "PopupCalendar.html", "calendar",
               "menubar=no,resizable=no,scrollbars=no," +
               "status=yes,toolbar=no," +
               ( isNav ? navSize : ieSize ) );
}
```

The one parameter that the openDatePicker() takes is the field in which the date value will be placed after the user chooses a date from the pop-up calendar. The second function,

```
function setDate( date )
{
  dateElement.value = date;
}
```

will fill in the form field with the date value after the pop-up window has closed.

You may have noticed that the setDate() function is never called from the page. There is a good reason for that—the function is called from the pop-up calendar after the user selects a date. In the previous examples, the onSelect() function for the pop-up window was not filled in. If you were to replace the blank function with

```
function onSelect()
{
  window.opener.setDate( document.theForm.date.value );
  self.close();
}
```

you would not only be completing the functionality of the pop-up calendar, but you would also allow the pop-up calendar to talk to its parent window. When a user selects a date on the pop-up calendar, the calendar temporarily stores the selected date in a hidden form field and then calls the `onSelect()` function. The `onSelect()` function calls the `setDate()` function on its parent window with the date value that was selected and then closes the pop-up calendar. Once the `setDate()` function is called on the parent window, the date has already been selected and the pop-up calendar has been closed, so the only thing remaining to do is fill in the form for the user.

Here is the complete source code for the pop-up calendar. It should be placed in a file named PopupCalendar.html in order to work with the examples in this chapter. Figure 15.4 illustrates this in action.

```html
<html>

  <head>
    <title>Date Chooser</title>

    <style type="text/css">
    <!--
      .mono{ font-family: monospace; }
    -->
    </style>

    <script language="JavaScript">
    <!--
      var now = new Date();
      var month = new Date( fixYear( now.getYear() ), now.getMonth(), 1 );
      var months = new Array( "January", "February", "March", "April",
                              "May", "June", "July", "August", "September",
                              "October", "November", "December" );

      var urlquery = location.href.split( "?" );
      if( urlquery[1] )
      {
        var params = urlquery[1].split( "&" );
        var m = ( params[0] ? params[0].split( "=" )[1] - 1 :
                              fixMonth( now.getMonth() ) );
        var y = ( params[1] ? params[1].split( "=" )[1] :
                              fixYear( now.getYear() ) );
        month = new Date( y, m, 1 );
      }
```

```
function fixYear( year )
{
  return( year < 1000 ?  year + 1900 : year );
}


function fixMonth( month )
{
  return( month < 0 ? month + 12 : (month > 11 ? month - 12 : month) );
}


function getNumberDays( d )
{
  switch( d.getMonth() + 1 )
  {
    case 1: case 3: case 5: case 7:
    case 8: case 10: case 12:
      return( 31 );
    case 4: case 6: case 9: case 11:
      return( 30 );
    case 2:
      return( 28 + ( d.getYear % 4 == 0 ? 1 : 0 ) );
  }
}


function getEnding( number )
{
  if( number > 10 && number < 20 ) return( "th" );

  switch( number % 10 )
  {
    case 0: case 4: case 5:
    case 6: case 7: case 8:
    case 9:
      return( "th" );
    case 1:
      return( "st" );
    case 2:
      return( "nd" );
```

```
      case 3:
        return( "rd" );
    }
  }

  function onSelect()
  {
    window.opener.setDate( document.theForm.date.value );
    self.close();
  }
 // -->
 </script>
</head>

<body>

  <form name="theForm">
    <table border="1" width="75%" style="border-collapse: collapse">
      <tr>
        <td align="left" colspan=2>
          <b>Month:</b>
          <input type="text" name="Month" size="5">
          <script language="JavaScript">
          <!--
            document.theForm.Month.value = fixMonth( month.getMonth() + 1 );
          // -->
          </script>
        </td>
        <td colspan=3>
          <center>
            <b><script language="JavaScript">
            <!--
              document.write( months[fixMonth( month.getMonth() )] + " " +
                              fixYear( month.getYear() ) );
            // -->
            </script></b><br>
            <input type="submit" value="Submit">
          </center>
```

```
    </td>
    <td align="right" colspan=2>
      <b>Year:</b>
      <input type="text" name="Year" size="5">
      <script language="JavaScript">
      <!--
        document.theForm.Year.value = fixYear( month.getYear() );
      // -->
      </script>
    </td>
  </tr>
  <tr>
    <td width="14%"><b><i>Sun</i></b></td>
    <td width="14%"><b><i>Mon</i></b></td>
    <td width="14%"><b><i>Tue</i></b></td>
    <td width="14%"><b><i>Wed</i></b></td>
    <td width="14%"><b><i>Thu</i></b></td>
    <td width="14%"><b><i>Fri</i></b></td>
    <td width="14%"><b><i>Sat</i></b></td>
  </tr>
  <tr>
    <script language="JavaScript">
    <!--
      var startDay = month.getDay();
      for( i = 0 ; i < startDay ; i++ )
      {
        document.write( "<td></td>" );
      }

      var numDays = getNumberDays( month );
      for( i = 1 ; i < numDays + 1 ; i++ )
      {
        if( ( i + startDay ) % 7 == 1 )
        {
          document.write( "</tr><tr>" );
        }
        document.write(
          "<td><center><input type='button' " +
```

```
                    "onClick='JavaScript: document.theForm.date.value=\"" +
                        fixMonth( month.getMonth() + 1 ) + "/" + i + "/" +
                        fixYear( month.getYear() ) + "\"; onSelect();' " +
                    "value='" + (i < 10 ? " " : "") + i + getEnding( i ) + "' " +
                    "class='mono'>" + "</center></td>" );
                }
            // -->
            </script>
        </tr>
    </table>
    <input type="hidden" name="date">
  </form>
</body>

</html>
```

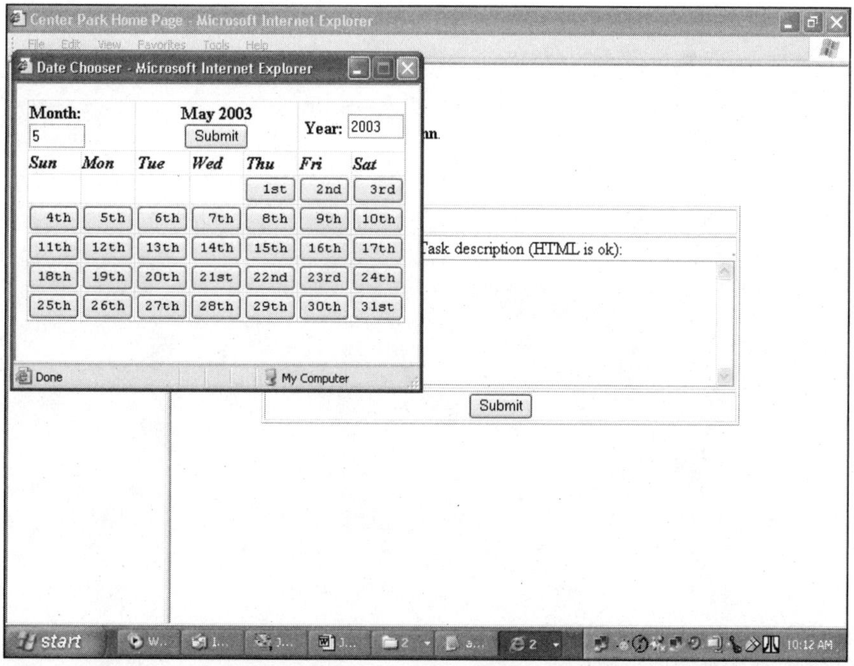

FIGURE 15.4 *By utilizing a pop-up calendar in this way, you can allow users an easy and accurate method of selecting a specific date. Note that this pop-up functionality can carry over to other form functions.*

Summary

Calendars can add a tremendous amount of functionality to your Web site, both in organization and presentation of information. For the Center Park project, it should be obvious how functional a well-designed calendar can be, in reaching the organizational needs of a varied audience (again, students, teachers, and parents). As you continue to build the Center Park site, you will see how the calendar functionality integrates with other components of your JavaScript, so that—for example—students are presented with a custom calendar listing their specific tasks and events, once they log in to the site. If you plan it correctly, the calendar can be the central launching point for a personalized Web experience, with all major informational aspects for the site building from what is presented on the calendar, be it specific to the user or general to all site visitors.

Chapter 16

Tests and surveys are wonderful sources of information. They can be used to test the knowledge of an individual or to elicit information from several people in an easy and useable manner. Online tests or surveys are no different in those respects. The benefits of an online test or survey are many. For starters, the test or survey taker can give you the information that you need from virtually any place there is a computer. This means that you can have a wide cross-section of responses, as the whole world has access to your test or survey. Additionally, many people find filling out online forms faster and easier than filling out paper tests and surveys.

What are the specific benefits to the online test (and survey) feature for the Center Park School? During the site-planning phase, the school administrators were quite specific in their request that the new Web site have "distance learning" capabilities, so that students (of all ages) could take advantage of Center Park instruction, even if they weren't in physical proximity of the school. Moreover, as noted in Chapter 15 and the discussion of the enhanced calendar functionality present within the site, the administrators wanted the site to present students with the ability to better organize their schoolwork: One tremendous feature of the Web, in this regard, is that it allows you to retrieve information at any time and place. Given the hectic lives of students, the school administrators wanted to experiment with the concept of "any time test taking" so that students could access quizzes and tests at home or after school hours (a particularly useful function to students who, for example, might be out sick on the day of a test, or are otherwise unable to come to school to complete an exam).

So, the online testing/survey component is of benefit to each particular section of the Center Park audience. Specifically:

- **Students**. Having the ability to utilize the site for test taking allows students to potentially study at their own pace: For example, an instructor might have "floating exam dates" throughout the semester, so that students are required to take an exam, but more in line with a typical college correspondence course where they study at their own pace, and then—when they are ready—take the exam.

- **Teachers**. By placing exams on the Web—and specifically within the calendar— teachers can be assured that students are aware of when important tests are to be taken, and can therefore (ideally) better plan for these exams. Moreover, teachers can place additional supporting material online with the exams (*e.g.* tests questions can include graphics, which the students can refer to); teachers can also use the power of the Web to do "electronic grading" so that as soon as students submit their answers, the tests are automatically graded and the results instantaneously presented back to them.

- **Parents**. By and large, most parents want to stay involved with their kid's education, but after-school PTA meetings or other events held in the evening/weekends can get in the way of already (very) busy lives. Again, using the "24/7/365" access features of the Web, parents can interact with the school at their leisure and convenience, thus allowing them to stay involved without having to physically be present for events and meetings at the school.

In this chapter I'll walk you through how I created an online test for the imaginary school Center Park. Because tests and surveys are so similar, we won't do an example survey. The only way in which a survey is different from a test is that there is no grading portion of a survey. The grading portion of a test is covered in the second half of this chapter.

Creating the Test

Creating the test portion of an online test (as apposed to the grading portion) is very simple. Using the knowledge you got from Chapter 8, you should be able to build a form and validate it prior to submission. Here is the complete source for the example I will explain afterwards:

```html
<html>

  <head>
    <title>Center Park - Computer Science Test</title>

    <script language="JavaScript">
    <!--
      function validate( form )
      {
        for( i = 0 ; i < form.elements.length ; i++ )
        {
          with( form.elements[i] )
          {
            if( type == "text" && value == "" )
            {
              alert( "Please answer all questions." );
              return( false );
            }
          }
        }
        return( true );
      }
    // -->
    </script>
  </head>

<body>
  <b><font size="5">Computer Science 101 - Midterm Test</font> </b>

  <br><br>

  <font face="Courier">
    All the questions are <b>compulsory</b>.
```

```
    Please read the questions <i>carefully</i> before answering.
    Do not spend too much time on any one question.
    You have 30 minutes to complete the test.  Good Luck!
</font>

<br><br>

<form name="TestForm" action="Grade.html"
      onSubmit="JavaScript: return( validate( this ) );">
  <table width="100%" cellpadding="2" cellspacing="2">
    <tr>
      <td>1)</td>
      <td>
        <font face="Courier">
          Imagine there was no precedence for arithmetic operators.
          Assuming left associativity for all operators, what is the value
          of the expression 5-3*4/2+6 ?
        </font>
      </td>
    </tr>
    <tr>
      <td>Answer</td>
      <td><input type="text" name="Q1" size="20"></td>
    </tr>
    <tr><td> </td><td> </td></tr>
    <tr>
      <td>2)</td>
      <td>
        <font face="Courier">
          What HTML tag must all JavaScript functions be nested in ie:
          HTML, BODY, TABLE?
        </font>
      </td>
    </tr>
    <tr>
      <td>Answer</td>
      <td><input type="text" name="Q2" size="20"></td>
    </tr>
```

```
<tr><td> </td><td> </td></tr>
<tr>
  <td>3)</td>
  <td>
    <font face="Courier">
      What event is spawned after a user has selected text or HTML
      elements on a Web page?
    </font>
  </td>
</tr>
<tr>
  <td>Answer</td>
  <td><input type="text" name="Q3" size="20"></td>
</tr>
<tr><td> </td><td> </td></tr>
<tr>
  <td>4)</td>
  <td>
    <font face="Courier">
      What type of variable scoping does JavaScript use?
    </font>
  </td>
</tr>
<tr>
  <td>Answer</td>
  <td><input type="text" name="Q4" size="20"></td>
</tr>
<tr><td> </td><td> </td></tr>
<tr>
  <td>5)</td>
  <td>
    <font face="Courier">
      What relational operator is used to determine if two variables
      of the same type are not equal to each other?
    </font>
  </td>
</tr>
<tr>
<tr>
```

```
      <td>Answer</td>
      <td><input type="text" name="Q5" size="20"></td>
    </tr>
  </table>

  <br>
  <input type="submit" value="Submit" name="B1">
</form>

<script language="JavaScript">
<!--
  window.setTimeout( "document.TestForm.SubmitButton.enabled=false",
                                1000 * 60 * 30 );
  // -->
  </script>
</body>

</html>
```

Figure 16.1 shows this code in action. Note that each question must be answered; otherwise, a warning pop-up appears to the test-taker, as seen in Figure 16.2

No aspect of this example should be new to you. The form contains five questions, each with a text form field in which the user should supply the answer. Before the form itself is submitted, the `validate()` function,

```
function validate( form )
{
  for( i = 0 ; i < form.elements.length ; i++ )
  {
    with( form.elements[i] )
    {
      if( type == "text" && value == "" )
      {
        alert( "Please answer all questions." );
        return( false );
      }
    }
  }
  return( true );
}
```

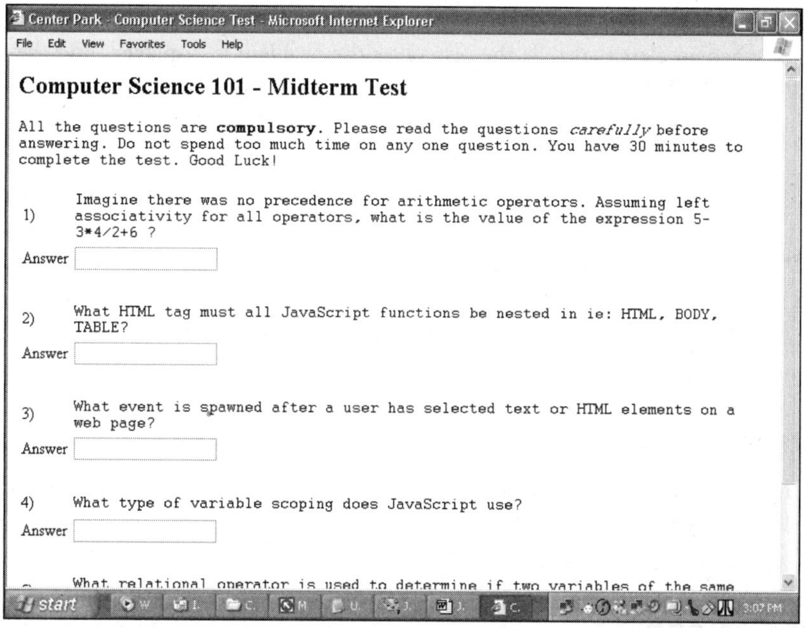

FIGURE 16.1 *A five-question online test. Utilizing the power of the Web, students can access the test at any time and have their results instantly returned to them.*

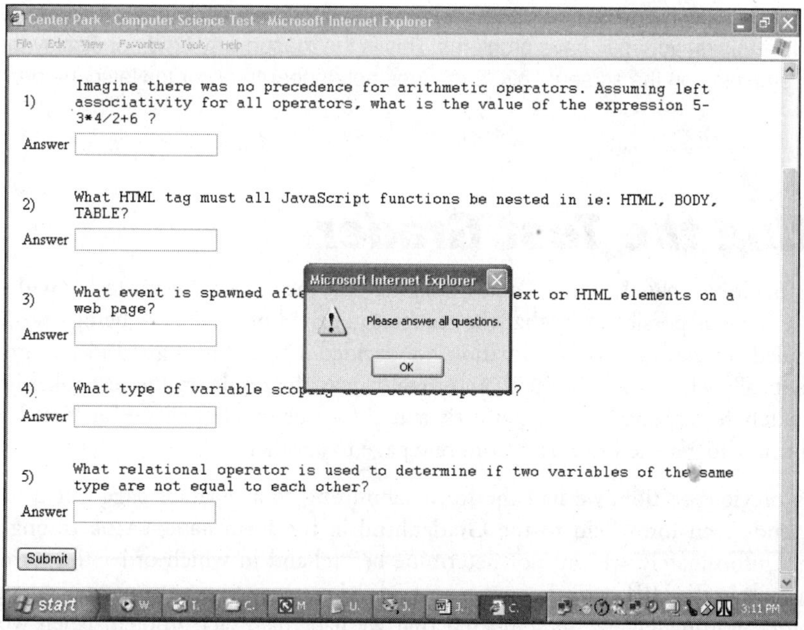

FIGURE 16.2 *All questions must be answered; otherwise, this pop-up message appears. This ensures consistency amongst the test takers.*

checks each answer text field to make sure an answer was provided. If a question was not answered, then an alert that tells the test-taker the problem is displayed, and the form is not submitted. If all of the questions were answered, the form is submitted to a separate HTML page named Grade.html. The functionality of this second page will be explained in the second half of the chapter.

One thing that you might not have seen on other pages is the time limit. The very last script tag,

```
<script language="JavaScript">
<!--
   window.setTimeout( "document.TestForm.SubmitButton.enabled=false",
                                  1000 * 60 * 30 );
// -->
</script>
```

using the Windows timer techniques discussed in Chapter 6, disables the Submit button on the form 30 minutes after the page loads.

> **NOTE**
>
> An interesting phenomenon occurs in Internet Explorer when the Submit button is pressed and the alert box is presented, asking the user to answer each question—the timer stops. If the user becomes aware of this (and time limits are a genuine concern to test-takers) you may have problems. This is the reason why I did not display the time remaining on the screen. This "bug" does not appear to occur in Netscape browsers.

Creating the Test Grader

In our made-up school Center Park, I imagine that the students want to know their score on a test as soon as possible, and that the teachers get tired of constantly being asked if the tests are graded yet. Because of this situation, we decided it would be a good idea to grade the test automatically when it is submitted, and then display the results to the test-taker immediately. Fortunately for us, JavaScript is perfectly suited for this functionality—but first I have to figure out how to get the form date from one page to another.

In the previous section, we had the form submitting to a separate page called Grader.html. This sends each form field to the Grader.html in the form name=value through the URL string. Unfortunately, we can not determine beforehand in which order the form fields will appear within the URL string, so we have to develop a way to get the name=value pairs out in any order. Fortunately, we remembered that we had this exact problem when working with cookie files, so we modified the getCookieValue() function for the URL string.

```
function getFormValue( name )
{
   var c = location.href.split( "?" )[1];
   var begin = c.indexOf( name );
   if( begin < 0 ) return( "" );
   begin += name.length + 1;
   var end = c.indexOf( "&", begin );
   if( end == -1 ) end = c.length;
   return( unescape( c.slice( begin, end ) ) );
}
```

Instead of looking in the cookie file for name=value pairs, this function searches the URL string for the desired information using the ampersand (&) as a delimiter. With the problem of retrieving the question answers from the previous page solved, all we have to do is check the given answers against the correct answers and generate a score.

Here is the complete source for the Grader.html page:

```
<html>

  <head>
    <title>Center Park - Test Grader</title>

    <script language="JavaScript">
    <!--
      var total = 0, correct = 0;

      function getFormValue( name )
      {
         var c = location.href.split( "?" )[1];
         var begin = c.indexOf( name );
         if( begin < 0 ) return( "" );
         begin += name.length + 1;
         var end = c.indexOf( "&", begin );
         if( end == -1 ) end = c.length;
         return( unescape( c.slice( begin, end ) ) );
      }
    // -->
    </script>
  </head>
```

```
<body>

<b><font size="5">Computer Science 101 - Midterm Test</font> </b>

<br><br>

<font face="Courier">
  All the questions are <b>compulsory</b>.
  Please read the questions <i>carefully</i> before answering.
  Do not spend too much time on any one question.
  You have 30 minutes to complete the test.  Good Luck!
</font>

<br><br>

<form>
  <table width="100%" cellpadding="2" cellspacing="2">
    <tr>
      <td>1)</td>
      <td>
        <font face="Courier">
          Imagine there was no precedence for arithmetic operators.
          Assuming left associativity for all operators, what is the value
          of the expression 5-3*4/2+6 ?
        </font>
      </td>
    </tr>
    <tr>
      <td>Answer</td>
      <td><b>10</b>     
        <script language="JavaScript">
        <!--
          if( parseInt( getFormValue( "Q1" ) ) == 10 )
          {
            document.write( "<font color='red'><b>CORRECT!</b></font>" );
            correct++
          }
          else
```

```
      {
         document.write( "<font color='red'><b>Wrong</b></font> " +
                           "You answered: " + getFormValue( "Q1" ) );
      }
      total++;
   // -->
   </script>
   </td>
</tr>
<tr><td> </td><td> </td></tr>
<tr>
   <td>2)</td>
   <td>
     <font face="Courier">
        What HTML tag must all JavaScript functions be nested in ie:
        HTML, BODY, TABLE?
     </font>
   </td>
</tr>
<tr>
   <td>Answer</td>
   <td><b>SCRIPT</b>     
     <script language="JavaScript">
     <!--
        if( getFormValue( "Q2" ).toUpperCase() == "SCRIPT" )
        {
           document.write( "<font color='red'><b>CORRECT!</b></font>" );
           correct++
        }
        else
        {
           document.write( "<font color='red'><b>Wrong</b></font> " +
                             "You answered: " + getFormValue( "Q2" ) );
        }
        total++;
     // -->
     </script>
   </td>
```

```
  </tr>
<tr><td> </td><td> </td></tr>
<tr>
  <td>3)</td>
  <td>
    <font face="Courier">
      What event is spawned after a user has selected text or HTML
      elements on a Web page?
    </font>
  </td>
</tr>
<tr>
  <td>Answer</td>
  <td><b>OnSelect</b>     
    <script language="JavaScript">
    <!--
      if( getFormValue( "Q3" ).toUpperCase() == "ONSELECT" )
      {
        document.write( "<font color='red'><b>CORRECT!</b></font>" );
        correct++
      }
      else
      {
        document.write( "<font color='red'><b>Wrong</b></font> " +
                        "You answered: " + getFormValue( "Q3" ) );
      }
      total++;
    // -->
    </script>
  </td>
</tr>
<tr><td> </td><td> </td></tr>
<tr>
  <td>4)</td>
  <td>
    <font face="Courier">
      What type of variable scoping does JavaScript use?
    </font>
```

```
      </td>
  </tr>
  <tr>
    <td>Answer</td>
    <td><b>Static</b>     
      <script language="JavaScript">
      <!--
        if( getFormValue( "Q4" ).toUpperCase() == "STATIC" )
        {
          document.write( "<font color='red'><b>CORRECT!</b></font>" );
          correct++
        }
        else
        {
          document.write( "<font color='red'><b>Wrong</b></font> " +
                          "You answered: " + getFormValue( "Q4" ) );
        }
        total++;
      // -->
      </script>
    </td>
  </tr>
  <tr><td> </td><td> </td></tr>
  <tr>
    <td>5)</td>
    <td>
      <font face="Courier">
        What relational operator is used to determine if two variables
        of the same type are not equal to each other?
      </font>
    </td>
  </tr>
  <tr>
    <td>Answer</td>
    <td><b>!=</b>     
      <script language="JavaScript">
      <!--
        if( getFormValue( "Q5" ) == "!=" )
```

```
            {
                document.write( "<font color='red'><b>CORRECT!</b></font>" );
                correct++
            }
            else
            {
                document.write( "<font color='red'><b>Wrong</b></font> " +
                                "You answered: " + getFormValue( "Q5" ) );
            }
            total++;
        // -->
        </script>
        </td>
      </tr>
    </table>
  </form>

  <br><br>

  <script language="JavaScript">
  <!--
    document.write( "<font color='red'><b>You got " + correct +
                    " correct out of " + total +
                    " questions.  Your score is " +
                    (correct/total*100) + "%</b></font>" );
  // -->
  </script>

  </body>

</html>
```

Summary

Online tests and surveys are becoming ubiquitous at all levels of education. The convenience and freedom they provide to both teachers and students (and, as we've discussed here, to parents as well) bring a new level of functionality to a school's Web site. Additionally, by placing tests online, instructors can also include other supporting information, so that students can refer to graphics, maps, or other figures in order to answer a specific question. For the Center

Park site, the administrators wanted to stay current with emerging educational trends in technology and allow their online testing component to be customizable to specific students, so that when a student logs in to the site, they see links to tests that are specific to their schedule and curriculum. Moreover, the school administrators wanted JavaScript code that was easily configurable so that the test could quickly be turned into a online survey for gathering critical parent feedback. The code demonstrated in this chapter should allow for all of these functional requirements to be achieved.

Chapter 17

School bake sales not withstanding, you don't normally think e-commerce when someone mentions a K–12 school. In fact, the traditional bake sale or holiday fund-raiser is what most schools have normally relied upon in order to generate funds for special events.

Center Park School was (emphasis on the word "was") no different, prior to the design and implementation of their Web site. But the school administrators knew from an early stage that they wanted to take advantage of the generous (and technology savvy) nature of their community, so that describing "Center Park School" and "e-commerce" in the same sentence would not be a misnomer.

Indeed, very early in the site design meetings, you told the administrators that a functioning online store was something very much within their reach. You also said that by integrating it with the larger functionality of the site, the store could be seen as a natural component of the overall site, and not just a "gimmick" or something that was gratuitously placed just in order to try and raise money.

But the relative technical ease of implementing an online store masks the underlying complexity in the business processes needed to keep it functioning, and to satisfy customer relationship management (CRM) requirements. Put simply, just because you can list something for sale on a site doesn't mean that it's easy to actually sell it! You need to consider such things as billing, inventory control, shipping, and (as it relates to CRM) ensuring that the customer has a pleasant experience at your online store, and thus wants to come back for more. Granted, the Center Park store is fairly small potatoes compared to something like Amazon.com, but the basic principles still apply: presenting items for sale in a easy-to-access format, providing a smooth process from item selection to check out, and ensuring that the customer has a good experience.

You would be hard-pressed to visit a major Web site and not find a part of it dedicated to selling something. The everyday user doesn't know how much work goes into creating an online store. Because of the difficulty involved in creating an online shopping cart—due to the lack of a straightforward approach to doing so—there are almost as many different implementations of shopping carts as there are online stores. In this chapter, you'll learn one way of creating a shopping cart that resides solely on the client's computer. This chapter will use many techniques presented throughout this book, but will rely heavily on cookie processing, which was presented in Chapter 11.

There are really three different parts to a shopping cart. The first part is the page or pages wherein items are added to the cart. The second part is a page where the user can view the current contents of his cart and remove items from it, if necessary. Last is the checkout page—every good store needs a checkout counter, and online stores are no different.

> ### TIP
>
> The example provided in this chapter is a demonstration of JavaScript coding principles and not specific CRM principles and methodologies. For more information on CRM, see *Customer Relationship Management Essentials* published by Premier Press.

Item Selection and Addition to the Cart

The most important part of a shopping cart is its ability to hold things. You can think of an online shopping cart as a collection of those paper tags you take at certain stores so that you don't have to walk around with a plasma TV or lawn tractor in your arms. The virtual shopping cart does not hold the actual items themselves; it only holds *pointers* to or *reminders* of what will eventually be purchased. This makes your job as a programmer easier, believe it or not.

The first part of developing an online shopping cart is to decide where and how to store the data. URL parameters might be a logical choice for where to store the data: URL parameters take care of the "how" part and are fairly easy to use. Unfortunately, URL parameters have too many drawbacks for this type of problem. They have a limit to how long they can be, and their use can become tricky when multiple pages are involved.

Because file I/O in JavaScript is out, there is really only one option for storing shopping cart data—cookies. With cookies, you know that data is stored in a `name=value` pair, but with our online shopping cart, we need to know not only what the item is, but also how much it costs. As a solution to this problem, I chose the format `number=description,cost` to store data in. The `number` part of my format is the item number in the list of items, `description` is the name of the item, and `cost` is the cost of the item.

After deciding how to store the data, it would be a good idea to write a function that will add an item to the cart. If you used the preceding format, a function such as the following would work perfectly:

```
function addItem( name, price )
{
 var i = 1;
 for( ; getCookieValue( "item" + i ) != "" ; i++ );
 document.cookie = "item" + i + "=" + name + "," + price;
 document.cookie = "items=" + i;
}
```

This function puts items into the cookie-cart in the following format:

```
item# = Item description string,#.##
```

One thing to remember if you're using this format is that the item description string must not contain any commas in it. If your description string does contain commas, displaying a list of items later on will become tricky. The function above not only adds the item to the cookie-cart in the first available slot, but it also stores a running total of how many items are in the cart. This behavior will not become useful until later, but is used to make sure that all the items in the cart are displayed. The function also uses a separate function, `getCookieValue()`, which you should be familiar with and which is used in almost every program that uses cookies in this book:

```
function getCookieValue( name )
{
 var c = document.cookie;
 var begin = c.indexOf( name );
 if( begin < 0 ) return( "" );
 begin += name.length + 1;
 var end = c.indexOf( ";", begin );
```

```
  if( end == -1 ) end = c.length;
  return( c.slice( begin, end ) );
}
```

The problem of parsing our proprietary item format will be handled in the next section.

Once you have decided on an item format and have written a function to add items to the cookie-cart, creating the rest of the code for the online store becomes simple. Here is a complete example that we have developed for our Center Park project (Figure 17.1 illustrates this code):

```html
<html>

  <head>
    <title>Center Park - Store</title>

    <script language="JavaScript">
    <!--
      function addItem( name, price )
      {
        var i = 1;
        for( ; getCookieValue( "item" + i ) != "" ; i++ );
        document.cookie = "item" + i + "=" + name + "," + price;
        document.cookie = "items=" + i;
      }

      function getCookieValue( name )
      {
        var c = document.cookie;
        var begin = c.indexOf( name );
        if( begin < 0 ) return( "" );
        begin += name.length + 1;
        var end = c.indexOf( ";", begin );
        if( end == -1 ) end = c.length;
        return( c.slice( begin, end ) );
      }
    // -->
    </script>
  </head>
```

```
<body>
  <b><font size="6">Center Park School Store -</font></b>
  <font size="4">for all your school paraphernalia needs</font><br><br>

  <form>
    <table border="2" width="100%">
      <tr>
        <td>School Hat - One size fits all, school emblem on front.</td>
        <td>
          $9.99</td><td align="center">
          <input type="button" value="Add"
                  onClick="JavaScript: addItem( 'School Hat - One size fits '
                              + 'all school emblem on front.', 9.99 );">
        </td>
      </tr>
      <tr>
        <td>
          School T-Shirt - Small-Medium-Large, school emblem on front.</td>
        <td>
          $19.99</td><td align="center">
          <input type="button" value="Add"
                  onClick="JavaScript: addItem( 'School T-Shirt - ' +
                      'Small-Medium-Large school emblem on front.', 19.99 );">
        </td>
      </tr>
      <tr>
        <td>
          Football Season Tickets - Watch the Bobcats all season long.
        </td>
        <td>
          $12.99</td><td align="center">
          <input type="button" value="Add"
                  onClick="JavaScript: addItem( 'Football Season Tickets - '
                              + 'Watch the Bobcats all season long.', 12.99 );">
        </td>
      </tr>
      <tr><td colspan="3" align="center">
        <input type="button" value="View Cart"
```

```
                onClick="JavaScript: document.location='ViewCart.html';">
             
        <input type="button" value="Check Out"
                onClick="JavaScript: document.location='CheckOut.html';">
      </td></tr>
    </table>
  </form>
</body>

</html>
```

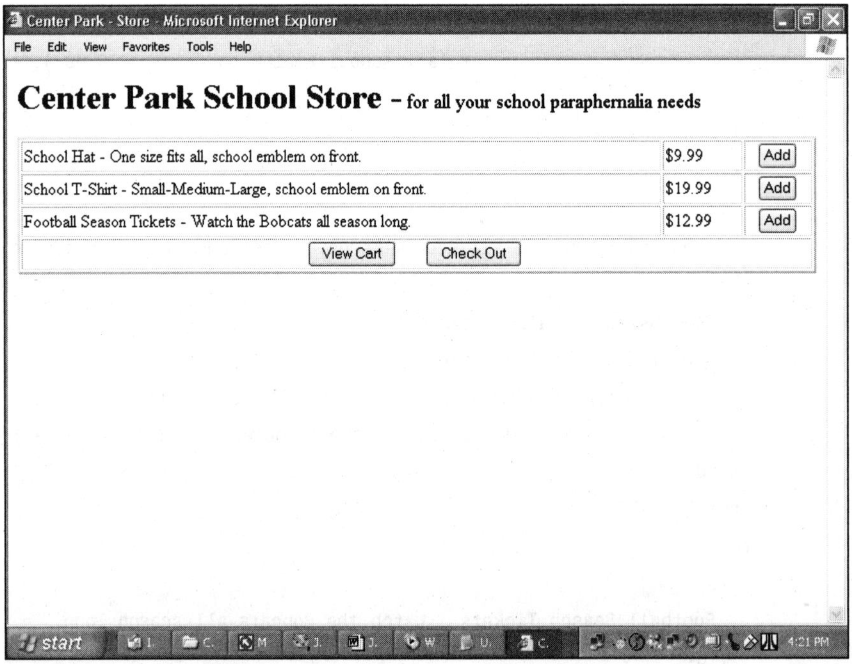

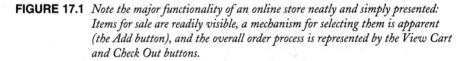

FIGURE 17.1 *Note the major functionality of an online store neatly and simply presented: Items for sale are readily visible, a mechanism for selecting them is apparent (the Add button), and the overall order process is represented by the View Cart and Check Out buttons.*

This online store offers three items that you might find in any online school store. A button next to each item lets a shopper add an item to the cart by calling the addItem() function. Additionally, two buttons at the bottom of the page allow the shopper to view his cart's contents and to check out when done shopping. The functionality of these two buttons is discussed in the next two sections.

Viewing Cart Contents

One part of the online shopping cart functionality that is not required, but is often expected, is the ability to view the contents of the cart. Before you can accomplish this functionality, however, you need to figure out how to get the item data out of the cookie file. If you are using the item format presented in the previous section, the following two functions would work:

```
function getItemName( item )
{
  var c = getCookieValue( item );
  if( c )
  {
    return( c.split( "," )[0] );
  }
  else return( "" );
}


function getItemPrice( item )
{
  var c = getCookieValue( item );
  if( c )
  {
    return( c.split( "," )[1] );
  }
  else return( "" );
}
```

These two functions are identical, except that the first one gets the item's description and the second one gets the cost of the item. After getting the value portion of the name=value pair from the cookie file, the two functions split it using a comma as a delimiter to return either the first or the second item in the array. After you write those two functions, displaying the cart's contents becomes an exercise in using for loops:

```
<html>

  <head>
    <title>Center Park - View Cart</title>

    <script language="JavaScript">
    <!--
      function getCookieValue( name )
```

```
        {
          var c = document.cookie;
          var begin = c.indexOf( name );
          if( begin < 0 ) return( "" );
          begin += name.length + 1;
          var end = c.indexOf( ";", begin );
          if( end == -1 ) end = c.length;
          return( c.slice( begin, end ) );
        }

        function getItemName( item )
        {
          var c = getCookieValue( item );
          if( c )
          {
            return( c.split( "," )[0] );
          }
          else return( "" );
        }

        function getItemPrice( item )
        {
          var c = getCookieValue( item );
          if( c )
          {
            return( c.split( "," )[1] );
          }
          else return( "" );
        }
      // -->
    </script>
  </head>

<body>
    <b><font size="6">Center Park School Store -</font></b>
    <font size="4">for all your school paraphernalia needs</font><br><br>

    <form>
```

```
<table width="100%" border="2">
  <script language="JavaScript">
  <!--
    for( i = 1 ; i <= parseInt( getCookieValue( "items" ) ) ; i++ )
    {
      document.write( "<tr><td>" );
      document.write( getItemName( "item" + i ) + "</td><td>" );
      document.write( "$" + getItemPrice( "item" + i ) );
      document.write( "</td></tr>" );
    }
  // -->
  </script>
  <tr><td colspan="3" align="center">
    <input type="button" value="Keep Shopping"
          onClick="JavaScript: document.location='Store.html';">
         
    <input type="button" value="Check Out"
          onClick="JavaScript: document.location='CheckOut.html';">
  </td></tr>
</table>
</form>
</body>

</html>
```

Sometimes a shopper may change his mind about purchasing an item, and as he probably wouldn't appreciate a "you touched it, you bought it" policy, it is a good idea to provide a way for him to remove items from his shopping cart. Like any useful functionality, this problem is best solved with a function. Here is one that does exactly what you need:

```
function removeItem( name )
{
  document.cookie = name + "=;";
  document.location = document.location;
}
```

Instead of trying to remove any trace of the item from the cookie file, this function removes the description and price from the file. This essentially removes the value part of the name=value pair. Because the item has not been removed completely from the shopping cart, you need to provide an extra check while displaying the cart so that empty items are not shown.

```
<script language="JavaScript">
<!--
  for( i = 1 ; i <= parseInt( getCookieValue( "items" ) ) ; i++ )
  {
    if( getItemName( "item" + i ) != "" &&
        getItemPrice( "item" + i ) != undefined )
    {
      document.write( "<tr><td>" );
      document.write( getItemName( "item" + i ) + "</td><td>" );
      document.write( "$" + getItemPrice( "item" + i ) );
      document.write( "</td></tr>" );
    }
  }
// -->
</script>
```

The if statement nested in the for loop checks to make sure that the item has not been removed from the cart and only displays the item if it still has its description and price.

The only task remaining in order to make the removal of items possible is a button that, when pushed, calls the removeItem() function with the appropriate item. Here is a complete example that contains buttons to do just that:

```
<html>

  <head>
    <title>Center Park - View Cart</title>

    <script language="JavaScript">
    <!--
      function removeItem( name )
      {
        document.cookie = name + "=;";
        document.location = document.location;
      }

      function getCookieValue( name )
      {
        var c = document.cookie;
        var begin = c.indexOf( name );
```

```
    if( begin < 0 ) return( "" );
    begin += name.length + 1;
    var end = c.indexOf( ";", begin );
    if( end == -1 ) end = c.length;
    return( c.slice( begin, end ) );
  }


  function getItemName( item )
  {
    var c = getCookieValue( item );
    if( c )
    {
      return( c.split( "," )[0] );
    }
    else return( "" );
  }


  function getItemPrice( item )
  {
    var c = getCookieValue( item );
    if( c )
    {
      return( c.split( "," )[1] );
    }
    else return( "" );
  }
 // -->
  </script>
</head>

<body>
  <b><font size="6">Center Park School Store -</font></b>
  <font size="4">for all your school paraphernalia needs</font><br><br>

  <form>
    <table width="100%" border="2">
      <script language="JavaScript">
      <!--
```

```
for( i = 1 ; i <= parseInt( getCookieValue( "items" ) ) ; i++ )
{
  if( getItemName( "item" + i ) != "" &&
      getItemPrice( "item" + i ) != undefined )
  {
    document.write( "<tr><td>" );
    document.write( getItemName( "item" + i ) + "</td><td>" );
    document.write( "$" + getItemPrice( "item" + i ) +
                    "</td><td align='center'>" );
    document.write( "<input type='button' value='Remove' " +
                    "onClick='JavaScript: removeItem( \"item" +
                    i + "\" );'>" );
    document.write( "</td></tr>" );
  }
}
// -->
</script>
<tr><td colspan="3" align="center">
  <input type="button" value="Keep Shopping"
         onClick="JavaScript: document.location='Store.html';">
       
  <input type="button" value="Check Out"
         onClick="JavaScript: document.location='CheckOut.html';">
</td></tr>
</table>
</form>
</body>

</html>
```

Checkout and Purchase

One of the most important parts of an online shopping cart is the purchase page. After all, without out this page, all the other parts would be pointless. The checkout and purchase part of an online store lists the items in the cart along with their prices and gives a running total of the cost at the end of the list. I'm sure you're familiar with this type of Web page, so let's start off with a complete working example:

```
<html>

<head>
  <title>Center Park - Store Checkout</title>

  <script language="JavaScript">
  <!--
    var total = 0;

    function getCookieValue( name )
    {
      var c = document.cookie;
      var begin = c.indexOf( name );
      if( begin < 0 ) return( "" );
      begin += name.length + 1;
      var end = c.indexOf( ";", begin );
      if( end == -1 ) end = c.length;
      return( c.slice( begin, end ) );
    }

    function getItemName( item )
    {
      var c = getCookieValue( item );
      if( c )
      {
        return( c.split( "," )[0] );
      }
      else return( "" );
    }

    function getItemPrice( item )
    {
      var c = getCookieValue( item );
      if( c )
      {
        return( c.split( "," )[1] );
      }
      else return( "" );
```

```
      }

      function fixTotal( n )
      {
        n *= 100;
        var good = parseInt( n );
        while( good < n ) good += 1;
        return( good / 100 );
      }
    // -->
    </script>
</head>

<body>
  <b><font size="6">Center Park School Store -</font></b>
  <font size="4">for all your school paraphernalia needs</font><br><br>

  <form>
    <table width="100%" border="2">
      <script language="JavaScript">
      <!--
        for( i = 1 ; i <= parseInt( getCookieValue( "items" ) ) ; i++ )
        {
          if( getItemName( "item" + i ) != "" &&
              getItemPrice( "item" + i ) != undefined )
          {
            document.write( "<tr><td>" );
            document.write( getItemName( "item" + i ) + "</td><td>" );
            document.write( getItemPrice( "item" + i ) );
            document.write( "</td></tr>" );

            total += parseFloat( getItemPrice( "item" + i ) );
          }
        }
      // -->
      </script>
      <tr>
        <td><b>Total</b></td>
```

```
        <td>$
          <script language="JavaScript">
          <!--
            document.write( fixTotal( total ) );
          -->
          </script>
         </td>
      </tr>
    </table>
  </form>
</body>

</html>
```

Most of this example should be familiar to you by now. Two functions, getItemName() and getItemPrice(),

```
function getItemName( item )
{
  var c = getCookieValue( item );
  if( c )
  {
    return( c.split( "," )[0] );
  }
  else return( "" );
}


function getItemPrice( item )
{
  var c = getCookieValue( item );
  if( c )
  {
    return( c.split( "," )[1] );
  }
  else return( "" );
}
```

retrieve the individual item information from the cookie file and place them in a table with the use of a for loop.

```
<script language="JavaScript">
    <!--
      for( i = 1 ; i <= parseInt( getCookieValue( "items" ) ) ; i++ )
        {
          if( getItemName( "item" + i ) != "" &&
             getItemPrice( "item" + i ) != undefined )
            {
              document.write( "<tr><td>" );
              document.write( getItemName( "item" + i ) + "</td><td>" );
              document.write( getItemPrice( "item" + i ) );
              document.write( "</td></tr>" );

              total += parseFloat( getItemPrice( "item" + i ) );
            }
        }
    // -->
    </script>
```

The very last row of the table contains the running total of item prices, which was calculated as they were being displayed with the following statement:

```
total += parseFloat( getItemPrice( "item" + i ) );
```

The variable total was declared in the head of the page and set to zero. After every item in the cart has been displayed, the value of the total is displayed at the end of the table, like so:

```
<tr>
  <td><b>Total</b></td>
    <td>$
      <script language="JavaScript">
        <!--
          document.write( fixTotal( total ) );
        -->
      </script>
     </td>
  </tr>
</table>
```

One thing that should be included on this page, but was omitted because it is outside the scope of this example, is a form for the shopper to fill in their shipping and billing address (including a form validating function). For a complete and working example, please refer to Chapter 8.

Summary

Online stores and "e-commerce" are viable additions to Web sites of all sizes, not just to large corporations or major online retailers. Indeed, the relatively simple example here for the Center Park school masks a fairly complex process, in that it allows visitors to browse items for sale, add them to a shopping cart, and then be presented with a total charge for all selected items. Again, however, the key issue to remember is that this functionality is not overly technically complicated; however, the underlying business processes and procedures necessary to make the online store a success can become quite complicated and burdensome for those who administer the site. Ensuring proper inventory and taking care of online billing are tasks outside the scope of this book, and require serious reflection on how an organization functions (well outside the "technicalities" of a Web site). However, presenting the visitor with a collection of items, allowing them to browse and select, and then presenting her with a total charge is achieving powerful functionality!

Chapter 18

The problem with JavaScript security is that it is neither secure nor part of JavaScript. Many solutions for creating a secure Web site using only HTML and JavaScript (that is, using no server-side languages or native programs) have circulated the Internet, but very few of them have actually accomplished what they set out to do.

Fortunately, there exists a very simple solution that uses only the basic JavaScript commands to create a very secure Web page or Web site. This chapter will show you that simple solution to the JavaScript security problem. It will also present many other possible solutions, so that you'll be completely aware of the issues associated with making a site secure.

What does security have to do with the Center Park School? In the context of the school, "security" means both ensuring only authorized persons have access, but also—once they log in to the site—presenting them with information that only they should see. In this context, "only they should see" is not meant to imply they are being unfairly blocked from full access, but rather that the information presented to them is customized to their specific interests (or in the case of a student, information pertaining to their specific curriculum). You will recall from Chapter 15 and the discussion of calendars, a key functionality requirement of the Center Park Web site is being able to organize and neatly present information to those who utilize the site. By also including a secure login, this adds to the ability to customize the information presented, and, in general, makes the site more user-friendly.

Simple Password Checking

The simplest technique for making a site password-protected with JavaScript is simply to request a password, verify it, and then allow the visitor to pass if the password is correct. The following example demonstrates this technique, and is illustrated in Figure 18.1. The file name of this example is Bad_Checking.html.

```html
<html>

  <head>
    <title>
      Password Protected Site
    </title>

    <script language="JavaScript">
    <!--
      function verifyPassword( word )
      {
        return( word == "sesame" );
      }
    -->
    </script>
  </head>

  <body>

    <form action="Continue.html"
          onSubmit="JavaScript: return(verifyPassword(this.password.value));">
      Please enter your password: 
```

```
    <input type="text" name="password" size="20"><br>
    <input type="submit" value="Submit">
  </form>

</body>

</html>
```

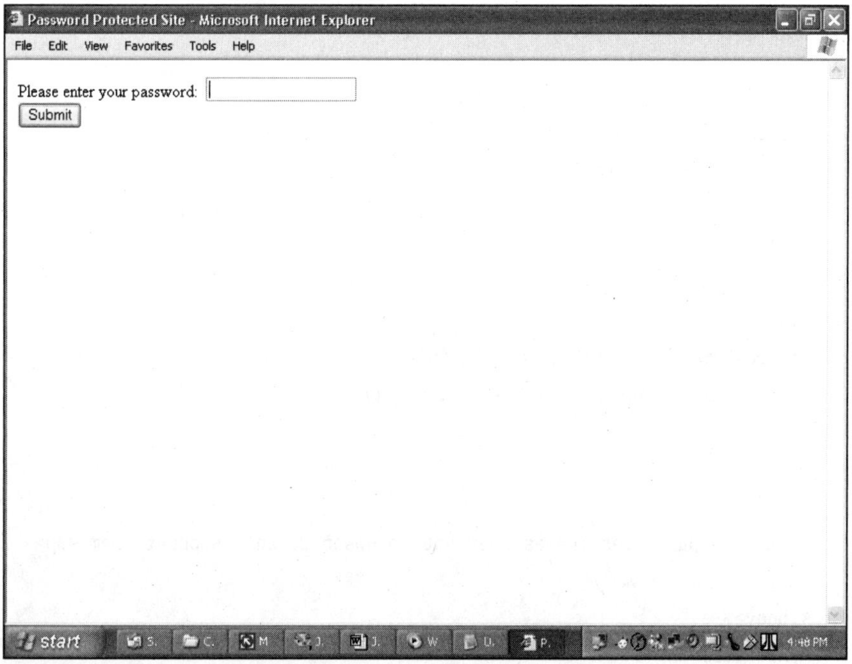

FIGURE 18.1 *A simple (but not very secure) password-protected site.*

At first glance, this might seem like a viable solution to creating a secure Web site. Once the visitor clicks the Submit button, the form validates the given password. If the password is correct, the form submits to `Continue.html`; if the password is not correct, then nothing happens. Unfortunately there is a very big flaw in this plan—all the visitor has to do to break into your site is to look at the source for the page! The problem is compounded by the fact that the browser itself allows the visitor to view the page source.

This technique might prevent an average surfer from breaking into your site (actually, they woudn't be average; they'd have to be someone who had never seen a computer, let alone surfed the Web!), but would do little to prevent even the least knowledgeable cracker from breaking in. So the problem is not how to create a password-protected Web site, but how to keep the visitor from viewing the source.

Hiding a Password in the Form Page

There is a way to prevent people from viewing the source for the page. If you place the password authentication page inside a form page, then simply clicking on File, View Source will bring up the source code for the frames page but not for the authentication page. Such a Web site might take the following form. Notice that Figure 18.2 appears just like 18.1, but in actuality it is utilizing frames to "hide" the password information. The file name for this example is Frames_Password.html:

```
Frames Page:
<html>

  <head>
    <title>
       Password Protected Site
    </title>
  </head>

  <frameset cols="0,*">
    <frame name="contents" target="main">
    <frame name="main" src="Authenticate.html">
    <noframes>
    <body>

      <p>This page uses frames, but your browser doesn't support them.</p>

    </body>
    </noframes>
  </frameset>

</html>


Authenticate.html:
<html>

  <head>
    <title>
       Password Protected Site
    </title>
```

```
<script language="JavaScript">
<!--
  function verifyPassword( word )
  {
    return( word == "sesame" );
  }
-->
</script>
</head>

<body>

<form action="Continue.html"
      onSubmit="JavaScript: return(verifyPassword(this.password.value));">
  Please enter your password: 
  <input type="text" name="password" size="20"><br>
  <input type="submit" value="Submit">
</form>

</body>

</html>
```

Terrific, now the Web site visitor cannot view the source code for the authentication page by clicking on the File menu and choosing View Source. But there is another problem. A determined visitor can still right-click on the authentication page in the browser and, by choosing View Source from the context menu, find out what the password is. Figure 18.3 shows the source for the frames page, which—at first glance—does the job (there is no password information). But Figure 18.4 is the source code for the authenticate.html page, which is easily accessible by right-clicking within the Web page itself. Once again, your security is easily broken.

Now the problem is not how to hide the source, but how to suppress the context menu event. Fortunately, that is possible.

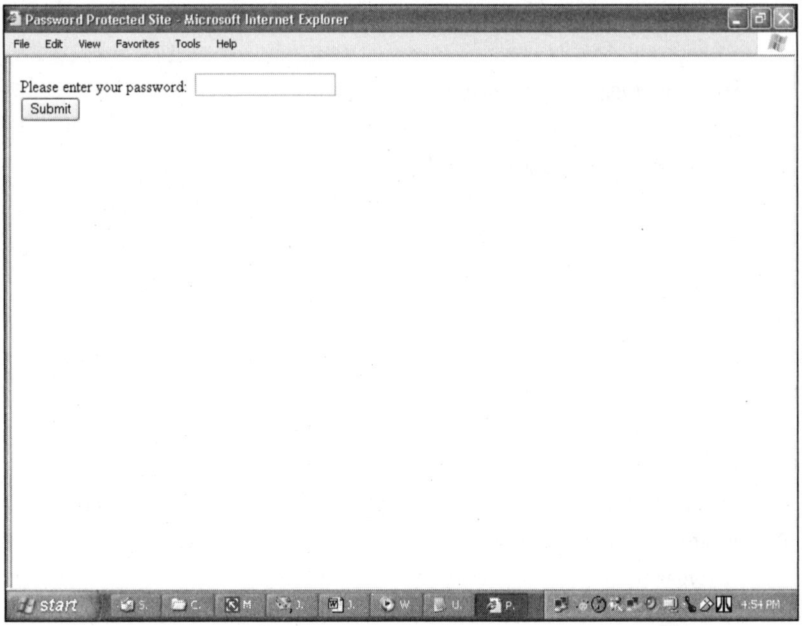

FIGURE 18.2 *This looks just like Figure 18.1, but in reality is utilizing frames in an attempt to give more security to the site.*

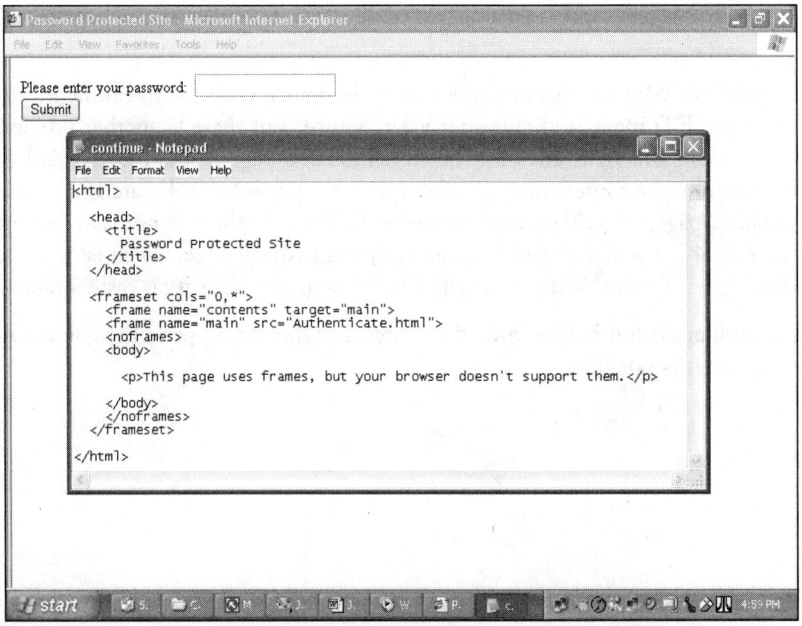

FIGURE 18.3 *Success! Security has been achieved via the use of frames*

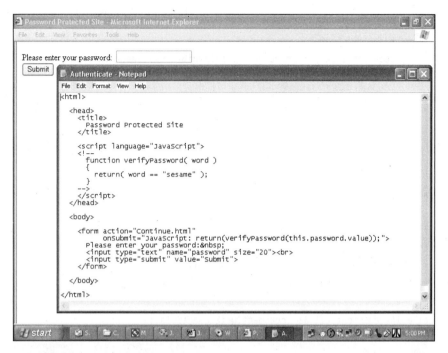

FIGURE 18.4 *Failure! Security is easily compromised by simply looking at the source code for the authenticate.html page.*

Suppressing a Context Menu for Web Pages

Suppressing the context menu for a Web page does take some work. You will have to capture every mouse event for the entire page, differentiate between context menu mouse clicks and normal mouse clicks, and then ask the browser not to show the context menu. The whole process might look something like this:

```
<script language=JavaScript>
<!--

  function clickIE4()
  {
    if( event.button==2 )
    {
      return( false );
    }
  }
```

```
function clickNS4(e)
{
  if( document.layers || document.getElementById && !document.all )
  {
    if( e.which == 2 || e.which == 3 )
    {
      return( false );
    }
  }
}


if( document.layers )
{
  document.captureEvents( Event.MOUSEDOWN );
  document.onmousedown = clickNS4;
}
else if( document.all && !document.getElementById )
{
  document.onmousedown = clickIE4;
}

document.oncontextmenu = new Function( "return( false );");

// -->
</script>
```

Applying this effect to a Web page is as simple as pasting the above code into the head of the page.

Here is the new and improved authentication page, which should be placed in the frames page presented above, which is named No_Context_Password.html:

```
<html>

  <head>
    <title>
      Password Protected Site
    </title>

    <script language="JavaScript">
    <!--
```

```
function clickIE4()
{
  if( event.button==2 )
  {
    return( false );
  }
}

function clickNS4(e)
{
  if( document.layers || document.getElementById && !document.all )
  {
    if( e.which == 2 || e.which == 3 )
    {
      return( false );
    }
  }
}

if( document.layers )
{
  document.captureEvents( Event.MOUSEDOWN );
  document.onmousedown = clickNS4;
}
else if( document.all && !document.getElementById )
{
  document.onmousedown = clickIE4;
}

document.oncontextmenu = new Function( "return( false );");

function verifyPassword( word )
{
  return( word == "sesame" );
}
-->
</script>
</head>
```

```
<body>

   <form action="Continue.html"
         onSubmit="JavaScript: return(verifyPassword(this.password.value));">
     Please enter your password: 
     <input type="text" name="password" size="20"><br>
     <input type="submit" value="Submit">
   </form>

</body>

</html>
```

Excellent, now you have a Web page that prevents the visitor from viewing its source in any way, as when you right-click within the page itself, no menu appears (and if you try and view the source code from the main browser menu, all you see is the source code for the frame container page, which doesn't contain the password information). But wait a minute, is your site now *really* secure? Read on…

The Problem with JavaScript Security

A Web page is always downloaded to the client's computer prior to being displayed in the browser. This means that even if a Web browser does not allow a visitor to view the source of a site, all a visitor would have to do is look in his temporary Internet folder for the source, and all your hard work is for naught.

It is possible to tell the browser to not download the Web page to a file before displaying it. This would alleviate the problem of having the password stored in every client's temporary Internet folder. I will not provide an example of doing this because it is a very convoluted process, and it still doesn't close up every security hole. For instance, if your client was dedicated enough, he might download or create a memory searcher that can find the password stored somewhere in the memory of the browser. Although this is relatively unlikely, it can be done, as Figure 18.4 proves.

Figure 18.5 shows a program that I wrote in a matter of hours that found the password in memory in less than a second. That brings me to the fundamental problem of JavaScript security—the password is always sent to the client's computer. No matter how you try, you will never manage to protect that password completely once it's on the client's computer. If you try to encrypt the password, the encryption algorithm is sent to the client, and he can reverse-engineer it. If you store the given password in the cookie file and use a second page to verify it, the client will still receive the source for the second file.

But rest assured, there *is* a perfectly simple way to create a secure Web site using only JavaScript.

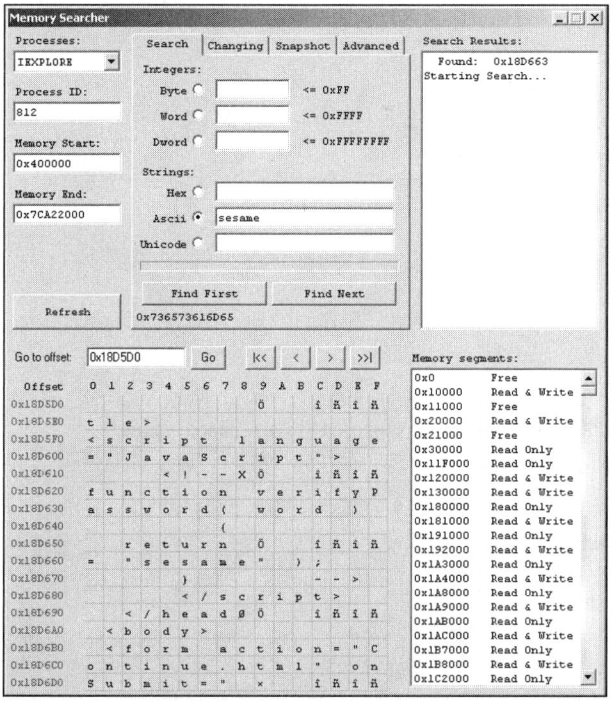

FIGURE 18.5 *The potential misnomer of describing JavaScript as secure.*

A Password-Protected Site

If you had thought about using a second Web page to verify the password after an initial page received it from the visitor, you came very close to the answer. What if, instead of using the second Web page to verify the password, the name of the second page was the password? If this were the case, the password would not need to be sent to the client at any time except after it is verified. In fact, if the visitor types in an incorrect password, all they will see is a 404 - Page Not Found error.

I am getting a little ahead of myself, so let me provide an example here to illustrate my point whose file name is Protected_Page.html:

```
<html>


<head>
  <title>
    Password Protected Site
  </title>


<script language="JavaScript">
```

```
<!--
  function verifyPassword( word )
  {
    document.location = word + ".html"
  }
-->
</script>
</head>

<body>

  <form onSubmit="JavaScript: verifyPassword( this.password.value );">
    Please enter your password: 
    <input type="text" name="password" size="20"><br>
    <input type="submit" value="Submit">
  </form>

</body>

</html>
```

I have removed all the worthless source code suppression functions and replaced the verifyPassword() function with

```
function verifyPassword( word )
{
  document.location = word + ".html"
}
```

If you imagine for a second that the password for my site is something very unusual, such as y7v2xu89, and I create a Web page called y7v2xu89.html and put it in the same directory as my authentication page, then my Web site would be as secure as the secret password. If the visitor to my site enters a correct password, he is taken to an actual page through which he would have access to all of the protected content of my site. If he were to enter an invalid password, he would see nothing except that 404 error.

Because security is a very big issue in the Center Park school Web site project, I have decided to implement this password-protection technique. First, here is the login page where the visitors of my site will enter their user names and passwords; its file name is LogIn.html.

```
<html>
  <head>
    <title>
```

```
    Center Park Home Page - Log In
  </title>

  <script language="JavaScript">
  <!--
    function LogIn( form )
    {
      // Store the student name in the cookie file for later reference
      document.cookie = "username=" + form.username.value;
      // Make sure the password is correct
      document.location = form.password.value + ".html";
    }

    function getCookieValue( name )
    {
      var c = document.cookie;
      var begin = c.indexOf( name );
      if( begin < 0 ) return( "" );
      begin += name.length + 1;
      var end = c.indexOf( ";", begin );
      if( end == -1 ) end = c.length;
      return( c.slice( begin, end ) );
    }

    function setCustoms()
    {
      var bg = getCookieValue( "bgColor" );
      var fg = getCookieValue( "fgColor" );
      if( bg != "" ) document.bgColor = bg;
      if( fg != "" ) document.fgColor = fg;
    }
  // -->
  </script>
</head>

<body onLoad="JavaScript: setCustoms();">

  <center>
```

```
  <font size=6><b>
    Welcome to Center Park Home Page
  </b></font>
</center>
<br><br>
To access the contents of this site, please log in using your student
username and the password provided to you:

<br><br>
<br><br>


<form name="login"
      onSubmit="JavaScript: LogIn( this ); return( false );" >
  <center>
    <table border="2" cellpadding="2" width="250">
      <tr>
        <td colspan="2"><b>Log In</b></td>
      </tr>
      <tr>
        <td>Username:</td>
        <td align="right"><input name="username" size="10"></td>
      </tr>
      <tr>
        <td>Password:</td>
        <td align="right"><input name="password" size="10"></td>
      </tr>
      <tr>
        <td colspan="2">
        <p align="center"><input type="submit" value="Submit"></td>
      </tr>
    </table>
  </center>
</form>

<script language="JavaScript">
<!--
  document.login.username.value = getCookieValue( "username" );
// -->
```

```
    </script>

  </body>
</html>
```

Now, using the same password that I used in the previous examples, here is the page a visitor will see if he or she enters a correct password. This example is y7v2xu89.html of the Center Park project:

```
<html>
  <head>
    <title></title>

    <script language="JavaScript">
    <!--
      var now = new Date();
      var months = new Array( "January", "February", "March", "April",
                              "May", "June", "July", "August", "September",
                              "October", "November", "December" );

      var yString = getCookieValue( "year" );
      var mString = getCookieValue( "month" );
      var y = fixYear( yString ? parseInt( yString ) : now.getYear() );
      var m = fixMonth( mString ? parseInt( mString ) : now.getMonth() );
      var month = new Date( y, m, 1 );

      function getCookieValue( name )
      {
        var c = document.cookie;
        var begin = c.indexOf( name );
        if( begin < 0 ) return( "" );
        begin += name.length + 1;
        var end = c.indexOf( ";", begin );
        if( end == -1 ) end = c.length;
        return( c.slice( begin, end ) );
      }

      function fixYear( year )
      {
        return( year < 1000 ?  year + 1900 : year );
```

```
}

function fixMonth( month )
{
  return( month < 0 ? month + 12 : (month > 11 ? month - 12 : month) );
}

function getNumberDays( d )
{
  switch( d.getMonth() + 1 )
  {
    case 1: case 3: case 5: case 7:
    case 8: case 10: case 12:
      return( 31 );
    case 4: case 6: case 9: case 11:
      return( 30 );
    case 2:
      return( 28 + ( d.getYear % 4 == 0 ? 1 : 0 ) );
  }
}

function getEnding( number )
{
  if( number > 10 && number < 20 ) return( "th" );

  switch( number % 10 )
  {
    case 0: case 4: case 5:
    case 6: case 7: case 8:
    case 9:
      return( "th" );
    case 1:
      return( "st" );
    case 2:
      return( "nd" );
    case 3:
      return( "rd" );
  }
}
```

```
      }

      // These should be loaded from a server-side language such as ASP
      var tasks = new Array( 30 );
      tasks[5] = "<a href='Test.html'>Take CS Test</a>";
      tasks[28] = "English Paper Due";

      function setCustoms()
      {
        var bg = getCookieValue( "bgColor" );
        var fg = getCookieValue( "fgColor" );
        if( bg != "" ) document.bgColor = bg;
        if( fg != "" ) document.fgColor = fg;
      }
    // -->
    </script>
</head>

<body onLoad="JavaScript: setCustoms(); document.cookie='loggedin=true';">
  <i>Welcome</i><b>
  <script language="JavaScript">
  <!--
    document.write( getCookieValue( "username" ) + "</b>!! " );
  // -->
  </script>
  <i>Here are your tasks for</i>

  <table width="75%">
    <tr><td align="center">
      <font size="6"><b>
        <script language="JavaScript">
        <!--
          document.write( months[m] );
        // -->
        </script>
      </b></font>
    </td></tr>
  </table>
```

```html
<table border="1" cellpadding="2" width="75%">
  <tr>
    <td width="14%"><b><i>Sunday</i></b></td>
    <td width="14%"><b><i>Monday</i></b></td>
    <td width="14%"><b><i>Tuesday</i></b></td>
    <td width="14%"><b><i>Wednesday</i></b></td>
    <td width="14%"><b><i>Thursday</i></b></td>
    <td width="14%"><b><i>Friday</i></b></td>
    <td width="14%"><b><i>Saturday</i></b></td>
  </tr>
  <tr>
    <script language="JavaScript">
    <!--
      var startDay = month.getDay();
      for( i = 0 ; i < startDay ; i++ )
      {
        document.write( "<td></td>" );
      }

      var numDays = getNumberDays( month );
      for( i = 0 ; i < numDays ; i++ )
      {
        if( ( i + startDay + 1 ) % 7 == 1 )
        {
          document.write( "</tr><tr>" );
        }
        document.write( "<td height='75' valign='top'" );
        if( fixYear( now.getYear() ) == fixYear( month.getYear() ) &&
            now.getMonth() == month.getMonth() && now.getDate() == i + 1 )
          document.write( " bordercolor='red'" );
        document.write( "><b>" + (i+1) + getEnding(i+1) + "</b><br>" );
        if( tasks[i+1] ) document.write( tasks[i+1] );
        document.write( "</td>" );
      }
    // -->
    </script>
  </tr>
</table>
```

```
<table width="75%">
  <tr>
    <td>
      <script language="JavaScript">
      <!--
        document.write( "<a href=\"" + document.location + "\" " );
        document.write( "onClick=\"JavaScript: document.cookie='month=" +
                        fixMonth(m-1) + "';\">" );
        document.write( months[fixMonth(m-1)] + "</a>" );
      // -->
      </script>
    </td>
    <td align="center">
      <a href="AddTask.html">Add task</a>
    </td>
    <td align="right">
      <script language="JavaScript">
      <!--
        document.write( "<a href=\"" + document.location + "\" " );
        document.write( "onClick=\"JavaScript: document.cookie='month=" +
                        fixMonth(m+1) + "';\">" );
        document.write( months[fixMonth(m+1)] + "</a>" );
      // -->
      </script>
    </td>
  </tr>
</table>

  </body>
</html>
```

My job is not finished yet, however. You'll notice that as soon as the page loads, a value that remembers that the user has logged in is set in the cookie file. In order for my site to be completely secure, I will need to check that value in each page that has sensitive data on it. Here is another actual page from the Center Page Web site that does just that. The name of this Web page is AddTask.html:

```
<html>

  <head>
```

```
<title>Center Park - Add Task</title>

<script language="JavaScript">
<!--
  if( getCookieValue( "loggedin" ) != "true" )
    document.location = "Main.html";

  var dateElement;
  function openDatePicker( target )
  {
    dateElement = target;
    var ieSize = "width=380,height=255";
    var navSize = "width=480,height=295";
    var isNav = navigator.appName == "Netscape";
    window.open( "PopupCalendar.html", "calendar",
            "menubar=no,resizable=no,scrollbars=no, " +
            "status=yes,toolbar=no,"
            + ( isNav ? navSize : ieSize ) );
  }


  function setDate( date )
  {
    dateElement.value = date;
  }


  function getCookieValue( name )
  {
    var c = document.cookie;
    var begin = c.indexOf( name );
    if( begin < 0 ) return( "" );
    begin += name.length + 1;
    var end = c.indexOf( ";", begin );
    if( end == -1 ) end = c.length;
    return( c.slice( begin, end ) );
  }


  function setCustoms()
  {
```

```
        var bg = getCookieValue( "bgColor" );
        var fg = getCookieValue( "fgColor" );
        if( bg != "" ) document.bgColor = bg;
        if( fg != "" ) document.fgColor = fg;
      }
  // -->
  </script>
</head>

<body onLoad="JavaScript: setCustoms();">
  <br>
  <br>
  <i>Center Park Task Scheduler for</i><b>
  <script language="JavaScript">
  <!--
    document.write( getCookieValue( "username" ) );
  // -->
  </script></b>.

  <br><br>
  <br><br>

  <form name="taskForm" onSubmit="JavaScript: return( false );">
    <center>
      <table border="1" width="75%">
        <tr>
          <td width="100%" colspan="2"><b>Schedule Task</b></td>
        </tr>
        <tr>
          <td width="50%">
            Date of task: 
            <input type="text" name="date" size="10">
            <input type="button" value="..."
              onClick="JavaScript: openDatePicker(document.taskForm.date);">
          </td>
          <td width="50%">
            Task description (HTML is ok):<br>
            <textarea rows="7" cols="35"></textarea>
```

```
        </td>
      </tr>
      <tr>
        <td align="center" colspan="2">
          <input type="submit" value="Submit" name="B1">
        </td>
      </tr>
    </table>
  </center>
  </form>
  </body>

</html>
```

The very first script command that executes,

```
if( getCookieValue( "loggedin" ) != "true" )
    document.location = "Main.html";
```

checks the `loggedin` cookie value and redirects the visitor to the main page if he or she has not logged in. This will prevent somebody from finding out the URL directly to the site and creating tasks as somebody else. At long last, I have created a secure, password-protected site using nothing but JavaScript!

Summary

This chapter has shown that JavaScript security is not that very, well, secure. While there are ways of providing some amount of basic security by combining your scripting with HTML (*e.g.* "hiding" your password information within a frame), these techniques are dubious at best, and can be easily broken by someone with even a modicum of technical skill. Moreover, applications can be quickly written or downloaded (see Figure 18.5) that can locate "secure" password information within seconds. The best way, then, to think about JavaScript security is as an interim step to a more secure solution. For example, utilizing server-side security—where no sensitive password information is either passed to or otherwise stored on the client computer, is the far better option. Still, as was shown in this chapter, there are relatively secure methods for protecting your site via JavaScript. However, this should only be trusted for information that is not overly sensitive (*i.e.* not passwords to bank accounts!) and should again be seen as a deterrent but not as a full-proof method of blocking access.

Chapter 19

Creating
Hyperlinked
Ad Rotators

If you have experience working with Web pages, you may have noticed that there never seems to be enough room in the browser. With all those tables, images, frames, and text there's hardly any space left for the advertisements that you may depend on to keep your site running. While designing the Center Park Web site, imagine that over a dozen student organizations come to you requesting space on the main page of the site. Obviously, you can't accommodate all of them—at least not at the same time.

Displaying a Different Ad
Each Time a Web Page Loads

Fortunately for you, Internet Explorer allows a Web page to change its content on-the-fly, through the use of the `innerHTML` property. You immediately started devising a way to rotate separate text advertisements each time a page loads. You can see how the code listing below is reflected in Figures 19.1 and 19.2, as the announcements are different between the two figures.

NOTE

As stated here, this example is for use only within Internet Explorer.

```html
<html>

  <head>
    <title>Center Park Home Page - Main Page</title>

    <script language="JavaScript">
    <!--
        var ads = new Array( "Come watch the Center Park Bobcats!<br>Get your" +
                             " schedules at the Union Building.",
                             "Join us at the June Bug festival June 12-14th!" +
                             "See you there.",
                             "July 3rd is the first annual Adopt a Nerd" +
                             " Day!<br>They are people too.<br>Be kind adopt" +
                             " a nerd." );

        function getAd()
        {
          var ad = parseInt( Math.random() * ads.length );
          return( ads[ad] );
        }

        function rotateAd()
        {
          document.all.adCell.innerHTML = getAd();
```

```
      }

      function getCookieValue( name )
      {
        var c = document.cookie;
        var begin = c.indexOf( name );
        if( begin < 0 ) return( "" );
        begin += name.length + 1;
        var end = c.indexOf( ";", begin );
        if( end == -1 ) end = c.length;
        return( c.slice( begin, end ) );
      }

      function setCustoms()
      {
        var bg = getCookieValue( "bgColor" );
        var fg = getCookieValue( "fgColor" );
        if( bg != "" ) document.bgColor = bg;
        if( fg != "" ) document.fgColor = fg;
      }
    // -->
    </script>
</head>

<body onLoad="JavaScript: setCustoms(); rotateAd();">
  <center>
    <font color="red" size="6"><b>
      Center Park Home Page
    </b></font></center>

  <br><br>

  <table width="100%">
    <tr>
      <td ID="adCell" width="50%">
      </td>
      <td width="50%">
        <a href="login.html">Log In</a><br>
```

```
        <a href="store.html">Store</a><br>
        <a href="customize.html">Customize</a>
      </td>
    </tr>
    <tr>
      <td width="100%" colspan="2">
        <hr>
        <font face="Courier" size="5">*** School News ***</font> <br>
        <br>
        <b>July 4th</b> - Fireworks on the mall! 
        Come enjoy the holiday with the Center Park faculty,
        staff and students.<br>
        <br>
        <b>July 3rd</b> - First annual Adopt a Nerd Day! 
        They are people too.<br>
        <br>
        <b>June 12th</b> - June Bug festival begins.
      </td>
    </tr>
  </table>
</body>

</html>
```

Each time it loads, this page will choose a random advertisement from a list of predefined advertisements and display it in the table.

Creating a Self-Changing Hyperlinked Text Ad

After studying how the students at Center Park use their Web site, you decide that each ad isn't getting enough screen time because students tend not to reload the page over and over again. Not only that, they need a way to hyperlink the text so that they can go directly to the page that the ad describes.

With a little more work, you can create self-changing and hyperlinked text ads. By using the Window object's setTimeout() function, you can set the ads to change every 10 seconds. By simply changing the content of the ads themselves, you can make them hyperlinked. See page 482 for the result of the changes.

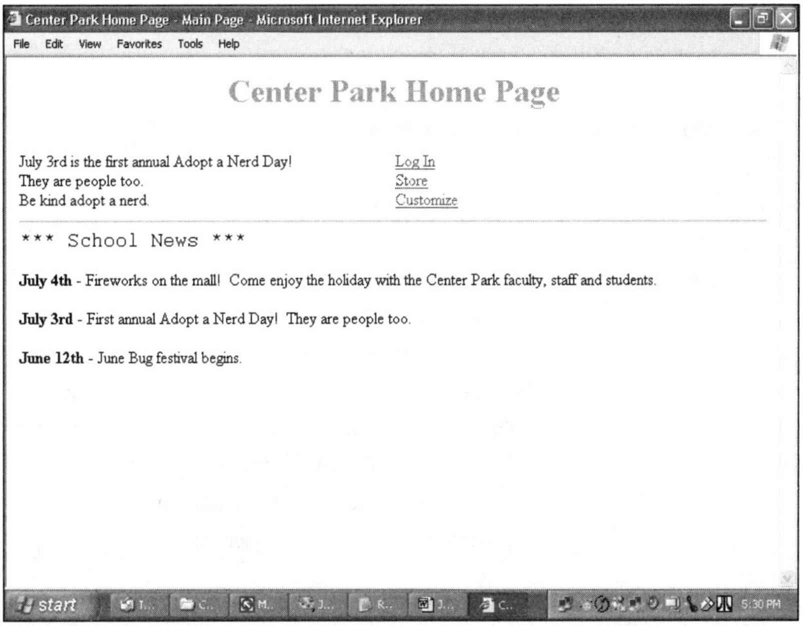

FIGURE 19.1 *In this shot, we see the nerds getting a little publicity.*

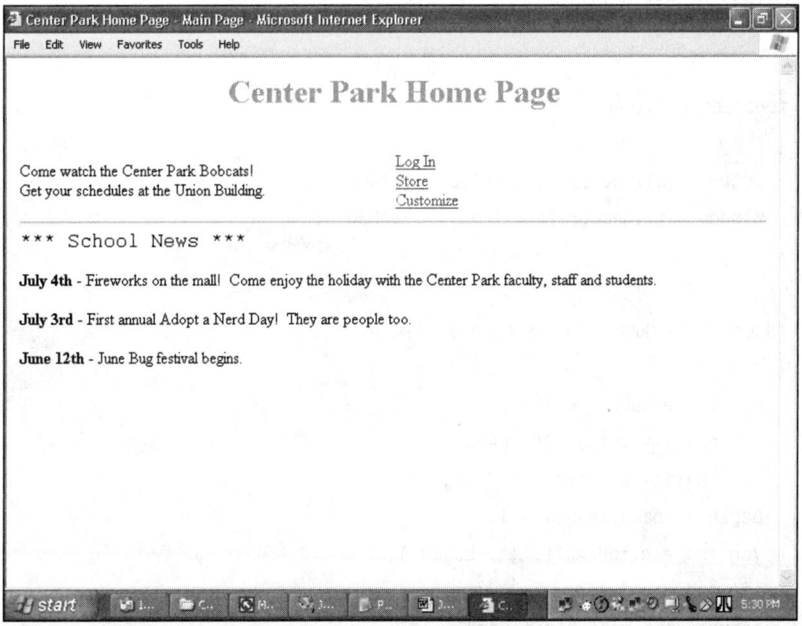

FIGURE 19.2 *In this view, the advertisement has switched from the nerds to the school sports team.*

```html
<html>

<head>
  <title>Center Park Home Page - Main Page</title>

  <script language="JavaScript">
  <!--
    var ads = new Array( "<a href='Bobcats.html'>Come watch the Center " +
                         " Park Bobcats!<br>Get your schedules at the" +
                         " Union Building.</a>",
                         "<a href='JuneBug.html'>Join us at the June" +
                         " Bug festival June 12-14th!  See you there.</a>",
                         "<a href='SchoolEvents.html'>July 3rd is the" +
                         " first annual Adopt a Nerd Day!<br>They are" +
                         " people too -- be kind adopt a nerd.</a>" );

    function getAd()
    {
      var ad = parseInt( Math.random() * ads.length );
      return( ads[ad] );
    }

    function rotateAd()
    {
      document.all.adCell.innerHTML = getAd();
      window.setTimeout( "rotateAd()", 10000 );
    }

    function getCookieValue( name )
    {
      var c = document.cookie;
      var begin = c.indexOf( name );
      if( begin < 0 ) return( "" );
      begin += name.length + 1;
      var end = c.indexOf( ";", begin );
      if( end == -1 ) end = c.length;
      return( c.slice( begin, end ) );
    }
```

```
    function setCustoms()
    {
      var bg = getCookieValue( "bgColor" );
      var fg = getCookieValue( "fgColor" );
      if( bg != "" ) document.bgColor = bg;
      if( fg != "" ) document.fgColor = fg;
    }
  // -->
  </script>
</head>

<body onLoad="JavaScript: setCustoms(); rotateAd();">
  <center>
    <font color="red" size="6"><b>
      Center Park Home Page
    </b></font></center>

  <br><br>

  <table width="100%">
    <tr>
      <td ID="adCell" width="50%">
      </td>
      <td width="50%">
        <a href="login.html">Log In</a><br>
        <a href="store.html">Store</a><br>
        <a href="customize.html">Customize</a>
      </td>
    </tr>
    <tr>
      <td width="100%" colspan="2">
        <hr>
        <font face="Courier" size="5">*** School News ***</font> <br>
        <br>
        <b>July 4th</b> - Fireworks on the mall! 
        Come enjoy the holiday with the Center Park faculty,
        staff and students.<br>
        <br>
```

```
        <b>July 3rd</b> - First annual Adopt a Nerd Day! 
        They are people too.<br>
        <br>
        <b>June 12th</b> - June Bug festival begins.
      </td>
    </tr>
  </table>
</body>

</html>
```

As you can see in Figure 19.3, the advertisements not only rotate, but are also hyperlinked. This is quite useful (as will be seen in the completed Center Park Web site) in taking the most advantage of limited screen real estate: in other words, multiple groups and organizations can advertise in the same space (rotating their ads in and out every few seconds) with each ad hyperlinked to a page specific to that group, so if a visitor wants more information, he or she can click over to the hyperlinked page and get it.

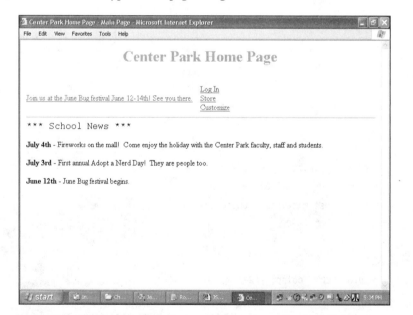

FIGURE 19.3 *Hyperlinking rotating ads is a great way to further take advantage of limited screen space.*

This site not only displays a different hyperlinked ad each time it is loaded, but it also automatically rotates the ads after a ten-second delay. The JavaScript statement

```
window.setTimeout( "rotateAd()", 10000 );
```

creates a timer to rotate the ad after ten seconds by calling the `rotateAd()` function, which then calls the same statement again. Technically, this is an infinite loop, but since there is a ten-second delay between each iteration, it is acceptable.

Creating a Self-Changing Hyperlinked Image Ad

As soon as the students see what you are capable of doing, they immediately start sending you ads in the form of images to replace their non-eye-catching text ads. Replacing their text ads with images is a very easy task. Because the `innerHTML` field of the HTML elements allows you to replace any HTML, all you need to do is put image tags where the text is. Here is an example of just that:

```
<html>

  <head>
    <title>Center Park Home Page - Main Page</title>

    <script language="JavaScript">
    <!--
      var ads = new Array( "<a href='Bobcats.html'>" +
                             "<image src='Bobcats.jpg' border='0'>" +
                           "</a>",
                           "<a href='JuneBug.html'>" +
                             "<image src=' JuneBug.jpg' border='0'>" +
                           "</a>" );


      function getAd()
      {
        var ad = parseInt( Math.random() * ads.length );
        return( ads[ad] );
      }


      function rotateAd()
      {
        document.all.adCell.innerHTML = getAd();
        window.setTimeout( "rotateAd()", 10000 );
      }


      function getCookieValue( name )
      {
        var c = document.cookie;
```

```
        var begin = c.indexOf( name );
        if( begin < 0 ) return( "" );
        begin += name.length + 1;
        var end = c.indexOf( ";", begin );
        if( end == -1 ) end = c.length;
        return( c.slice( begin, end ) );
    }

    function setCustoms()
    {
        var bg = getCookieValue( "bgColor" );
        var fg = getCookieValue( "fgColor" );
        if( bg != "" ) document.bgColor = bg;
        if( fg != "" ) document.fgColor = fg;
    }
  // -->
  </script>
</head>

<body onLoad="JavaScript: setCustoms(); rotateAd();">
  <center>
    <font color="red" size="6"><b>
      Center Park Home Page
    </b></font></center>

  <br><br>

  <table width="100%">
    <tr>
      <td ID="adCell" width="50%">
      </td>
      <td width="50%">
        <a href="login.html">Log In</a><br>
        <a href="store.html">Store</a><br>
        <a href="customize.html">Customize</a>
      </td>
    </tr>
    <tr>
      <td width="100%" colspan="2">
```

```
        <hr>
        <font face="Courier" size="5">*** School News ***</font> <br>
        <br>
        <b>July 4th</b> - Fireworks on the mall! 
        Come enjoy the holiday with the Center Park faculty,
        staff and students.<br>
        <br>
        <b>July 3rd</b> - First annual Adopt a Nerd Day! 
        They are people too.<br>
        <br>
        <b>June 12th</b> - June Bug festival begins.
      </td>
    </tr>
  </table>
</body>

</html>
```

At last, you have an ad rotator that is exactly what the students wanted (See Figure 19.4). Not only is each ad made up of an image, but the ads are also hyperlinked and self-rotating. Now, if only this technique were platform-independent.

FIGURE 19.4 *Rotating image ads can bring a new sense of urgency to your information, thus encouraging visitors to pay more attention to what you have to say.*

Platform-Independence

The problem with the previous examples is that they only work in an Internet Explorer browser. Netscape browsers are unable to reference HTML elements directly through an ID attribute. Thankfully, there is a workaround, but it is slightly more complicated than the previous examples. Instead of replacing HTML in a table cell, this time around I will have to replace HTML tag parameter values. In the following example, all of the link and image tags are already in place once the page loads:

```
<html>

  <head>
    <title>Center Park Home Page - Main Page</title>

    <script language="JavaScript">
    <!--
      var ads = new Array( 2 );
      ads[0] = new Array( "Bobcats.html", "Bobcats.jpg" );
      ads[1] = new Array( "JuneBug.html", "JuneBug.jpg" );

      function getAd()
      {
        var ad = parseInt( Math.random() * ads.length );
        return( ads[ad] );
      }

      function rotateAd()
      {
        var newAd = getAd();

        with( document )
        {
          for( i = 0 ; i < links.length ; i++ )
          {
            if( links[i].name == "ad" )
            {
              links[i].href = newAd[0];
            }
          }
          for( i = 0 ; i < images.length ; i++ )
```

```
          {
            if( images[i].name == "ad" )
            {
               images[i].alt = images[i].src = newAd[1];
            }
          }
        }
        window.setTimeout( "rotateAd()", 10000 );
      }


      function getCookieValue( name )
      {
        var c = document.cookie;
        var begin = c.indexOf( name );
        if( begin < 0 ) return( "" );
        begin += name.length + 1;
        var end = c.indexOf( ";", begin );
        if( end == -1 ) end = c.length;
        return( c.slice( begin, end ) );
      }


      function setCustoms()
      {
        var bg = getCookieValue( "bgColor" );
        var fg = getCookieValue( "fgColor" );
        if( bg != "" ) document.bgColor = bg;
        if( fg != "" ) document.fgColor = fg;
      }
    // -->
    </script>
  </head>


<body onLoad="JavaScript: setCustoms(); rotateAd();">
  <center>
    <font color="red" size="6"><b>
      Center Park Home Page
    </b></font></center>
```

```
<br><br>

<table width="100%">
  <tr>
    <td ID="adCell" width="50%">
      <a href="Main.html" name="ad">
        <img src="Bobcats.jpg" border="0" name="ad">
      </a>
    </td>
    <td width="50%">
      <a href="login.html">Log In</a><br>
      <a href="store.html">Store</a><br>
      <a href="customize.html">Customize</a>
    </td>
  </tr>
  <tr>
    <td width="100%" colspan="2">
      <hr>
      <font face="Courier" size="5">*** School News ***</font> <br>
      <br>
      <b>July 4th</b> - Fireworks on the mall! 
      Come enjoy the holiday with the Center Park faculty,
      staff and students.<br>
      <br>
      <b>July 3rd</b> - First annual Adopt a Nerd Day! 
      They are people too.<br>
      <br>
      <b>June 12th</b> - June Bug festival begins.
    </td>
  </tr>
</table>
</body>

</html>
```

Every ten seconds, the anchor tag and image tag gets updated with a new href or src value respectively. This provides the same functionality as the previous examples, but is slightly longer and harder to read than before.

Summary

As we noted at the beginning of the chapter, the Center Park Web site has limited screen "real estate"; indeed, most if not all Web sites have this same problem. From more Windows-like menu systems to utilizing graphical image maps, savvy Web designers have tried—since the early days of the Web—to present as much information onscreen as possible, but without it being overbearing or otherwise appearing overly busy to the reader.

Rotating images can be a great way to address this problem, as each group or issue being advertised gets as much space on the screen as the next—they just have to share it with their allotted amount of "screen time." For the Center Park school this works very well, as it allows the school administrators to give each group (and whoever audience they might want to reach) an equal amount of space on the Web site; but by using rotating images they refute any argument of bias, as everyone really does get their "fair share" of screen time.

By using JavaScript and other features of the Web browser (and as we've seen in this chapter, with special focus on Internet Explorer), you can utilize the rotation image to serve the informational requirements of your site and make it attractive in the process. As we've discussed throughout this project, form needs to follow function, but that doesn't mean (especially with the visual and other media-rich presentation qualities of the Web) either the "function" or the "form" have to be boring.

As we'll see in the next chapter, by combing rotating images with some DHTML (and additional JavaScript) you can elevate even the most rudimentary Web site into something that is visually appealing, or in other words has a high "eye candy" quality without again being overly busy, or appearing unorganized.

Chapter 20

Up to this point, the chapters have been focused on extending the functionality of the Center Park Web site. So far you have designed and implemented a login page, a store, an online test, and two different kinds of calendars—everything a good Web site of this type requires. This chapter will focus not on the design and implementation of new features, but on the improvement of the Web site visuals. Most professional Web sites have some type of dynamic content, also referred to as "eye-candy." Although eye-candy is not required in order for a Web site to be fully functional, it make a site more inviting and does encourage the Web site visitor to come back again.

Unfortunately, most dynamic effects on a Web site take tremendous time to create and finalize. There is no straightforward approach to adding the eye-candy that Web site visitors have come to expect. Because of this, this chapter will only focus on two types of dynamic content: mouseover image rotations and custom color schemes for the entire site.

The Center Park school administrators were quite specific in that they did not want a site that was overly "flashy," but at the same time wanted something that was still visually appealing. On several occasions, they had used the old design phrase of "form follows function," that is, they wanted the site's functionality to be at the forefront. By that they wanted a site that was easy to access, customizable to the end user, and informational across different audiences (parents, teachers, students). In your early meetings with the administrative group, you told them that through some rather straightforward visual effects, you could achieve all of these functional requirements but still make the site look good. That goal is the focus of the information presented in this chapter.

Mouseover Image Rotations

Mouseover image rotations are probably the most common dynamic effect on the Web. Due to its simplicity, there are many different ways to implement this effect. For our Center Park Web site project you'll simply use the built-in mouse event handler for the IMG tag, but I will present several other ways in which the same effect could be accomplished.

I wrote the example below, which uses simple text links, in order to demonstrate the significant improvements that occur just by adding this simple effect. We'll compare it with the mouseover links later on. Figure 20.1 illustrates this very basic Web page.

```
<html>

  <head>
    <base target="main">
  </head>

  <body>
    <font color="red" size="4"><b>
      Center Park<br>
    </b></font>
    <table width="100%">
      <tr><td>
        <a href="Main.html" target="main">
          Home
        </a>
      </td></tr>
```

```
    <tr><td>
      <a href="LogIn.html" target="main">
        Login
      </a>
    </td></tr>
    <tr><td>
      <a href="Store.html" target="main">
        Store
      </a>
    </td></tr>
    <tr><td>
      <a href="Customize.html" target="main">
        Customize
      </a>
    </td></tr>
    </table>
  </body>

</html>
```

Notice that this example is completely devoid of any JavaScript whatsoever. I placed this Web page in the left frame of the following frames page:

```
<html>

  <head>
    <title>Center Park Home Page</title>
  </head>

  <frameset cols="150,*">
    <frame name="contents" target="main"
           src="MenuBar.html" scrolling="no" noresize>
    <frame name="main" src="Main.html" scrolling="auto" noresize>
    <noframes>
      <body>

        <p>This page uses frames, but your browser doesn't support them.</p>

      </body>
```

```
     </noframes>
   </frameset>


</html>
```

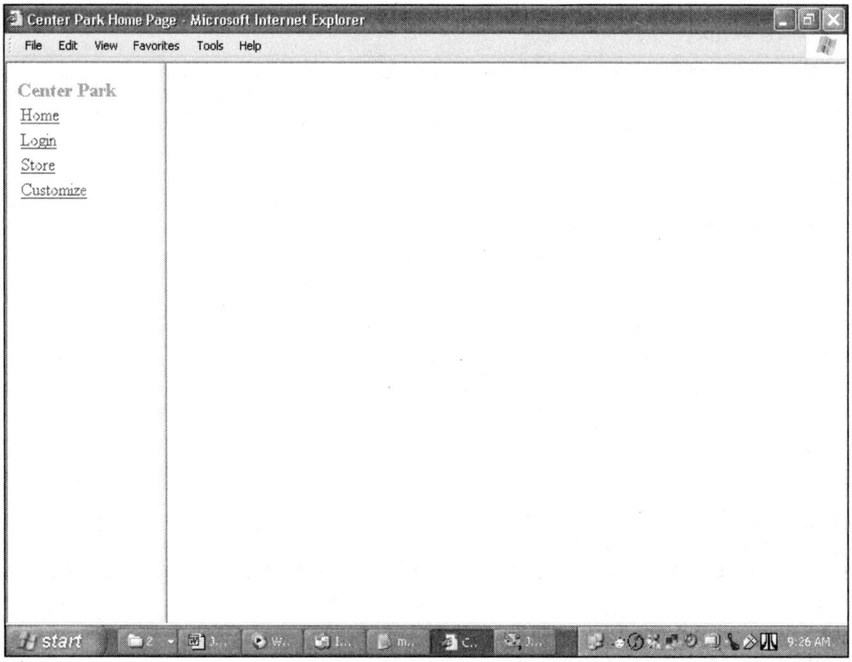

FIGURE 20.1 *A typical (boring?) frames-based Web page, highlighting the usual navigation frame (the left frame) where links are placed that, when clicked, open information in the main content frame (the right frame).*

As you can see in Figure 20.1, this Web page is very plain indeed. Anybody with basic knowledge of HTML could design and build this page in about an hour. There are literally millions of Web sites that look nearly identical to this one. In other words, they're boring.

One very easy way to spice things up a bit is to replace the text links with image links, as follows. Note that in Figure 20.2, the text links are now graphic links.

```
<html>


  <head>
    <base target="main">
  </head>
```

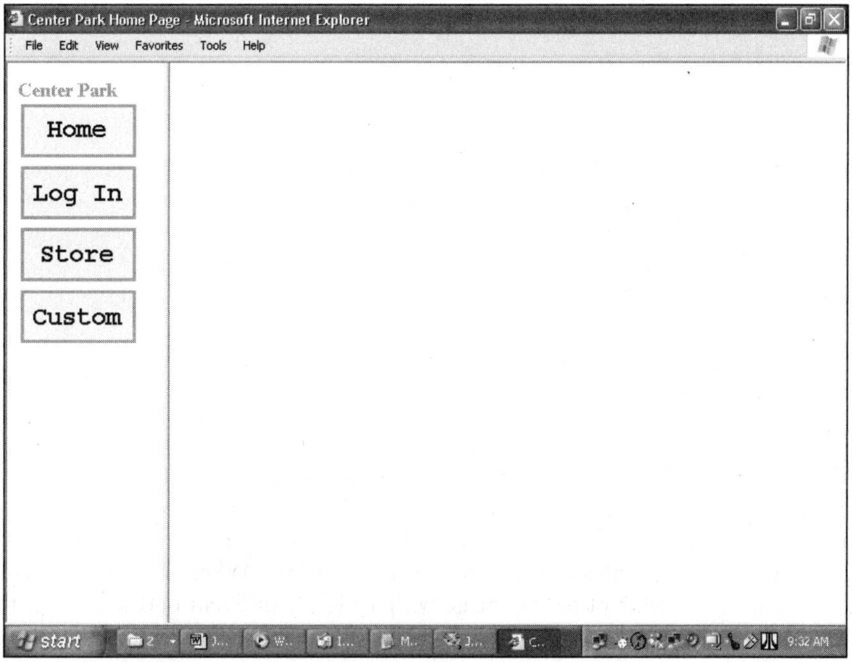

FIGURE 20.2 *The plain text links have now been "spiced up" with some simple graphics.*

```
<body>
  <font color="red" size="4"><b>
    Center Park<br>
  </b></font>
  <table width="100%">
    <tr><td>
      <a href="Main.html">
        <img border="0" src="home1.bmp">
      </a>
    </td></tr>
    <tr><td>
      <a href="LogIn.html" target="main">
        <img border="0" src="login1.bmp">
      </a>
    </td></tr>
    <tr><td>
      <a href="Store.html" target="main">
```

```
              <img border="0" src="store1.bmp">
          </a>
      </td></tr>
      <tr><td>
        <a href="Customize.html" target="main">
          <img border="0" src="customize1.bmp">
        </a>
      </td></tr>
    </table>
  </body>

</html>
```

Although this site is significantly more interesting, it is still not flashy enough to make it stand out in any way. What I really need to take my site to the head of the pack is some dynamism. I'd like to make the image change slightly when my mouse hovers over it. To do that, I will use the onMouseOver and onMouseOut image event handlers. When the mouse cursor is moved over the image, I will replace the image with a slightly different one; and when the cursor is moved off the image, I will return it to its original state. Here is a template for doing just that:

```
<img src="image1.bmp" border="0"
    onMouseOver="JavaScript: this.src='image2.bmp';"
    onMouseOut="JavaScript: this.src='image1.bmp';">
```

If I apply this template to the images in the Center Park menu bar, it would look something like Figure 20.3. Note that in this figure, the mouse cursor is hovering over the Log In button, causing it (via the OnMouseOver image event) to change color and appear highlighted).

Here is the complete source that makes it look that way:

```
<html>

  <head>
    <base target="main">
  </head>

  <body>
    <font color="red" size="4"><b>
      Center Park<br>
    </b></font>
    <table width="100%">
      <tr><td>
```

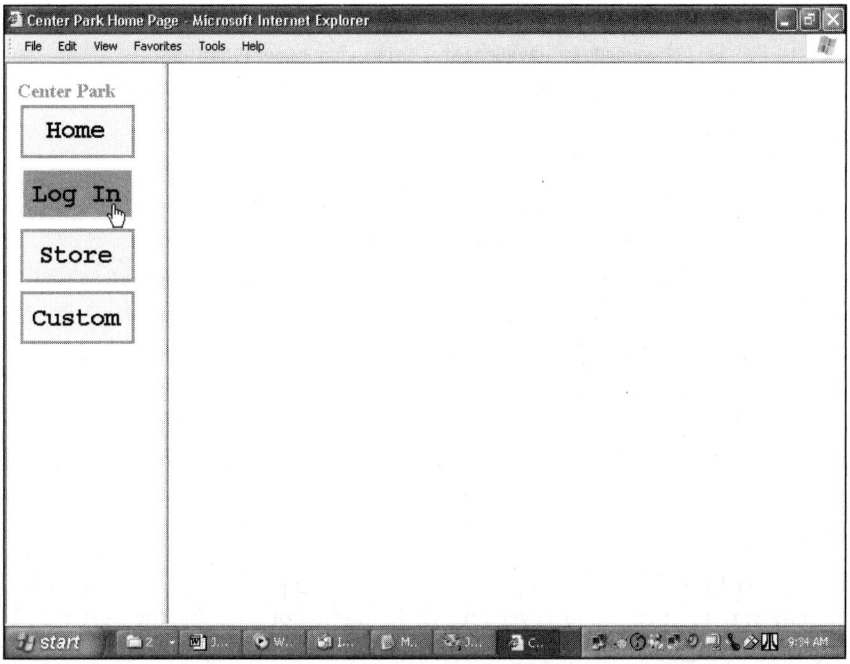

FIGURE 20.3 *The* onMouseOver *image event can highlight specific functionality, as well as bring a more visually appealing quality to your Web design.*

```html
<a href="Main.html" target="main">
  <img border="0" src="home1.bmp"
       onMouseOver="JavaScript: this.src='home2.bmp';"
       onMouseOut="JavaScript: this.src='home1.bmp';">
</a>
</td></tr>
<tr><td>
  <a href="LogIn.html" target="main">
    <img border="0" src="login1.bmp"
         onMouseOver="JavaScript: this.src='login2.bmp';"
         onMouseOut="JavaScript: this.src='login1.bmp';">
  </a>
</td></tr>
<tr><td>
  <a href="Store.html" target="main">
    <img border="0" src="store1.bmp"
```

```
              onMouseOver="JavaScript: this.src='store2.bmp';"
              onMouseOut="JavaScript: this.src='store1.bmp';">
        </a>
      </td></tr>
      <tr><td>
        <a href="Customize.html" target="main">
          <img border="0" src="customize1.bmp"
              onMouseOver="JavaScript: this.src='customize2.bmp';"
              onMouseOut="JavaScript: this.src='customize1.bmp';">
        </a>
      </td></tr>
    </table>
  </body>

</html>
```

At long last I have a site that is as aesthetically pleasing as it is useful. This, of course, is not the only way to create mouseover effects. It might not even be the best way, but it is the simplest. If you have a very large number of buttons or if you wanted to incorporate the onMouseDown event with yet another image, you would soon realize that doing so requires a very large amount of code. The more code there is, the longer the download time will be, so I will present one alternative that you may find more useful than hard-coding each image.

I stated earlier that every good bit of functionality requires an equally good function, and mouseover events are no exception. What you need is a function that can handle each image change for every image, regardless of the event that caused it. This may seem like daunting requirements, but with the aid of the document object model (DOM), it's really not difficult at all. First I will present a working example and then I will explain it in detail.

```
<html>

  <head>
    <base target="main">

    <script language="JavaScript">
    <!--
      function change( image, event )
      {
        image.src = image.name + event + ".bmp";
      }
    // -->
    </script>
```

```
</head>

<body>
  <font color="red" size="4"><b>
    Center Park<br>
  </b></font>
  <table width="100%">
    <tr><td>
      <a href="Main.html" target="main">
        <img border="0" src="home1.bmp" name="home"
            onMouseDown="JavaScript: change( this, 3 );"
            onMouseOver="JavaScript: change( this, 2 );"
            onMouseOut="JavaScript: change( this, 1 );">
      </a>
    </td></tr>
    <tr><td>
      <a href="LogIn.html" target="main">
        <img border="0" src="login1.bmp" name="login"
            onMouseDown="JavaScript: change( this, 3 );"
            onMouseOver="JavaScript: change( this, 2 );"
            onMouseOut="JavaScript: change( this, 1 );">
      </a>
    </td></tr>
    <tr><td>
      <a href="Store.html" target="main">
        <img border="0" src="store1.bmp" name="store"
            onMouseDown="JavaScript: change( this, 3 );"
            onMouseOver="JavaScript: change( this, 2 );"
            onMouseOut="JavaScript: change( this, 1 );">
      </a>
    </td></tr>
    <tr><td>
      <a href="Customize.html" target="main">
        <img border="0" src="customize1.bmp" name="customize"
            onMouseDown="JavaScript: change( this, 3 );"
            onMouseOver="JavaScript: change( this, 2 );"
            onMouseOut="JavaScript: change( this, 1 );">
      </a>
```

```
        </td></tr>
      </table>
    </body>

</html>
```

All of the image events are handled by a single function, change(),

```
function change( image, event )
{
   image.src = image.name + event + ".bmp";
}
```

which takes two parameters. The first parameter is a pointer to the image that created the event. The second parameter is an integer that specifies the event type. I have chosen the value 3 for the onMouseDown event, the value 2 for the onMouseOver event, and the value 1 for the onMouseOut event. For each button, you will need to create a separate image for each event type. One thing you may have noticed is that I added a name attribute to each image element. This value is used in the change() function to make sure the correct image is displayed on the element. The format required by the image elements in order to use this function is as follows:

```
<img src="image1.bmp" name="image" border="0"
     onMouseDown="JavaScript: change( this, 3 );"
     onMouseOver="JavaScript: change( this, 2 );"
     onMouseOut="JavaScript: change( this, 1 );">
```

This method is somewhat easier to read than the previous one, and it will decrease download time with a large number of images. Both techniques are identical in function, however. It is completely up to you as to which one you use.

Custom Color Schemes

Another frivolous yet eye-pleasing dynamic feature you can add to almost any site is a custom color scheme. By storing custom color values in the cookie file, you can set them for any page that is loaded. This feature was first introduced in Chapter 11, but I will elaborate on it now to make it a fully functional, dynamic HTML effect.

The first part of implementing a custom color scheme for an entire Web site is to create a page where the color variables can be set in the cookie file. Because this is such an easy task to do and because it has been explained in previous chapters, I will simply present you with the working source code. Figure 20.4 shows the simple user interface, which allows site visitors the ability to "customize" the color scheme to their liking.

```html
<html>

  <head>
    <title>
      Center Park - Customization
    </title>

    <script language="JavaScript">
    <!--
      function saveCustoms( form )
      {
        document.cookie = "bgColor=" + form.bgColor.value;
        document.cookie = "fgColor=" + form.fgColor.value;
      }
    // -->
    </script>
  </head>

<body>

    <form onSubmit="JavaScript: saveCustoms( this );">
      <table>
        <tr>
          <td>
            <b><font size="5">Customize <br>
            Web site colors:<br>
            <br></font></b>
          </td>
        <tr>
          <td>
            <b>Background Color:    </b>
          </td>
          <td>
            <input type="text" name="bgColor" size="15">
          </td>
        </tr>
        <tr>
          <td>
```

```
        <b>Foreground Color:</b>
      </td>
      <td>
        <input type="text" name="fgColor" size="15">
      </td>
      <td>
        <input type="submit" value="Submit">
      </td>
    </tr>
  </table>
</form>


</body>


</html>
```

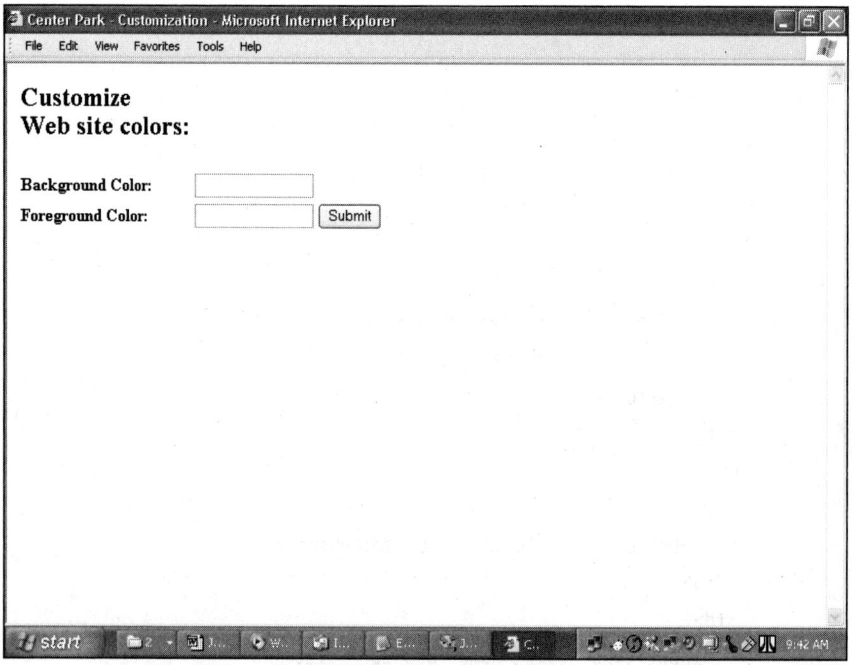

FIGURE 20.4 *Even simple user-customizable options such as this can bring a real sense of personalization to your Web site, encouraging users to feel a stronger sense of ownership (translation: they will be more inclined to return to your site).*

This is the bare minimum code required to store a custom color scheme. A simple function, saveCustoms():

```
function saveCustoms( form )
{
   document.cookie = "bgColor=" + form.bgColor.value;
   document.cookie = "fgColor=" + form.fgColor.value;
}
```

is called when the Submit button on the form is pressed, and it stores the custom color variables in the cookie file. From that point on, any page that has access to that cookie file and has the proper code to retrieve the custom color variable can have the color scheme that the visitor desires.

The code to load the custom color variables is equally simple. All that is required is to read the variables from the cookie file and set the document fields accordingly. Figure 20.5 illustrates this functionality by customizing the background to black and setting the foreground to white.

```
<html>

  <head>
    <title>
      Center Park - Customization
    </title>

    <script language="JavaScript">
    <!--
      function saveCustoms( form )
      {
         document.cookie = "bgColor=" + form.bgColor.value;
         document.cookie = "fgColor=" + form.fgColor.value;
      }

      function getCookieValue( name )
      {
         var c = document.cookie;
         var begin = c.indexOf( name );
         if( begin < 0 ) return( "" );
         begin += name.length + 1;
         var end = c.indexOf( ";", begin );
```

```
      if( end == -1 ) end = c.length;
      return( c.slice( begin, end ) );
    }


    function setCustoms()
    {
      var bg = getCookieValue( "bgColor" );
      var fg = getCookieValue( "fgColor" );
      if( bg != "" ) document.bgColor = bg;
      if( fg != "" ) document.fgColor = fg;
    }
  // -->
  </script>
</head>

<body onLoad="JavaScript: setCustoms();">

  <form onSubmit="JavaScript: saveCustoms( this );">
    <table>
      <tr>
        <td>
          <b><font size="5">Customize <br>
          Web site colors:<br>
          <br></font></b>
        </td>
      <tr>
        <td>
          <b>Background Color:    </b>
        </td>
        <td>
          <input type="text" name="bgColor" size="15">
        </td>
      </tr>
      <tr>
        <td>
          <b>Foreground Color:</b>
```

```
        </td>
        <td>
          <input type="text" name="fgColor" size="15">
        </td>
        <td>
          <input type="submit" value="Submit">
        </td>
      </tr>
    </table>
  </form>


  </body>


</html>
```

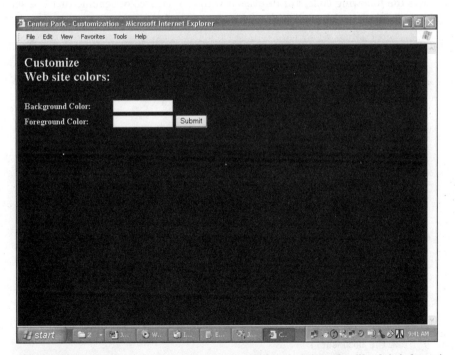

FIGURE 20.5 *Individual users can be quite particular about how they like their information displayed. A customization feature such as this can go a long way towards making their experience on your Web site a happier one.*

This slightly modified example not only saves the custom colors, but loads and applies them the next time the page is loaded. The `setCustoms()` function,

```
function setCustoms()
{
   var bg = getCookieValue( "bgColor" );
   var fg = getCookieValue( "fgColor" );
   if( bg != "" ) document.bgColor = bg;
   if( fg != "" ) document.fgColor = fg;
}
```

which is called from the body tag's `onLoad` event handler,

```
<body onLoad="JavaScript: setCustoms();">
```

reads the color variables from the cookie file and applies them to the document's color fields. The same exact approach can be applied to any page that has access to the cookie file. Figure 20.6 utilizes the following code, but displays it with the same color scheme that was set above (in this case, a black background with a white foreground).

```
<html>

  <head>
    <title>Center Park Home Page - Main Page</title>

    <script language="JavaScript">
    <!--
      function getAd()
      {
        var ad = "ad";
        ad += parseInt( Math.random() * 2 ) + 1;
        return( ad + ".jpg" );
      }

      function rotateAd()
      {
        with( document )
        {
          for( i = 0 ; i < images.length ; i++ )
          {
            if( images[i].name == "adImage" )
```

```
        {
          images[i].alt = images[i].src = getAd();
        }
      }
    }
    window.setTimeout( "rotateAd()", 10000 );
  }

  function getCookieValue( name )
  {
    var c = document.cookie;
    var begin = c.indexOf( name );
    if( begin < 0 ) return( "" );
    begin += name.length + 1;
    var end = c.indexOf( ";", begin );
    if( end == -1 ) end = c.length;
    return( c.slice( begin, end ) );
  }

  function setCustoms()
  {
    var bg = getCookieValue( "bgColor" );
    var fg = getCookieValue( "fgColor" );
    if( bg != "" ) document.bgColor = bg;
    if( fg != "" ) document.fgColor = fg;
  }
  // -->
  </script>
</head>

<body onLoad="JavaScript: setCustoms(); rotateAd();">
  <center>
    <font color="red" size="6"><b>
    Center Park Home Page
    </b></font></center>

  <br><br>
```

```
<table width="100%">
  <tr>
    <td width="50%">
      <img name="adImage" border="0" width="345" height="200">
    </td>
    <td width="50%">
      <a href="login.html">Log In</a><br>
      <a href="store.html">Store</a><br>
      <a href="customize.html">Customize</a>
    </td>
  </tr>
  <tr>
    <td width="100%" colspan="2">
      <hr>
      <font face="Courier" size="5">*** School News ***</font> <br>
      <br>
      <b>July 4th</b> - Fireworks on the mall!  Come enjoy the
      holiday with the Center Park faculty, staff and students.<br>
      <br>
      <b>July 3rd</b> - First annual Adopt a Nerd Day!  They are
      people too.<br>
      <br>
      <b>June 12th</b> - June Bug festival begins.</td>
  </tr>
</table>
</body>

</html>
```

This example is the default content for the frames page presented earlier in this chapter. It utilizes the setCustoms() function to apply the user's desired color scheme. All pages in the Center Park site are similarly equipped to apply the user's desired color scheme.

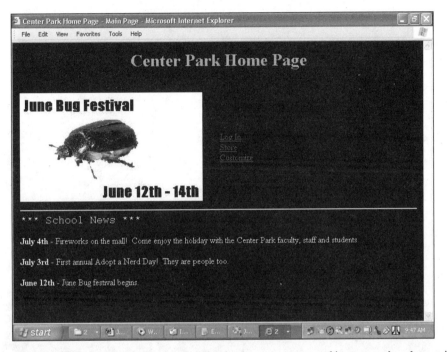

FIGURE 20.6 *While perhaps not visually pleasing to one person, this custom color scheme might be just the ticket for someone else.*

Summary

Giving your Web site visitors the ability to customize display settings, as well as providing a more visually appealing experience can only make the time spent on your site more enjoyable. Through a bit of JavaScript and DHTML effects, you can achieve both of these aims relatively easily. Moreover, by utilizing cookies, you can integrate many of these effects across your entire site, so that if, for example, a custom color scheme is set on one page, it can be applied across the entire site. While form should follow function even in a dynamic, graphically rich medium such as the Web, this doesn't mean your site has to be plain or otherwise "boring." Indeed, as this chapter has shown, by utilizing some simple, tasteful graphics in addition to some basic HTML (*e.g.* frames), you can achieve an attractive site that looks good, but at the same time delivers all the required information and in an accessible, well-organized format.

Chapter 21

Now that you've seen each of the functions of the Center Park site individually constructed, you should now see the entire site as a completed entity. In this final chapter you will

◆ See the entire Center Park Web site in action, including a top-down tour of all the functionality presented therein.

◆ Explore the individual code components (as described in the previous project chapters) to see how they function in relation to the rest of the site.

◆ Determine, as the consultant hired to build the site, the change control and long-term administrative needs of the site; remember, a critical issue in any design (utilizing JavaScript or otherwise) is thinking of how the end user—*i.e.* the customer—will utilize all the great functionality you've build into your site. In this regard, we'll review the Center Park site from a usability perspective and determine whether it meets all the needs as set down in Chapter 14.

JavaScript-Specific Features of the Center Park Web Site

As you've seen over the past few chapters, the Center Park Web site has several JavaScript-specific features that elevate it above a regular "static" Web site. Specifically, and as you've seen over the past few chapters, those features are as follows:

> **NOTE**
>
> The following list was originally presented in Chapter 14, which was the Center Park "preview" chapter. We are presenting this list once again, so you can use it as a "review checklist" for how the described functionality was actually implemented within the Center Park Web site. Then, the individual headings in this chapter will discuss each functional component in more detail.

- **Dynamic calendars**. Students have asked to be able to view their homework assignments "at a glance," and to be able to do so in weekly and monthly increments; moreover, important dates for the operation of the school year (start/ending dates, vacations, meetings, etc.) need to be communicated via the site. The site will require several dynamic calendars, so that users of the site can locate the information when they want and in the fashion (weekly, monthly) they want.

- **A test and survey feature**. Administrators of the school recently visited a sister school in another district and were impressed to see that school performing online testing. This feature has proven very useful as a method of assessment for advanced-standing students in continuing education, as well as (through some fairly simple modification of the code) a means of gathering information via online surveys. The Center Park administrators would like such a feature for their Web site.

- **An online store**. As with all things education, fund-raising is critical to ensuring that the important programs and initiatives of the school continue despite the omnipresent red pen of the local, state, and federal legislature. Center Park administrators have requested that the site feature some type of online store at which orders for various fund-raising items can be placed at any time of day or night. To help further facilitate this online store, the administrators have also requested that basic financial calculators be included on the site so that visitors and members can perform quick price calculations.

- **Secure, members-only access**. Many of the features of the site, while open to the general public (*e.g.* the online store), will require secure access for current students and faculty only. In order to ensure that the information deemed confidential can remain as such, you will need to utilize some of the security features of JavaScript coding.

♦ **Rotating banner advertisements.** Not surprisingly, several organizations within the school (*e.g.* the sports teams, the band, and various student clubs) have asked for advertising space on the site so that visitors can be aware of their activities. Several of the rotating-banner ads will provide links to specific sections of the site, so being able to hyperlink within the ads will be a critical.

♦ **Bold, attractive appearance.** Finally, all of the above-mentioned functionality, as well as the general look and feel of the site, must be as eye-pleasing as possible. To that end, the site will also include various dynamic HTML (DHTML) effects.

Within each of the sections in this chapter, the functionality will be reviewed; however, the focus will also be to determine if the project goal (*i.e.* the requested functionality) was met, and to determine what additional features might be added in the future (and—critically—what user functional requirements might drive the development of these additional features).

NOTE

This wrap-up chapter has been written as if it were a "post-project" review. As you read through it, imagine yourself in the role of JavaScript Web developer (which you now are, after reading this book!), meeting with the Center Park administrators. Your job in this customer follow-up meeting, then, is to "sell" your own work (that is, show how the final product has met their pre-project requirements) but at the same time keep an open ear for (and make note of) potential future changes, which would add to the functionality of the site.

Post-Project Review:
The Center Park Web Site

It is 9:00 a.m. on the Monday morning the Center Park Web site has gone live. As part of your initial project proposal, you are now in a critical meeting with the school administrators to review the functioning of the site to ensure that it meets all required functionality and to make a list of possible future updates.

Imagine, then, that the following sections are "meeting notes" from this discussion, as you—as the site developer—discuss your final product with the school administrators. Also, note that the final section contains a complete listing of each source file for the entire site (this type of source code listing might be something you would provide to the client, especially those who may have the expertise to modify functionality of the site on their own).

Review: The Site Home Page

The first thing to review in the completed site is the site home page. Figures 21.1 and 21.2 show the page and highlight the rotating banner functionality that has been built into the site.

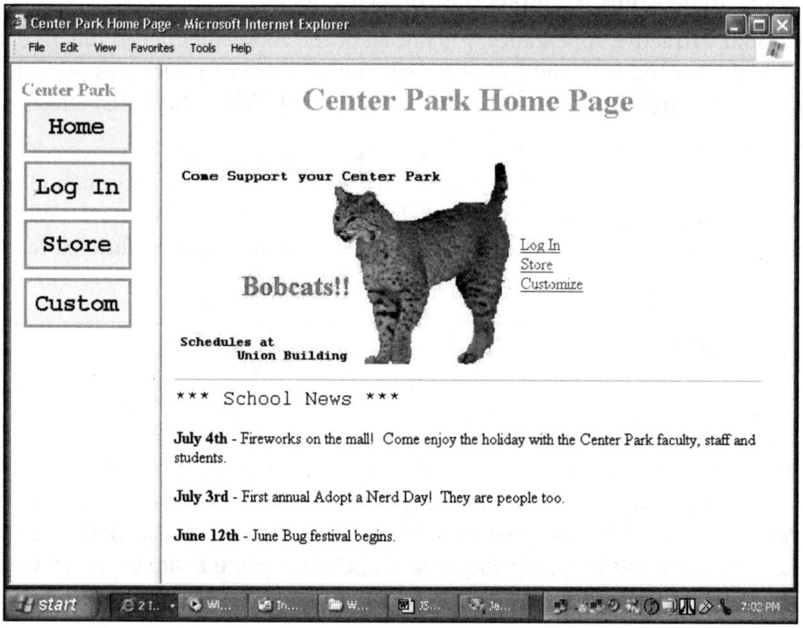

FIGURE 21.1 *The Center Park home page, highlighting the rotating banner functionality.*

Requirements Met: the Site Home Page

The home page meets many of the functionality requirements set forth in the initial project request:

◆   The rotating banner graphics (in this case, highlighting the general "Support Your Bobcats" message as shown in Figure 21.1, and the advertisement for the "June Bug Festival" as shown in Figure 21.2) help to answer the "screen real estate" issue, in that by displaying each ad for a few seconds, they allow multiple advertisements to share the same space, with each getting equal "air time." Note there is no limit to the number of graphics you can rotate; moreover, you can include hyperlinks within each one so that if a particular group/event being advertised has its own Web site, a link could be provided to it within the rotating ad.

◆   As shown in Figure 21.3, the navigation buttons utilize DHTML effects by changing color when the mouse is moved over them. Note as well that the functionality presented by these links is also presented in the right frame. Why do this? In case the user somehow was to get out of the site frame set (and thus lose the navigation buttons presented in the left frame), he or she could still access all the major functionality of the site.

FIGURE 21.2 *A different graphic is now being displayed. Also note that navigation buttons at the left of the screen are duplicated in the right frame as hyperlinks.*

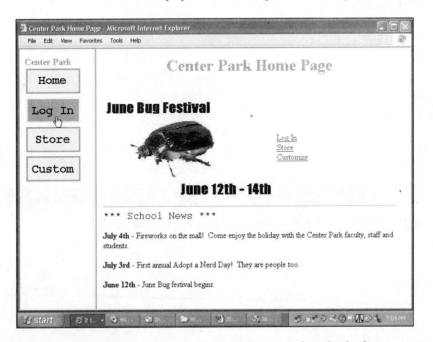

FIGURE 21.3 *When you move your mouse pointer over each navigation button, it changes color to indicate that it is active and ready to be selected.*

◆ While this is arguably a simple design (for illustrative purposes only; in the "real world" you might be asked to put a more aesthetic touch to your design), it works well from a functional perspective—all major site functionality is readily available and easy to find and understand, via the names given the button links.

Review: The Log In Function

Because of the omnipresent security concerns with Web sites, more and more organizations of all sizes are seeking to secure specific content. Sometimes, organizations will form "intranets"—versus an extranet or Internet site—in order to make information available only to employees or other authorized persons.

The Center Park Web site is no different. In this case, the secure Log In button, when clicked, presents users with a user name and password sign-in, as illustrated in Figure 21.4.

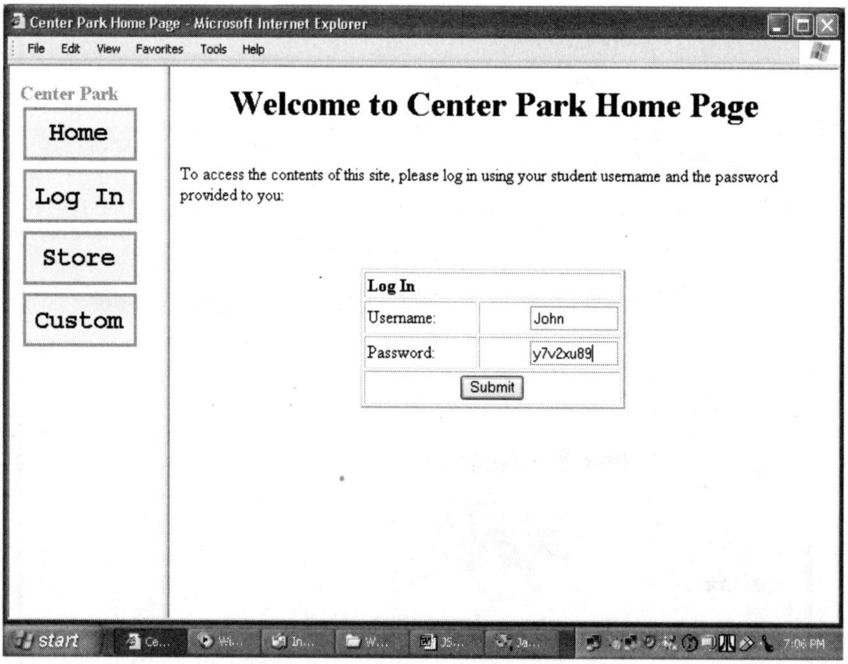

FIGURE 21.4 *The Log In functionality allows users to access private or otherwise secure content within the Center Park Web site.*

Requirements Met: the Login Function

JavaScript doesn't have a lot of built-in security functionality, and this "secure" login is indicative of that. Still, the page does have some basic attributes that you could—in a real-world situation—develop in a more robust manner:

◆ The password field could be changed to a regular form password field, where the characters that are entered are marked out and represented only by asterisks (this is still only very basic security, but it would prevent, for example, someone from gaining your password while looking over your shoulder as you keyed it in).

◆ If this were a production site, each user would have a specific user name and password; however, even in this basic example, you can see the inherent security that is possible by locking out unauthorized access via a user name and password.

Review: The Task Calendar

Once users log in to the site (via the user name and password shown in Figure 21.4), they are presented with their customized calendar of tasks and events, as shown in Figure 21.5.

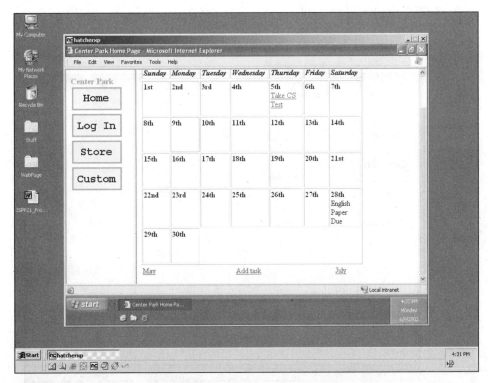

FIGURE 21.5 *The "customized calendar", which is presented to the users after they successfully log in to the Center Park site.*

The calendar function, even in this most basic form, is a virtual cornucopia of JavaScript functionality. The following subsection describes how this coding meets many of the defined requirements of the Web site.

Requirements Met: the Task Calendar

The Center Park administrators wanted their site to present users of all types (teachers, students, and parents) an easy and convenient way to keep in organized touch with the Center Park School.

That said, the Task Calendar fits the bill for many of these function requirements:

- As shown in Figure 21.5, the calendar is specific to each user login ("Welcome John!!).
- The calendar defaults to the current month and day (the current day is highlighted with a box around it).
- "Navigation" buttons are presented at the bottom of the calendar, so users can move forward or backward one month in order to view that month's respective calendar.
- The ability to add a task to the calendar is presented via the "Add task" link at the bottom of the calendar.

Adding a task to the calendar is an important functional component. When the user clicks on the "Add task" link illustrated in Figure 21.5, he or she is presented with the Schedule Task form, as shown in Figure 21.6 below.

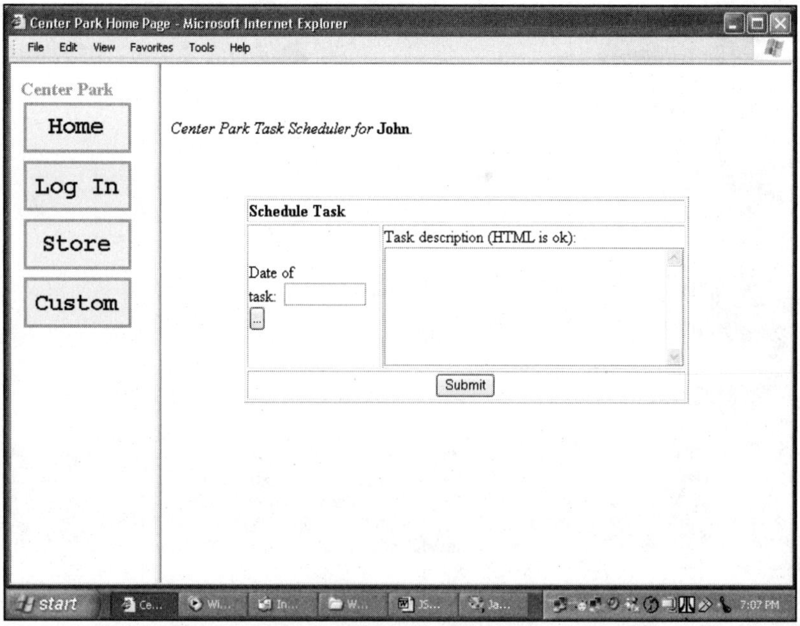

FIGURE 21.6 *Users can add a task to their calendar via this "Schedule Task" function of the Task Calendar.*

To add a task, the user would follow these steps:

1. First, the user would click on the "Add task" button as shown in Figure 21.5. This presents the Schedule Task screen, as shown in Figure 21.6.

2. At this point, the first thing to do is select the date of the task. As shown in Figure 21.6, the user would click on the button underneath the "Date of task" text, which in turn brings up the Date Chooser pop-up calendar, as shown in Figure 21.7.

3. Once a date is selected in the Date Chooser pop-up calendar, it is automatically inserted back into the initial form, as shown in Figure 21.8. Also, the description of the task is also entered. Note that in this case, the following HTML is entered:

```
<a href="http://www.centerparkschool.edu/tests/test1.html">Click here to take the
    first exam.</a>
```

so that when the task is placed on Donald's calendar for 5/30/2003, it will actually be a hyperlink to the an exam.

4. Once the date and task description are entered, the user clicks the Submit button and the task is entered on his calendar.

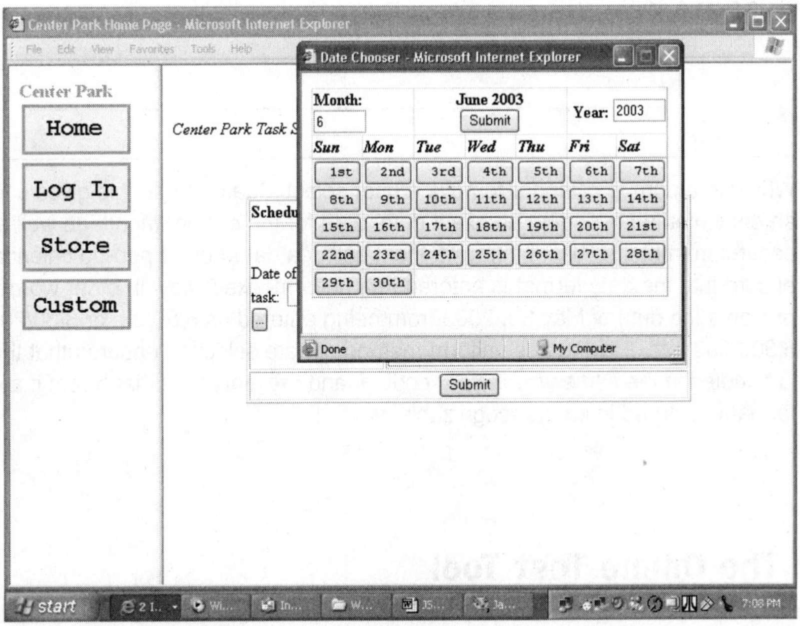

FIGURE 21.7 *The Date Chooser pop-up allows a user to select a specific date for their task. Note that the date and month can be changed so that the task can be assigned to any date, not just during the current month.*

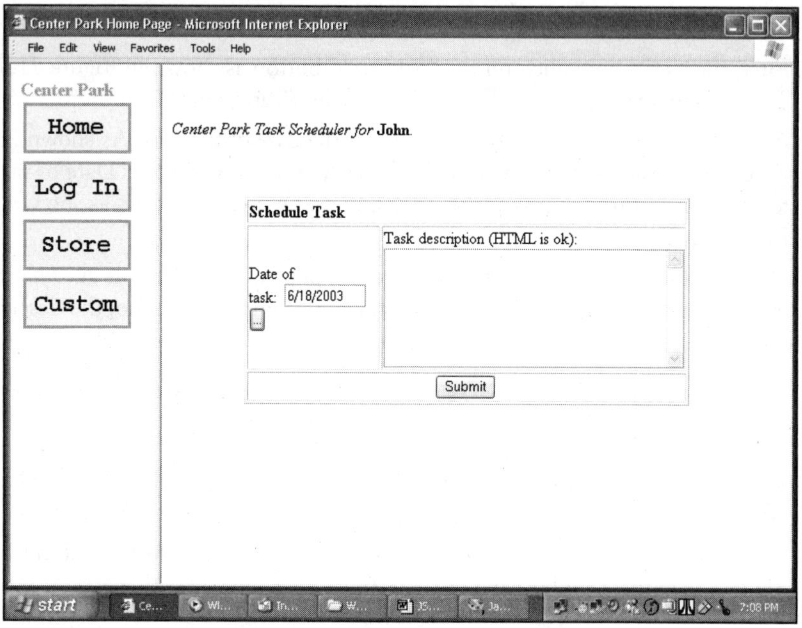

FIGURE 21.8 *Once a date is chosen in the Date Chooser, it is placed into the Date of task field.*

TIP

Why use a pop-up calendar to have a user select a date? First, this gives users an easy method of finding an exact date, both for the current month as well as past/future months. Also, by having them select a date from a pop-up calendar, you ensure that the date format is entered in a uniform, exact way: in other words, this prevents the date of May 30, 2003 from being entered as 5/30/03, or 5/30/2003, or 5.30.2003, etc. Having this uniform method of date selection ensures that the data is handled in the same way in your coding, and prevents potential errors if a data format is entered in an unrecognizable way.

Review: The Online Test Tool

While the Center Park administrators have their reservations about going to a purely online testing environment, they are interested in working with this functionality in the new site.

If you look back to Figure 21.5, you can see that on May 5th, there is a task entitled "Take CS Test." If you click on this link, you will be presented with a glimpse of the online testing component, as shown in Figure 21.9.

FUNCTIONALITY, YES...BUT FOR "ILLUSTRATIVE PURPOSES" ONLY

The code for the Center Park site that is presented in this chapter, while functional, is for illustrative purposes only.

What's the catch, you say? The data entered in the Task Calendar (as well as the online store, which is illustrated a bit later in this chapter) doesn't really go anywhere when the user clicks the various submit buttons. Why is this so? The answer is simple: the data has nowhere to go; specifically, it doesn't have a database to be inserted into.

Integrating a database with your Web site can be a complicated task, depending on the type of functionality you wish to present. However, you will quickly find that you will need this type of functionality if you are to move beyond the most basic functionality. Unfortunately, database integration goes beyond the scope of this book (focusing as it does purely on JavaScript); moreover, there are different programming methods that can be utilized to integrate a database with your site.

That said, then, much of the advanced functionality of the Center Park site is just an illustration of potential functionality that could be achieved if the site were integrated with a database.

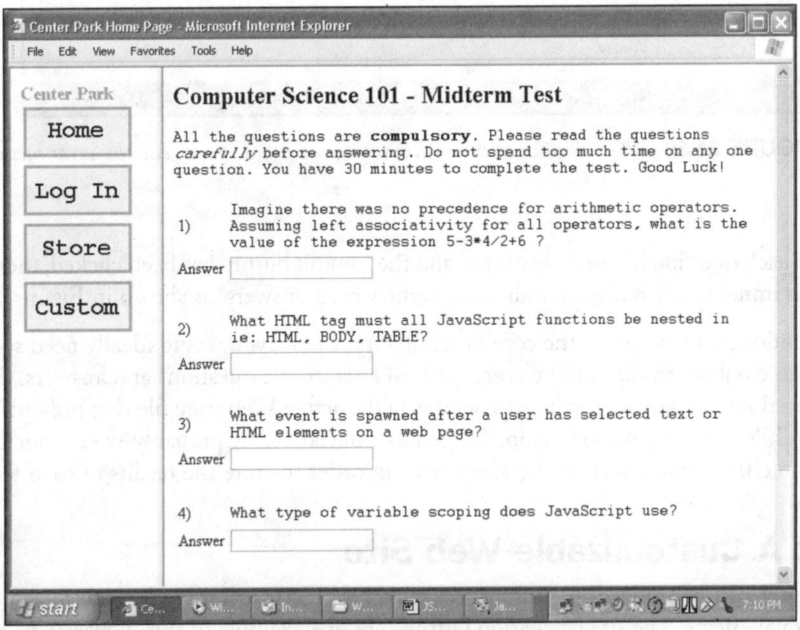

FIGURE 21.9 *An example of a five-question online test, made possible via JavaScript!*

Requirement Met: Online Testing Capability

Figure 21.9 illustrates a simple five-question Computer Science test. The user is presented with answer fields, and at the bottom of the screen (not visible in Figure 21.9) is a Submit button for them to click when they have answered all questions. Note that if they do not enter something in each answer field, they will be presented with a warning prompt (more JavaScript functionality here…) as shown in Figure 21.10.

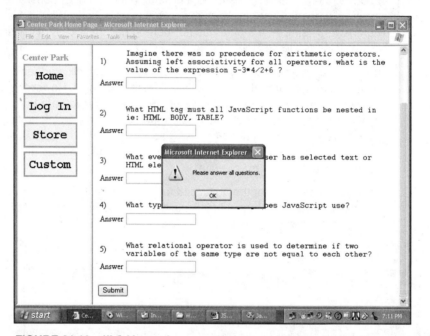

FIGURE 21.10 *All fields must have something entered into them, or else this error message appears.*

When each question has been answered and the Submit button has been clicked, the test-taker's score is immediately returned, indicating right/wrong answers, as shown in Figure 21.11.

As mentioned above, while the core functionality is here, you would ideally need some type of backend database to capture the scores as well as store the questions and answers. Right now, the questions and answers are hard-coded into the actual Web page file that presents the online test. While this is good for, again, "illustrative purposes," it probably would not be the best solution either from a security perspective or in order to store the results of each test.

Review: A Customizable Web Site

JavaScript can be utilized in conjunction with DHTML in order to produce some neat and functional effects. The site navigation buttons are one example of this; however, an even better example is how the site allows the visitor to set both the foreground and background colors.

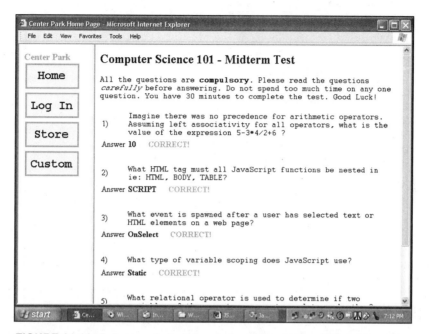

FIGURE 21.11 *Instant analysis of the submitted answers is possible via the JavaScript functionality of the testing feature of the Web site.*

When the user clicks on the Custom Navigation button, he or she is presented with the options shown in Figure 21.12.

Requirement Met: Customizable Features

As shown in Figure 21.12, the user can select the foreground and background colors of the site. Figure 21.13 illustrates how choosing black as the background and white as the foreground changes the appearance of the Center Park site.

While this is again a simple example, it hints at the possibilities in Web page customization features that are possible with JavaScript. Moreover, giving the user this type of control is good customer relationship management and indicates that you—as site designer and/or administrator—are interested in catering to your customers' specific needs and interests.

Review: The Center Park Web Store

The final piece of required functionality, as set forth by the Center Park school administrators, was to have some type of basic Web store, so that visitors could shop for school merchandise (and thus, again, potentially alleviate the need for all those bake sales). Figures 21.14 through 21.16 illustrate the base functionality of the Web Store.

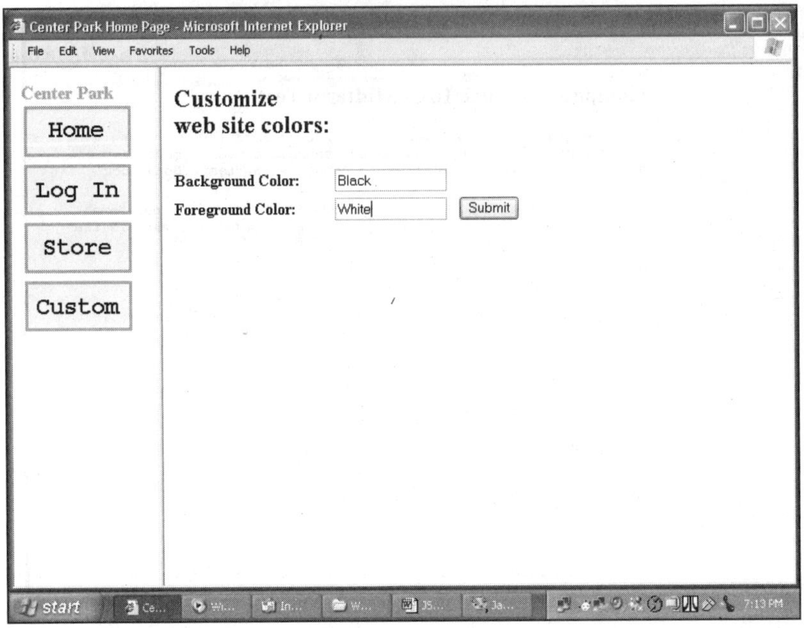

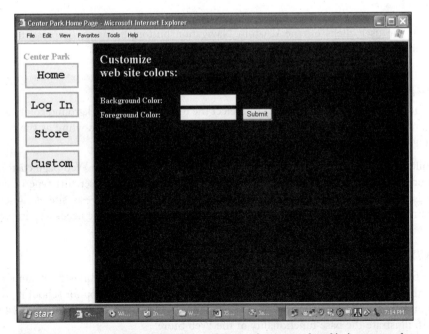

FIGURE 21.12 *Users can customize the appearance of the Center Park site.*

FIGURE 21.13 *A simple custom feature, but one that can make a big impact on the appearance of the site.*

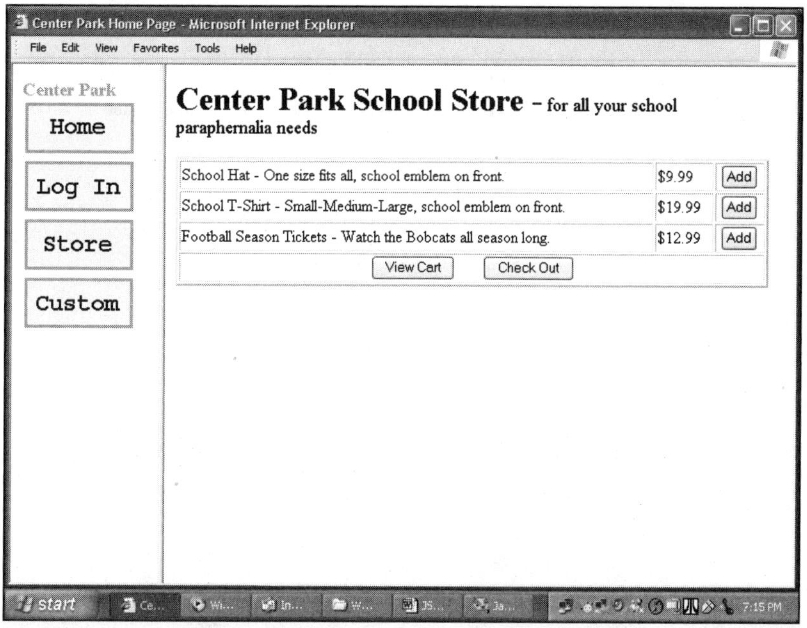

FIGURE 21.14 *The home page of the store, listing all the items for sale.*

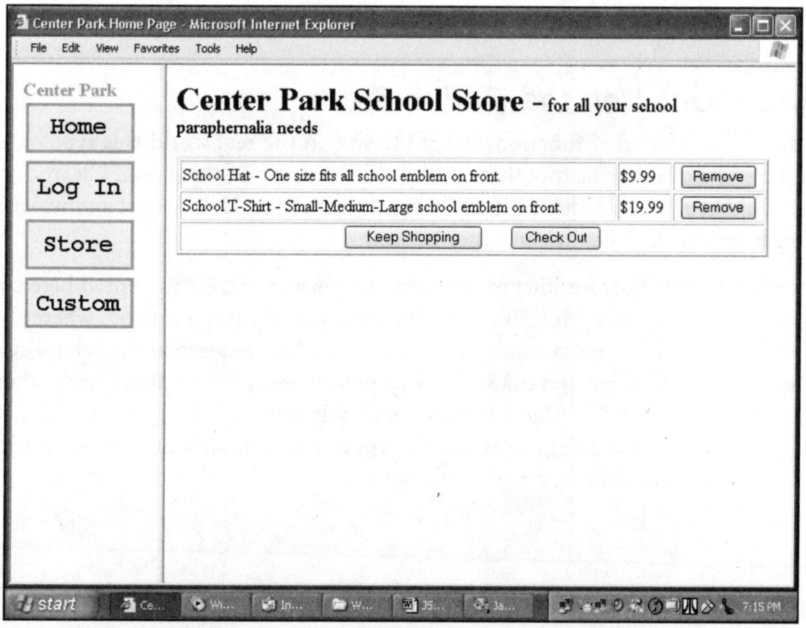

FIGURE 21.15 *In this example, the visitor has added one school hat and one school T-shirt.*

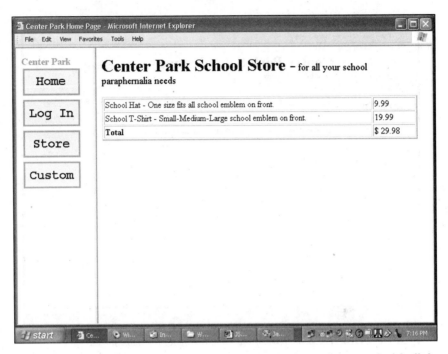

FIGURE 21.16 *By clicking on the Check Out button, the shopper is presented with all the items they have selected and the total charge for the items.*

Requirement Met: the Online Store

As with some of the other functionality of the site, in the real world this type of online store would have several other factors that go beyond the scope of this book. Clearly, one of those factors would be how individuals actually pay for their items: Do they get an invoice via e-mail? Are they asked to enter credit card information?

However, even in its "just for illustrative purposes" form, the code presented here could still be considered an online store. How? Perhaps the store is really just a catalog, where shoppers can browse what is available, get a total, and then e-mail their request to the school store or print out a hard copy order form and mail it in. The point here is that— along with other functionality shown in this chapter—the core functionality is provided, and with some customization (as well as integration of a database), the site could easily fit all requirements set forth by the school administrators, even in a real-world setting.

The Center Park Web Site: Complete Code Listing

The following sections list each of the pages that make up the site. If you were to code and then save them, with the name provided, into a single directory, you could then see the site in action as it has been illustrated here.

MenuBar.html

This is the code for the left-hand frame of the site home page:

```html
<html>

  <head>
    <base target="main">

    <script language="JavaScript">
    <!--
      function change( image, event )
      {
        image.src = image.name + event + ".bmp";
      }
    // -->
    </script>
  </head>

<body>
  <font color="red" size="4"><b>
    Center Park<br>
  </b></font>
  <table width="100%">
    <tr><td>
      <a href="Main.html" target="main">
        <img border="0" src="home1.bmp" name="home"
            onMouseDown="JavaScript: change( this, 3 );"
            onMouseOver="JavaScript: change( this, 2 );"
            onMouseOut="JavaScript: change( this, 1 );">
      </a>
    </td></tr>
```

```
<tr><td>
  <a href="LogIn.html" target="main">
    <img border="0" src="login1.bmp" name="login"
         onMouseDown="JavaScript: change( this, 3 );"
         onMouseOver="JavaScript: change( this, 2 );"
         onMouseOut="JavaScript: change( this, 1 );">
  </a>
</td></tr>
<tr><td>
  <a href="Store.html" target="main">
    <img border="0" src="store1.bmp" name="store"
         onMouseDown="JavaScript: change( this, 3 );"
         onMouseOver="JavaScript: change( this, 2 );"
         onMouseOut="JavaScript: change( this, 1 );">
  </a>
</td></tr>
<tr><td>
  <a href="Customize.html" target="main">
    <img border="0" src="customize1.bmp" name="customize"
         onMouseDown="JavaScript: change( this, 3 );"
         onMouseOver="JavaScript: change( this, 2 );"
         onMouseOut="JavaScript: change( this, 1 );">
  </a>
</td></tr>
  </table>
</body>

</html>
```

Main.html

This is the code for the right-hand frame of the home page:

```
<html>

  <head>
    <title>Center Park Home Page - Main Page</title>

    <script language="JavaScript">
```

```
<!--
  function getAd()
  {
    var ad = "ad";
    ad += parseInt( Math.random() * 2 ) + 1;
    return( ad + ".jpg" );
  }


  function rotateAd()
  {
    with( document )
    {
      for( i = 0 ; i < images.length ; i++ )
      {
        if( images[i].name == "adImage" )
        {
          images[i].alt = images[i].src = getAd();
        }
      }
    }
    window.setTimeout( "rotateAd()", 10000 );
  }


  function getCookieValue( name )
  {
    var c = document.cookie;
    var begin = c.indexOf( name );
    if( begin < 0 ) return( "" );
    begin += name.length + 1;
    var end = c.indexOf( ";", begin );
    if( end == -1 ) end = c.length;
    return( c.slice( begin, end ) );
  }


  function setCustoms()
  {
    var bg = getCookieValue( "bgColor" );
    var fg = getCookieValue( "fgColor" );
```

```html
        if( bg != "" ) document.bgColor = bg;
        if( fg != "" ) document.fgColor = fg;
      }
    // -->
    </script>
</head>

<body onLoad="JavaScript: setCustoms(); rotateAd();">
  <center>
    <font color="red" size="6"><b>
      Center Park Home Page
    </b></font></center>

  <br><br>

  <table width="100%">
    <tr>
      <td width="50%">
        <img name="adImage" border="0" width="345" height="200">
      </td>
      <td width="50%">
        <a href="login.html">Log In</a><br>
        <a href="store.html">Store</a><br>
        <a href="customize.html">Customize</a>
      </td>
    </tr>
    <tr>
      <td width="100%" colspan="2">
        <hr>
        <font face="Courier" size="5">*** School News ***</font> <br>
        <br>
        <b>July 4th</b> - Fireworks on the mall!  Come enjoy the holiday
        with the Center Park faculty, staff and students.<br>
        <br>
        <b>July 3rd</b> - First annual Adopt a Nerd Day!  They are people
        too.<br>
        <br>
        <b>June 12th</b> - June Bug festival begins.</td>
```

```
        </tr>
      </table>
    </body>

  </html>
```

LogIn.html

This code represents the login page, which users complete in order to gain access to their personalized task calendar:

```html
<html>
  <head>
    <title>
      Center Park Home Page - Log In
    </title>

    <script language="JavaScript">
    <!--
      function LogIn( form )
      {
        // Store the student name in the cookie file for later reference
        document.cookie = "username=" + form.username.value;
        // Make sure the password is correct
        document.location = form.password.value + ".html";
      }

      function getCookieValue( name )
      {
        var c = document.cookie;
        var begin = c.indexOf( name );
        if( begin < 0 ) return( "" );
        begin += name.length + 1;
        var end = c.indexOf( ";", begin );
        if( end == -1 ) end = c.length;
        return( c.slice( begin, end ) );
      }

      function setCustoms()
```

```
      {
        var bg = getCookieValue( "bgColor" );
        var fg = getCookieValue( "fgColor" );
        if( bg != "" ) document.bgColor = bg;
        if( fg != "" ) document.fgColor = fg;
      }
    // -->
    </script>
</head>

<body onLoad="JavaScript: setCustoms();">

  <center><font size=6><b>Welcome to Center Park Home Page</b></font></center>
  <br><br>
  To access the contents of this site, please log in using your student
  username and the password provided to you:

  <br><br>
  <br><br>

  <form name="login" onSubmit="JavaScript: LogIn( this ); return( false );" >
    <center>
      <table border="2" cellpadding="2" width="250">
        <tr>
          <td colspan="2"><b>Log In</b></td>
        </tr>
        <tr>
          <td>Username:</td>
          <td align="right"><input name="username" size="10"></td>
        </tr>
        <tr>
          <td>Password:</td>
          <td align="right"><input name="password" size="10"></td>
        </tr>
        <tr>
          <td colspan="2">
          <p align="center"><input type="submit" value="Submit"></td>
        </tr>
```

```
      </table>
    </center>
  </form>

  <script language="JavaScript">
  <!--
    document.login.username.value = getCookieValue( "username" );
  // -->
  </script>

  </body>
</html>
```

y7v2xu89.html

For illustrative purposes, this page has been given the name of the password that is required to be entered in the login screen (the username doesn't matter). Again, this is obviously not the most secure design (to put it mildly!) but has been created as it is purposely, to ensure that you understand how information is passed between one page and another.

```
<html>
  <head>
    <title></title>

    <script language="JavaScript">
    <!--
      var now = new Date();
      var months = new Array( "January", "February", "March", "April",
                              "May", "June", "July", "August", "September",
                              "October", "November", "December" );

      var yString = getCookieValue( "year" );
      var mString = getCookieValue( "month" );
      var y = fixYear( yString ? parseInt( yString ) : now.getYear() );
      var m = fixMonth( mString ? parseInt( mString ) : now.getMonth() );
      var month = new Date( y, m, 1 );

      function getCookieValue( name )
      {
```

```javascript
  var c = document.cookie;
  var begin = c.indexOf( name );
  if( begin < 0 ) return( "" );
  begin += name.length + 1;
  var end = c.indexOf( ";", begin );
  if( end == -1 ) end = c.length;
  return( c.slice( begin, end ) );
}


function fixYear( year )
{
  return( year < 1000 ?  year + 1900 : year );
}


function fixMonth( month )
{
  return( month < 0 ? month + 12 : ( month > 11 ? month - 12 : month ) );
}


function getNumberDays( d )
{
  switch( d.getMonth() + 1 )
  {
    case 1: case 3: case 5: case 7:
    case 8: case 10: case 12:
      return( 31 );
    case 4: case 6: case 9: case 11:
      return( 30 );
    case 2:
      return( 28 + ( d.getYear % 4 == 0 ? 1 : 0 ) );
  }
}


function getEnding( number )
{
  if( number > 10 && number < 20 ) return( "th" );

  switch( number % 10 )
```

```
      {
        case 0: case 4: case 5:
        case 6: case 7: case 8:
        case 9:
          return( "th" );
        case 1:
          return( "st" );
        case 2:
          return( "nd" );
        case 3:
          return( "rd" );
      }
    }


    // These should be loaded from a server-side language such as ASP
    var tasks = new Array( 30 );
    tasks[5] = "<a href='Test.html'>Take CS Test</a>";
    tasks[28] = "English Paper Due";


    function setCustoms()
    {
      var bg = getCookieValue( "bgColor" );
      var fg = getCookieValue( "fgColor" );
      if( bg != "" ) document.bgColor = bg;
      if( fg != "" ) document.fgColor = fg;
    }
  // -->
  </script>
</head>

<body onLoad="JavaScript: setCustoms(); document.cookie='loggedin=true';">
  <i>Welcome</i><b>
  <script language="JavaScript">
  <!--
    document.write( getCookieValue( "username" ) + "</b>!! " );
  // -->
  </script>
  <i>Here are your tasks for</i>
```

```html
<table width="75%">
  <tr><td align="center">
    <font size="6"><b>
      <script language="JavaScript">
      <!--
        document.write( months[m] );
      // -->
      </script>
    </b></font>
  </td></tr>
</table>

<table border="1" cellpadding="2" width="75%">
  <tr>
    <td width="14%"><b><i>Sunday</i></b></td>
    <td width="14%"><b><i>Monday</i></b></td>
    <td width="14%"><b><i>Tuesday</i></b></td>
    <td width="14%"><b><i>Wednesday</i></b></td>
    <td width="14%"><b><i>Thursday</i></b></td>
    <td width="14%"><b><i>Friday</i></b></td>
    <td width="14%"><b><i>Saturday</i></b></td>
  </tr>
  <tr>
    <script language="JavaScript">
    <!--
      var startDay = month.getDay();
      for( i = 0 ; i < startDay ; i++ )
      {
        document.write( "<td></td>" );
      }

      var numDays = getNumberDays( month );
      for( i = 0 ; i < numDays ; i++ )
      {
        if( ( i + startDay + 1 ) % 7 == 1 )
        {
          document.write( "</tr><tr>" );
        }
```

```
            document.write( "<td height='75' valign='top'" );
            if( fixYear( now.getYear() ) == fixYear( month.getYear() ) &&
now.getMonth() == month.getMonth() && now.getDate() == i + 1 )
document.write( " bordercolor='red'" );
            document.write( "><b>" + (i+1) + getEnding( i + 1 ) + "</b><br>" );
            if( tasks[i+1] ) document.write( tasks[i+1] );
            document.write( "</td>" );
          }
        // -->
        </script>
      </tr>
    </table>


    <table width="75%">
      <tr>
        <td>
          <script language="JavaScript">
          <!--
            document.write( "<a href=\"" + document.location + "\" " );
            document.write( "onClick=\"JavaScript: document.cookie='month=" +
fixMonth(m-1) + "';\">" );
            document.write( months[fixMonth(m-1)] + "</a>" );
          // -->
          </script>
        </td>
        <td align="center">
          <a href="AddTask.html">Add task</a>
        </td>
        <td align="right">
          <script language="JavaScript">
          <!--
            document.write( "<a href=\"" + document.location + "\" " );
            document.write( "onClick=\"JavaScript: document.cookie='month=" +
fixMonth(m+1) + "';\">" );
            document.write( months[fixMonth(m+1)] + "</a>" );
          // -->
          </script>
        </td>
```

```
      </tr>
    </table>

  </body>
</html>
```

AddTask.html

The following page presents the ability for a user to add a task to his or her personal calendar:

```html
<html>

  <head>
    <title>Center Park - Add Task</title>

    <script language="JavaScript">
    <!--
      if( getCookieValue( "loggedin" ) != "true" ) document.location = "Main.html";

      var dateElement;
      function openDatePicker( target )
      {
        dateElement = target;
        var ieSize = "width=380,height=255";
        var navSize = "width=480,height=295";
        var isNav = navigator.appName == "Netscape";
        window.open( "PopupCalendar.html", "calendar", "menubar=no,resizable=no,scroll-
bars=no,status=yes,toolbar=no," + ( isNav ? navSize : ieSize ) );
      }

      function setDate( date )
      {
        dateElement.value = date;
      }

      function getCookieValue( name )
      {
        var c = document.cookie;
        var begin = c.indexOf( name );
```

```
      if( begin < 0 ) return( "" );
      begin += name.length + 1;
      var end = c.indexOf( ";", begin );
      if( end == -1 ) end = c.length;
      return( c.slice( begin, end ) );
   }


   function setCustoms()
   {
     var bg = getCookieValue( "bgColor" );
     var fg = getCookieValue( "fgColor" );
     if( bg != "" ) document.bgColor = bg;
     if( fg != "" ) document.fgColor = fg;
   }
  // -->
  </script>
</head>

<body onLoad="JavaScript: setCustoms();">
  <br>
  <br>
  <i>Center Park Task Scheduler for</i><b>
  <script language="JavaScript">
  <!--
    document.write( getCookieValue( "username" ) );
  // -->
  </script></b>.


  <br><br>
  <br><br>


  <form name="taskForm" onSubmit="JavaScript: return( false );">
    <center>
      <table border="1" width="75%">
        <tr>
          <td width="100%" colspan="2"><b>Schedule Task</b></td>
        </tr>
        <tr>
```

```
        <td width="50%">
          Date of task: 
          <input type="text" name="date" size="10">
          <input type="button" value="..." onClick="JavaScript: openDatePicker(
document.taskForm.date );">
        </td>
        <td width="50%">
          Task description (HTML is ok):<br>
          <textarea rows="7" cols="35"></textarea>
        </td>
      </tr>
      <tr>
        <td align="center" colspan="2">
          <input type="submit" value="Submit" name="B1">
        </td>
      </tr>
    </table>
  </center>
 </form>
 </body>
</html>
```

PopUpCalendar.html

The following code allows the pop-up calendar to appear, so that users can pick a specific date
on which to schedule their task:

```
<html>

  <head>
    <title>Date Chooser</title>

    <style type="text/css">
    <!--
      .mono{ font-family: monospace; }
    -->
    </style>

    <script language="JavaScript">
```

```
<!--
  var now = new Date();
  var month = new Date( fixYear( now.getYear() ), now.getMonth(), 1 );
  var months = new Array( "January", "February", "March", "April",
                          "May", "June", "July", "August", "September",
                          "October", "November", "December" );

  var urlquery = location.href.split( "?" );
  if( urlquery[1] )
  {
    var params = urlquery[1].split( "&" );
    var m = ( params[0] ? params[0].split( "=" )[1] - 1 : fixMonth( now.getMonth() ) );
    var y = ( params[1] ? params[1].split( "=" )[1] : fixYear( now.getYear() ) );
    month = new Date( y, m, 1 );
  }

  function fixYear( year )
  {
    return( year < 1000 ?  year + 1900 : year );
  }

  function fixMonth( month )
  {
    return( month < 0 ? month + 12 : ( month > 11 ? month - 12 : month ) );
  }

  function getNumberDays( d )
  {
    switch( d.getMonth() + 1 )
    {
      case 1: case 3: case 5: case 7:
      case 8: case 10: case 12:
        return( 31 );
      case 4: case 6: case 9: case 11:
        return( 30 );
      case 2:
        return( 28 + ( d.getYear % 4 == 0 ? 1 : 0 ) );
    }
```

```
}

function getEnding( number )
{
  if( number > 10 && number < 20 ) return( "th" );

  switch( number % 10 )
  {
    case 0: case 4: case 5:
    case 6: case 7: case 8:
    case 9:
      return( "th" );
    case 1:
      return( "st" );
    case 2:
      return( "nd" );
    case 3:
      return( "rd" );
  }
}


function onSelect()
{
  window.opener.setDate( document.theForm.date.value );
  self.close();
}

function getCookieValue( name )
{
  var c = document.cookie;
  var begin = c.indexOf( name );
  if( begin < 0 ) return( "" );
  begin += name.length + 1;
  var end = c.indexOf( ";", begin );
  if( end == -1 ) end = c.length;
  return( c.slice( begin, end ) );
}
```

```
      function setCustoms()
      {
        var bg = getCookieValue( "bgColor" );
        var fg = getCookieValue( "fgColor" );
        if( bg != "" ) document.bgColor = bg;
        if( fg != "" ) document.fgColor = fg;
      }
    // -->
    </script>
</head>

<body onLoad="JavaScript: setCustoms();">

  <form name="theForm">
    <table border="1" width="75%" style="border-collapse: collapse">
      <tr>
        <td align="left" colspan=2>
          <b>Month:</b>
          <input type="text" name="Month" size="5">
          <script language="JavaScript">
          <!--
            document.theForm.Month.value = fixMonth( month.getMonth() + 1 );
          // -->
          </script>
        </td>
        <td colspan=3>
          <center>
            <b><script language="JavaScript">
            <!--
              document.write( months[fixMonth( month.getMonth() )] + " " + fixYear(
month.getYear() ) );
            // -->
            </script></b><br>
            <input type="submit" value="Submit">
          </center>
        </td>
        <td align="right" colspan=2>
          <b>Year:</b>
```

```
      <input type="text" name="Year" size="5">
      <script language="JavaScript">
      <!--
        document.theForm.Year.value = fixYear( month.getYear() );
      // -->
      </script>
    </td>
  </tr>
  <tr>
    <td width="14%"><b><i>Sun</i></b></td>
    <td width="14%"><b><i>Mon</i></b></td>
    <td width="14%"><b><i>Tue</i></b></td>
    <td width="14%"><b><i>Wed</i></b></td>
    <td width="14%"><b><i>Thu</i></b></td>
    <td width="14%"><b><i>Fri</i></b></td>
    <td width="14%"><b><i>Sat</i></b></td>
  </tr>
  <tr>
    <script language="JavaScript">
    <!--
      var startDay = month.getDay();
      for( i = 0 ; i < startDay ; i++ )
      {
        document.write( "<td></td>" );
      }

      var numDays = getNumberDays( month );
      for( i = 1 ; i < numDays + 1 ; i++ )
      {
        if( ( i + startDay ) % 7 == 1 )
        {
          document.write( "</tr><tr>" );
        }
        document.write( "<td><center>" +
                          "<input type='button' " +
                          "onClick='JavaScript: document.theForm.date.value=\"" +
fixMonth( month.getMonth() + 1 ) + "/" + i + "/" + fixYear( month.getYear() ) + "\";
onSelect();' " +
```

```
                                    "value='" + ( i < 10 ? " " : "" ) + i + getEnding( i )
        + "' " +

                                    "class='mono'>" +
                                    "</center></td>" );

                }
            // -->
            </script>
        </tr>
      </table>
      <input type="hidden" name="date">
    </form>
  </body>

</html>
```

Test.html

The following code presents the online test:

```
<html>

  <head>
    <title>Center Park - Computer Science Test</title>

    <script language="JavaScript">
    <!--
      if( getCookieValue( "loggedin" ) != "true" )
        document.location = "Main.html";

      function validate( form )
      {
        for( i = 0 ; i < form.elements.length ; i++ )
        {
          with( form.elements[i] )
          {
            if( type == "text" && value == "" )
            {
              alert( "Please answer all questions." );
              return( false );
```

```
          }
        }
      }

      return( true );
    }

    function getCookieValue( name )
    {
      var c = document.cookie;
      var begin = c.indexOf( name );
      if( begin < 0 ) return( "" );
      begin += name.length + 1;
      var end = c.indexOf( ";", begin );
      if( end == -1 ) end = c.length;
      return( c.slice( begin, end ) );
    }

    function setCustoms()
    {
      var bg = getCookieValue( "bgColor" );
      var fg = getCookieValue( "fgColor" );
      if( bg != "" ) document.bgColor = bg;
      if( fg != "" ) document.fgColor = fg;
    }
  // -->
  </script>
</head>

<body onLoad="JavaScript: setCustoms();">
  <b><font size="5">Computer Science 101 - Midterm Test</font> </b>

  <br><br>

  <font face="Courier">
    All the questions are <b>compulsory</b>.
    Please read the questions <i>carefully</i> before answering.
    Do not spend too much time on any one question.
```

```
        You have 30 minutes to complete the test.  Good Luck!
     </font>


     <br><br>


     <form name="TestForm" action="Grade.html" onSubmit="JavaScript: return( validate(
this ) );">
        <table width="100%" cellpadding="2" cellspacing="2">
          <tr>
            <td>1)</td>
            <td>
              <font face="Courier">
                  Imagine there was no precedence for arithmetic operators.  Assuming left
associativity for all operators, what is the value of the expression 5-3*4/2+6 ?
              </font>
            </td>
          </tr>
          <tr>
            <td>Answer</td>
            <td><input type="text" name="Q1" size="20"></td>
          </tr>
          <tr><td> </td><td> </td></tr>
          <tr>
            <td>2)</td>
            <td>
              <font face="Courier">
                What HTML tag must all JavaScript functions be nested in ie:
HTML, BODY, OR TABLE?
              </font>
            </td>
          </tr>
          <tr>
            <td>Answer</td>
            <td><input type="text" name="Q2" size="20"></td>
          </tr>
          <tr><td> </td><td> </td></tr>
          <tr>
            <td>3)</td>
```

```
      <td>
        <font face="Courier">
            What event is spawned after a user has selected text or HTML
elements on a web page?
        </font>
      </td>
    </tr>
    <tr>
      <td>Answer</td>
      <td><input type="text" name="Q3" size="20"></td>
    </tr>
    <tr><td> </td><td> </td></tr>
    <tr>
      <td>4)</td>
      <td>
        <font face="Courier">
          What type of variable scoping does JavaScript use?
        </font>
      </td>
    </tr>
    <tr>
      <td>Answer</td>
      <td><input type="text" name="Q4" size="20"></td>
    </tr>
    <tr><td> </td><td> </td></tr>
    <tr>
      <td>5)</td>
      <td>
        <font face="Courier">
            What relational operator is used to determine if two variables of the
same type are not equal to
            each other?
        </font>
      </td>
    </tr>
    <tr>
      <td>Answer</td>
      <td><input type="text" name="Q5" size="20"></td>
```

```
      </tr>
    </table>

    <br>
    <input type="submit" value="Submit" name="SubmitButton">
  </form>

  <script language="JavaScript">
  <!--
    window.setTimeout( "document.TestForm.SubmitButton.enabled=false", 1000 * 60 * 30
);
    // -->
  </script>

  </body>

</html>
```

Grade.html

Once the test is submitted, it is "graded" via the use of the following page:

```
<html>

  <head>
    <title>Center Park - Test Grader</title>

    <script language="JavaScript">
    <!--
      var total = 0, correct = 0;

      function getFormValue( name )
      {
        var c = location.href.split( "?" )[1];
        var begin = c.indexOf( name );
        if( begin < 0 ) return( "" );
        begin += name.length + 1;
        var end = c.indexOf( "&", begin );
        if( end == -1 ) end = c.length;
```

```
        return( unescape( c.slice( begin, end ) ) );
    }

    function getCookieValue( name )
    {
      var c = document.cookie;
      var begin = c.indexOf( name );
      if( begin < 0 ) return( "" );
      begin += name.length + 1;
      var end = c.indexOf( ";", begin );
      if( end == -1 ) end = c.length;
      return( c.slice( begin, end ) );
    }

    function setCustoms()
    {
      var bg = getCookieValue( "bgColor" );
      var fg = getCookieValue( "fgColor" );
      if( bg != "" ) document.bgColor = bg;
      if( fg != "" ) document.fgColor = fg;
    }
  // -->
  </script>
</head>

<body onLoad="JavaScript: setCustoms();">

  <b><font size="5">Computer Science 101 - Midterm Test</font> </b>

  <br><br>

  <font face="Courier">
    All the questions are <b>compulsory</b>.
    Please read the questions <i>carefully</i> before answering.
    Do not spend too much time on any one question.
    You have 30 minutes to complete the test.  Good Luck!
  </font>
```

```
<br><br>

<form>
   <table width="100%" cellpadding="2" cellspacing="2">
     <tr>
       <td>1)</td>
       <td>
         <font face="Courier">
             Imagine there was no precedence for arithmetic operators.  Assuming left
associativity for all operators, what is the value of the expression 5-3*4/2+6 ?
         </font>
       </td>
     </tr>
     <tr>
       <td>Answer</td>
       <td><b>10</b>     
         <script language="JavaScript">
         <!--
           if( parseInt( getFormValue( "Q1" ) ) == 10 )
           {
             document.write( "<font color='red'><b>CORRECT!</b></font>" );
             correct++
           }
           else
           {
             document.write( "<font color='red'><b>Wrong</b></font> You answered:
" + getFormValue( "Q1" ) );
           }
           total++;
         // -->
         </script>
       </td>
     </tr>
     <tr><td> </td><td> </td></tr>
     <tr>
       <td>2)</td>
       <td>
         <font face="Courier">
```

```
                    What HTML tag must all JavaScript functions be nested in ie:
HTML, BODY, TABLE?
                </font>
            </td>
        </tr>
        <tr>
            <td>Answer</td>
            <td><b>SCRIPT</b>     
                <script language="JavaScript">
                <!--
                    if( getFormValue( "Q2" ).toUpperCase() == "SCRIPT" )
                    {
                        document.write( "<font color='red'><b>CORRECT!</b></font>" );
                        correct++
                    }
                    else
                    {
                        document.write( "<font color='red'><b>Wrong</b></font> You answered:
" + getFormValue( "Q2" ) );
                    }
                    total++;
                // -->
                </script>
            </td>
        </tr>
        <tr><td> </td><td> </td></tr>
        <tr>
            <td>3)</td>
            <td>
                <font face="Courier">
                    What event is spawned after a user has selected text or HTML
elements on a Web page?
                </font>
            </td>
        </tr>
        <tr>
            <td>Answer</td>
            <td><b>OnSelect</b>     
```

```html
<script language="JavaScript">
<!--
  if( getFormValue( "Q3" ).toUpperCase() == "ONSELECT" )
  {
    document.write( "<font color='red'><b>CORRECT!</b></font>" );
    correct++
  }
  else
  {
    document.write( "<font color='red'><b>Wrong</b></font> You answered:
" + getFormValue( "Q3" ) );
  }
  total++;
// -->
</script>
</td>
</tr>
<tr><td> </td><td> </td></tr>
<tr>
  <td>4)</td>
  <td>
    <font face="Courier">
      What type of variable scoping does JavaScript use?
    </font>
  </td>
</tr>
<tr>
  <td>Answer</td>
  <td><b>Static</b>     
    <script language="JavaScript">
<!--
  if( getFormValue( "Q4" ).toUpperCase() == "STATIC" )
  {
    document.write( "<font color='red'><b>CORRECT!</b></font>" );
    correct++
  }
  else
  {
```

```
                    document.write( "<font color='red'><b>Wrong</b></font> You answered:
" + getFormValue( "Q4" ) );
                }
                total++;
            // -->
            </script>
          </td>
        </tr>
        <tr><td> </td><td> </td></tr>
        <tr>
          <td>5)</td>
          <td>
            <font face="Courier">
                What relational operator is used to determine if two variables of the
same type are not equal to each other?
            </font>
          </td>
        </tr>
        <tr>
          <td>Answer</td>
          <td><b>!=</b>     
            <script language="JavaScript">
            <!--
                if( getFormValue( "Q5" ) == "!=" )
                {
                  document.write( "<font color='red'><b>CORRECT!</b></font>" );
                  correct++
                }
                else
                {
                  document.write( "<font color='red'><b>Wrong</b></font> You answered:
" + getFormValue( "Q5" ) );
                }
                total++;
            // -->
            </script>
          </td>
        </tr>
```

```
        </table>
      </form>


      <br><br>


      <script language="JavaScript">
      <!--
        document.write( "<font color='red'><b>You got " + correct + " correct out of " +
total + " questions.  Your score is " + (correct/total*100) + "%</b></font>" );
        // -->
      </script>


    </body>


</html>
```

Customize.html

The following page allows the user to customize the foreground and background colors of the
Center Park site:

```
<html>

  <head>
    <title>Center Park - Customization</title>

    <script language="JavaScript">
    <!--
      function saveCustoms( form )
      {
        document.cookie = "bgColor=" + form.bgColor.value;
        document.cookie = "fgColor=" + form.fgColor.value;
      }

      function getCookieValue( name )
      {
        var c = document.cookie;
        var begin = c.indexOf( name );
        if( begin < 0 ) return( "" );
```

```
          begin += name.length + 1;
          var end = c.indexOf( ";", begin );
          if( end == -1 ) end = c.length;
          return( c.slice( begin, end ) );
      }

      function setCustoms()
      {
        var bg = getCookieValue( "bgColor" );
        var fg = getCookieValue( "fgColor" );
        if( bg != "" ) document.bgColor = bg;
        if( fg != "" ) document.fgColor = fg;
      }
   // -->
   </script>
</head>

<body onLoad="JavaScript: setCustoms();">
  <form onSubmit="JavaScript: saveCustoms( this );">
    <table>
      <tr>
        <td><b><font size="5">Customize <br>
        web site colors:<br>
        <br></font></b></td>
      <tr>
        <td><b>Background Color:    </b></td>
        <td><input type="text" name="bgColor" size="15"></td>
      </tr>
      <tr>
        <td><b>Foreground Color:</b></td>
        <td><input type="text" name="fgColor" size="15"></td>
        <td>  <input type="submit" value="Submit"></td>
      </tr>
    </table>
  </form>
</body>
</html>
```

Store.html

The home page of the site store, the following presents the items available, and the ability to add them to your shopping cart:

```html
<html>

  <head>
    <title>Center Park - Store</title>

    <script language="JavaScript">
<!--
      function addItem( name, price )
      {
        var i = 1;
        for( ; getCookieValue( "item" + i ) != "" ; i++ );
        document.cookie = "item" + i + "=" + name + "," + price;
        document.cookie = "items=" + i;
      }

      function getCookieValue( name )
      {
        var c = document.cookie;
        var begin = c.indexOf( name );
        if( begin < 0 ) return( "" );
        begin += name.length + 1;
        var end = c.indexOf( ";", begin );
        if( end == -1 ) end = c.length;
        return( c.slice( begin, end ) );
      }

      function setCustoms()
      {
        var bg = getCookieValue( "bgColor" );
        var fg = getCookieValue( "fgColor" );
        if( bg != "" ) document.bgColor = bg;
        if( fg != "" ) document.fgColor = fg;
      }
    // -->
```

```
        </script>
    </head>

    <body onLoad="JavaScript: setCustoms();">
        <b><font size="6">Center Park School Store -</font></b>
        <font size="4">for all your school paraphernalia needs</font><br><br>

        <form>
            <table border="2" width="100%">
                <tr>
                    <td>School Hat - One size fits all, school emblem on front.</td>
                    <td>
                        $9.99</td><td align="center">
                        <input type="button" value="Add" onClick="JavaScript: addItem( 'School
Hat - One size fits all school emblem on front.', 9.99 );">
                    </td>
                </tr>
                <tr>
                    <td>School T-Shirt - Small-Medium-Large, school emblem on front.</td>
                    <td>
                        $19.99</td><td align="center">
                        <input type="button" value="Add" onClick="JavaScript: addItem( 'School
T-Shirt - Small-Medium-Large school emblem on front.', 19.99 );">
                    </td>
                </tr>
                <tr>
                    <td>Football Season Tickets - Watch the Bobcats all season long.</td>
                    <td>
                        $12.99</td><td align="center">
                        <input type="button" value="Add" onClick="JavaScript: addItem( 'Football
Season Tickets - Watch the Bobcats all season long.', 12.99 );">
                    </td>
                </tr>
                <tr><td colspan="3" align="center">
                    <input type="button" value="View Cart" onClick="JavaScript: document.
location='ViewCart.html';">
                             
```

```
        <input type="button" value="Check Out" onClick="JavaScript: document.
location='CheckOut.html';">
          </td></tr>
        </table>
      </form>
    </body>

</html>
```

ViewCart.html

The following page displays the items that the visitor has selected and placed into her shopping cart:

```
<html>

  <head>
    <title>Center Park - View Cart</title>

    <script language="JavaScript">
    <!--
      function removeItem( name )
      {
        document.cookie = name + "=;";
        document.location = document.location;
      }

      function getCookieValue( name )
      {
        var c = document.cookie;
        var begin = c.indexOf( name );
        if( begin < 0 ) return( "" );
        begin += name.length + 1;
        var end = c.indexOf( ";", begin );
        if( end == -1 ) end = c.length;
        return( c.slice( begin, end ) );
      }

      function getItemName( item )
      {
```

```
      var c = getCookieValue( item );
      if( c )
      {
        return( c.split( "," )[0] );
      }
      else return( "" );
    }

    function getItemPrice( item )
    {
      var c = getCookieValue( item );
      if( c )
      {
        return( c.split( "," )[1] );
      }
      else return( "" );
    }

    function setCustoms()
    {
      var bg = getCookieValue( "bgColor" );
      var fg = getCookieValue( "fgColor" );
      if( bg != "" ) document.bgColor = bg;
      if( fg != "" ) document.fgColor = fg;
    }
  // -->
  </script>
</head>

<body onLoad="JavaScript: setCustoms();">
  <b><font size="6">Center Park School Store -</font></b>
  <font size="4">for all your school paraphernalia needs</font><br><br>

  <form>
    <table width="100%" border="2">
      <script language="JavaScript">
      <!--
        for( i = 1 ; i <= parseInt( getCookieValue( "items" ) ) ; i++ )
```

```
                {
                    if( getItemName( "item" + i ) != "" && getItemPrice( "item" + i )
        != undefined )
                    {
                        document.write( "<tr><td>" );
                        document.write( getItemName( "item" + i ) + "</td><td>" );
                        document.write( "$" + getItemPrice( "item" + i ) + "</td><td
        align='center'>" );
                        document.write( "<input type='button' value='Remove'
        onClick='JavaScript: removeItem( \"item" + i + "\" );'>" );
                        document.write( "</td></tr>" );
                    }
                }
            // -->
            </script>
            <tr><td colspan="3" align="center">
                <input type="button" value="Keep Shopping" onClick="JavaScript:
        document.location='Store.html';">
                     
                <input type="button" value="Check Out" onClick="JavaScript:
        document.location='CheckOut.html';">
                </td></tr>
            </table>
        </form>
    </body>

</html>
```

Checkout.html

Finally, the following page displays all items currently in the shopping cart along with the total price for all items:

```
<html>

    <head>
        <title>Center Park - Store Checkout</title>

        <script language="JavaScript">
```

```
<!--
  var total = 0;

  function getCookieValue( name )
  {
    var c = document.cookie;
    var begin = c.indexOf( name );
    if( begin < 0 ) return( "" );
    begin += name.length + 1;
    var end = c.indexOf( ";", begin );
    if( end == -1 ) end = c.length;
    return( c.slice( begin, end ) );
  }

  function getItemName( item )
  {
    var c = getCookieValue( item );
    if( c )
    {
      return( c.split( "," )[0] );
    }
    else return( "" );
  }

  function getItemPrice( item )
  {
    var c = getCookieValue( item );
    if( c )
    {
      return( c.split( "," )[1] );
    }
    else return( "" );
  }

  function fixTotal( n )
  {
    n *= 100;
    var good = parseInt( n );
```

```
       while( good < n ) good += 1;
       return( good / 100 );
     }


     function setCustoms()
     {
       var bg = getCookieValue( "bgColor" );
       var fg = getCookieValue( "fgColor" );
       if( bg != "" ) document.bgColor = bg;
       if( fg != "" ) document.fgColor = fg;
     }
   // -->
   </script>
</head>


<body onLoad="JavaScript: setCustoms();">
   <b><font size="6">Center Park School Store -</font></b>
   <font size="4">for all your school paraphernalia needs</font><br><br>


   <form>
     <table width="100%" border="2">
       <script language="JavaScript">
       <!--
         for( i = 1 ; i <= parseInt( getCookieValue( "items" ) ) ; i++ )
         {
           if( getItemName( "item" + i ) != "" && getItemPrice( "item" + i )
!= undefined )
           {
             document.write( "<tr><td>" );
             document.write( getItemName( "item" + i ) + "</td><td>" );
             document.write( getItemPrice( "item" + i ) );
             document.write( "</td></tr>" );

             total += parseFloat( getItemPrice( "item" + i ) );
           }
         }
       // -->
       </script>
```

```html
<tr>
  <td><b>Total</b></td>
  <td>$
    <script language="JavaScript">
    <!--
      document.write( fixTotal( total ) );
    -->
    </script>
   </td>
</tr>
</table>
</form>
</body>

</html>
```

Summary

And there you have it—a functioning Web site that is replete with JavaScript examples. While it would have been possible (maybe...) to create the site sans JavaScript, the overall effect and functionality would not have been nearly as good. Indeed, the Center Park administrators presented you, as designer, with some fairly significant challenges. What you have delivered to them—if you've been following along with all the project chapters, including this wrap-up chapter—is a strong foundation, a Web site that meets their initial requirements but is flexible enough (and well coded) to allow them a strong avenue for future customization. Also, all of the target audiences have been addressed, so that students, teachers, and parents all have a (good) reason to visit the site, and visit it often. By using the code in the Center Park Project as a functional reference, as well as reviewing the fundamental JavaScript instruction presented in Part I, you should be able to neatly and efficiently implement JavaScript into your own projects. Happy coding!

Index

Symbols

A

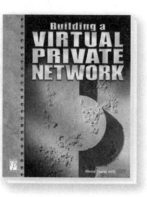